D1551133

Web Engineering:
Principles and Techniques

Woojong Suh
Inha University, Korea

IDEA GROUP PUBLISHING
Hershey • London • Melbourne • Singapore

Acquisitions Editor:	Mehdi Khosrow-Pour
Senior Managing Editor:	Jan Travers
Managing Editor:	Amanda Appicello
Development Editor:	Michele Rossi
Copy Editor:	Jennifer Young
Typesetter:	Kristin Roth
Cover Design:	Lisa Tosheff
Printed at:	Integrated Book Technology

Published in the United States of America by
Idea Group Publishing (an imprint of Idea Group Inc.)
701 E. Chocolate Avenue, Suite 200
Hershey PA 17033
Tel: 717-533-8845
Fax: 717-533-8661
E-mail: cust@idea-group.com
Web site: http://www.idea-group.com

and in the United Kingdom by
Idea Group Publishing (an imprint of Idea Group Inc.)
3 Henrietta Street
Covent Garden
London WC2E 8LU
Tel: 44 20 7240 0856
Fax: 44 20 7379 3313
Web site: http://www.eurospan.co.uk

Library of Congress Cataloging-in-Publication Data

Web engineering : principles and techniques / Woojong Suh, editor.
p. cm.
Includes bibliographical references and index.
ISBN 1-59140-432-0 (hard cover) -- ISBN 1-59140-433-9 (soft cover) -- ISBN 1-59140-434-7 (Ebook)
1. Web site design. 2. Web servers. 3. Application software--Development. I. Suh, Woojong.
TK5105.888.W3727 2004
006.7--dc22
2004022144

British Cataloguing in Publication Data
A Cataloguing in Publication record for this book is available from the British Library.

Web Engineering: Principles and Techniques

Table of Contents

Preface

About this Book

Since the advent of the Web, every aspect of our lives and organizational activities has changed dramatically. Organizations' expectations and dependencies on the use of Web technologies have increased rapidly over the years. Most organizations have conceived these Web technologies as a critical instrument for enhancing their performance; they have made every effort to develop, use, and maintain Web-based applications successfully. Nevertheless, such efforts are faced with various complexity and diversity caused by the demands for not only developing large-scale systems but also extending their applications into various domains. In most cases, these challenges are handled in an ad hoc manner rather than systematically. This phenomenon is a result of the fact that the progress of development and maintenance processes of Web applications have not kept up sufficiently with the rapid expansion of the challenges.

As a new approach to solve such challenges, Web Engineering has recently drawn great attention. Web Engineering is a multidisciplinary field encompassing diverse principles primarily based on management information systems and computer science. Its major specific areas include systems analysis and design, software engineering, hypermedia engineering, human-computer interaction, requirement engineering, data mining, project management, artificial intelligence, and Web programming. Web Engineering has the purpose of effectively supporting the organizational activities concerned with the lifecycle of Web applications or Web projects. Such activities include the following issues primarily: development and maintenance process, quality assessment, Web intelligence, Web resource management, and Web project management. These issues are often dealt with in terms of methodology, process, model, technique, or technology.

For the past few years, the researchers' interests in Web Engineering have significantly increased; an international conference on Web Engineering has been held since 2001, and the first journal on Web Engineering, *Journal of Web Engineering*, was published in 2002. Nevertheless, the concept or perspective of Web Engineering does not seem to have been introduced widespread yet; now it is the early stage of Web Engineering. This is the fundamental motivation for publishing this book.

This book aims to enhance the professional insights and capabilities of researchers and technical professionals. Hence, it places emphasis on serving both theoretical understanding and the latest research results in the major sub-areas of Web Engineering. It is expected that this book will be used as a useful educational textbook for classes in graduate schools, as well as helpful material for current and future research by researchers in universities and research institutions. In addition, it will serve a variety of technologies, methodologies, and techniques to help Web projects from practical perspectives, so it also is expected to help Web professionals in various industries improve their business capabilities.

This book is organized into six sections: Web Engineering: Concepts and Reference Model; Web Application Development: Methodologies and Techniques; Web Metrics and Quality: Models and Methods; Web Resource Management: Models and Techniques; Web Maintenance and Evolution: Techniques and Methodologies; and Web Intelligence: Techniques and Applications.

Section I: Web Engineering: Concepts and Reference Model

The two chapters in this section are designed to provide readers with the introduction to Web Engineering and a reference model for the Web engineers. Chapter 1, *Web Engineering: Introduction and Perspectives*, raises the issues and considerations in large, complex Web application development, and introduces Web Engineering as a way of managing complexity and diversity of large-scale Web development. Chapter 2, *Web Engineering Resources Portal (WEP): A Reference Model and Guide*, provides the Web Engineering Resources Portal (WEP) as a basic reference model and guide, to serve several cross-referenced taxonomies of technologies, research results, and tools for the Web engineers.

Section II: Web Application Development: Methodologies and Techniques

This section includes three chapters related to the development of Web applications. Chapter 3, *Web Application Development Methodologies*, discusses the challenges in relation to Web application development and proposes a Modified Prototyping Method (MPM) for developing the system. Chapter 4, *Relationship Analysis: A Technique to Enhance Systems Analysis for Web Development*, presents a comprehensive, systematic, domain-independent analysis technique, Relationship Analysis (RA), which can help the design of the navigational links in developing Web applications. Chapter 5, *Engineering Location-Based Services in the Web*, discusses the state of the art of location-based services and presents an object-oriented design approach for engineering location-based applications that effectively supports the evolution of these applications.

Section III: Web Metrics and Quality: Models and Methods

The three chapters in this section focus on the measurement concerning Web business, Web applications, and Web projects. Chapter 6, *Architectural Metrics for E-Commerce: A Balance between Rigor and Relevance*, proposes six dimensions of architectural metrics for Internet businesses and reports the results of large-scale empirical studies to validate the proposed metrics and to explore their relevance across four Internet business domains. Chapter 7, *The eQual Approach to the Assessment of E-Commerce Quality: A Longitudinal Study of Internet Bookstores*, introduces eQual, an instrument for assessing the quality for Web sites, and examines online bookshops, one based on eQual 2.0 and the other on eQual 4.0, to evaluate the use of the instrument and the benchmarking of the bookshops on two separate occasions. Chapter 8, *Web Cost Estimation: An Introduction*, introduces a literature review of Web cost estimation, then compares the literature according to set criteria, and discusses Web size measures.

Section IV: Web Resource Management: Models and Techniques

The two chapters in this section propose applications of theoretical models and techniques to manage and use Web resources. Chapter 9, *Ontology-Supported Web Content Management*, describes how to exploit ontology to manage Web contents and resources and introduces case studies on personalization from user-specific content and a comparison-shopping mall system in electronic commerce. Chapter 10, *Design Principles and Applications of XRML*, proposes a language eXtensible Rule Markup Language (XRML) which is an emerging architecture to share Web resources between human and software agents, and identifies its potential application areas and challenges.

Section V: Web Maintenance and Evolution: Techniques and Methodologies

The three chapters included in this section focus on the maintenance and evolution of Web applications. Chapter 11, *Program Transformations for Web Application Restructuring*, discusses the role of restructuring Web applications in a highly dynamic and rapidly evolving development environment, and examines specific examples in several different contexts to investigate the possibility to automate restructuring. Chapter 12, *The Requirements of Methodologies for Developing Web Applications,* identifies the main requirements of methodologies for developing e-commerce applications, and introduces Internet Commerce Development Methodology (ICDM) which considers evolutionary development of systems. Chapter 13, *A Customer Analysis-Based Methodology for Improving Web Business Systems,* discusses the challenges in the development of Web business systems, explores the previous methodologies by comparing them, and proposes a Customer Analysis-based Improvement Methodology (CAIM) to help evolve customer-oriented Web business systems, employing scenario-based and object-oriented approaches.

Section VI: Web Intelligence: Techniques and Applications

The two chapters included in this section deal with various techniques and applications related to Web intelligence. Chapter 14, *Analysis and Customization of Web-*

Based Electronic Catalogs, presents a Personalized Electronic Catalog (PEC) system to synthesize the Web-based electronic catalog customization on information content, organization and display for electronic catalogs, and applies the system to electronic catalogs in an industrial application to demonstrate the analysis and improvement of information access. Chapter 15, *Data Mining Using Qualitative Information on the Web*, proposes a Web mining application, KBNMiner (Knowledge-Based News Miner), to predict interest rates by employing qualitative information on the Web, and makes an experiment by the use of Web news information to validate the effectiveness of the KBNMiner.

Woojong Suh
Inha University, Korea
December 2004

Acknowledgments

This book could not come into the world without great help from numerous individuals who contributed. First of all, I would like to thank all of the authors for their insights and excellent contributions. They accepted my comments and suggestions for the scope of chapter themes, the balances in the chapter structure, and other requirements for accomplishing the goal of the book. I am sure that such cooperation was the most critical factor in publishing the book successfully.

Web engineering is an emerging area, so establishing its scope and identifying practical needs are important in creating value in this book. I could confirm my decision on these points through professional opinions by San Murugesan of Southern Cross University and Heeseok Lee of Korea Advanced Institute of Science and Technology from the academic standpoint and by Dr. Choongseok Lee of Samsung SDS Co. and Dr. Jaewoo Jung of IBM BCS Korea from the practical standpoint. I wish to give special thanks to all of them. Also I would especially like to thank San Murugesan, General Chair of International Conference on Web Engineering(ICWE) 2005, who gave an opportunity to introduce the book to ICWE 2004 in Munich.

In addition, I wish to thank all the people who helped me throughout the process of the publishing project. I am very grateful to everyone who assisted me in the reviewing process, including Gyoogun Lim of Sejong Univiersity, Kyoungjae Kim of Dongguk University, Changhee Han of Hanyang University, Hwagyoo Park, Kyungdong University, and Taeho Hong of Pusan University. Special thanks also goes to the publishing team at Idea Group, Inc. In particular, Dr. Mehdi Khosrow-Pour invited me to take an opportunity to work with IGP, and Jan Travers, Amanda Appicello, Michele Rossi, Jennifer Sundstrom, and Amanda Phillips provided me with ongoing professional support throughout this project. Their enthusiasm was strong enough for the book to be published successfully. Finally, I want to thank my wife for her love and support during this project.

Woojong Suh
Inha University, Korea
December 2004

Section I

Web Engineering:
Concepts and Reference Model

Chapter I

Web Engineering: Introduction and Perspectives

San Murugesan
Southern Cross University, Australia

Athula Ginige
University of Western Sydney, Australia

Abstract

Web-based systems and applications now deliver a complex array of functionality to a large number of diverse groups of users. As our dependence and reliance on the Web has increased dramatically over the years, their performance, reliability and quality have become paramount importance. As a result, the development of Web applications has become more complex and challenging than most of us think. In many ways, it is also different and more complex than traditional software development. But, currently, the development and maintenance of most Web applications is chaotic and far from satisfactory. To successfully build and maintain large, complex Web-based systems and applications, Web developers need to adopt a disciplined development process and a sound methodology. The emerging discipline of Web engineering advocates a holistic, disciplined approach to successful Web development. In this chapter, we articulate and raise awareness of the issues and considerations in large, complex Web application development, and introduce Web engineering as a way of managing complexity and diversity of large-scale Web development.

Introduction

Within a decade, the World Wide Web has become ubiquitous, and it continues to grow unabated at exponential rate. Web-based systems and applications now deliver a complex array of varied content and functionality to a large number of heterogeneous users. The interaction between a Web system and its backend information systems has also become more tight and complex.

As we now increasingly depend on Web-based systems and applications, their performance, reliability and quality have become paramount importance, and the expectations of and demands placed on Web applications have increased significantly over the years. As a result, the design, development, deployment and maintenance of Web-based systems have become more complex and difficult to manage.

Though massive amounts of Web development and maintenance continue to take place, most of them are carried out in ad hoc manner, resulting in poor quality Web systems and applications. Problems such as outdated or irrelevant information, difficulties in using the Web site and finding relevant information of interest, slow response, Web site crashes, and security breaches are common. We encounter these kinds of problems because Web developers failed to address users' needs and issues such as content management, maintenance, performance, security, and scalability of Web applications. They also often overlook important non-technical considerations such as copyright and privacy.

Many Web developers seem to think that Web application development is just simple Web page creation using HTML or Web development software such as *Front Page* or *Dreamweaver* and embodying few images and hyperlinking documents and Web pages. Though certain simple applications such as personal Web pages, seminar announcements, and simple online company brochures that call for simple content presentation and navigation fall into this category, many Web applications are complex and are required to meet an array of challenging requirements which change and evolve. There is more to Web application development than visual design and user interface. It involves planning, Web architecture and system design, testing, quality assurance and performance evaluation, and continual update and maintenance of the systems as the requirements and usage grow and develop.

Hence, ad hoc development is not appropriate for large, complex Web systems, and it could result in serious problems: the delivered systems are not what the user wants; they are not maintainable and scalable, and hence have short useful life; they often do not provide desired levels of performance and security; and/or most Web systems are often much behind schedule and overrun the budget estimates.

More importantly, many enterprises and organisations cannot afford to have faulty Web systems or tolerate downtime or inconsistent or stale content/information. The problems on the Web become quickly visible and frustrate the users, possibly costing the enterprises heavily in terms of financial loss, lost customer and loss of reputation. As is often said, "We cannot hide the problems on the Web."

Unfortunately, despite being faced with these problems and challenges, most Web application development still continues to be ad hoc, chaotic, failure-prone, and unsatisfactory. And this could get worse as more inherently complex Web systems and applications that involve interaction with many other systems or components pervade us and our dependence on them increases.

To successfully build large-scale, complex Web-based systems and applications, Web developers need to adopt a disciplined development process and a sound methodology, use better development tools, and follow a set of good guidelines.

The emerging discipline of Web engineering addresses these needs and focuses on successful development of Web-based systems and applications, while advocating a holistic, disciplined approach to Web development.

Web Engineering uses scientific, engineering, and management principles and systematic approaches to successfully develop, deploy, and maintain high-quality Web systems and applications (Murugesan et al., 1999). It aims to bring Web-based system development under control, minimise risks and improve quality, maintainability, and scalability of Web applications.

The essence of Web engineering is to successfully manage the diversity and complexity of Web application development, and hence, avoid potential failures that could have serious implications.

This chapter aims to articulate and raise awareness of the issues and considerations in large-scale Web development and introduce Web engineering as a way of managing complexity and diversity of large-scale Web development.

Following a brief outline of the evolution of the Web and the categorisation of Web applications based on their functionality, this chapter examines current Web development practices and their limitations, and emphasises the need for a holistic, disciplined approach to Web development. It then presents an overview of Web engineering, describes an evolutionary Web development process, discusses considerations in Web design and recommends ten key steps for successful development. In conclusion, it offers perspectives on Web Engineering and highlights some of the challenges facing Web developers and Web engineering researchers.

Evolution of the Web

The Web has become closely ingrained with our life and work in just a few years. From its initial objective of facilitating easy creation and sharing of information among a few scientists using simple Web sites that consisted primarily of hyperlinked text documents, the Web has grown very rapidly in its scope and extent of use, supported by constant advances in Internet and Web technologies and standards. In 10 years, the number of Web sites dramatically has grown from 100 to over 45 million (Figure 1).

Enterprises, travel and hospitality industries, banks, educational and training institutions, entertainment businesses and governments use large-scale Web-based systems and applications to improve, enhance and/or extend their operations. E-commerce has become global and widespread. Traditional legacy information and database systems are being progressively migrated to the Web. Modern Web applications run on distributed

Figure 1. Growth of Web sites

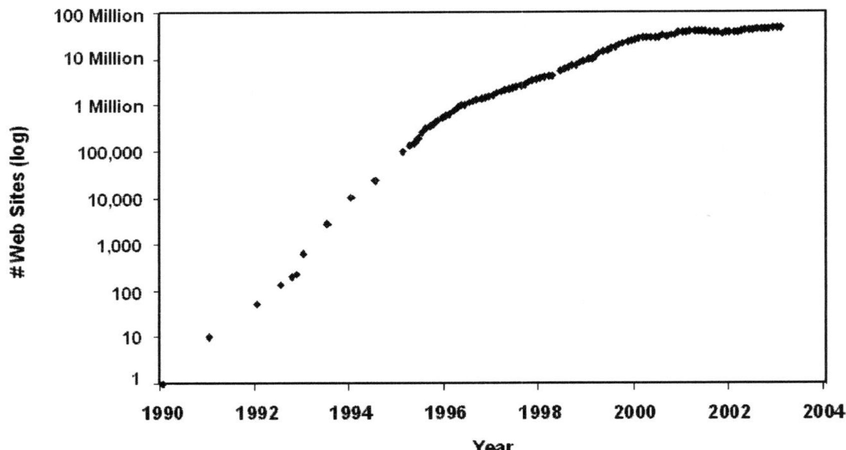

Note: Web Sites = Number of Web servers; one host may have multiple sites by using different domains or port numbers.

Source: Hobbes' Internet Timeline, 2004, www.zakon.org/robert/internet/timeline/

hardware and heterogeneous computer systems. Furthermore, fuelled by recent advances in wireless technologies and portable computing and communication devices, a new wave of mobile Web applications are rapidly emerging. The Web has changed our lives and work at every level, and this trend will continue for the foreseeable future.

The evolution of the Web has brought together some disparate disciplines such as media, information science, and information and communication technology, facilitating easy creation, maintenance, sharing, and use of different types of information from anywhere, any time, and using a variety of devices such as desktop and notebook computers, pocket PCs, personal digital assistants (PDAs), and mobile phones. Contributions of each of these disciplines to the evolution and growth of the Web are:

- **Media:** integration of different types of media such as data, text, graphics, images, audio and video, and their presentation (animation, 3D visualisation); different types of interaction and channels of communications (one-to-one, one-to-many, many-to-one, and many-to-many).
- **Information science:** information organisation, presentation, indexing, retrieval, aggregation, and management; and collaborative and distributed content creation.
- **Information and communication technology and networking:** efficient and cost-effective storage, retrieval, processing, and presentation of information; infrastructures that facilitate transfer and sharing of data and information; wired and wireless Internet communication; and personalised and context-aware Web applications.

Table 1. Categories of Web applications based on functionality

Functionality/Category	Examples
Informational	Online newspapers, product catalogues, newsletters, manuals, reports, online classifieds, online books
Interactive	Registration forms, customized information presentation, online games
Transactional	Online shopping (ordering goods and services), online banking, online airline reservation, online payment of bills
Workflow oriented	Online planning and scheduling, inventory management, status monitoring, supply chain management
Collaborative work environments	Distributed authoring systems, collaborative design tools
Online communities, marketplaces	Discussion groups, recommender systems, online marketplaces, e-malls (electronic shopping malls), online auctions, intermediaries

Many new Web technologies and standards have emerged in the last couple of years to better support new, novel Web applications: XML, Web services, the Semantic Web, Web personalisation techniques, Web mining, Web intelligence, and mobile and context-aware services.

The advances in Internet and Web technologies and the benefits they offer have led to an avalanche of Web sites, a diverse range of applications, and phenomenal growth in the use of the Web.

Categories of Web Applications

The scope and complexity of Web applications vary widely: from small scale, short-lived (a few weeks) applications to large-scale enterprise applications distributed across the Internet, as well as via corporate intranets and extranets. Web applications now offer vastly varied functionality and have different characteristics and requirements. Web applications can be categorised in many ways — there is no unique or widely accepted way. Categorisation of Web applications based on functionality (Table 1) is useful in understanding their requirements and for developing and deploying Web-based systems and applications.

Web Development Practices

Web development has a very short history, compared to the development of software, information systems, or other computer applications. But within a period of few years, a large number of Web systems and applications have been developed and put into widespread use.

The complexity of Web-based applications has also grown significantly — from information dissemination (consisting of simple text and images to image maps, forms, common gateway interface [CGI], applets, scripts, and style sheets) to online transactions, enterprise-wide planning and scheduling systems, Web-based collaborative work environments, and now multilingual Web sites, Web services and mobile Web applications.

Nevertheless, many consider Web development primarily an authoring work (content/page creation and presentation) rather than application development. They often get carried away by the myth that "Web development is an art" that primarily deals with "media manipulation and presentation." Sure, like the process of designing and constructing buildings, Web development has an important artistic side. But Web development also needs to follow a discipline and systematic process, rather than simply hacking together a few Web pages.

Web applications are not just Web pages, as they may seem to a causal user. The complexity of many Web-based systems is often deceptive and is not often recognised by many stakeholders — clients who fund the development, Web development managers and Web developers — early in the development.

Several attributes of quality Web-based systems such as usability, navigation, accessibility, scalability, maintainability, compatibility and interoperability, and security and reliability often are not given the due consideration they deserve during development. Many Web applications also fail to address cultural or regional considerations, and privacy, moral and legal obligations and requirements. Most Web systems also lack proper testing, evaluation, and documentation.

While designing and developing a Web application, many developers fail to acknowledge that Web systems' requirements evolve, and they do not take this into consideration while developing Web systems. Web-based systems development is not a one-time event as perceived and practiced by many; it is a process with an iterative lifecycle.

Another problem is that most Web application development activities rely heavily on the knowledge and experience of individual (or a small group of) developers and their individual development practices rather than standard practices.

Anecdotal evidence and experience suggest that the problems of ad hoc development (outlined above and in the Introduction section) continue to be faced by developers, users, and other stakeholders. As a result, these are increasing concerns about the manner in which complex Web-based systems are created as well as the level of performance, quality, and integrity of these systems.

> *"Many organisations are heading toward a Web crisis in which they are unable to keep the system updated and/or grow their system at the rate that is needed. This crisis involves the proliferation of quickly 'hacked together' Web systems that are kept running via continual stream of patches or upgrades developed without systematic approaches." (Dart, 2000)*

Poorly developed Web-based applications have a high probability of low performance and/or failure. Recently, large Web-based systems have had an increasing number of failures (Williams, 2001). In certain classes of applications such as supply-chain management, financial services, and digital marketplaces, a system failure can propagate broad-based problems across many functions, causing a major Web disaster. The cost of bad design, shabby development, poor performance, and/or lack of content management for Web-based applications has many serious consequences.

The primary causes of these failures are a lack of vision, shortsighted goals, a flawed design and development process, and poor management of development efforts — not technology (Ginige & Murugesan, 2001a). The way we address these concerns is critical to successful deployment and maintenance of Web applications.

Therefore, one might wonder whether development methodologies and processes advocated over the years for software or information systems development and software engineering principles and practices could be directly used for developing Web applications. Though the valuable experiences gained and some of processes and methodologies used in software engineering (and other domains) could be suitably adapted for Web development as appropriate, they are not adequate, as Web development is rather different from software development in several aspects.

Web Development is Different

It is important to realise that Web application development has certain characteristics that make it different from traditional software, information system, or computer application development (Deshpande et al., 2002; Deshpande & Hansen, 2001; Ginige & Murugesan, 2001a, 2001b; Glass, 2001; Lowe 2003; Murugesan et al., 1999; Pressman, 2001 and 2004).

Web applications have the following characteristics:

- Web applications constantly evolve. In many cases, it is not possible to fully specify what a Web site should or will contain at the start of the development process, because its structure and functionality evolve over time, especially after the system is put into use. Further, the information contained within and presented by a Web site will also change. Unlike conventional software that goes through a planned and discrete revision at specific times in its lifecycle, Web applications continuously evolve in terms of their requirements and functionality (instability of requirements). Managing the change and evolution of a Web application is a major technical, organisational and management challenge — much more demanding than a traditional software development.
- Further, Web applications are inherently different from software. The content, which may include text, graphics, images, audio, and/or video, is integrated with procedural processing. Also, the way in which the content is presented and organised has implications on the performance and response time of the system.
- Web applications are meant to be used by a vast, variable user community — a large number of anonymous users (could be many millions like in the cases of eBay and the 2000 Sydney Olympics Web site) with varying requirements, expectations, and

skill sets. Therefore, the user interface and usability features have to meet the needs of a diverse, anonymous user community to whom we cannot offer training sessions, thus complicating human-Web interaction (HWI), user interface, and information presentation.

- Nowadays, most Web-based systems are content-driven (database-driven). Web-based systems development includes creation and management of the content, as well as appropriate provisions for subsequent content creation, maintenance, and management after the initial development and deployment on a continual basis (in some applications as frequently as every hour or more).
- In general, many Web-based systems demand a good "look and feel," favouring visual creativity and incorporation of multimedia in presentation and interface. In these systems, more emphasis is placed on visual creativity and presentation.
- Web applications have a compressed development schedule, and time pressure is heavy. Hence, a drawn-out development process that could span a few months to a year or more is not appropriate.
- Ramifications of failure or dissatisfaction of users of Web-based applications can be much worse than conventional IT systems.
- Web applications are developed by a small team of (often young) people with diverse backgrounds, skills, and knowledge compared to a team of software developers. Their perception of the Web and the quality of Web-based systems also differ considerably, often causing confusion and resulting in misguided priorities.
- There are rapid technological changes — constant advances in Web technologies and standards bring their own challenges — new languages, standards, and tools to cope with; and lots of errors and bugs in early versions of new mark-up languages, development tools, and environments (technology instability).
- Web development uses cutting-edge, diverse technologies and standards, and integrates numerous varied components, including traditional and non-traditional software, interpreted scripting languages, HTML files, databases, images, and other multimedia components such as video and audio, and complex user interfaces (Offurt, 2002).
- The delivery medium for Web applications is quite different from that of traditional software. Web applications need to cope with a variety of display devices and formats, and supporting hardware, software, and networks with vastly varying access speeds.
- Security and privacy needs of Web-based systems are more demanding than that of traditional software.
- The Web exemplifies a greater bond between art and science than generally encountered in software development.

These unique characteristics of the Web and Web applications make Web development different and more challenging than traditional software development.

Web Engineering

Web engineering is way of developing and organising knowledge about Web application development and applying that knowledge to develop Web applications, or to address new requirements or challenges. It is also a way of managing the complexity and diversity of Web applications.

A Web-based system is a *living* system. It is like a garden — it continues to evolve, change, and grow. A sound infrastructure must be in place to support the growth of a Web-based system in a controlled, but flexible and consistent manner. Web engineering helps to create an infrastructure that will allow evolution and maintenance of a Web system and that will also support creativity.

Web engineering is application of scientific, engineering, and management principles and disciplined and systematic approaches to the successful development, deployment and maintenance of high quality Web-based systems and applications (Murugesan et al., 1999).

It is a holistic and proactive approach to the development of large Web-based systems, and it aims to bring the current chaos in Web-based system development under control, minimise risks, and enhance the maintainability and quality of Web systems.

Since its origin and promotion as a new discipline in 1998 (Deshpande, Ginige, Murugesan & Hansen, 2002; Murugesan, 1998), Web engineering is receiving growing interest among the stakeholders of Web-based systems, including developers, clients, government agencies, users, academics, and researchers. In addition, this new field has attracted professionals from other related disciplines such as multimedia, software engineering, distributed systems, computer science, and information retrieval.

Web Engineering is Multidisciplinary

Building a large, complex Web-based system calls for knowledge and expertise from many different disciplines and requires a diverse team of people with expertise in different areas. Web engineering is multidisciplinary and encompasses contributions from diverse areas: systems analysis and design, software engineering, hypermedia/hypertext engineering, requirements engineering, human-computer interaction, user interface, information engineering, information indexing and retrieval, testing, modelling and simulation, project management, and graphic design and presentation.

"Contrary to the perception of some professionals, Web Engineering is not a clone of software engineering, although both involve programming and software development" (Ginige & Murugesan, 2001a). While Web Engineering uses software engineering principles, it encompasses new approaches, methodologies, tools, techniques, and guidelines to meet the unique requirements of Web-based systems. As previously stated, development of Web-based systems is much more than traditional software development. There are subtle differences in the nature and lifecycle of Web-based and software systems, as well as the way in which they're developed and maintained. "Web development is a mixture between print publishing and software development, between marketing and computing, between internal communications and external relations, and between art and technology" (Powell, 2000).

Evolution of Web Engineering

Web Engineering is progressively emerging as a new discipline addressing the unique needs and challenges of Web-based systems development. Since 1998, when the First Workshop on Web Engineering was held in Brisbane, Australia, in conjunction with the World Wide Web Conference (WWW7), there has been series of workshops and special tracks at major international conferences (WWW conferences 1999-2005, HICS 1999-2001, SEKE 2002 and 2003 and others), and a dedicated annual International Conference on Web Engineering (ICWE) 2002-2005.

There also have been a few special issues of journals on topics related to Web Engineering. There are two new dedicated journals, *Journal of Web Engineering* (www.rintonpress.com/journals/jweonline.html) and *Journal of Web Engineering and Technology* (www.inderscience.com), as well as an edited book, *Web Engineering: Managing Diversity and Complexity of Web Application Development* (Murugesan & Deshpande, 2001).

The bibliography at the end of this chapter gives details of special issues, conferences, books, and journal articles on Web engineering and other related areas.

New subjects and courses on Web engineering are now being taught at universities, both at undergraduate and postgraduate levels, and more research is being carried out on various aspects of Web engineering. Also, not surprisingly, there is growing interest among Web developers in using Web engineering approaches and methodologies.

Evolutionary Web Development

Web-applications are evolutionary. For many Web applications, it is not possible to specify fully what their requirements are or what these systems will contain at the start of their development and later, because their structure and functionality will change constantly over time. Further, the information contained within and presented by a Web site often changes — in some applications as often as every few minutes to a couple of times a day. Thus, the ability to maintain information and to scale the Web site's structure (and the functions it provides) is a key consideration in developing a Web application.

Given this Web environment, it seems the only viable approach for developing sustainable Web applications is to follow an evolutionary development process where change is seen as a norm and is catered to. And, this also mandates adoption of a disciplined process for successful Web development.

Web Development Process

A Web development process outlines the various steps and activities of Web-based systems development. It should clearly define a set of steps that developers can follow and must be measurable and trackable (Ginige & Murugesan, 2001c).

Characteristics of Web applications that make their development difficult — and uniquely challenging — include their real-time interaction, complexity, changeability, and the desire to provide personalised information. In addition, the effort and time required to design and develop a Web application is difficult to estimate with a reasonable accuracy.

Based on our practical experience in building Web applications, we recommend an evolutionary process for Web development, shown in Figure 2. This process assists developers in understanding the context in which the application will be deployed and used; helps in capturing the requirements; enables integration of the know-how from different disciplines; facilitates the communication among various members involved in the development process; supports continuous evolution and maintenance; facilitates easier management of the information content; and helps in successfully managing the complexity and diversity of the development process (Ginige & Murugesan 2001c).

Context Analysis

The first essential step in developing a Web-based system is "context analysis," where we elicit and understand the system's major objectives and requirements, as well as the

Figure 2. Web development process

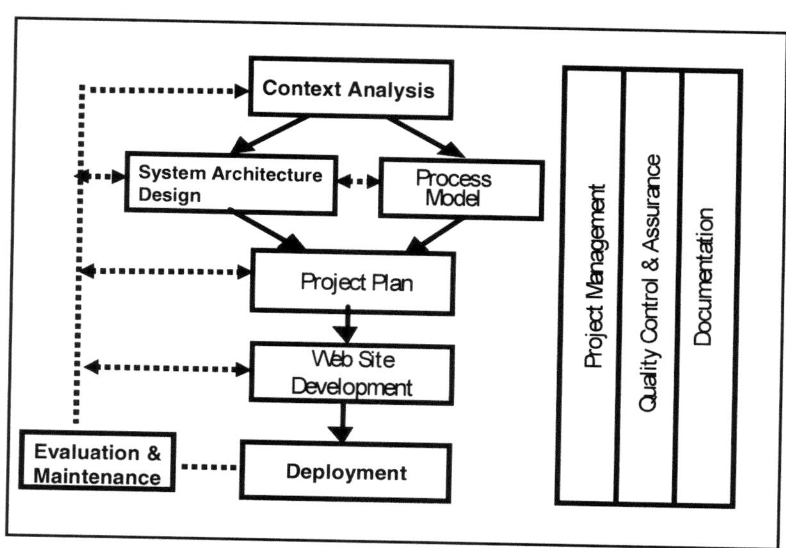

needs of the system's typical users and the organisation that needs the system. It is important to realise at this stage that requirements will change and evolve — even during system development and after its deployment. It is also important to study briefly the operation for which a Web application is to be developed, and the potential implications of introduction of the new system on the organisation. This study should normally include: how information (to be made available on the Web) is created and managed; organisational policy on ownership and control (centralised or decentralised) of information; its current and future plans and business objectives; possible impact of the introduction of Web-based applications on the organisation; the resulting changes in its business and business processes; and emerging trends in the industry sector.

As the Web applications evolve and need to be modified to cater to new requirements — some of which arise from changes or improvements in the business process as a result of deployment of the new Web-based system — an understanding of a big picture about the organisation and its information management policies and practices is a prerequisite for successful design, development, and deployment of Web-based applications.

Before starting Web development, therefore, developers need to elicit and understand the system's major objectives and requirements, gather information about the operational and application environment, and identify the profile of typical system users.

In addition to the functional requirements, potential demands on the scalability, maintainability, availability, and performance of the system need to be specifically elicited and understood by the developers at the beginning of the development process. Based on this information, developers then arrive at the system's functional, technical, and non-technical requirements, which, in turn, influence the system's architectural design.

For instance, if the information content and the system's functions are going to evolve considerably, like in most e-business systems, the system needs to be designed for scalability. On the other hand, if the information changes frequently — like in weather reports, special sales offerings, job vacancies, product price list, brochures, and latest news or announcements — to keep the information current and consistent, the system needs to be designed for easy information maintainability (Merialdo et al., 2003). Moreover, where the application demands very high availability and needs to cater for high peak or uncertain demands, the system may be required to run on multiple Web servers with load balancing and other performance enhancement mechanisms (Almedia & Menasce, 2002; Menasce & Almedia, 2002; Oppenheimer & Patterson, 2002). Examples of this category of applications are online stock trading, online banking, and high volume near-real-time sports and entertainment Web sites such as the Olympics, Wimbledon, and Oscar Web sites.

Thus, it is very important to recognise that scalability, maintainability, and/or performance need to be built into the initial system architecture. It would be very hard, or impossible, to incorporate these features if the initial architecture is not designed to support them. To illustrate this, consider an e-business Web site that provides product information, such as price and availability, which appears on many different pages and changes frequently. If the Web site is designed as static Web pages, then every time a product's information changes, one has to incorporate the change in every page that contains this information. This is a cumbersome and laborious task, and often changes are only made to a few pages, instead of all relevant pages. As a consequence of this, the same information appearing on different pages will be inconsistent.

A better approach to ensure consistency of information across all Web pages is to automatically retrieve the information, when and where needed, from a single information source. If product information is stored in a single central database, then by extracting the relevant information from this database, we can dynamically create various Web pages that contain this information. In the database-driven approach, we need to change the information only in one place: the database. Further, the database-driven Web sites can have a back-end system to allow an authorised person, who may not be skilled in Web page development, to make information changes easily through a Web interface, from anywhere. A database-driven Web site requires a completely different architecture than a Web site that has only static Web pages. Hence, an appropriate architecture that would meet the system's requirements needs to be chosen early in the system development.

Thus, as highlighted in Table 2, the objective of context analysis is to capture and derive the key information required to develop the Web application. In addition, it can also identify non-technical issues that have to be addressed for successful implementation and application of the system. These may include reengineering of business processes where required, organisational and management policies, staff training, and legal, cultural and social aspects.

Context analysis can minimise or eliminate the major problems plaguing large Web-based system development. But, many developers and project managers overlook this essential first step in Web system development and face the problems later when it is hard to correct them.

Based on the context analysis, we then arrive at the system's technical and non-technical requirements (Lowe, 2003), which, in turn, influence the system architecture design.

Architecture Design

In system architecture design, we decide on various components of the system and how they are linked. At this stage, we design:

Table 2. Objectives of context analysis of Web applications

The objectives of context analysis, the first step in Web development, are to:

- Identify the stakeholders and their broader requirements and experiences.
- Identify the functions the Web site needs to provide (immediately, and in the short, medium, and long term).
- Establish what information needs to be on the Web site, how to get this information, and how often this information may change.
- Identify the corporate requirements in relation to look and feel, performance, security, and governance.
- Get a feel of the number of users (typical and peak) and anticipated demands on the system.
- Study similar (competitive) Web sites to gain an understanding of their functionalities, strengths, and limitations.

Table 3. Means of fulfilling the requirements of Web application

Requirement	**Means of Fulfilment**
Uniform look and feel across all Web pages that can easily be modified	Creation of Web pages using templates and style sheets
Consistency of information that may appear in different places or pages	Storing information in a single place (such as in a database or as an XML file), without duplication of information in different places or databases, and retrieving the required information for presentation where and when needed
Ease of information update and maintenance	Provision of a back-end system to edit information in a data repository; could have Web interface for easy access from anywhere
Ability to add new Web pages easily	Dynamic generation of navigational links, rather than predetermined static navigational links
Decentralised system administration	Provision of a multi-user login system to access back-end systems and inclusion of a "user administration system" that can assign specific functions and data sets to content managers and other developers/administrators
Mechanisms for quality control and assessing the relevance of information	Inclusion of metadata for Web pages; use of a Web robot for gathering salient information, processing the information gathered and taking appropriate action(s) for ensuring quality or relevance of information presented.
Increased probability of being found through search engines	Using meta tags and registering with search engines

- An overall system architecture describing how the network and the various servers (Web servers, application servers and database servers) interact;
- An application architecture depicting various information modules and the functions they support; and
- A software architecture identifying various software and database modules required to implement the application architecture.

Table 3 summarises the means of fulfilling some of the requirements of Web-based applications (Ginige & Murugesan, 2001c).

We then decide on an appropriate development process model (Uden, 2002; Pressman, 2004) and develop a project plan. To successfully manage Web development, a sound project plan and a realistic schedule are necessary. Progress of development activities must be monitored and managed. Project planning and scheduling techniques that are commonly used in other disciplines can be used for Web development. Following this, the various components of the system and Web pages are designed, developed and tested.

Figure 3. Web page design

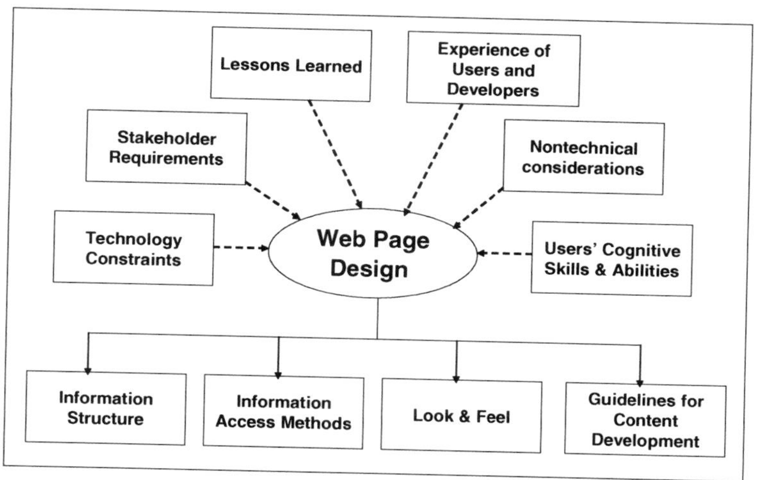

Web Page Design

Web page design is an important activity; it determines what information is presented and how it is presented to the users. A prototype usually contains a set of sample pages to evaluate the page layout, presentation, and navigation (within and among different pages). Based on the feedback from the stakeholders, the page design is suitably modified. This process may go through a few iterations until the stakeholders and designers are satisfied with the page layout, presentation and the navigation structure.

Web page content development needs to take into consideration the stakeholders' requirements, users' cognitive abilities (Cloyd, 2001), technical issues and considerations, nontechnical issues, earlier experiences of developers and users, and lessons learned from similar Web applications (Figure 3).

If the Web system is intended for global use, by users from different countries, the Web content and presentation may have to be localised; there also may be a need for multilingual Web sites (for details, see Becker & Mottay, 2001; Collins, 2002). Also, the Web site's content and usability have to be designed from a global perspective and be responsive to cultural sensitivity in language along with appropriate use of colour, presentation, and animation (Becker & Mottay, 2001).

Web Maintenance

After a Web-based system is developed and deployed online for use, it needs to be maintained. As outlined earlier, content maintenance is a continual process. We need to formulate content maintenance policies and procedures, based on the decision taken at the system architecture design stage on how the information content would be maintained, and then we need to implement them. Further, as the requirements of Web systems grow and evolve, the system needs to be updated and also may be redesigned to cater to the new requirements.

It is important to periodically review Web-based systems and applications regarding the currency of information content, potential security risks, performance of the system, and usage patterns (by analysing Web logs), and take suitable measures to fix the shortcomings and weaknesses, if any.

Project Management

The purpose of project management is to ensure that all the key processes and activities work in harmony. Building successful Web-based applications requires close coordination among various efforts involved in the Web development cycle. Many studies, however, reveal that poor project management is the major cause of Web failures both during development and subsequently in the operational phase. Poor project management will defeat good engineering; good project management is a recipe for success. Successfully managing a large, complex Web development is a challenging task requiring multidisciplinary skills and is, in some ways, different from managing traditional IT projects.

Quality control, assurance and documentation are other important activities, but they are often neglected. Like project management, these activities need to spread throughout the Web development lifecycle.

Steps to Successful Development

Successful development of Web systems and applications involves multiple interactive steps which influence one another. We recommend the following key steps for successful development and deployment of Web applications (Ginige & Murugesan, 2001c):

1. Understand the system's overall function and operational environment, including the business objectives and requirements, organisation culture and information management policy.
2. Clearly identify the stakeholders — that is, the system's main users and their typical profiles, the organisation that needs the system, and who funds the development.
3. Elicit or specify the (initial) functional, technical, and nontechnical requirements of the stakeholders and the overall system. Further, recognise that these requirements may not remain the same; rather, they are bound to evolve over time during the system development.
4. Develop overall system architecture of the Web-based system that meets the technical and nontechnical requirements.

5. Identify subprojects or subprocesses to implement the system architecture. If the subprojects are too complex to manage, further divide them until they become a set of manageable tasks.
6. Develop and implement the subprojects.
7. Incorporate effective mechanisms to manage the Web system's evolution, change, and maintenance. As the system evolves, repeat the overall process or some parts of it, as required.
8. Address the nontechnical issues, such as revised business processes, organisational and management policies, human resources development, and legal, cultural, and social aspects.
9. Measure the system's performance, analyse the usage of the Web application from Web logs, and review and address users' feedback and suggestions.
10. Refine and update the system.

Web System Design: Challenges

The Internet is an open platform that provides unparalleled opportunities. But it has virtually no control over visitor volume, or when and how they access a Web system. This makes developing Web applications that exhibit satisfactory performance even under a sudden surge in number of users a nebulous and challenging task.

Satisfying the expectations and needs of different types of users with varying skills is not easy. When users find a site unfriendly, confusing, or presented with too much information, they will leave frustrated. Worse yet, these frustrated users may spread the bad news to many others. Web site usability factors include good use of colours, information content, easy navigation, and many more. They also include evaluation from an international perspective so that you can reach a global audience. Web usability factors that impact the Web user experience are (Becker & Berkemeyer, 2002): page layout, design consistency, accessibility, information content, navigation, personalisation, performance, security, reliability, and design standards (naming conventions, formatting, and page organisation).

A Web-based system also has to satisfy many different stakeholders besides the diverse range of users, including: persons who maintain the system, the organisation that needs the system, and those who fund the system development. These may pose some additional challenges to Web-based system design and development.

Today's Web-savvy consumers do not tolerate much margin of error or failure. Web system slow down, failure, or security breach may cause a loss of its customers — probably permanently. A whopping 58 percent of first time customers would not return to a site that crashed (Electronic Hit and Run, USA Today, 10 Feb 2000). According to a study (Inter@ctive Week, 6 Sep 1999), US$4.35 billion may be lost in e-business due to poor Web download speeds alone.

As Web applications are becoming mission-critical, there is greater demand for improved reliability, performance, and security of these applications.

Poor design and infrastructure have caused many Web applications to be unable to support the demands placed on them, so they have therefore failed. Many Web sites have suffered site crashes, performance failures, security breaches, and outages — resulting in irate customers, lost revenue, devalued stocks, a tarnished reputation (bad publicity, lack of customer confidence), permanent loss of customers, and law suits (Williams, 2001). Stock prices have become inextricably linked to the reliability of a company's e-commerce site.

The recent major failures and their impact on enterprises have served as a forceful reminder of the need for capacity planning, and improved performance, quality, and reliability. Successful Web application deployment demands consistent Web site availability, a better understanding of its performance, scalability, and load balancing. Proactive measures are needed to prevent grinding halts and failures from happening in the first place.

Large-scale Web system design is a complex and a challenging activity as it needs to consider many different aspects and requirements, some of which may have conflicting needs (Ivory & Hearst, 2002; Siegel, 2003; Cloyd, 2001).

We use terms like scalability, reliability, availability, maintainability, usability, and security to describe how well the system meets current and future needs and service-level expectations. These *-ilities* characterise (Williams, 2000) a Web system's architectural and other qualities. In the face of increasingly complex systems, these system qualities are often more daunting to understand and manage.

Scalability refers to how well a system's architecture can grow, as traffic, demand for services, or resource utilisation grows. As Web sites grow, small software weaknesses that had no initial noticeable effects can lead to failures, reliability problems, usability problems, and security breaches. Developing Web applications that scale well represents one of today's most important development challenges.

Flexibility is the extent to which the solution can adapt as business requirements change. A flexible architecture facilitates greater reusability and quicker deployment.

Thus, the challenge is to design and develop sustainable Web systems for better:

- Usability — interface design, navigation (Becker & Mottay 2001),
- Comprehension,
- Performance — responsiveness,
- Security and integrity,
- Evolution, growth, and maintainability, and
- Testability.

Web Testing and Evaluation

Testing plays a crucial role in the overall development process (Becker & Berkemeyer, 2002; Hieatt & Mee, 2002; Lam, 2001). However, more often than not, testing and evaluation are neglected aspects of Web development. Many developers test the system only after it had met with failures or limitations have become apparent, resorting to what is known as *retroactive testing*. What is desired in the first place is *proactive testing* at various stages of the Web development lifecycle. Benefits of proactive testing include assurance of proper functioning and guaranteed performance levels, avoidance of costly retroactive fixes, optimal performance, and lower risk.

Testing and validating a large complex Web system is a difficult and expensive task. Testing should not be seen as a one-off activity carried out near the end of development process. One needs to take a broad view and follow a more holistic approach to testing — from design all the way to deployment, maintenance, and continual refinement.

The test planning needs to be carried out early in the project lifecycle. A test plan provides a roadmap so that the Web site can be evaluated through requirements or design stage. It also helps to estimate the time and effort needed for testing — establishing a test environment, finding test personnel, writing test procedures before any testing can actually start, and testing and evaluating the system.

Lam (2001) groups Web testing into the following broad categories and provides excellent practical guidelines on how to test Web systems:

- Browser compatibility
- Page display
- Session management
- Usability
- Content analysis
- Availability
- Backup and recovery
- Transactions
- Shopping, order processing
- Internalisation
- Operational business procedures
- System integration
- Performance
- Login and security

Experience shows that there are many common pitfalls in Web testing and attempts should be made overcome them (Lam, 2001). Testing and evaluation of a Web application may be expensive, but the impact of failures resulting from lack of testing could be more costly or even disastrous.

Knowledge and Skills for Web Development

The knowledge and skills needed for large, complex Web application development are quite diverse and span many different disciplines. They can be broadly classified as:

- Technologies supporting and facilitating Web applications
- Design methods
    - Design for usability — interface design, navigation
    - Design for comprehension
    - Design for performance — responsiveness
    - Design for security and integrity
    - Design for evolution, growth and maintainability
    - Design for testability
    - Graphics and multimedia design
    - Web page development
- System architecture
- Web development methods and processes
- Web project management
- Development tools
- Content management
- Web standards and regulatory requirements

Web Development Team

As previously mentioned, development of a Web application requires a team of people with diverse skills and backgrounds (Hansen, 2004). These individuals include programmers, graphic designers, Web page designers, usability experts, content developers, database designers and administrators, data communication and networking experts, and Web server administrators. A Web development team is multidisciplinary, like a film production team, and must be more versatile than a traditional software development team.

Hansen et al. (2001) presents a classification of the participants in a Web development team and a hierarchy for their skills and knowledge. This classification helps in forming a team and in devising a strategy for successful reskilling of the development team.

Conclusion

Web engineering is specifically targeted toward the successful development, deployment and maintenance of large, complex Web-based systems.

It advocates a holistic and proactive approach to developing successful Web applications. As more applications migrate to the Web environment and play increasingly significant roles in business, education, healthcare, government, and many day-to-day operations, the need for a Web engineering approach to Web application development will only increase. Further, as we now place greater emphasis on the performance, correctness, and availability of Web-based systems, the development and maintenance process will assume greater significance.

Web Engineering is an emerging discipline having both theoretical and practical significance. It is gaining the interest among researchers, developers, academics, and clients. This is evidenced by increased research activities and publications in this area, hosting of dedicated international conferences and workshops, publication of new journals devoted to Web Engineering, and universities offering special courses and programmes on the subject. It is destined for further advancement through research, education, and practice.

> *"To advance Web engineering, it is essential to define its core body of knowledge, to identify the areas in need of greater research and to develop a strategy to tackle the new technologies, new applications and the various technical, methodological, and societal issues that arise in tandem with such developments." (Deshpande, Olsina & Murugesan, 2002)*

Some of the areas that need further study, in no particular order, include:

- Web application delivery on multiple devices — desktop and pocket PCs, mobile phones, PDAs, TVs and refrigerators
- Context-aware Web applications and context-sensitive responses
- Device-independent Web access and content presentation

- Modelling and simulation of Web applications and systems
- Performance evolution and enhancement
- Testing and validation of systems
- Effort and cost estimation
- Web personalisation
- Quality control and assurance

No Silver Bullet!

Web Engineering will not make the problems and the risks go away. But, it can help you plan, monitor, control, and cope with the challenging task of developing large, complex Web applications. It will also facilitate making more informed decisions and developing better quality and better-engineered Web systems and applications.

It is important to understand the wider context in which a Web-based system or application will be used, and design an architecture that will support the development, operation, and maintenance as well as evolution of the Web application in that context, addressing the key issues and considerations. We strongly recommend that Web developers and project managers move away from an ad hoc, hacker-type approach to a well-planned, systematic, and documented approach for the development of large, high-performance, evolutionary, and/or mission-critical Web sites and applications.

Our key recommendations for successfully developing and implementing large, complex Web application are to:

- Adopt a sound strategy and follow a suitable methodology to successfully manage the development and maintenance of Web systems.
- Recognise that, in most cases, development of a Web application is not an event, but a process, since the applications' requirements evolve. It will have a start, but it will not have a predictable end as in traditional IT/software projects.
- Within the continuous process, identify, plan, and schedule various development activities so that they have a defined start and finish.
- Remember that the planning and scheduling of activities is very important to successfully manage the overall development, allocate resources, and monitor progress.
- Consider the big picture during context analysis, planning, and designing a Web application. If you do not, you may end up redesigning the entire system and repeating the process all over again. If you address the changing nature of requirements early on, you can build into the design cost-effective ways of managing change and new requirements.

- Recognise that development of a large Web application calls for teamwork and shared responsibility among the team members, so motivate a team culture.

Web engineering has been successfully applied in a number of Web applications. A well-engineered Web system is:

- Functionally complete and correct
- Usable
- Robust and reliable
- Maintainable
- Secure
- Perform satisfactorily even under flash and peak loads
- Scalable
- Portable, where required perform across different common platforms; compatible with multiple browsers
- Reusable
- Interoperable with other Web and information systems
- Universal accessibility (access by people with different kinds disabilities)
- Well-documented

Time to deploy an online Web system, though still important, is no longer a dominant process driver, as more emphasis is now placed on quality Web systems in terms of functionally, usability, content maintainability, performance, and reliability.

Web engineering can help enterprises and developers to convert their Web systems and applications from a potential costly mess into powerful resource for gaining sustainable competitive advantage.

Acknowledgments

The authors would like to thank Yogesh Deshpande and Steve Hansen, both from University of Western Sydney, Australia, for their contribution in origination and development of the Web engineering discipline and for their input on various aspects of Web development reported in this chapter which evolved through our collaborative efforts over the years. We would also like to thank our graduate students Anupama Ginige and Indra Seher who contributed to formulation and presentation some of the ideas presented in this chapter.

References

Almeida, V.A.F., & Menasce, D.A. (2002). Capacity planning for Web services: An essential tool for managing Web services. *IT Professional*, (July-August), 33-38.

Becker S., & Berkemeyer, A. (2002). Rapid application design and testing for usability. *IEEE Multimedia*, (Oct-Dec), 38-46.

Becker, S., & Mottay, F. (2001). A global perspective of Web usability for online business applications. *IEEE Software, 18*(1), 54-61.

Cloyd, M.H. (2001). Designing user-centered Web applications in Web time. *IEEE Software, 18*(1), 62-69.

Collins, R.W. (2002). Software localization for Internet software: Issues and methods. *IEEE Software,* (March/April), 74-80.

Dart, S. (2001). *Configuration management: A missing link in Web engineering.* Norwood, MA: Arttech House.

Deshpande, Y. et al. (2002). Web engineering. *Journal of Web Engineering, 1*(1), 3-17.

Deshpande, Y., Ginige, A., Murugesan, S., & Hansen, S., (2002). Consolidating Web engineering as a discipline. *SEA Software*, (April), 32-34.

Deshpande, Y., & Hansen, S. (2001). Web engineering: creating a discipline among disciplines. *IEEE Multimedia,* (April - June), 82-87.

Deshpande Y., Olsina, L., & Murugesan, S. (2002). Web engineering. Report on the *Third ICSE Workshop on Web Engineering, ICSE2002,* Orlando, FL, USA.

Ginige, A., & Murugesan, S. (2001a). Web engineering: An introduction. *IEEE Multimedia, 8*(1), 14-18.

Ginige, A. & Murugesan, S. (2001b). The essence of Web engineering: Managing the diversity and complexity of Web application development. *IEEE Multimedia, 8*(2), 22-25.

Ginige, A., & Murugesan, S. (2001c). Web engineering: A methodology for developing scalable, maintainable Web applications. *Cutter IT Journal, 14*(7), 24-35.

Glass, R. (2001). Who's right in the Web development debate? *Cutter IT Journal, 14*(7), 6-10.

Hansen, S. (2002). Web information systems: The changing landscape of management models and Web applications. *Proceedings of the 14th international conference on software engineering and knowledge engineering* (pp. 747-753). ACM.

Hansen, S., Deshpande, Y. & Murugesan S. (2001). A skills hierarchy for Web-based systems development. In S. Murugesan & Y. Deshpande (Eds.), *Web Engineering – Managing Diversity and Complexity of Web Application Development* (LNCS Vol 2016, pp. 223-235). Berlin: Springer.

Hieatt, E., & Mee, R. (2002). Going faster: Testing the Web application. *IEEE Software*, (March - April), 60-65.

Ivory, M.Y, & Hearst, M.A. (2002). Improving Web site design. *IEEE Internet Computing*, (March - April), 56-63.

Lam, W. (2001). Testing e-commerce systems: A practical guide. *IT Professional, 3*(2), 19-27.

Lowe, D. (2003). Web system requirements: An overview. *Requirements Engineering, 8*, 102-113.

Menasce, D.A, & Almeida, V.A.F. (2002). *Capacity planning for Web services: Metrics, models, and methods.* Upper Saddle River, NJ: Prentice Hall.

Merialdo, P. et al. (2003). Design and development of data-intensive Web sites: The Araneus Atzeni. *ACM Transactions on Internet Technology, 3*(1), 49-92.

Murugesan, S. (1998). *Web engineering.* Presentation at the *First Workshop on Web Engineering, World Wide Web Conference (WWW7),* Brisbane, Australia.

Murugesan, S. et al. (1999). Web engineering: A New Discipline for Development of Web-based systems. In *Proceedings of the First ICSE Workshop on Web Engineering,* Los Angeles (pp. 1-9).

Murugesan, S., & Deshpande, Y. (Eds) (2001). *Web engineering: Managing diversity and complexity of Web application development.* Lecture Notes in Computer Science – Hot Topics, 2016. Berlin: Springer Verlag.

Offutt, J. (2002). Quality attributes of Web software applications. *IEEE Software, Special Issue on Software Engineering of Internet Software, 19*(2), 25-32.

Oppenheimer, D., & Patterson, D.A. (2002). Architecture and dependability of large-scale Internet services. *IEEE Internet Computing*, September-October, 41-49.

Pressman, R.S. (2001). What a tangled Web we weave. *IEEE Software, 18*(1), 18-21.

Pressman, R.S. (2004). Applying Web Engineering, Part 3. *Software Engineering: A Practitioner's Perspective* (6th ed.). New York: McGraw-Hill.

Reifer, D.J. (2000). Web development: Estimating quick-to-market software. *IEEE Software, 17*(6), 57-64.

Siegel, D.A. (2003). The business case for user-centered design: Increasing your power of persuasion. *Interactions, 10*(3).

Uden, L. (2002). Design process for Web applications. *IEEE Multimedia,* (Oct-Dec), 47-55.

Williams, J. (2000). Correctly assessing the "ilities" requires more than marketing hype. *IT Professional, 2*(6), 65-67.

Williams, J. (2001). Avoiding CNN moment. *IT Professional, 3*(2), 68-70.

Bibliography on Web Engineering

For further information on many different aspects of Web development and Web Engineering, we have listed below some useful resources such as books, special issues, journal articles, and Web sites.

Books

Burdman, J. (1999). *Collaborative Web development: Strategies and best practices for Web teams.* Addison-Wesley.

Dart, S. (2001), *Configuration management: A missing link in Web engineering.* Norwood, MA: Arttech House.

Dustin, E., Rashka, J., & McDiarmid, D. (2001). *Quality Web systems: Performance, security, and usability.* Reading, MA: Addison-Wesley.

Friedlein, A. (2000). *Web project management: Delivering successful commercial Web sites.* Morgan Kaufmann.

Friedlein, A. (2003). *Maintaining and evolving successful commercial Web sites.* Morgan Kaufmann.

Gerrad, P. & Thompson, N. (2002). *Risk-based e-business testing.* Artech Publishers.

Hackos, J.T. (2002). *Content management for dynamic Web delivery.* John Wiley & Sons.

Lowe, D. & Hall, W. (1999). *Hypermedia and the Web: An engineering approach.* New York: John Wiley & Sons.

Menasce, D.A. & Almeida, V.A.F. (2002). *Capacity planning for Web services: Metrics, models, and methods.* Upper Saddle River, NJ: Prentice Hall.

Nakano, R. (2002). *Web content management: A collaborative approach.* Boston: Addison Wesley.

Nguyen, H. Q. (2001). *Testing applications on the Web: Test planning for Internet-based systems.* John Wiley.

Nielsen, J. (1999). *Designing Web usability: The practice of simplicity.* Indianapolis, IN: New Riders Publishing.

Powell, T.A. (1998). *Web site engineering: Beyond Web page design.* Upper Saddle River, NJ: Prentice Hall.

Powell, T.A. (2000). *Web design: The complete guide.* New York: McGraw-Hill.

Pressman, R.S. (2004). Applying Web engineering. In *Software engineering: A practitioner's perspective.* New York: McGraw-Hill.

Rosenfeld, L. & Morville, P. (2002). *Information architecture for the World Wide Web: Designing large-scale Web sites.* O'Reilly & Associates.

Scharl, A. (2000). *Evolutionary Web Development.* Springer.

Shklar, L. & Rosen, R. (2003). *Web application architecture: Principles, protocols and practices.* John Wiley & Sons.

Stottlemyer, D. (2001). *Automated Web testing toolkit: Expert methods for testing and managing Web applications.* John Wiley.

Vidgen, R. et al (2002). *Developing Web information systems: From strategy to implementation.* Butterworth Heinemann.

Wodtke, C. (2002). *Information architecture: Blueprints for the Web.* New Riders.

Journals

IEEE Internet Computing. www.computer.org/internet

IEEE Software. www.computer.org/software

Journal of Web Engineering, Rinton Press. www.rintonpress.com/journals/jwe

Journal of Web Engineering and Technology. www.inderscience.com

Web Information Systems Engineering. http://www.i-wise.org

World Wide Web, Kluwer Academic Publishers. http://www.kluweronline.com/issn/1386-145X

Special Issues

Engineering Internet Software, *IEEE Software*, March-April 2002.

Testing E-business Applications, *Cutter IT Journal,* September 2001.

Usability and the Web, *IEEE Internet Computing*, March-April 2002.

Usability Engineering, *IEEE Software*, January-February 2001.

Web Engineering, *Cutter IT Journal*, 14(7), July 2001.

Web Engineering, *IEEE MultiMedia*, Jan.–Mar. 2001 (Part 1) and April–June 2001 (Part 2).

Journal Articles

Almedia, V.A.F., & Menasce, D.A. (2002). Capacity planning for Web services: An essential tool for managing Web services. *ITPro*, July-August 2002, 33-38.

Arlitt, M., et al. (2001). Characterizing the scalability of a large Web-based shopping system. *ACM Transactions on Internet Technology, 1*(1), 44-69.

Barnes, S. & Vidgen, R. (2002). An integrative approach to the assessment of e-commerce quality. *Journal of Electronic Commerce Research, 3*(3). http://www.webqual.co.uk/papers/jecr_published.pdf

Baskerville. et al. (2003). Is Internet-speed software development different? *IEEE Software*, Nov-Dec, 70-77.

Becker, S. & Mottay, F. (2001). A global perspective of Web usability for online business applications. *IEEE Software, 18*(1), 54-61.

Brewer, E.A. (2002). Lessons from giant-scale services. *IEEE Internet Computing,* July, 46-55.

Cardellini, V. et al. (1999). Dynamic balancing on Web server systems. *IEEE Internet Computing,* May-June, 2839.

Ceri, S., Fraternali, P., & Bongio, A. (2000, May). Web modelling language (WebML): A modelling language for designing Web sites. *Proceedings of the World Wide Web WWW9 Conference,* Amsterdam.

Cloyd, M.H. (2001). Designing user-centered Web applications in Web time. *IEEE Software, 18*(1), 62-69.

Collins, R.W. (2002). Software localization for Internet software: Issues and methods. *IEEE Software*.

Davison, B.D. (2002). A Web catching primer. *IEEE Internet Computing*.

Deshpande et al. (2002). Web engineering. *Journal of Web Engineering, 1*(1), 3-17.

Deshpande, Y. et al. (2002). Consolidating Web engineering as a discipline. *SEA Software*.

Deshpande, Y. et al. (2002, July). Web site auditing – The first step towards reengineering. *Proc 14th International Conference on Software Engineering and Knowledge Engineering,* Italy, 2002, pp. 731 – 737.

Deshpande, Y. & Hansen, S. (2002). Web Engineering: Creating a discipline among disciplines. *IEEE Multimedia,* 82-87.

Fewster, R. & Mendes, E. (2001, April 4-6). Measurement, prediction and risk analysis for Web applications. *IEEE Seventh International Software Metrics Symposium* London, England, pp. 338-348.

Ginige, A. & Murugesan, S. (2001) Web engineering: An introduction. *IEEE Multimedia, 8*(1), 14-18.

Ginige, A. & Murugesan, S. (2001). Web engineering: A methodology for developing scalable, maintainable Web applications. *Cutter IT Journal, 14*(7) 24–35.

Ginige, A. & Murugesan, S. (2001). The essence of Web engineering: Managing the diversity and complexity of Web application development. *IEEE Multimedia, 8*(2), 22-25.

Glass, R. Who's right in the Web development debate? *Cutter IT Journal, 14*(7), 6-10.

Goeschka, K.M. & Schranz, M.W. (2001). Client and legacy integration in object-oriented Web engineering. *IEEE Multimedia, Special issues on Web Engineering, 8*(1), 32-41.

Hieatt, E. & Mee, R. (2002). Going faster: Testing the Web application. *IEEE Software,* 60-65.

Ingham, D.B., Shrivastava, S.K., & Panzieri, F. (2000). Constructing dependable Web services. *IEEE Internet Computing*, 25-33.

Isakowitz, T., Stohr, E. & Balasubmmnian, P. (1995). RMM: A methodology for structured hypermedia design. *Comm A CM, 38*(8), 35-44.

Ivory, M.Y & Hearst, M.A. (2002). Improving Web site design. *IEEE Internet Computing*, 56-63.

Kirda, E., Jazayeri, M., Kerer, C. & Schranz, M. (2001). Experiences in engineering flexible Web services. *IEEE Multimedia, Special issues on Web Engineering, 8*(1), 58-65.

Lam, W. (2001). Testing e-commerce systems: A practical guide. *IT Professional, 3*(2), 19-27.

Liu, S., et al. (2001). A practical approach to enterprise IT security. *IT Professional, 3*(5) 35-42.

Lowe, D. (2003). Web system requirements: An overview. *Requirements Engineering, 8,* 102-113.

Lowe, D. & Henderson-Sellers, B. (2001). OPEN to change. *Cutter IT Journal, 14*(7), 11-17.

Maurer, F. & Martel, S. (2002). Extreme programming: Rapid development for Web-based applications. *IEEE Internet Computing*, 86-90.

Menasce, D.A. (1993). Load testing of Web sites. *IEEE Internet Computing,* 89-92.

Merialdo. P. et al. (2003). Design and development of data-intensive Web sites: The Araneus Atzeni. *ACM Transactions on Internet Technology, 3*(1), 49-92.

Mich, L. et al. (2003). Evaluating and designing Web site quality. *IEEE Multimedia*, 34-43.

Offutt, J. (2002). Quality attributes of Web software applications. *IEEE Software, Special Issue on Software Engineering of Internet Software, 19*(2), 25-32.

Olsina, L., Lafuente, G. & Rossi, G. (2001). Specifying quality characteristics and attributes for Websites. In S. Murugesan & Y. Deshpande (Eds), *Web engineering – managing diversity and complexity of Web application development* (pp. 266-278). Berlin: Springer.

Oppenheimer, D., & Patterson, D.A. (2002). Architecture and dependability of large-scale Internet services. *IEEE Internet Computing*, 41-49.

Perlman, G. (2002). Achieving universal usability by designing for change. *IEEE Internet Computing,* 46-55.

Powel, T.A. (1998). *Web site engineering: Beyond Web page design.* Prentice Hall.

Pressman, R.S. (2001). What a tangled Web we weave. *IEEE Software, 18*(1), 18-21.

Pressman, R.S. (2001). Can Internet-based applications be engineered? *IEEE Software, 15*(5), 104-110.

Reifer, D.J. (2000). Web development: Estimating quick-to-market software. *IEEE Software.*

Roe, V. & Gonik, S. (2002). Server-side design principles for scalable Internet systems. *IEEE Software*, 34-41.

Scalable Internet Services (2001). *Internet Computing.*

Schwabe, D. & Rossi, G. (1998). An object oriented approach to Web-based application design. *Theory and Practice of Object Systems (TAPOS), special issue on the Internet, 4*(4), 207-225.

Schwabe, D., Esmemldo, L., Rossi, G. & Lyardet, F. (2001). Engineering Web application for reuse. *IEEE Multimedia, 8*(1), 20-31.

Scott, D., & Sharp, R. (2002). Developing secure Web applications, *IEEE Internet Computing*, 38-45.

Siegel, D.A. (2003). The business case for user-centred design: Increasing your power of persuasion. *Interactions, 10*(3).

Upchurch, L. et al. (2001). Using card sorts to elicit Web page quality attributes. *IEEE Software.*

Williams, J. (2000). Correctly assessing the "ilities" requires more than marketing hype. *IT Professional, 2*(6), 65-67.

Web sites

ACM SIGWEB: www.acm.org/sigweb

Jakob Nielsen's Website: www.useit.com

NIST Web Usability: zing.ncsl.nist.gov/WebTools/index.html

Universal Usability Guide: www.universalusability.org

Usability Professional Association: www.upassoc.org

Usable Web: www.usableweb.com

Web Engineering Resources, R.S. Pressman and Associates: www.ispa.com/spi/index.html#webe

Web Engineering.org Community Homepage: www.webengineering.org

Web Information System Development Methodology: www.wisdm.net

Web Information Systems Engineering: http://www.i-wise.org

Web Quality: www.webqual.co.uk

World Wide Web Consortium: www.w3.org

Conferences

International Conference on Web Engineering (ICWE) 2004 and 2005. www.icwe2004.org; www.icwe2005.org

Web Information Systems Engineering Conference. http://www.i-wise.org/

World Wide Web Conference. www.www2004.org; www.www2005.org

Chapter II

Web Engineering Resources Portal (WEP): A Reference Model and Guide

Sotiris P. Christodoulou
University of Patras, Greece

Theodore S. Papatheodorou
University of Patras, Greece

Abstract

This chapter introduces the Web Engineering Resources Portal (WEP) as a basic reference model and guide for Web Engineers. WEP provides a general classification of Web Engineering resources under technologies, research results, and tools. It consists of a reference model and a resources portal. The objective of the WEP reference model is to provide a common basic terminology, a technical-oriented classification of Web applications (WebApps), a specification of WebApps Logical and Physical Architectures, a classification of skills needed in Web projects and a generic and adaptable Web lifecycle process model. The WEP reference model provides the framework upon which Web Engineering resources are classified and presented. The WEP portal provides several and cross-referenced taxonomies of technologies, research results, and tools whereas its objective is to facilitate Web Engineers to comprehend available resources, understand their role and appropriately use them during development and operation/maintenance of Web information systems.

Introduction

Web Engineering is defined in Deshpande, Murugesan, Ginige, Hansen, Schwbe, Gaedke and White (2002), by experienced researchers in the field as: "The application of systematic, disciplined and quantifiable approaches to development, operation, and maintenance of Web-based Information Systems (WIS). It is both a pro-active approach and a growing collection of theoretical and empirical research in Web application development." In the same work, Web engineering is essentially defined as "matching the problem domains properly to solution methods and the relevant mix of technologies" (Deshpande et al., 2002).

But, what is WIS[1]? Holck (2003) provides a good survey of WIS definitions around the literature, where there is some confusion because of diverse perspective and terms used. Thus, we conclude that the first thing Web Engineers really need is a common terminology on WIS and its components. To address this need, we include in the WEP Reference Model a specific part entitled: *WEP-Terms: WEP Basic Terminology & Definitions.* We replicate the definitions of WIS and Web applications here as well.

WIS is an information system utilizing Web technologies to provide information (data) and functionality (services) to end-users through a hypermedia-based presentation/interaction user interface on web-enabled devices.

WebApps are the different functionality-oriented components of a WIS. A WebApp is actually a small-scale WIS, providing very specific information or functionality. Many developers use these terms as synonymous, especially for small WISs.

Moreover, we define the "planning, development, operation, and maintenance of WIS" as a *Web project.* Basically, it is a lifecycle process model to ensure successful WIS development and evolving through a number of stages from investigation of initial requirements through analysis, design, implementation, testing, and operation/maintenance.

In each stage, the process model specifies the activities that are carried out, the relationships between these activities, the skills needed (roles), the resources that are used, the results that are created, etc. The activities are carried out by teams of developers who are based on selected *Web technologies*, take advantage of selected *research results,* and use a number of *tools*. This triplet constitutes the Web Engineering Resources (WER), which includes anything available to developers to support the Web project. Figure 1 shows how they are produced and related to each other. However, WERs are not easily discoverable and understandable by developers, so they are often not used appropriately or at all during the Web projects for reasons outlined in the next section.

The main objective of this chapter is to put Web Engineering Resources in use and to provide a reference model and guide for Web Engineers. We call it the Web Engineering Resources Portal (shortly WEP), because it provides several and cross-referenced taxonomies of these resources, just like an information portal does. WEP provides a WEP reference model and WER portal. The *WEP reference model* includes:

Figure 1. Web engineering resources

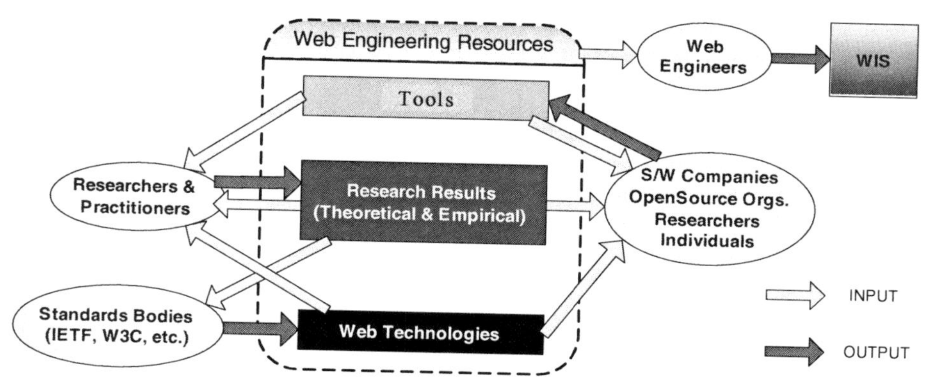

(a) **WEP-Terms:** WEP basic terminology and definitions. We define the main terms used in WEP in order to determine the semantics of the terms used in it.

(b) **WEP-Arch:** Identification and technical-oriented classification of common WIS components (namely WebApps). Specification of the three *WebApps' logical layers*: content, logic and interface, and the *WebApps' physical architecture.*

(c) **WEP-Teams:** Specification and classification of skills needed in the WIS project under abstract team classes of stakeholders.

(d) **WEP-Process:** A WIS lifecycle process model with three phases: planning, deployment and evolution. It is a generic process model through which WEP-Teams are using WERs to deliver and maintain a WIS based on the WEP-Arch. We keep this high-level process generic, easy for the developers to follow, comprehend and adapt to specific WIS requirements.

(e) **WER-Portal:** Several Web Engineering Resources taxonomies through which Web engineers will be able to easily and meaningfully locate research resources, web technologies, and tools and understand their role during WIS development and WIS operation/maintenance. The objective of the WER portal is to help Web Engineers to comprehend and appropriately use available and emerging Web technologies/tools and to provide means to transfer knowledge (research results) and experience (patterns/good practices) in an easy and understandable way. The WER portal should be regularly updated in order to include new WERs.

Background: Web Development Status

"Web development" is a global term used for development of either a few HTML pages or a large-scale WIS. Moreover, the word "development" refers only to design and implementation issues, while the lifecycle of a WIS is bigger. Thus, we usually prefer using the term "Web project" instead. Moreover, instead of "Web developer" we often use the term "Web Engineer" whenever we have to emphasize the strong engineering skills needed.

In the literature (Holck, 2003) concerning Web development, quite a number of special characteristics (comparing to other information systems) have been addressed. Four of the perhaps most often mentioned are: the new, incremental development process, the time pressure, the new professions, and a diverse and remote user group. Some other special characteristics include: a much more fine-grained ongoing maintenance process (actually an evolution), strong integration requirements with legacy systems, unpredicted end-users and an emphasis on the content (content management and personalized/adaptive information). For more information on the topic refer to Deshpande et al. (2002).

To address these special characteristics, several Web-oriented lifecycle processes have been proposed. Some of them come from the area of software engineering and are tailored to the WIS special needs (we provide the taxonomy of them inside WEP). A Web Engineer's first choice for a Web project is the lifecycle process among many and similar ones. Additionally, in several stages of the process, they also must choose among several software tools, technologies, and research resources. Especially when it comes to the implementation phase, several issues concerning Web technologies are coming up, and Web Engineers has to carefully pick the right ones.

The problem is getting even bigger if we consider that tools and technologies (i.e., standards) are shifting extremely fast in the Web world and their volume is big. As Nambisan and Wang (1999) state, "Technology-related knowledge barriers are intensified by the fact that much of the Web technologies are not yet mature, making the task of choosing from among alternative technological solutions a challenging one." Furthermore, Web projects span a variety of application domains and involve stakeholders of different backgrounds. Thus, they have very different requirements for methodologies, tools and technologies, even for different parts of the same WIS.

Finally, some research results, like Hansen, Deshpande and Murugesan (2001) specify required skills for developers working on different parts of WIS development. However, many real projects today are carried out with crucial roles or skills missing. Thus, unskilled or inexperienced developers need help to quickly understand what Web Engineering can offer to them.

Conclusions

Based on our extended experience for several years on building large-scale Web-based systems and on our studies and research (Christodoulou, Styliaras & Papatheodorou, 1998; Christodoulou, Zafiris & Papatheodorou, 2001) and above analysis, we have concluded the following:

- In several stages of all proposed Web development processes, developers are asked to consider carefully and choose correctly the appropriate technologies to base on their development. However, these processes are not providing any way to help achieve it. They assume that developers have the appropriate technology knowledge and experience, but this is not true for most Web developers.

- Very few research results are transferred to real-life projects. Web Engineers need time to study all research results in the fields of Web Engineering and others affecting it, like multimedia, data management, software engineering, network engineering, etc.
- Emerging technologies are often used hesitantly in the beginning, and it takes a lot of time for them to be adopted by a large part of web development community. Developers need time to study and understand new emerging technologies in such a broad field.
- Developers need time to use and understand new tools, like development platforms and emerging languages.

It is clear that Web Engineers have to continually be in a process of studying, understanding, using, and testing emerging tools and technologies. They need to exhaustively study the recent research results, in order to gain the knowledge, experience, and skills to decide correctly. This is a very time consuming task and it is very difficult for most Web Engineers to follow in the strict timeline of a Web project. The effect of this is the fact that WERs are not used appropriately or at all during current WIS projects. Cutter Consortium (2000) provides some statistical data on Web projects that prove this.

We strongly believe that there are solutions out there but are not easily discoverable and understandable by Web Engineers. Web Engineers need help and guidance in accessing the knowledge and experience of web development. Current solutions include: design patterns, good practices, and tutorials on technologies and tools. What is missing is an overall view and structure of WERs under several taxonomies that helps you find what you need, and then you have to study and explore it yourself. By studying WERs, we concluded that there is a very complex information space that needs to be engineered, in order to provide WERs to developers through a meaningful way. To this end we introduce WEP.

WEP Reference Model

The objective of the WEP reference model is to provide a common basic terminology (WEP-Terms), a technical-oriented classification of WebApps, a specification of WebApps logical and physical architectures (WEP-Arch), a classification of skills needed in WIS Project (WEP-Teams), and a generic and adaptable WIS lifecycle process model (WEP-Process) through which WEP-Teams are using WERs to deliver, maintain and evolve a WIS based on the WEP-Arch. This reference model will provide the base and framework on which the WERs will be classified and presented.

WEP-Terms: WEP Basic Terminology and Definitions

Throughout this chapter, several Web and non-Web terms are used. In order for the readers to perceive the concepts outlined in this chapter, we have to share the same understanding of basic terms. Let us start by defining the general terms: data, information, software, program and application.

Anything that can be stored electronically is either data or software.

Data[2] are distinct pieces of information in digital form, formatted in a special way that can be read, manipulated, or transmitted on some digital channel by software. Data can be related with other data. These relations or links are part of the data that facilitate its efficient manipulation. Data on its own has no meaning. Only when interpreted by some kind of data processing system does it take on meaning and become *information*. People or computers can find patterns in data to perceive information, and information can be used to enhance knowledge.

Software is a collection of instructions in a form that can be read and executed by a computer. Software can be divided in two general categories: systems software and programs (application software). Systems software includes the operating system and all the utilities that enable the computer to function and support the production and execution of programs.

An *application* is a composition of one or more programs that do real work for humans. One of the programs is responsible for providing the user interface, through which humans can interact with the application, in order to generally do two things: (1) get data as information (specific programs to read, listen, or watch data) or (2) get functionality over data as services.

Figure 2 visualizes the meaning of some of the above terms. The following Web-oriented terms are used here as defined in W3C "Web Characterization Terminology & Definitions Sheet[3]" (W3C Working Draft 24-May-1999): *URI*, *link*, *anchor*, *user*, *Web client*, *Web request*, *explicit Web request*, *implicit Web request*, *Web server*, *Web response*, *cookie*, *Web resource*, *Web page*, and *Web site*. We suggest studying these definitions before reading this chapter.

Web Architecture[4]

The *World Wide Web*, known as "WWW", "the Web" or "W3") as defined by W3C, is "the universe of network-accessible information, available through Web-enabled devices, like computer, phone, television, or networked refrigerator." The Web is a network-spanning information space in which the information objects, referred to collectively as *Web resources*, are identified by global identifiers called URIs and are interconnected by links defined within that space.

A *Web agent* is software acting on this information space on behalf of a person, entity, or process. Agents include servers, proxies, browsers, spiders, multimedia players, and other user agents.

Figure 2. Basic terms relations

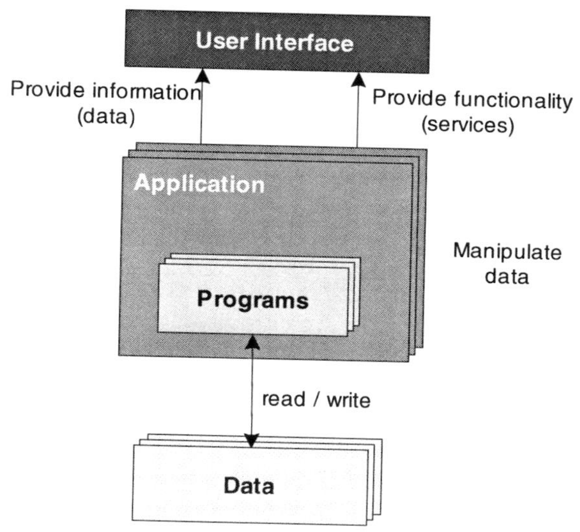

Web architecture encompasses both protocols that define the information space, by way of identification and representation, and protocols that define the interaction of agents within the Web. We further explore these three dimensions of Web architecture:

- **Identification:** Each Web resource is identified by a URI. A URI should be assigned to each resource that is intended to be identified, shared, or described by reference (linked). The fragment identifier of a URI allows indirect identification of a secondary resource by reference to a primary resource and additional information. URI is used to access a resource. Access may take many forms, including retrieving a representation (e.g., using HTTP GET or HEAD), modifying the state of the resource (e.g., using HTTP POST or PUT), and deleting the resource (e.g., using HTTP DELETE).
- **Interaction:** Web agents exchange information via messages that are constructed according to a non-exclusive set of messaging protocols (e.g., HTTP, FTP, NNTP, SMTP, etc.). These messages arise as the result of actions requested by a user or called for by a rendering engine while processing hypermedia-aware data formats. A message consists of representation data and possibly resource metadata (e.g., HTTP 'alternates' and 'vary' headers), representation metadata (e.g., HTTP content-Type field), and/or message metadata (e.g., the HTTP transfer-encoding header).
- **Representation:** Messages carry representations of a resource. A resource communicates the overall information about its state through these representations,

which are built from a non-exclusive set of data formats, used separately or in combination (including XHTML, CSS, PNG, XLink, RDF/XML, SVG, and SMIL animation). A data format is defined by a format specification, which also governs the handling of fragment identifiers. The first data format that was used to build representations was HTML. Since then, data formats for the Web have flourished. The Web architecture does not apply constraints which data formats can be used to build representations.

WIS and WebApps

We define a *Web-based Information System*, or *WIS*, as an information system, utilizing Web architecture to provide information (data) and functionality (services) to end-users through a hypermedia-based presentation/interaction user interface on web-enabled devices. WISs vary widely in their scope, from informational systems to e-business transaction systems, to network-distributed Web Services and beyond. A high-level functionality-oriented taxonomy of WISs was provided by Isakowitz, Bieber and Vitali (1998): "There are four general kinds of WISs: Intranets, to support internal work, Web-presence sites which are marketing tools designed to reach consumers outside the firm, electronic commerce systems that support consumer interaction such as online shopping, and a blend of internal and external systems to support business to business communication commonly called extranets."

Generally, a WIS deals with vast amounts of data — in heterogeneous sources and formats — and distributed functionality coded in different programming languages and platforms. Like traditional information systems, beyond a delivering (run-time) infra-

Figure 3. From Web resources to WWW

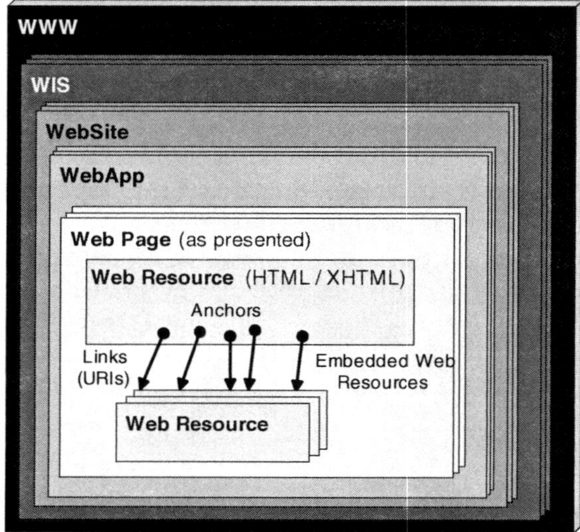

structure, WISs should provide a development and maintenance infrastructure to allow the managing of its data, s/w functionality and agents.

WISs are designed, developed, and maintained in order to fulfill specific goals of targeted end-users. These goals are the cornerstones of a WIS project. We define a Web Application, or *WebApp*, as a WIS component that covers at least one of end-users' goals. WebApps are the different functionality-oriented components of a WIS. At run-time, a WebApp is comprehended by the end-users as a set of *WebPages*, that provides very specific information (e.g., the WebPages of a tutorial on JavaScript) or functionality (e.g., the collection of WebPages through which an end-user can order goods and pay with his credit card). A WebPage may provide access to more than one WebApp, for example, an informative page that also includes at the top a form box for querying the search engine of the WIS, which is a separate WebApp. Actually a WIS is a large-scale WebApp that fulfills several end-users' goals. That is why most developers use these terms as synonymous, especially for small WISs. Figure 3 "visualizes" the meaning of these terms.

WebPages

According to the definitions of WIS and WebApps, the cornerstone of both is the WebPage. A WebPage is a collection of information, consisting of one or more Web resources, intended to be rendered simultaneously, and identified by a single URI. More specifically, a Web page consists of a Web resource with zero, one, or more embedded Web resources intended to be rendered as a single unit, and referred to by the URI of the *main Web resource* which is not embedded.

Any software or data in any digital form under a WebServer can be "downloaded" via HTTP to a WebClient. However, we consider *Web data* to be data in any format that can be delivered over Web and viewed or heard within the context of a WebPage on a WebClient. *Web software* is a software code in any language that can be executed within a WebClient or on server-side (locally or distributed) in order to provide components of a WebPage.

WebPages are built from a non-exclusive set of data formats, used separately or in combination (like [X]HTML, CSS, PNG, Real Audio, SVG, JPG, or MPEG). The main resource of a WebPage should be in a data format that can support linking mechanisms, identifying links to embedding resources or links to other WebPages worldwide. The data format of this main resource is only limited to the WebClients' implementations. Currently, the supported formats are: HTML and XHTML family markup document types (see technologies section for a summarizing of current ones). Thus, we also refer to the main resource as (X)HTML Page.

All these mark-up document types provide tag elements that can be grouped under tag sets of a specific functionality. After studying the current (e.g., HTML, XHTML 1.0, XHTML Basic) and the near future ones (XTHML 2.0) we provide a general classification of WebPage's tag sets in Table 1.

Table 1. HTML 4.01, XHTML 1.0 and Basic tag elements

General Tags	
Structure	**html, head, body,** frameset(frame), noframes e.g., html (head, body) or html (head, frameset(frame), noframes)
Head	**title, base, meta**, style (StyleLang), script (ScriptLang), **object(param)** (share objects across frames' WebPages) **link**: Links to alternate versions of a current document (written in another human language, designed for different media, for instance a version especially suited for printing), Links to the starting page of a collection of documents, Links an external style sheet or script to a document, etc. *Link Types* supported by HTML: Alternate, Stylesheet, Start, Next, Prev, Contents, Index, Glossary, Copyright, Chapter, Section, Subsection, Appendix, Help, Bookmark (plus Script in XHTML).

Body and noframes tags can include the following tag sets:

Structure & Presentation Tag Elements			
Core Text	Text	**P, pre, blockquote, div, h1-h6, address**	B
		span, br, em, strong, dfn, code, samp, kbd, var, cite, abbr, acronym, q	I
	List	**ul(li), ol(li), dl(dt,dd),** *dir, menu*	B
Extra Text	Table	**table (caption**, thead, tfoot, tbody, colgroup, col, **tr, th, td)**	B
	Presentation	tt, i, b, big, small, sub, sup, strike, *s, u, font, fontbase*	I
		hr, *center*	B
	Misc	Edit: ins, del, Bi-directional text: bdo	B,I
Hypertext		**A**	I
MediaObject		**img, object(param)**, map(area), iframe Any multimedia format supported by Web Clients (natively or via Plug-ins) like, Raster Images (GIF, JPG, PNG), Vector Images (SVG, WebCGM), Animated Images (GIF), Animated Video (Flash, ShockWave), Video (MPEG, AVI, DIVX, MOV), Audio (MP3, WAV), Streamming Video (RealVideo), Streaming Audio (Real Audio), Documents (PDF, PS, MSOffice), or (X)HTML files.	I
ClientProgram		**object(param)**, *applet(param)* Small programs (except client scripts) that can be executed on Web Clients via Plug-ins, like: Java Applets, Flash, ShockWave, Active-X Controls.	I
Interact Tag Elements & Events Attributes			
Form		**form**, fieldset(legend),*isindex*	B
		input, select (optgroup, **option), textarea, label,** button	I
ClientScript		script (ScriptLang)	B,I
		Noscript	B
Events (attributes)		onload, onunload, onclick, ondblclick, onmousedown, onmouseup, onmouseover, onmousemove, onmouseout, onfocus, onblur, onkeypress, onkeydown, onkeyup, onsubmit, onreset, onselect, onchange These events attributes may be used with most elements, especially with Form ones. It is possible to associate an action with a certain number of events that occur when a user interacts with a Web page. Each of the "intrinsic events" listed above takes a value that is a script. The script is executed whenever the event occurs for that element. The syntax of script data depends on the scripting language.	
Embedded code of StyleLangs and ScriptLangs			
StyleLang		Any style sheet language (either embedded or in separate files) that attaches style (e.g. fonts, colors, content positioning) to different elements of structured documents (e.g., HTML, XHTML, XHTMLBasic and XML), such as HTML headers, links, tables or XML elements. Basic features: Input languages and Output devices. The most famous StyleSheetLangs are: **CSS** (we refer to CSS2 which build on CSS1) and **XSL/FO**. CSS can be applied to HTML and XML languages (like XHTML), while XSL/FO only to XML languages. Both support media-specific style sheets for visual browsers, aural devices, printers, Braille devices, handheld devices, etc.	
ScriptLang		Tiny program code (either embedded or in separate files linked through link tag or src attribute of style) that can be executed on Web Clients natively, like: JavaScript, VBScript, JScript. Script data can be the content of the script element and the value of intrinsic event attributes.	

Elements in ***Bold****: XHTML Basic 1.0 Tag Elements; B: Block level elements*

Elements in Italics: *Deprecated elements; I: Inline or "text-level" elements*

WebPages at WebServer Side (Static and Dynamic)

A WebPage and its embedded resources may be stored under the WebServer as they delivered (*static WebPage*) or produced dynamically (partly or as a whole), at run-time, upon user request (*dynamic WebPage*). Note that a static WebPage can be "dynamic" and "active" on client-side, via the usage of client-side scripting, embedded ClientPrograms or MediaObjects. End-users do not care whether a WebPage is static or dynamic. They request a series of WebPages in order to fulfill a goal. The decision whether a WebPage is better to be implemented as static or dynamic is a development issue.

Dynamic WebPages are produced dynamically on server-side by a *Server-Side Script (SSS)*, i.e., a SESLPage, a CGIProgram, or a JavaServlet. All these technologies provide means to access various local or distributed data sources (e.g., DBs, directory servers, e-mail servers, XML repositories, legacy systems), call local or distributed programs (e.g., Web services) and manage workflow process (e.g., produce and manage cookies) whilst being able to respond back to the client any information necessary as WebPages.

A *SESLPage* (server-side embedded scripting language page) combines fixed or static data of (X)HTML with scripting code enclosed in special tags. This code can be in various languages (C, Perl, VBasic, etc.). When the SESLPage is requested by a WebClient, the SESL code is executed on the server and the dynamic content is mixed with (X)HTML static content to produce the WebPage to be sent back to the client. Famous SESLs include: PHP, JSP, WebServer SSI, ASP, ASP.NET, and ColdFucionML.

A *CGIProgram* is any program designed to accept and return data that conforms to the CGI specification. CGI is a specification transferring information between a WebServer and a CGIProgram. The program could be written in any programming language, including C, Perl, Java, or VBasic. Many (X)HTML pages that contain forms, for example, use a CGI program to process the form's data once it is submitted. One problem with CGI is that each time a CGI script is executed, a new process starts. For busy Web sites, this can slow down the server noticeably. A more efficient solution, and increasingly popular is to use JavaServlets.

A *JavaServlet* is a small program that runs on a Web server. The term usually refers to a Java applet that runs within a Web server environment. This is analogous to a Java applet that runs within a Web client environment. JavaServlets are becoming increasingly popular as an alternative to CGI programs. The biggest difference between the two is that a servlet is persistent. This means that once it is started, it stays in memory and can fulfill multiple requests.

WebPages at WebClient Side

Regarding the contents of WebPages delivered to WebClients, we classify them as Table 2 shows.

Users can request a WebPage through a WebClient by typing a URI, by clicking on a link or by clicking on a button. They can request for either a static WebPage, using an (X)HTML URI or a dynamic WebPage, using an SSS URI. The response they get in both cases is a WebPage. However, in the case of a dynamic WebPage request, WebClient

Table 2. Client-side WebPages classes

WebPage()	An (X)HTML file which may include the followings: (1) embedded StyleLang code (2) embedded ScriptLang code (3) link(s) to external StyleLang file(s) (4) link(s) to external ScriptLang file(s) (5) link(s) to embedded MediaObject file(s)
WebPage(F)	A WebPage() which also includes one or more Forms
WebPage(P)	A WebPage() which also includes one or more embedded ClientPrograms
WebPage	Any of the above

may also get a *cookie*, a text message produced by the SSS and transparently sent by the WebServer to the WebClient. This message is stored locally and it is sent back to the WebServer each time the WebClient requests a WebPage from the WebServer. Cookies are used for implementing personalization features of WebApps. Other kind of information may be also exchanged transparently between WebClients and WebServers, like user preferences and WebServer policy (e.g., P3P), at the first request.

Starting from a WebPage() users can follow the embedded links to request more WebPages. From a WebPage(F), they can either follow a hyperlink or fill the forms fields and press the submit button. ClientScripts may help them at this point. By pressing the submit button, they always request for a dynamic WebPage, but their request includes also the form data. From a WebPage(P), users can interact with the ClientProgram which is running locally within the WebClient. Some ClientProgram languages like Java, provide capabilities to create forms and hyperlinks within the programs GUI, and send requests back to the server.

To summarize, a WebRequest can be: (X)HTML URI, SSS URI or SSS URI plus form data. All types of requests may include cookies. The WebResponse is a WebPage and may include a cookie.

Web Meta-Architectures

Web Architecture is extended by Web meta-architectures. Currently, the most important ones are semantic Web and Web services.

Semantic Web

The semantic Web is not a separate Web but an extension of the current one, in which information is given a well-defined meaning, better enabling computers and people to work in cooperation. The principal technologies of the semantic Web fit into a set of layered specifications called the RDF. The current components of that framework are the RDF Model & Syntax, the RDF Vocabulary Description Language (VDL) and the Web Ontology Language (OWL). All these languages are built on the foundation of URIs, XML, and XML namespaces. Figure 4 presents semantic Web architecture and core technologies.

RDF is a data model (represented in an XML syntax) for resources and relations among them and provides semantics for this data model. RDF schema is a vocabulary describing properties and classes of RDF resources, with semantics for generalization-hierarchies of them.

OWL is built upon the RDF and defines structured Web-based ontologies. Ontology is a machine-readable collection of RDF entity relationship terms, and how they related to each other. OWL adds more vocabulary describing resources properties and classes, relations between classes (e.g., disjointness), cardinality (e.g., "exactly one"), equality, richer typing of properties, characteristics of properties (e.g., symmetry), and enumerated classes.

Figure 4. Semantic Web architecture and core technologies

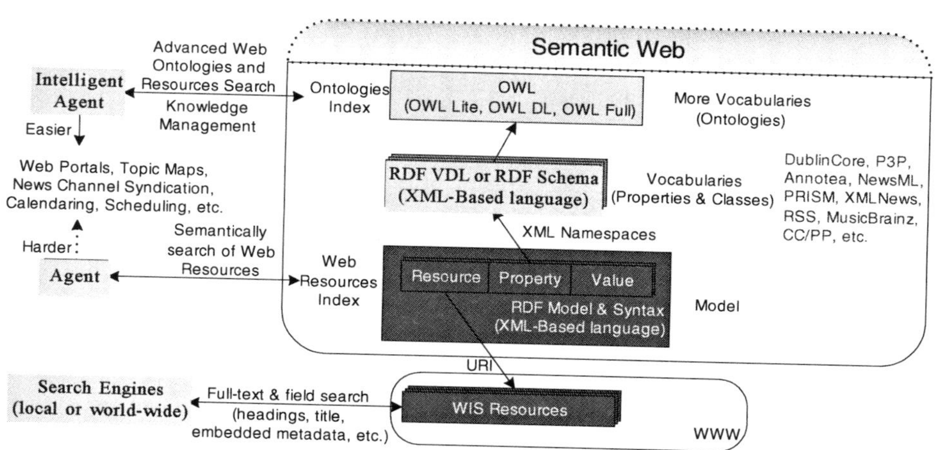

Any technology, which involves information about web resources, should be expressed in compliance to the RDF model, e.g., HTML LINK relationships will be transitioned into RDF properties. Given a worldwide semantic web of assertions, the search engine technology currently applied to HTML pages will presumably translate directly into indexes not of words, but of RDF or OWL objects. This by itself will allow much more efficient searching of the Web as though it were one giant database, rather than one giant book.

The semantic Web is designed to be a universal medium for the exchange of data. It enables vocabulary semantics to be defined and reused by communities of expertise. There are a variety of domain specific communities that are using RDF/XML to publish their data on the Web. These notably include the Dublin Core Metadata Initiative (dublincore.org) focused on developing interoperable metadata standards, the Creative Commons (creativecommons.org) work describing digital rights and providing the basis for an "intellectual property conservancy," XMLNews, PRISM, the RDF Site Summary (RSS) supporting news syndication and MusicBrainz (musicbrainz.org) cataloging and cross referencing music.

Web Services

Web services are standard-based interfaces for software functionality, implemented as discoverable services on the Internet. While semantic Web infrastructure is for discovering and consuming URI addressable data, Web services infrastructure is for discovering and consuming URI addressable software logic.

A Web service is a software system, whose public interfaces and bindings are defined and described in a machine-processable format (WSDL). Its definition can be discovered (in a UDDI registry) by other software systems. These systems may then interact with the Web service in a manner prescribed by its definition, using XML based messages

Figure 5. Web services architecture and core technologies

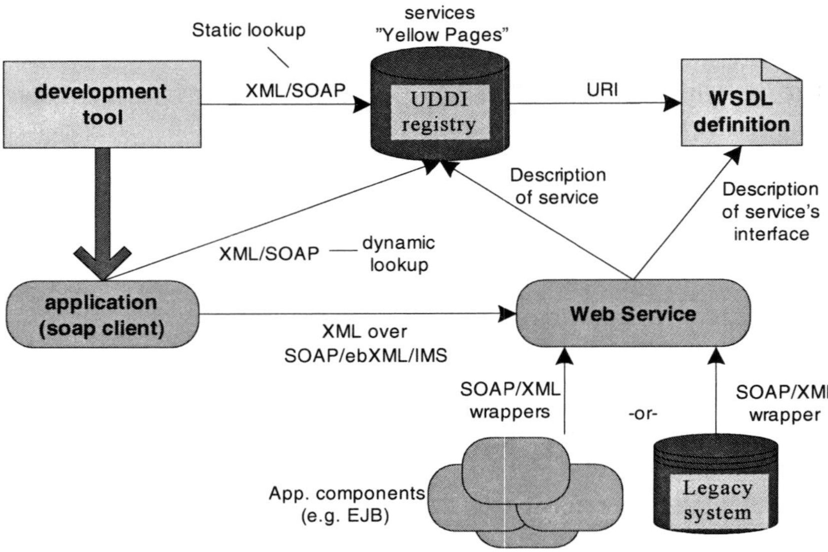

based on a messaging protocol (SOAP) conveyed by Internet protocols (like HTTP). Figure 5 presents Web services architecture and core technologies.

SOAP is a lightweight XML-based messaging protocol used to encode the information in a Web service request and response messages before sending them over a network. SOAP messages are independent of any operating system or protocol and may be transported using a variety of Internet protocols, including SMTP, FTP, MIME, and HTTP.

WSDL is an XML-based language used to describe public interfaces and bindings of a Web service. WSDL is the language that UDDI uses.

UDDI is a Web-based distributed registry that has two kinds of clients: businesses that wish to publish a service (and its usage interfaces in WSDL), and clients who want to discover services of a certain kind, and bind programmatically to them.

A Web service is a URI addressable web resource, but it is not designed to be consumed directly by a WebClient. They do not provide the user with a GUI. Web services instead share business logic, data and processes through a programmatic interface across a network. Developers can develop specific intermediary programs (like CGI, JavaServlets, etc.) to communicate with web services logic and offer their functionality through a GUI (such as a Web page) to end-users.

WEP-Arch: WebApps' Logical and Physical Architectures

WEP-Arch is a technology-independent reference model for the WebApps' technical-oriented classes, logical and physical architectures. With this component of WEP reference model we want to facilitate WIS project stakeholders, i.e., WIS domain people (content/service providers), Web developers and end-users to comprehend:

- The diversity and complexity of WISs and WebApps.
- The logical architecture of WIS and WebApps
- The physical (run-time) architecture of WIS and WebApps

WEP-Arch provides a model and a context for understanding WIS, WebApps, its logical and physical components and the relationships among them. It integrates different conceptions of WebApps classes under a common "reference architecture." While the concepts and relationships of WEP-Arch represent a full-expanded enumeration of the architecture components, the stakeholders are able to understand how the architecture could be adapted to meet the goals and requirements of a specific WIS project.

WebApps' Technical-Oriented Classes

Deshpande et al. (2002) provide a *functionality-oriented classification* of WebApps that includes the following classes: informational, interactive, transaction, workflow, collaborative work environments, online communities/marketplaces, Web portals and Web services. It is clear that WebApps vary widely from small-scale, short-lived services to large-scale enterprise information systems distributed across the network, incorporating different Web technologies and data from heterogeneous sources and in various formats. It is obvious that the diversity and complexity of WebApps is high.

End-users classify a WebApp according to its functionality, which should facilitate them to achieve a specific goal. However, developers need to classify WebApps under "technical-oriented" classes, according to the skills, technologies and tools needed for designing, developing and maintaining them. After thorough study of current WebApps architecture and based on our experience in developing large-scale WISs, we provide such an abstract technical-oriented classification of WebApps as follows.

WIS is perceived as a large-scale *Web Hyperspace* (Hypermedia Information Space) that provides information and services to fulfill goals of targeted end-users. Information (as multimedia content in various formats, linked via hypertext metaphor and navigational structures) is provided by *Web hypermedia applications* through a collection of static and/or dynamic WebPages and services are provided within these WebPages as *Web front-end applications (WFA)*, through WebForms, ClientScripts & result WebPages and as *Web interactive applications (WIA)*, through ClientPrograms.

- **Web Front-End Application (WFA):** It is an integration application that uses the Web technologies to provide a Web front-end (through WebPages[F]) to back-end information systems, business logic or legacy applications, such as registration forms, booking systems, Web e-mail, transaction applications etc. In this case, the application logic is mainly implemented using Web forms and client-side scripting on WebClient (e.g., Javascript code to validate users' input) and SSS and programs on a WebServer (e.g., PHP to query back-end data sources, call local or distributed Web services, mix the results with [X]HTML code and send it to the user). A WFA may consist of one WebForm, many individual WebForms or a pipeline of WebForms (the results of a WebForm interaction is another WebForm page).
  - **Main Scope:** Provide services (and content) of back-end systems over the web to end-users through WebForms interaction paradigm.
  - **Important Part:** The application logic (service-oriented applications).
  - **Skills Needed:** S/W engineering, network engineering (distributed computing, Web services), DB/information engineering, Web publishing (Web forms), Web programming (server-side scripting, client-side scripting).

- **Web Interactive Application (WIA):** It is one or many ClientPrograms that use the Web infrastructure in order to reach end-users through a Web-based GUI (that usually requires a plug-in installed on WebClient). Examples of such applications include interactive games, chats, interactive geographic maps, etc.
  - **Main Scope:** Provide interactive experience over the Web to the end-users.
  - **Important Part:** GUI and performance (interaction-oriented applications).
  - **Skills Needed:** S/W engineering, human-computer interaction, multimedia.

- **Web Hypermedia Application (WHA):** it is the structuring of an information space in concepts of nodes (chunks of information), links (relations among nodes), anchors, navigation contexts (indexes, site maps, guided tours, etc.) and the delivery of this structure over the Web as WebPages. At server-side a WHA is a collection of static and dynamic WebPages() which incorporate the links and anchors of the WHA. A WHA can allow the navigation through the content of structured data sources like DB or XML repositories. Note though, that searching the same data sources through a WebForm is not part of the WHA, but it is a WFA. Users interact with a WHA by following links. However, a WHA may include WebForms of WFA and ClientPrograms of WIA as embedded components in its WebPages. Interacting with these components is part of the other applications.
  - **Main Scope:** Diffuse content over the Web to the end-users.
  - **Important Part:** The content (content-oriented applications).
  - **Skills Needed:** Hypermedia engineering, DB/information engineering, Web publishing ([X]HTML, XML/XSL, CSS, RDF/metadata, Web server administration), Web programming (SSS), multimedia.

WIS Hyperspace is a large-scale WHA, incorporating service-oriented (WFAs), interaction-oriented (WIAs) and content-oriented applications (WHAs).

WebApps' Logical Architecture

Let us move inside WebApps. We break down WebApps into logical components (parts of WebApps) that can be designed and implemented to some extend independent. These components can be grouped into layers. Research results, practice and technology evolution shows that WebApps should be broken-down to three logical layers: *content, logic and interface*. Table 3 describes the layers and components of WebApps' logical architecture.

This three-layered architecture can also be expanded to a multi-layered one, where different layers of software implement the WebApp logic and content is spitted to data and navigation layers. This isolated architecture facilitates Web developers to define, design and implement several reusable components in each layer (content, logic or interface components) and reuse them across several WebApps or even different WISs. Figure 6 shows the logical layers and their approximate importance for each class of WebApps.

WebApps' Physical Architecture

The physical architecture describes the components of the WebApp at run-time. The physical components include implementations of logical components (like data sources, data files, programs, stylesheets, etc.) and the run-time infrastructure of the WebApp (Web client types, communication protocols, Web server and its modules, run-time environment of logic components, network infrastructure to access distributed resources, etc.). Contrary to logical architecture of WebApps, which is simple and generic, the physical architecture is more complex, multi-tiered and specific. The physical

Table 3. WebApps' logical architecture (layers & components)

Logical Layers	Layers' Description & Components
Content	Content layer includes the designs of data, metadata and WebApp navigation. For unstructured data it includes the type (e.g., image, video, animation, etc.). For structured and semistructured data, it includes the data schemata (like ER, XSD, OO, tree structure, etc.). Moreover, and for WHAs, it includes the navigational design as WebPages (nodes and navigational structure) and hyperlinks across them. Finally, it includes the metadata schemata for the WebPages and the individual Web Resources of the WebApp. Each data, metadata and navigation design constitutes a Content Component.
Logic	Logic layer includes the logical designs of all s/w components (program and script code) of the WebApp, like SSSs, ClientScripts, ClientPrograms, and server-side Programs. These Logic Components are designed to provide: data access logic, server-side logic (services of WFA), client-side logic (WIA ClientPrograms and WFA ClientScripts) and rendering logic (SSS of WHA and WFA).
Interface	Interface layer includes the designs of WebApp GUI through which end-users have access to the content and interact with the logic of the WebApp. Interface Components include the layout designs of the WebPages (WHA), the look-and-feel graphical designs of WebPages (WHA), the presentation designs of multimedia resources like video, animation, audio, etc. (WHA), the Web Forms designs (WFA) and the GUI design of ClientPrograms (WIA).

Figure 6. Logical layers in each WebApps' class

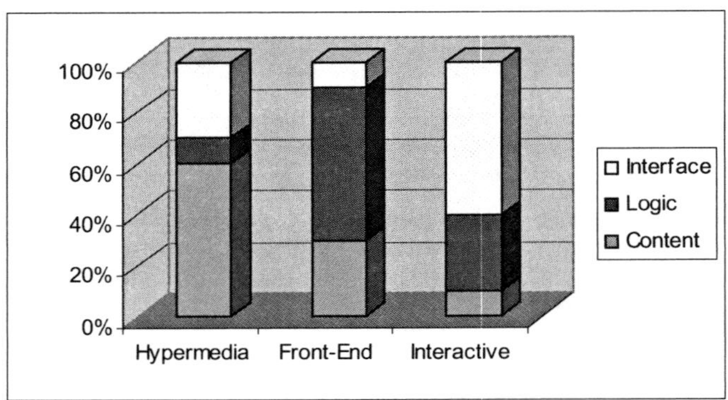

Table 4. Physical tiers of WebApps

Physical Tiers	Tiers' Description
Data	Data physical tier includes the actual content of the WebApp, digitized and stored in a specific data format under certain systems/tools able to store and manage it (e.g., content management system, RDBMS, XML repository, directory server, (X)HTML files on filesystem, etc.). Legacy systems belong to this tier, as WebApps use them as black-boxes providing data. According to the data format and management system of data we distinguish three types: MediaObjects, semi-structureddata, StructuredData. Moreover, this tier includes data that does not correspond to Content Components, like XSL, CSS, ClientScripts, ClientPrograms. These are perceived as "data" for the WebApp at run-time, even though they implement Logic and Interface components, because they are delivered by the WebServer as files and used on WebClient side.
DataAccess	DataAccess physical tier includes the technologies (like SQL) and programs implementing the data access logic (e.g., ODBC, XML Parser, specific programs, etc.) which are used in order to access data at WebApp run-time. This physical tier implements the data access logic components.
AppLogic	AppLogic physical tier includes all programs that implement the core (local with regard to WebServer) logic components of WebApp (server-side Logic Components) and their run-time environment (e.g. an application server, J2EE, .NET, etc.).
Distribution	Distribution physical tier includes all technologies (e.g., CORBA, SOAP) and software programs (e.g., distributed web services) that implement the distributed logic components of WebApp and their run-time environment.
Rendering	Rendering physical tier includes the code and the run-time environment of CGIPrograms, SESLPages and JavaServlets.
WebServer	WebServer physical tier includes the software and run-time environment of WebServer plus the administration and management tools (administration environment, log analysis tools, etc.). This tier may include the policy profile of the WIS stored in a format like P3P.
Communication	Communication physical tier includes the communication protocols and the supported data formats of the WebApp plus the network infrastructure to support the communication with web-enabled devices and Web clients.
WebClient	WebClient physical tier includes the set of WebClients (browsers and devices) that are supported by the WebApp. Moreover, it includes all necessary plug-ins for MediaObjects and ClientPrograms and user preferences.
GUI	GUI physical tier includes the WebApp GUI through which end-users access content (view on screen, hear on speakers, etc.) and interact (with mouse, keyboard, etc.) with the WebApp client-side logic physical components. GUI Components include WebPages (layout and presentation style) and their embedded MediaObjects, Web Forms, ClientScripts and ClientPrograms.

architecture tiers do not associate directly to the logical layers. Instead, one physical component may implement logical components from all three logical layers. The physical tiers, components and composite components of WebApps are defined in Table 4, 5 and 6 respectively.

The tiers of the physical architecture and their mapping to logical layers is shown in Figure 7. Figure 8 presents the physical components and composite components of each physical tier and shows how components are interoperate at high-level.

Finally, in Table 7 we present the physical components for each class of WebApps. WebServer and WebClient physical components are common to all.

Table 5. Physical components of WebApps

Physical Components		Description	Map to Logical Components
Data Sources	**SemiStructData**	(X)HTML files, XML Native DB, XML Server/Repository, XML files (they may provide links to MediaObjects, ClientScripts, ClientPrograms, Stylesheets)	Content (data, links, metadata)
	StructData	DBs, Directory server, email server, Index server, legacy EIS, etc. (they may include or link to MediaObjects, ClientScripts, ClientPrograms, Stylesheets)	Content (data, links, metadata)
MediaObjects		Media files (like images, video, animations, etc.), Documents (PDF, MSOffice, etc.)	Interface
MetaData		Metadata about the WebApp Web Resources (RDF/XML, OWL, RSS, etc.)	Content (metadata)
WebForm		(X)HTML tags, XForms, etc.	Interface
StyleSheet		CSS, XSL, etc.	Interface
ClientScript		JavaScript, VBScript, Jscript, etc.	Logic (light or form client-side)
ClientProgram		Java Applets, Flash, ShockWave, Active-X Controls, etc.	Logic (heavy client-side) Interface
SSS		SESL (PHP, ASP.NET, ASP, JSP, ColdFusion, etc.), CGIPrograms (Perl, C/C++, Java, etc.), Servlets (Java)	Logic (rendering)
AccessProgram		Data Sources Access Programs or technologies, like XML parser, XQuery program, ADO.NET, LdapSearch, etc. These programs are based on a Data Source Querying technology, like SQL, XQuery, LDAP and asynchronous messaging services (for legacy EIS) like JDO, JMS, MQSeries, etc.	Logic (data access)
ServerProgram		Any kind of S/W component that implements the core server-side logic (either local or distributed). One of them is invoked by a SSS and returns an output (possibly after invoking several others ServerPrograms). ServerPrograms include: • Individual Programs in any programming language (like JavaBeans, .NET Managed Classes etc.) • Infrastructure Servers (Application server like J2EE Server, .NET Framework, etc.) • Distributed Programs (like WebServices, etc.)	Logic (local/distributed)
WebServer		Fundamental component for every WebApp responsible to provide responds to WebClient requests. Moreover, it provides security (e.g., SSL) and policy (e.g., P3P) features of the WebApp.	Logic
WebClient		Fundamental component for every WebApp responsible to provide requests to the WebServer of the WebApp. Moreover, it provides security (e.g., SSL) and policy (e.g. user preferences) features	Logic

Table 6. Physical composite components of WebApps

Physical Composite Components	Description	Map to Logical Components
Static WebPage()	(X)HTML) + (1) embedded StyleLang code (2) embedded ScriptLang code (2) link(s) to external StyleSheets (3) link(s) to external ClientScripts (4) link(s) to embedded MediaObjects	Content (data, links, metadata), Logic (light client-side) Interface
StaticWebPage(F)	StaticWebPage() + WebForms (link to an SSS URI)	Content (data, links, metadata), Logic (form client-side) Interface
StaticWebPage(P)	StaticWebPage() + ClientPrograms	Content (data, links, metadata), Logic (heavy client-side) Interface
DynamicWebPage()	a StaticWebPage() produced by an SSS (Input: SSS URI)	Content (data, links, metadata), Logic (data access, light client-side) Interface
DynamicWebPage(P)	a StaticWebPage(P) produced by an SSS (Input: SSS URI)	Content (data, links, metadata), Logic (data access, heavy client-side) Interface
DynamicWebPage(F)	a StaticWebPage(F) produced by an SSS (Input: SSS URI)	Content (data, links, metadata), Logic (data access, form client-side) Interface
DynamicWebPage(FR)	a StaticWebPage () or (F) produced by an SSS (Input: SSS URI + form data)	Content (data, links, metadata), Logic (data access, local/distributed, client-side) Interface

Figure 7. Physical tiers and their mapping to logical layers

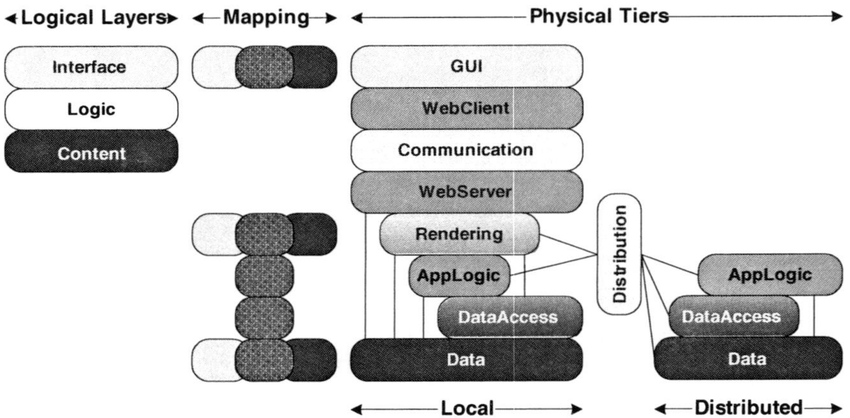

Figure 8. Interoperation of physical components and composite components

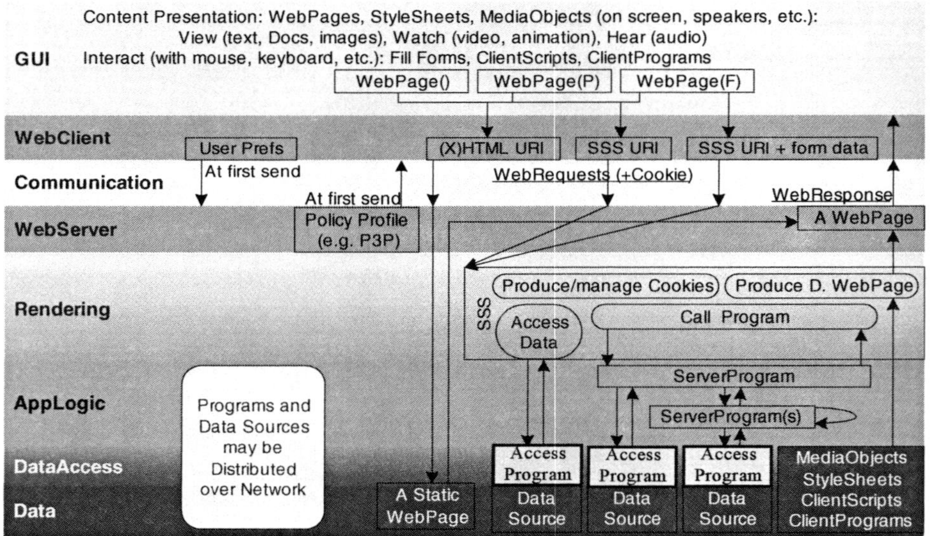

WEP-Teams: WIS Project Teams

In this section, we outline the main stakeholders involved in the lifecycle of a WIS project. We classify them under generic teams according to their skills on specific areas of expertise. We included this classification in WEP, because the composition of the project team is crucial for the success of the project and WEP goal is to give developers a roadmap

Table 7. Physical components and composite components per WebApps' class

Physical Tiers		Hyperspace	Front-End	Interactive
Data (CLI)	Distribution	DataSources, MediaObjects, StaticWebPages(), StyleSheets, ClientScripts	DataSources, MediaObjects, StaticWebPages(F), StyleSheets, ClientScripts	DataSources, MediaObjects, StaticWebPages(P), StyleSheets, ClientScripts ClientPrograms
Data Access (L)		AccessPrograms	AccessPrograms	AccessPrograms
AppLogic (L)			ServerPrograms	
Rendering (CLI)		DynamicWebPages()	DynamicWebPages(F) or (FR)	DynamicWebPages(P)
GUI (CLI)		WebPages() with: • StyleSheets • ClientScripts (light)	WebPages(F) or () with: • StyleSheets • ClientScripts (form)	WebPages(P) with: • StyleSheets • ClientScripts (light) • ClientPrograms

C= Content; L=Logic; I=Interface

how to do it. There are some research papers, like Hansen et al. (2001), that specify in more detail the required skills for developers working on different parts of a WIS project.

The basic goal of the Web is to allow content/services providers to easily diffuse content and services over the Internet and make it available to the end-users. Web Developers are in-between.

Two main bodies provide people for WIS project teams:

- **Customer:** the body that pays for the project and incorporates the content / service providers. It often represents the end-users during requirements gathering and testing stages.
- **IT Organization:** the body responsible for deployment, operation and maintenance of the WIS. It often cooperates with external consultants or partners, providing additional skills not found in IT organization personnel. It provides people with either a technical or creative design background.

First, we construct the basic teams (expertise-oriented) with a leader and several members (see Table 8). The leader should have team management skills. A member may cover more than one skill. The number of the members and the priority of the required skills depend on the nature and the scale of the project. We recommend forming small but high-skilled teams. A survey (McDonald & Welland, 2003) across seven IT organizations shows that: a development team of eight people incorporates: two from a technical background; two from a creative design background; two lead the team and the other two are a domain and a business expert.

Moreover, and based on the basic teams, we construct some very important hybrid teams (Table 8), the importance of which, we will see in the next section. Notice, that all leaders of basic teams participate in analysis and quality assurance teams, because each basic team has a unique perspective of the WIS design and its relationship to project objectives.

Table 8. WEP-teams: Basic and hybrid WIS project teams

BASIC TEAMS	
Project Manager: Project Management Skills **Domain Team** Leader: Domain Overall Knowledge Members' skills: S1. Business Domain Expertise (legacy systems, guidance on achieving the business objectives) S2. Content Domain Expertise (legacy content) S3. Content Providers (textual content authoring, other content providing like photos, videotapes, etc.) S4. Marketing Expertise in the Domain S5. Legal, social, ethical issues of the domain **Web Team** Leader: Web Engineering Members' skills: S1. Requirements Engineering (analysis of Requirements, functional specifications / use-case modeling) S2. Web-enabled device Publishing (in (X)HTML) S3. Web Integration - Server-side Scripting (integration with data sources, programs or legacy systems) S4. Client-side Scripting S5. Web Testing Engineering (test platform design / implementation, metrics, acceptance criteria, etc.) S6. Web metadata design implementation and maintenance S7. Web Site Administration • Install, configure and maintain Web Servers • Develop and Maintain "policies" (security/access rights) for the operation of the site • Collection and collation of feedback on site • Monitor/access log files to produce statistics	**Content Team** Leader: Hypermedia, DB and Information Engineering Members' skills: S1. Textual and Multimedia DB Engineering (Logical/Physical Designing, Data Access, Legacy Data Integration, DB Programming, DB Testing) S2. XML Engineering S3. Hypermedia Engineering (esp. Navigational Aspects) **Logic Team** Leader: S/W & Network Engineering Members' skills: S1. S/W Engineering (Logic / Physical Designing, Programming, Legacy systems integration, Testing) S2. Network Engineering (Distributed Computing – inter-application communication, web services) **Interface Team** Leader: Human – web-enabled devices interaction and Creative Design Skills (research, technologies, tools) Members' skills: S1. Electronic Publishing S2. Web-enabled device Interface and Interaction Expertise S3. Multimedia Engineering (Graphics Designing, Multimedia Content Digitizing, Animation Expertise) *Note: Engineering = experience and knowledge of research, technologies and tools*
HYBRID TEAMS	
Project Planning Team Project Manager, Web Leader, Domain Leader **Project Management and Quality Assurance Team** Project Manager, Web Leader (Technical Manager), Domain Leader, Content Leader, Logic Leader, Interface Leader	**Analysis Team** Web Leader, Web Team (S1), Domain Team, Content Leader, Logic Leader, Interface Leader **Test Team** Web Team (S5), Domain Team, End-users **Evolution Team** Web Team (Leader, S2, S6, S7) Domain Team (Leader, S3, S4, S5)

WEP-Process: A Lifecycle Process Model

In this section and based on the WebApps classes, logical layers and physical tiers, we specify WEP-Process, a lifecycle process model, that supports developers during a WIS project. It is a work discipline that describes *who* is doing *what* and *how* in order to ensure successful WIS development and evolving. WEP-Process emphasizes on modularity, component-based development, extensibility, reusing, easy maintenance, interoperability and metadata support (semantic web). It is a data-centric and service-centric, rather than application-centric, development process. We kept WEP-Process generic, adaptable and easy for the developers to follow in order to achieve our main target: to transfer good practices and research results of web engineering to real web projects.

There are three cornerstones of WEP-Process:

1. WIS structure design as a set of interconnected and interoperable WebApps, according to the WebApps' classes defined earlier, i.e. WIS hyperspace, WHAs, WFAs and WIAs.
2. Identification and design of WebApps' logical components.
3. Design and implementation of WebApps' physical components.

From developer perspective, it is very useful to break-down WebApps into a set of overlapping components, each one having the following characteristics: (1) it can be developed, to some extend, independently of the others; (2) it is based on specific technologies and tools and (3) requires specific development skills. Components of the same class can be deployed by the same team, thus better exploiting the team skills, achieving level best integration in each layer and tier, constructing easily maintainable WebApps and reusing design / implementation artifacts and experience.

WEP-Process consists of three *phases:* (1) WIS planning phase; (2) WIS deployment phase; and (3) WIS evolution phase. We use the term "evolution" instead of "maintenance," which is used in software engineering literature, because in Web engineering we have to think more about evolution and less about maintenance. If a WIS, no matter how good it is, it is just maintained and not evolved, after two or three years may become obsolete. Each phase consists of several *stages*. Stages include several *activities* that incorporate a *workflow* that diverse team members may go through to produce a particular set of output *artifacts* based on results artifacts of other activities (input artifacts). The workflows, at a more detailed level, describe a step-by-step procedure of how team members collaborate and how they use and produce artifacts, based on WERs. Throughout the workflow the developers have to use WERs, for example, to take advantage of research results, to base on Web technologies and to use tools with specific guidelines. This will help developers understand the mission of each activity and make clearer to them how they can better exploit the available WERs.

WEP-Process is outlined in Tables 9-13 (A. Phases, A1. Stages, a. Activities). *Project management*, incorporating *quality assurance* is a special stage running in parallel with the Phases B and C. The activities are briefly but clearly described. In the context of a real project the activities (i.e., team members, workflows, WERs used, input & output artifacts) should be described in detail.

Web Engineering Resources Portal

In this section, we outline the Web Engineering Resources that a web developer may use for developing and maintaining a WIS. These resources include (1) technologies; (2) research results in the diverse areas and topics; and (3) tools ranging from complete solutions to small-scale programs. In the next sections we will provide taxonomies of WERs in each category and references to some of them.

Table 9. WEP-Process: WIS project planning phase

A. WIS Project Planning Phase *(Planning Team)*

a. Definition of *Scope and general Objectives* of the WIS, including urgency of need, business value, degree of alliance with current mission of the Customer organization.

b. Definition of the *WIS Goals*. Initial requirements of the WIS are identified and documented in a preliminary requirements report. WIS Goals should be explicitly stated, since they will lead the entire Deployment Process.
- Identify the *Users' Classes* and their profile, i.e., domain expertise, background, preferences, age, access devices (desktop browsers, voice devices, PDAs, mobiles, etc.) and their capabilities, connection speed, etc.
- Identify the *Users' Goals* for each user's class. A user goal is achieved through a navigation session within the WIS Hyperspace & WHAs and/or interaction with incorporated WFAs and WIAs. We define two general types of goals:
  - *Information-oriented Goals*: access and navigate through specific information of WHAs and
  - *Service-oriented Goals*: perform a complex task through interaction with WFAs and/or WIAs.

c. *Current Situation*. Identify existing data sources, legacy systems, S/W and H/W infrastructure of the Customer Organization. Identify existing Human resources in Customer and IT Organizations.

d. Detail specification of the *WIS Deployment process model* (Planning and Timetables). In Phase B, we provide a general process model, which should be adapted to specific Project constraints and needs.

e. Select a *Project Management Model* to control and track Project: Management structure, Decision-making structure, Quality Assurance mechanisms, progress monitoring, collaboration, ethical/legal/intellectual property issues, etc.

f. Deploy the *Project Teams*. Specify what skills are required, identify roles and associate them to people within Customer and IT Organizations (see WEP-Teams in previous section).

g. *Budget estimation*.

h. *Feasibility Analysis* – The major areas of concerns, are usually economic justification, technical feasibility, legal considerations and evaluation of alternative approaches (Pressman, 1997), including time-related and marketing issues. Moreover it includes Risk Analysis to assess technical and management risks.

Milestones: **WIS Goals, Current Situation, WIS Deployment process model, Project Management Model, Project Teams, Feasibility Analysis**

Table 10. WEP-Process: Deployment phase: Requirements specification & analysis stage

B. WIS Deployment Phase
carried out by *Project Teams* based on *WIS Deployment process model* and *Project Management Model*

Stage B1. Requirements Specification & Analysis *(Analysis Team)*

a. *Requirements Capturing*:
- *Functional Requirements* capturing based on WIS Goals.
- *Non-Functional Requirements*, i.e., usability, reliability, security, performance, extensibility, maintainability, compatibility, etc.
- Address the *Non-Technical Issues* such as business processes, legal, cultural and social aspects.
- *Implementation Constraints*: required standards, implementation languages, resource limits, operation environments, required data formats, etc.

b. *Use-case model* of Functional Requirements. It consists of users and use cases (in a modeling language like UML) and it is the integrated view of functional requirements analysis. Each use case (one per User Goal) shows step-by-step how WIS interacts with the users and what the WIS does. This activity specifies the functionality-oriented components of WIS, i.e., user-oriented WebApps.

c. *Prototyping*: If the functional requirements specified by the use-case model are not very clear, you may consider including prototypes development: Prototypes serve as a representation of requirements and facilitate the communication between developers and end-users. Prototypes could include: construction of representative WebPages, WebForms and their results pages, ClientPrograms short demo, etc.

d. *WIS Structure*: A high-level preliminary structural design of the WIS as a set of *WebApps*. Usually, an Information-oriented Goal is served by one WHA, while Service-oriented Goals are served by WFAs and WIAs incorporated in WebPages of the WHAs. Notice that the WIS Hyperspace is considered as a WHA. WIS Hyperspace structure design includes the Home Page and second level WebPages (i.e., entry pages to WHAs) plus the individual WebPages that include WebForms of WFAs and ClientPrograms of WIAs.

e. *Technical Specifications* of WIS: The construction of a technical report describing the following:
- Analysis of *Non-Functional Requirements* and *Non-Technical Issues*.
- Analysis of *Current Situation* (existing data sources and legacy systems).
- *Content Specification*. Specification of kind and amount of content need to be developed within Project, possibly by reverse-engineering of the existing logical schemas of legacy data sources.
- *Logic Specification*. Specification of logic components (programs) need to be developed within Project (over Content and legacy systems) in order to satisfy the Service-oriented User Goals.
- *Interface Specification*. Specification of targeted WebClients on specific web-enabled devices plus their presentation and interaction capabilities and constraints.
- Analysis of *Implementation Constraints* and analysis of *Industry and Web standards* specific for the application domain. Core technologies selection, required development infrastructure and tools, etc.

f. *Acceptance Criteria Specification*. These will be used later during testing stage in order to validate the implemented WIS against Users' Goals and Non-Functional Requirements.

Milestones: **Use Case Model, Prototypes, WIS Structure, WIS Technical Specifications, Acceptance Criteria**

Table 11. WEP-Process: Deployment phase: Logical design & physical design stages

Stage B2. Logical Design
Content/Logic/Interface Teams based on *WIS Structure*, *WIS Technical Specifications* and *Use-case Model*

a. *Content Components Design* for each WebApp.
   - *Data Components* are: UnstructData type specification (e.g., images, video, docs, etc.), SemiStructData designs (e.g., XML Schemata), StructData designs (e.g., ER, OO). Choose the better design methodology based on research results, good practices and data types. Some data components may be common across several WebApps (like copyright statement, etc.). These components belong to WIS Hyperspace.
   - *WHA Navigation Components* are: WebPages of WHAs (specify the data of each WHA WebPage based on the Data Components, specify classes of WebPages according to the semantics of their data, high-level links across WHA WebPages – low-level linking will be made during the authoring activity of implementation stage later), Navigational Structures of WHAs (design of WHA local access structures like menus, index pages, guided tours, etc.).
   - *WIS Navigation Components* are: Global WebPages (e.g., home page), global access structures (e.g., site map), cross-WHA high-level links, etc.
   - *Metadata Components* are: Metadata schemata per class of WebPages of WHAs, metadata schemata per individual WIS WebPages, metadata schemata per class of other WIS resources (like images).

b. *Logic Components Design* for each WebApp (see *Logic Layer* description).

c. *Interface Components Design* for each WebApp (see *Interface Layer* description).

Milestones: **Content Components, Logic Components, Interface Components**

Stage B3. Physical Design (based on *Logical Design* Components)
Team (Activities) : Web (a,d,f,g,h), Content (b,c,d,f), Logic (a,c,d,e) and Interface (a,b,f)

This is the main development stage where the physical architecture of the WIS is designed and it will drive the implementation stage' activities. The following activities are not considered to be carried out sequentially but in parallel, as a decision in one tier may influence others. Thus, all basic development teams, i.e., Web, Content, Logic and Interface Teams should work in close cooperation. The objective of these activities is to contribute to the overall *WIS Physical Architecture Diagram*, which is the Milestone of this stage. In many cases, developers may consider purchasing off-the-shelf development frameworks or re-using them from prior Web projects. Famous ones are IBM's WebSphere, Sun ONE (J2EE), BEA Logic and Microsoft's .NET framework. Many non-functional requirements of the WIS are usually provided by these frameworks, and the developers do not have to implement them. However, non-functional requirements should be considered within each activity separately and at the WIS level.

a. *WebClient Physical Components*: specify the set of WebClients (browsers and devices) that can access the WebApps and all necessary plug-ins for MediaObjects and ClientPrograms. Specify the delivery markup language (type of (X)HTML) of WebApps. Specify the ClientScript and ClientPrograms language to implement the client-side Logic Components. Specify the StyleSheet language to use.

b. *Data Physical Components*: for each Content Component and some Interface Components (e.g., MediaObjects) specify the data formats and their storage systems (data sources or repositories) able to develop, store it and manage it (e.g. content management system, RDBMS, XML repository, directory server, filesystem, etc.). Content Components of the same design methodology (e.g. ER or XML), is better to be physically designed under a common storage system, even though they belong to different WebApps. This will reduce the cost and complexity of the WIS development. During this activity we specify the structure and interface of the Static WebPages ((X)HTML files).

c. *DataAccess Physical Components*: for each Data Physical Component specify the data access technologies (like SQL, XQuery) and the data AccessPrograms (e.g., ODBC, XML Parser, specific programs, etc.) which will be used by other physical components in order to access data sources at run-time.

d. *Distributed Physical Components*: specify which server-side Logic Components will be physically implemented distributed with regard to WebServer. For these, specify the technologies (e.g., CORBA, Web Services, etc.), programming languages, and development / run-time environments. Moreover, specify which Data Physical Components will be distributed and what technologies will be used.

e. *AppLogic Physical Components*: for each server-side Logic Component specify the programming language, and their development and run-time environments (e.g., an application server like Sun ONE (J2EE) or .NET Framework, etc.). It is recommended to base your design on few languages and a common environment. Moreover, extract common functionality of Logic Components and design them as common AppLogic Physical Components (like EJBs) that are reused across different WebApps.

f. *Rendering Physical Components*: specify the SSS technologies for the implementation of rendering Logic Components, plus its development and run-time environment. During this activity we specify the structure and interface of the Dynamic WebPages ((X)HTML files).

g. *WebServer Physical Components:* specify the WebServer features, its modules, its run-time environment, its administration and management tools (administration environment, log analysis tools, etc.)

h. *Communication Physical Components:* specify the communication protocols and the supported data formats of the WebApps plus the network infrastructure to support the communication with specified WebClients.

Milestone: **WIS Physical Architecture Diagram**

Technologies Taxonomies

In this section, we provide an overview of the technologies relative to Web Engineering, based on WIS physical architecture, upon which most of the acronyms and concepts of WWW are presented. To summarize all these technologies in one figure is a hard task but we think it is of great importance for developers. The main mission of this map is to provide an easy and fast way to developers for:

Table 12. Deployment phase: Implementation & unit testing and acceptance testing stages

Stage B4. Implementation & Unit Testing (based on *Physical Design* Components)
Implementation and Unit Testing activities include the same activities' structure and Teams association as in *Physical Design*, except that content authoring is carried out by *Domain Team*. Integration activity is carried out by the *Web Team*.

a. *Implementation* of *WIS Physical Architecture Diagram* Components as specified in *Physical Design* stage. This is not a sequential procedure, as some components may need to be developed before others. Such dependencies among components should be identified at the beginning of this activity. This activity includes run-time environments installing and configuring, programming, multimedia production and content authoring.
b. *Unit Testing* of each component against the functional and non-functional (e.g., stress/capacity testing) requirements. This activity includes the design of test cases, the actual testing and the reporting of the results.
c. *Integration* of all implemented components into the WIS and its WebApps.

Milestone: **WIS up and running**

Stage B5. Acceptance Testing (*Test Team* based on *Acceptance Criteria*)

a. *Test Cases Design* for WIS and per WebApps, based on methodologies and tools (e.g., stressing tools, etc.)
b. *Test each WebApp* separately against Acceptance Criteria.
c. *Test WIS* as a whole against Acceptance Criteria.
d. *Report the results* of the testing activities. If the results are not what we expect we move back to either the logical design, physical design or implementation stage.

Milestone: **Testing Reports**

Table 13. WEP-Process: WIS evolution phase

C. WIS Evolution Phase (*Evolution Team*)

a. Content update (data, metadata, links).
b. WIS Infrastructure maintenance and support, e.g., correction of software bugs, new hardware and software installation and configuration, etc.
c. *Enhancement:* lightly extends system functionality, minor adaptations to new technologies, etc.
d. Logs analysis and statistics production.
e. Collection and collation of end-users' feedback. Report emerging requirements for the WIS.
f. Technologies, tools and research results monitoring. Report emerging technical requirements for the WIS.

The results of the two last activities may indicate the need of a new Project, if the emerging requirements are by far different from the ones current WIS address.

- Understanding the scope and role of a technology by just locating it on the figure.
- Understanding the similar and complementary technologies.

An overview of the technologies during run-time and in all physical tiers is presented in Figure 9 (client-side) and Figure 10 (server-side).

At the *data tier*, we distinguish three classes of data: media objects, semi-structured data and structured data. Structure means that the data can be parsed and manipulated by machines' programs.

MediaObjects technologies are basically the multimedia formats supported by WebClients (natively or via plug-ins), like raster images (GIF, JPG, PNG), vector images (SVG, WebCGM), animated images (GIF), animated video (Flash, ShockWave), video (MPEG, AVI, DIVX, MOV), audio (MP3, WAV), streaming video (RealVideo), streaming audio (Real Audio) or documents (PDF, PS, MSOffice formats).

Semi-structured data technologies include mark-up meta-languages like SGML, XML and mark-up languages like HTML, XML Languages (see Figure 11).

SGML is not a markup language itself, but a meta-language for the specification of an unlimited number of markup languages, each optimized for a particular category of

Figure 9. Client-side technologies

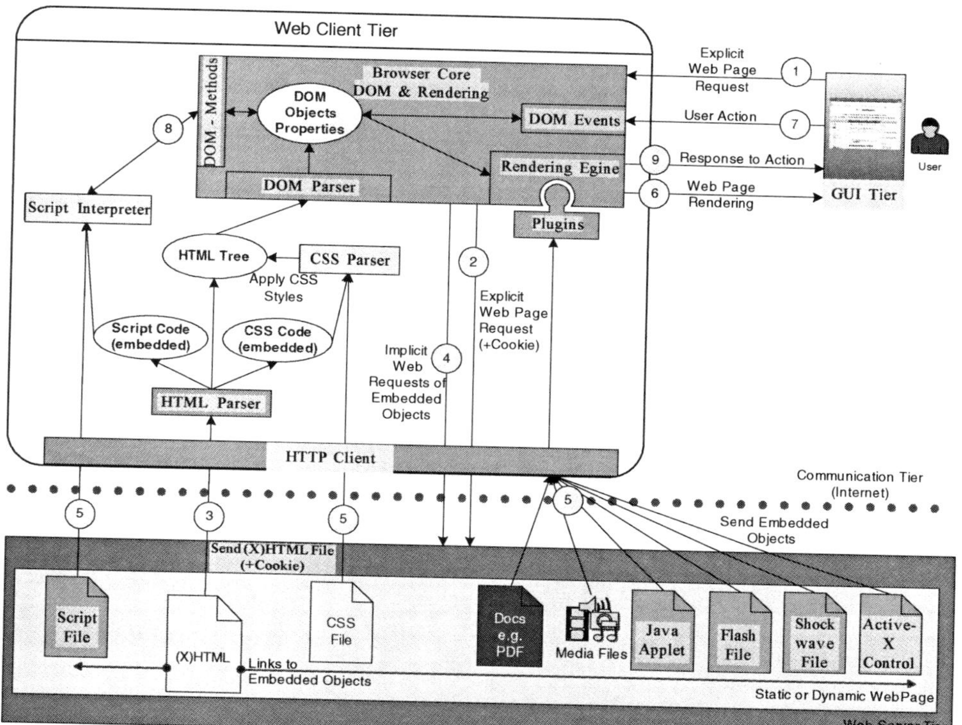

documents. The SGML description of a markup language is called a DTD. *XML* is a pared-down version of SGML developed by the W3C designed especially for Web documents. It is also a meta-language for the specification of an unlimited number of markup languages. It allows designers to create their own customized tags, enabling the definition, transmission, validation, and interpretation of data between applications and between organizations. In Figure 11, you can observe only a set of the more important XML languages and their wide application.

Beyond XML, the *XML family* is a growing set of technologies that offer useful services to accomplish important and frequently demanded tasks. Sophisticated linking mechanisms have been invented for XML formats. XML Namespaces (XMLNS) provides a mechanism for establishing a globally unique name that can be understood in any context. XPointer allows links to address content that does not have an explicit, named anchor. To define fragment identifier syntax, use the XPointer Framework and XPointer element() Schemes. XLink describes a standard way to add hyperlinks to an XML file. XLink allows links to have multiple ends and to be expressed either inline or in "link bases" stored external to any or all of the resources identified by the links it contains. CSS, the style sheet language, is applicable to XML as it is to HTML. XSL is the advanced language for expressing style sheets. It is based on XSLT, a transformation language used for rearranging, adding and deleting tags and attributes. The DOM is a standard

Figure 10. Server-side technologies

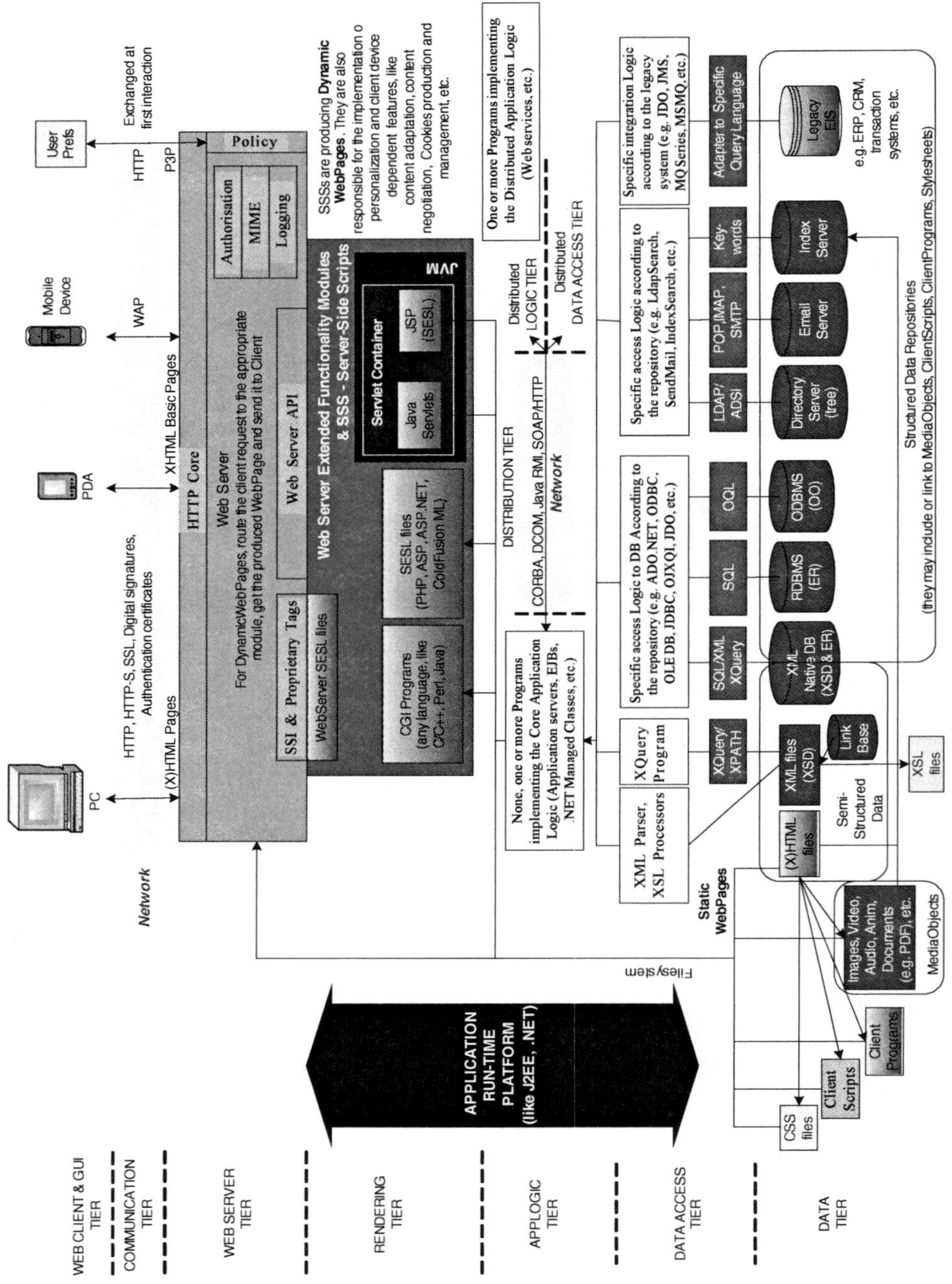

Figure 11. Mark-up languages and meta-languages

Schemas	XML Schemas, RDF Schemas	Style & Transformation	XSL, XSLT, XSL/FO
WebPages	XHTML, XForms, XFrames	XML-based Protocols	SOAP, JXTA, BXXP, XMPP
Mobile WebPages	XHTML Basic, WML	Web Services Descr.	WDML
Graphics	SVG, WebCGM	Multimedia Sync	SMIL
Mobile Graphics	SVG Profiles	Metadata	RDF, OWL, RSS
Maths, 3D, Geographic Data	MathML, X3D, GML	Voice Interaction	VoiceXML (SRGS, SSML, CCXML), SALT
E-commerce data	ebXML, FIX, OFX, XAML, XBRL, xCBL, FinXML, FpML	Security	SAML, XACML, WS Security XMLEncryption, XMLSignature
Mobile Profiles	CC/PP	Web Site Policy	P3P

Presentation-oriented Data
XML Languages
HTML
Mark-up Languages
SGML (DTD)
Pare-down version
XML (XML Schema or DTD)
XML Namespaces
URI and Unicode (UTF-8)
Mark-up Meta-Languages

Figure 12. XML family technologies

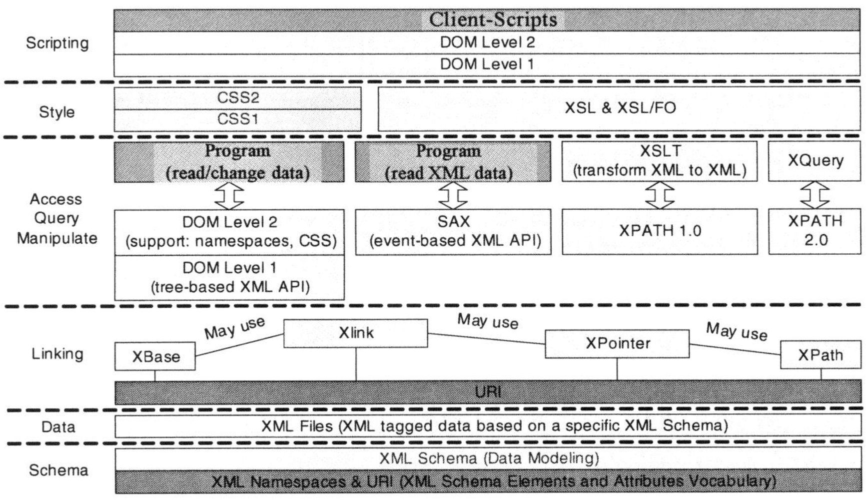

set of function calls for manipulating XML (and HTML) files from a programming language. XML Schemas help developers to precisely define the structures of their own XML-based formats. There are several more modules and tools available or under development and you have to frequently visit W3C's technical reports pages. Figure 12 shows all XML family technologies in the different tiers and their relevance.

Structured data technologies include the mature DB technologies (ER, OO, etc.), directory servers protocols and formats (LDAP/tree), index servers, etc.

At *GUI* tier the most important technologies are the publishing mark-up languages (currently HTML and XHTML) that WebClients support. Let us discuss more XHTML emerging family of technologies (refer to HTML Working Group Roadmap[5] for latest news).

The *Extensible HyperText Markup Language (XHTML)* is a family of current and future document types and modules that reproduce (XHTML 1.0), subset (XHTML Basic), and extend (XHTML 1.1) HTML, reformulated in XML. XHTML family document types are all XML-based. XHTML is the successor of HTML, and a series of specifications has been developed for it.

Currently it consists of:

- *XHTML 1.0* (in three flavors) is a reformulation of HTML 4 in XML, and combines the strength of HTML 4 with the power of XML. Three DTDs are provided: strict, transitional, and frameset.
- *XHTMLMOD* (Modularization of XHTML). A decomposition of XHTML 1.0 into a collection of abstract modules that provide specific types of functionality — allow subsets, extensions (a feature needed for extending XHTML's reach onto emerging platforms), and combinations with other XML vocabularies (for things like vector graphics, multimedia, math, electronic commerce, and more). Also defines a way to develop your own modules that can be combined with XHTML modules.
    - There are four Core Modules, which are required to be an XHTML family member: *Structure Module* (html, head, body, title), *Text Module* (abbr, acronym, address, blockquote, br, cite, code, dfn, div, em, h1-h6, kbd, p, pre, q, samp, span, strong, var), *Hypertext Module* (a) and *List Module* (dl, dt, dd, ol, ul, li).
    - Other XHTML modules: *Text Extension Modules* (presentation module, edit, bi-directional text), *Forms Modules* (basic forms, forms), *Table Modules* (basic tables, tables), *Miscellaneous Modules* (image, client-side image map, server-side image map, object, frames, target, iframe, intrinsic events, metainformation, scripting, style sheet, style attribute, link, base), and *Deprecated Modules* (applet, name identification, legacy).
- *XHTML Host Language* document type. A document type which uses XHTML as a host language, at a minimum, must include structure, text, hypertext and list modules. Examples defined by W3C: XHTML Basic, XHTML 1.1, XHTML + MathML + SVG etc. and examples defined by other organizations: WML 2.0, XHTML-Print etc.
- *XHTML Integration Set* document type. A document type that integrates XHTML modules into another host language. At a minimum, a document type must include text, hypertext and list modules (structure module is not required). Possible use cases: XHTML inside SVG/SMIL/NewsML, etc.

- The *XHTML Basic* document type includes the minimal set of modules required to be an *XHTML Host Language* document type, and in addition it includes images, basic forms, basic tables, and object support. It is designed for Web clients that do not support the full set of XHTML features; for example, Web clients such as mobile phones, PDAs, pagers, and settop boxes. The document type is rich enough for content authoring. Provides support for attached (not-embedded) device-specific StyleLangs (e.g., WAP CSS) to create a presentation that is appropriate for the device. No support for scripts and frames.
- *XHTML 1.1* is reformulation and clean-up of XHTML 1.0 Strict using XHTML modules, avoiding many of the presentation features. Additionally it includes Ruby Annotation Module (ruby, rbc, rtc, rb, rt, rp). It is designed to serve as the basis for future extended XHTML Family document types, and its modular design makes it easier to add other modules as needed or integrate itself into other markup languages. XHTML 1.1 plus *SVG* for scalable vector graphics, *MathML* for mathematics and *SMIL* for multimedia synchronization is an example of such XHTML family document type. Accordingly, XHTML Basic 1.1 plus SVG document type supports embedded images like *SVGProfiles* (*SVG Tiny* for cellphones and *SVG Basic* for PDAs) for scalable vector graphics.
- *XHTML 2* (still a working draft) is a member of the XHTML family of markup languages. It is an XHTML host language but updates many of the modules defined in XHTMLMOD, and includes the updated versions of all those modules and their semantics. XHTML 2 also uses modules that integrates new technologies: *XML events*, and *XForms*. XTMHL 2.0 objective is to totally redesign HTML and replace it. The aims of XHTML2 include: as generic XML as possible, less presentation/more structure, more usability, more accessibility, better internationalization, more device independence (single authoring), less scripting.

Several emerging specifications are coming soon, like *XFrames,* a new XML application to replace HTML frames with similar functionality but with fewer usability problems and *HLink*, link recognition mechanism for the XHTML family.

At AppLogic and rendering tier, main technologies are the Programming Languages. Most popular ones are: C, C++, Java, Perl, VisualBasic, VC++, VJ++, Delphi, Python, Ruby, SmallTalk, .NET (C#, VB.NET, J#).

Semantic Web and Web services technologies have been presented in Figures 4 and 5.

For e-commerce specific technologies refer to Medjahed et al. (2003). They have made a great survey of the main techniques, products, and standards for B2B interactions.

Java Family Technologies. J2EE specification provides a set of java-based technologies serving several purposes:

- **Component-Based Development:** EJB component model simplifies the development of middleware applications by providing automatic support for services such as transactions, security, database connectivity, and more

- **Web Services:** Java API for XML processing (JAXP), Java API for XML registries (JAXR), Java API for XML-based remote procedure call (JAX-RPC), SOAP with attachments API for Java (SAAJ), Java architecture for XML binding (JAXB), Java API for XML messaging (JAXM)
- **Web Specific Technologies:** JavaServer faces, JavaServer pages, JavaServer pages standard tag library (JSTL), JavaServlets
- **DB Connectivity:** JDBC
- **Integration with EIS:** J2EE connector architecture, JMS
- **Security:** Java authorization contract for containers — Java ACC
- **Distribution:** CORBA and Java IDL
- **Mobile-Oriented Technologies:** J2EE client provisioning, J2EE CC/PP processing, J2ME
- **Guidelines, Patterns and Code:** Java blueprints
- **Benchmark to Measure Performance and Scalability:** ECperf
- **Peer-to-Peer Protocol:** JXTA

Research Results Taxonomies

The definition of Web Engineering provided in the introduction of this chapter is a generic one and reflects the multidisciplinary nature of the field. The word "approaches" mainly refers to research results, both theoretical and empirical, originated from several research areas and topics. The main research areas (partly based on (Whitehead, 2002)) and topics that contribute useful research results to Web Engineering are outlined in Table 14.

Efficient Web development should take advantage of all applicable parts of these research areas and topics. As Powell (1998) writes: "WISs involve a mixture between print publishing and software development, between marketing and computing, between internal communications and external relations, and between art and technology." In the context of this chapter, we cannot provide references to all relevant research results (i.e., papers, books, etc.) because we would need many pages just for this. The complete list of research results and corresponding references will be included in the implementation of WEP. However, we provide in this section a brief description and representative references for the most important topics.

- **Designing techniques & notations:** For the designing of the three logical layers of the WebApps, the developer may utilize well-known and adopted conceptual designing techniques and notations that mainly derive from software engineering and DB concepts, like object-oriented (OO), entity-relational (ER), labeled directed graph, use-case modeling and component-based design. A very popular modeling

Table 14. Research areas and topics contributing research results

Research Topics applied to research areas	**Research Areas** and some highlighted specific topics
• Development methods & process modeling • Requirements capturing, analysis & modeling • Designing techniques & notations • Design patterns & good practices • Testing methodologies • Evaluation & metrics • Maintenance issues • Domain specific research (e-commerce, education, business processes, etc.) • Security and authentication • Social and legal aspects (like copyright, privacy, accessibility, ethical issues) • Quality assurance & project management techniques	• **Web Specific Research** Web publishing in (X)HTML, XML, semantic web, web services, client-side scripting and programming, server-side scripting, web testing techniques, accessibility, rapid development, integration, personalization • **DataBases & Information Management** Data conceptual designing & notations, digitization techniques & authoring aspects, data retrieval & querying techniques, multimedia design & production techniques • **Hypermedia engineering** Linking, navigational design, presentation aspects, development methods, evaluation & metrics • **Software engineering** Process models, requirements analysis, use-cases, system architecture, programming, maintenance, integration • **Network engineering** Network architecture, protocols, distributed computing • **Human-computer interaction** Design and evaluation of user interfaces, graphics design, interaction techniques, electronic & print publishing, mobile and handheld computers access

notation is UML (Rumbaugh, Jacobson & Booch, 1999). UML, through the proposition of a Web application extension (Conallen, 1999) or works such as WebML (Ceri, Fraternali & Bongio, 2000), have shown to offer WIS designers a suited way to formalize WIS concepts.

- **Web Development Methods & Processes:** Several process models have emerged for ensuring successful WIS development. Some of them come from the area of software engineering and they are tailored to the WIS special needs, like rational unified process (Kruchten, 1999), adaptable process model (Pressman, 2001) and OPEN framework (Lowe & Henderson-Sellers, 2001). Moreover, there are some hypermedia research originated design methodologies for the construction of the conceptual, navigational and interface designs of Web hyperspaces. They distinguished to workflow-based, scenario-based and content-based methods. Such methods include OOHDM (Schwabe and Rossi, 1998), RMM (Isakowitz, Stohr & Balasubramanian, 1995), WebML (Ceri et al., 2000), W-Model (Sherrell & Chen, 2001), the process of Flavio and Price (1998), Conallen's UML adaptation to Web (1999) and adaptation of RMM (Kirda, Jazayerei, Kerel & Schranz, 2001). Finally, agile processes are lately applied to Web, like AWE (McDonald & Welland, 2003).
- **S/W Development Processes**, like Rational Unified Process, Adaptable Process Model and OPEN Framework. Moreover, there are some mature software process models like: waterfall, fountain, spiral, build and fix, rapid prototyping, incremental and joint application development (JAD). Lately, big attention is given to agile processes, including: extreme programming, adaptive software development, feature-driven development, etc.
- **Domain Specific Research:** Especially for e-commerce domain there are many research results like a workflow-based hypermedia development methodology especially adapted for e-commerce WISs introduced by Lee and Suh (2001). Another good work for the beginner in the field of e-commerce is the one provided by Medjahed, Benatallah, Bouguettaya, Ngu, and Elmagarmid (2003) that summarizes all technologies, tools and some research in the domain.

- **Design Patterns & Good Practices:** Design patterns address the reuse of design experience at any of the several aspects of design and development: conceptual, navigation, logic and interface modeling; application specific patterns (include domain specific implementations, e.g., cultural content). German and Cowan (2000) have reported on more than fifty design patterns, most of them concerning navigation at the hypertext level. Examples of navigational design patterns realizing contextual navigation, i.e., navigation from a given object to a related object in a certain semantic context, are guided tours which support linear navigation across pages, and indexes, allowing to navigate to the members of an index and vice versa (Ceri, Fraternali & Paraboschi, 1999). More design patterns on hypermedia navigation are provided by Gaedke, Lyardet and Werner-Gellersen (1999) and Gillenson, Sherrell and Chen (2000). Several good practices are disseminated across the research communities.

Several good practices are disseminated across the research communities. For instance, NASA developed a site[6] for Web good practices. Finally, RUP provides an extensive catalog of architectural, analysis and design patterns. It also highlights some good practices for development of software and hypermedia: (1) develop iteratively, (2) use component architectures both for S/W and content and (3) model visually both S/W and content e.g. with UML. Some good practices for management include (1) model and manage requirements, (2) continuously verify quality, and (3) manage changes. The delivery of good practices is made through guidelines, templates and tool specific guidance.

- **Testing, Metrics and Evaluation:** Web testing has many dimensions in addition to conventional software testing. Each physical component of a WebApp must be tested. Usability testing is also very important. Services like W3C's HTML, CSS and XHTML certification, and Bobby for accessibility are freely available to Web developers. Some Web metrics and quality research results are provided by Mendes, Mosley and Counsell (2001) and Olsina, Lafuente and Pastor (2002).
- **Requirement and Analysis:** Insufficient requirements specification is a major problem in Web development. Thus, several researchers try to address this aspect. Gnaho (2001) proposes a user-centered engineering approach, where user goals are modeled during requirements analysis and drive the design and implementation phases. Retschitzegger and Schwinger (2000) have proposed a framework of requirements, covering the design space of DataWeb modeling methods in terms of three orthogonal dimensions: levels, aspects and phases.

Tools Taxonomies

A large amount of diverse tools exist that can be used by developers during WEP-Process. Developers have to choose the right tools, install and configure them in order to construct the development and the run-time infrastructure of the WIS.

Tools were built to support one or more activities of development processes or the interoperation of physical components during WIS run-time. A tool may incorporate and support one or more research results and/or technologies. For instance OOHDM-Web tool supports OOHDM research result and OO technology among others. Some research results and almost every technology are supported by a set of tools. These tools can range from complete solutions (e.g., .NET Framework) to small scripts (e.g., W3C HTML Tidy).

It is not possible to provide the full list of available tools in the context of this chapter. In the implementation of the WEP, for each single technology and research result we will provide all available tools and taxonomies of them according to their capabilities. For instance, a taxonomy of tools that support XML family of technologies is presented in our past work (Christodoulou et al., 2001), where we propose an abstract RDF/XML architecture of modules to support the developers throughout the development process. Some examples of XML tools include: XML parsers, XML editors, XSLT processors, XSL/FO processors, XML utilities or toolkits, XML query implementations, XML-DB tools.

High-level classes of tools include the logical layers and physical tiers tools:

- **Content Design Tools** (e.g., UML, OO, ER, XML & RDF Schemas design tools)
- **Logic Design Tools** (e.g., UML & OO design tools)
- **Interface Design Tools** (e.g., graphics design tools)
- **Data Management Tools** (e.g., multimedia production and management, HTML editors, RDBMS, XML repositories, XML toolkits, Directory Servers, metadata automatic extraction tools, automatic links extraction tools)
- **DataAccess Tools** (e.g., XQuery programs, ADO.NET, JDO implementations, LdapSearch program, adapters to legacy systems)
- **AppLogic Tools** (e.g., Application Servers, Compilers/Interpreters, SOAP implementations, UDDI registries, JVM, and many more)
- **Rendering Tools** (e.g., Compilers/Interpreters, SESL tools, JVM, Java Servlets Container)
- **WebServer Tools** (e.g., Web Server, Web Server modules, log analysis tools, administration tools)
- **GUI Tools** (e.g., forms design tools, ClientScripts debuggers, plug-ins, CSS editors, Java/Flash/Shockwave/Active X Controllers development tools)

Another class of tools is the process support tools, like the rational unified process environment, project management and monitoring tools, requirements analysis and modeling tools, testing tools, etc. A tool may be part of more than one class. For instance a RDBMS is a data management and content design tool.

Full-Scale Development and Run-Time Platforms

In this section we provide an enumeration and a brief description of the most popular full-scale development and run-time platforms.

J2EE Tools

Several commercial and open-source products have developed based on J2EE specifications. For a brief description of J2EE see Java family technologies above. These products usually include a suite of tools like, application servers, development studios, portal servers, etc. The most popular ones include: Sun ONE, BEA WebLogic, IBM WebSphere, Apple Web Objects, Novell extend and Oracle Application Server.

.NET

Microsoft's *.NET* includes: Visual Studio.NET, .NET framework, and a .NET server infrastructure.

Visual Studio.NET supports all languages supported by earlier releases of Visual Studio (*Visual Basic*, *Visual C++*) with the notable exception of Java. In its place, it supports *C#*, Microsoft's new object-oriented programming language, similar to Java. Visual Studio.NET has some interesting productivity features including WebForms, a web-based version of Windows Forms.

The .NET Framework consists of two main parts:

- **Common Language Runtime:** A run-time environment (interpreter) that executes code in Microsoft's Intermediate Language (IL). Programs can be written in about every language, including C, C++, C#, and Visual Basic. These programs are compiled in IL byte code and then they are ready to be executed in CLR.
- **.NET Framework class Library:** The library includes prepackaged sets of functionality that developers can use to more rapidly extend the capabilities of their own software. The library includes three key components:
  - **ASP.NET** to help build Web applications and Web services
  - **Windows Forms** and **WebForms** to facilitate smart client user interface development.
  - **ADO.NET** to help connect applications to databases

.NET server infrastructure includes several servers. Some of the most important include: Application Center, BizTalk Server, Host Integration Server, SQL Server, etc.

Table 15 shows some analogies between J2EE and .NET technologies.

Apache Software Foundation Projects

The Apache Software Foundation provides support of open-source software projects. The most important ones and their sub-projects are summarized in Table 16.

Table 15. Analogies between J2EE and .NET technologies

Feature	J2EE	Microsoft .NET
Object-oriented Language	Java	C#
Byte Code	Java Byte Code	IL (Intermediate Language)
Interpreter – runtime environment	JRE (Java Runtime Environment)	CLR (Common Language Runtime)
Dynamic Web Pages	JSP	ASP.NET
Logic Components	EJB (Enterprise Java Beans)	.NET Managed Classes or components
Data Access Logic	JDBC, JMS, Java XML Libraries	ADO.NET

Table 16. Apache Software Foundation important projects and sub-projects

Project	Description
HTTP Server	An open-source, secure, efficient and extensible HTTP Server
Ant	Java-based build tool
James	Java Apache Mail Enterprise Server
Maven	Java Project Management and Comprehension Tools
Perl	The Apache/Perl integration project brings together the full power of the Perl programming language and the Apache HTTP server
Avalon	Framework and components for Java applications
Cocoon	Apache Cocoon is an XML publishing framework built around the concepts of separation of concerns (content, logic and style) and component-based web development. It is based on Xalan XSLT Engine and Xerces XML Parser. Cocoon is a Java servlet and it can be run in every servlet container or J2EE application server that supports Java Servlets 2.2 and above, like Tomcat, Jetty, JBoss JRun, Resin, Websphere, Weblogic, etc. Cocoon relies on the pipeline model: an XML document is pushed through a pipeline that exists in several transformation steps of your document. Every pipeline begins with a generator, continues with zero or more transformers, and ends with a serializer. The Generator is is responsible for delivering SAX events down the pipeline. A Transformer gets an XML document (or SAX events), and generates another XML document (or SAX events). A Serializer is responsible for transforming SAX events into binary or char streams for final client consumption (a presentation format). Cocoon provides Serializers for generating HTML, XML, XHTML, PDF, OpenOffice.org/StarOffice, MS Excel, RTF, Postscript, Plain text, SVG and of course you can create your own.
• Lenya	A Java-based Open-Source Content Management System
DB	Software related to Database access
• Torque	A persistence layer and it includes a JDBC connection pool to DBs
• OJB	ObJectRelationalBridge (OJB) is an Object/Relational mapping tool that allows transparent persistence for Java Objects against relational databases
Jakarta	Server-side Java
• Taglibs	A collection of JavaServer Pages (JSP) custom tag libraries useful in building web applications
• Cactus	A simple test framework for unit testing server-side Java code (servlets, EJBs, tag libraries, filters)
• Lucene	A high-performance, full-featured text search engine written entirely in Java
• Struts	A model-view-controller framework for constructing web applications with servlets and JSP
• Tapestry	A Web application framework based on reusable components within a pure Model-View-Controller pattern
• Turbine	A model-view-controller framework for constructing web applications with either Velocity or JSP
• Velocity	A general purpose Java-based template engine
• Jetspeed	A Java user customizable portal system based on Turbine framework
• Slide	A WebDAV aware content management system
• Tomcat 5	The official Reference Implementation of the Servlet 2.4 and JSP 2.0 technologies.
Web Services	Apache WebServices (WS) Project is a collaborative software development project dedicated to providing robust, full-featured, commercial-quality, and freely available Web Services support on a wide variety of platforms
• Axis	An implementation of the SOAP
• WSIF	The Web Services Invocation Framework (WSIF) is a simple Java API for invoking Web services, no matter how or where the services are provided
• WSIL	The Web Services Inspection Language (WS-Inspection) provides a distributed Web service discovery method, by specifying how to inspect a web site for available Web services
• XML-RPC	A Java implementation of XML-RPC, a popular protocol that uses XML over HTTP to implement remote procedure calls
• WSRP4J	The OASIS Web Services for Remote Portlets (WSRP) standard simplifies integration of remote applications/content into portals so that portal administrators can pick from a rich choice of services and integrate it in their portal without programming effort. The Apache WSRP4J open source project was initiated by IBM to facilitate quick adoption of the WSRP standard by content and application providers and portal vendors.
JaxMe	JaxMe 2 is an open source implementation of JAXB, the specification for Java/XML binding
XML	XML solutions focused on the Web
• Xerces	XML parsers in Java, C++ (with Perl and COM bindings)
• Xalan	XSLT stylesheet processors, in Java and C++
• AxKit	XML-based web publishing, in mod_perl
• FOP	XSL formatting objects, in Java
• Xang	Rapid development of dynamic server pages, in JavaScript
• Batik	A Java based toolkit for Scalable Vector Graphics (SVG)
• XML Security	Java and C++ implementations of the XML signature and encryption standards
• Xindice	A native XML database

Future Trends

The future trends of WEP can be summarized in the following three points:

- Get feedback from researchers and web developers on WEP reference model. Work more on it together with other researchers in order to make it a stable "standard" for Web Engineering community.
- Implementation of the WEP Portal and evaluation of its usage in real-life WIS projects.
- Maintenance of WEP Portal, in order to include emerging technologies, research results and tools.

Conclusion

Based on our extended experience on building large-scale WISs and on our research and analysis of current Web development we have outlined the main difficulties Web developers have on exploiting the Web Engineering resources such as technologies, research results and tools. WERs are not used appropriately or at all during current WIS projects. By studying WERs we concluded that there is a very complex information space that needs to be engineered, in order to provide WERs to developers through a meaningful way. To this end we introduced WEP.

In order to put Web Engineering resources in use by developers, which is the main objective of this chapter, we provide a Reference Model and Guide. We call it the Web Engineering Resources Portal (WEP), because it provides several and cross-referenced taxonomies of these resources, just like an information portal does. WEP consists of a WEP Reference Model and a WER Portal. The WEP Reference Model includes: (1) WEP-Terms: WEP Basic Terminology and Definitions; (2) WEP-Arch: technical-oriented classification of WebApps, WebApps' Logical Layers and the WebApps' Physical Tiers; (3) WEP-Teams: classification of skills; and (4) WEP-Process: A WIS lifecycle process model with three phases: Planning, Deployment and Evolution. WER-Portal provides several WERs Taxonomies based on WEP Reference Model, and acts as a guide through which Web Engineers will be able to easily and meaningfully locate research resources, web technologies and tools and understand their role during (1) WIS Development and (2) WIS Operation/Maintenance. The objective of WER-Portal is to facilitate Web Engineers to comprehend and appropriately use available and emerging Web technologies/tools and as well as to provide a means to transfer knowledge (research results) and experience (patterns/good practices) in an easy and understandable way.

The next step is to implement WEP portal and evaluate it in real-life WIS projects. Furthermore, we have to well-maintain it, in order to always be up-to-date in incorporating every emerging technologies, research results and tools. Finally, in order to achieve its objective, WEP must be enhanced by the contribution of other researchers in the field and work together to make it a stable "standard" for the Web Engineering community.

References

Ceri, S., Fraternali, P., & Bongio, A. (2000). Web Modelling Language (WebML): A modelling language for designing Web sites. *Proceedings of WWW9 Conference,* Amsterdam, The Netherlands.

Ceri, S., Fraternali, P., & Paraboschi, S. (1999). Data-driven one-to-one Web site generation for data-intensive applications. *Proceedings of VLDB'99,* Edinburgh.

Christodoulou, S., Styliaras, G., & Papatheodorou, T. (1998). Evaluation of hypermedia application development and management systems. *ACM Hypertext '98,* Pittsburgh, PA, USA.

Christodoulou, S., Zafiris, P., & Papatheodorou, T. (2001). Web Engineering: The developers' view and a practitioner's. In *Web Engineering: Managing Diversity and Complexity in Web Application Development* (LNCS Vol.2016) Springer-Verlag.

Conallen, J. (1999). *Building Web applications with UML.* Object Technology Series. Addison Wesley.

Cutter Consortium. (2000). *Research briefs.*

Deshpande, Y., Murugesan, S., Ginige, A., Hansen, S., Schwbe, D., Gaedke, M., & White, B. (2002). Web Engineering. *Rinton Press Journal of Web Engineering, 1*(1), 3-17.

Flavio, A., & Price, R. (1998). Towards an integrated design methodology for Internet-based information systems. *Proceedings of HTF5: The 5th Workshop on Engineering Hypertext Functionality into Future Information System,* Kyoto, Japan.

Gaedke, M., Lyardet, F., & Werner-Gellersen, H. (1999). Hypermedia development: Design patterns in hypermedia. *Proc. of Hypertext'99 Workshop on Hypermedia Patterns and Components for Building better Web Information Systems.*

German, D., & Cowan, D. (2000). Towards a unified catalog of hypermedia design patterns. *Proc. of 33rd Hawaii International Conference on System Sciences (HICSS 2000),* Maui, Hawaii.

Gillenson, M., Sherrell L., & Chen, L. (2000). A taxonomy of Web site traversal patterns and structures. *Communications of the AIS, 3*(4).

Gnaho, C. (2001). Web-based information systems development - A user centered engineering approach. *Lecture Notes in Computer Science*, 2016, 105-118.

Hansen, S., Deshpande, Y., & Murugesan, S. (2001). A skill hierarchy for Web-based systems development. In *Web Engineering: Managing diversity and complexity in Web application development,* LNCS 2016, Springer-Verlag.

Holck, J. (2003). 4 perspectives on Web information systems. *36th HICSS (Hawaii International Conference on System Sciences).*

Isakowitz, T., Bieber, M., & Vitali, F. (1998). Web information systems. *Communications of the ACM.* 41(7), 78-80.

Isakowitz, T., Stohr, E., & Balasubramanian, P. (1995). RMM, A methodology for structured hypermedia design. *Communications of the ACM, 38*(8), 34-44.

Kirda, E., Jazayeri, M., Kerer, C., & Schranz, M. (2001). Experiences in engineering flexible Web services. *IEEE Multimedia - Special issues on Web Engineering, 8*(1), 58-65.

Kruchten, P. (1999). *The rational unified process: An introduction* (Addison-Wesley Object Technology Series, 1999). Available online: *http://www.rational.com//products/rup/index.jsp*

Lee, H., & Suh, W. (2001). A workflow-based methodology for developing hypermedia information systems. *Journal of Organizational Computing and Electronic Commerce, 11*(2), 77-106.

Lowe, D., & Henderson-Sellers, B. (2001). OPEN to change. *Cutter IT Journal, 14*(7), 11-17.

McDonald, A., & Welland R. (2003). Agile Web Engineering (AWE) process: Multidisciplinary stakeholders and team communication. *Third International Conference on Web Engineering*, ICWE 2003, LNCS 2722 (pp. 515-518).

Medjahed, B., Benatallah, B., Bouguettaya, A., Ngu, A.H.H., & Elmagarmid, A. (2003). Business-to-business interactions: Issues and enabling technologies. *The VLDB Journal , 12*(1).

Mendes, E., Mosley, N. & Counsell, S. (2001). Web metrics: Estimating design and authoring effort. *IEEE Multimedia - Special issues on Web Engineering, 8*(1), 50-57.

Nambisan, S., & Wang, Y.-M. (1999). Roadblocks to Web technology adoption? *Communications of the ACM, 42*(1), 98-101.

Olsina, L., Lafuente, G., & Pastor, O. (2002). Towards a reusable repository for Web metrics. *Proceedings of the Third ICSE Workshop on Web Engineering,* Orlando, Florida.

Powell, T.A. (1998). *Web site engineering: Beyond Web page design.* Prentice Hall.

Pressman, R. (2001). Adaptable process model. Hypertext version available online: *http://www.rspa.com/apm/index.html*

Pressman, R.S. (1997). *Software engineering: A practitioner's approach.* New York: McGraw-Hill.

Retschitzegger, W., & Schwinger, W. (2000). Towards modeling of dataWeb applications: A requirements' perspective. *Proceedings of the Americas Conference on Information Systems, AMCIS 2000,* Long Beach, California (Vol. I, pp. 149-155).

Rumbaugh, J., Jacobson, I., & Booch, G. (1999). *The unified modeling language reference manual.* Addison-Wesley.

Schwabe, D., & Rossi, G. (1998). An object oriented approach to Web-based application design. *Theory and Practice of Object Systems Journal, 4*(4), 207-225.

Sherrell, L., & Chen, L. (2001). The W life cycle model and associated methodology for corporate Web site development. *Communication of the Association for Information Systems (CAIS), 5*(7).

Whitehead, E. J. (2002). A proposed curriculum for a masters in Web Engineering. *Rinton Press Journal of Web Engineering, 1*(1), 018-022.

Endnotes

1 Too many abbreviations are used throughout this chapter. For shake of readability and space saving the full-text of all abbreviations are provided in a table at the end of the chapter.

2 Definition partly based on http://www.hyperdictionary.com/dictionary/data

3 http://www.w3.org/1999/05/WCA-terms/

4 http://www.w3.org/TR/2003/WD-webarch-20031001/

5 http://www.w3.org/MarkUp/xhtml-roadmap/

6 http://nasa-wbp.larc.nasa.gov/devel/index.html

Appendix

Abbreviations

ADO	ActiveX Data Objects
ADSI	Active Directory Service Interface
ALICE	Artificial Linguistic Computer Entity
API	Application Program Interface
ASP	Active Server Page
AVI	Audio Video Interleave
AWE	Agile Web Engineering
B2B	Business to Business
B2C	Business to Customer
BXXP	Blocks Extensible Exchange Protocol
CBD	Component-Based Design
CC/PP	Composite Capabilities/ Preference Profiles
CCXML	Call Control XML
CFML	Cold Fusion Markup Language
CGI	Common Gateway Interface
CMP	Container Managed Persistence
CORBA	Common Object Request Broker Architecture
CRM	Customer Relatioship Management
CSS	Cascading Style Sheets

Abbreviations (cont.)

DB	DataBase
DCOM	Distributed Component Object Model
DHTML	Dynamic HTML
DIVX	DIgital Video eXpress
DOM	Document Object Model
DSDM	Dynamic Systems Development Method
DSML	Directory Service Markup Language
DTD	Document Type Definition
ebXML	electronic business eXtensible Markup Language
ECML	Electronic Commerce Modeling Language
EIS	Enterprise Information System
EIS	Enterprise Information System
EJB	Enterprise JavaBeans
EMMA	Extensible MultiModal Annotation Markup Language
ER	Entity-Relational
ERP	Enterprise Resource Planning
FinXML	Financial XML
FIX	Financial Information eXchange
FpML	Financial Products Markup Language
FTP	File Transfer Protocol
GIF	Graphics Interchange Format
GML	Geographic Mark-up Language
GML	Geography Markup Language
GUI	Graphical User Interface
H/W	HardWare
HTML	HyperText Markup Language
HTTP	HyperText Transfer Protocol
HTTP-S	HTTP Secure
IETF	Internet Engineering Task Force
IMAP	Internet Message Access Protocol
IRI	Internationalized Resource Identifiers
IT	Information Technology
J2EE	Java 2 Platform Enterprise Edition
J2ME	Java 2 Platform Micro Edition
JAD	Joint Application Development
JAXB	Java Architecture for XML Binding
JAXM	Java API for XML Messaging
JAXP	Java API for XML Processing
JAXR	Java API for XML Registries
JAX-RPC	Java API for XML-Based Remote Procedure Call
Java ACC	Java Authorization Contract for Containers
Java RMI	Java Remote Method Invocation
JDBC	Java DataBase Connectivity
JDO	Java Data Objects
JMS	Java Messaging Services
JPG	joint photographic experts group
JSP	Java Server Page
JSTL	JavaServer Pages Standard Tag Library
JVM	Java Virtual Machine
JXTA	comes from the word juxtapose, meaning side-by-side.
LAMP	Linux Apache MySQL and PHP
LDAP	Lightweight Directory Access Protocol
LDG	Labeled Directed Graph

Abbreviations (cont.)

MathML	Mathematics Mark-up Language
MIME	Multipurpose Internet Mail Extensions
MOV	QuickTime Video Format
MP3	MPEG Audio Layer 3
MPEG	Moving Pictures Experts Group
MSMQ	MicroSoft Message Queuing
NNTP	Network News Transport Protocol
ODBC	Open DataBase Connectivity
ODBMS	Object-oriented DataBase Management System
OFX	Open Financial eXchange
OJXQI	The Oracle Java XQuery API
OLE DB	Object Linking and Embedding DB
OO	Object-Oriented
OOHDM	Object-Oriented-HypermeDia-Model
OQL	Object Query Language
OWL	Web Ontology Languag
P3P	Platform for Privacy Preferences
PDA	Personal Digital Assistant
PDF	Portable Document Format
PHP	Hypertext Preprocessor
PNG	Portable Network Graphics
POP	Point Of Presence
PRISM	Publishing Requirements for Industry Standard Metadata
PS	PostScript
RDBMS	Relational Data Base Management System
RDF	Resource Description Framework
RDF VDL	RDF Vocabulary Description Language
RMM	Relationship Management Methodology
RSS	RDF Site Summary or Rich Site Summary
RUP	Rational Unified Process
S/W	SoftWare
SAAJ	SOAP with Attachments API for Java
SALT	Speech Application Language Tags
SAML	Security Assertion Markup Language
SAX	Simple API for XML
SESL	Server-side Embedded Scripting Language
SET	Secure Electronic Transaction
SGML	Standard Generalized Mark-up Language
SIMPLE	Session Initiation Protocol (SIP) for Instant Messaging and Presence Leveraging Extensions
SIP	Session Initiation Protocol
SMIL	Synchronized Multimedia Integration Language
SMTP	Simple Mail Transfer Protocol
SOAP	Simple Object Access Protocol
SQL	Structured Query Language
SRGS	Speech Regognition Grammar Specification
SSI	Server Side Include
SSL	Secure Sockets Layer
SSML	Speech Synthesis Mark-up Language
SSS	Server Side Script
SVG	Scalable Vecor Graphics

Abbreviations (cont.)

UDDI	Universal Description Discovery and Integration
UIML	User Interface Markup Language
UML	Unified Modeling Language
URI	Uniform Resource Identifier
URL	Uniform Resource Locator
vADS	Advertisement and Discovery of Services Protocol
VBasic	Visual Basic
vXAML	Transaction Authority Markup Language
vXFS	Xmethods File System
vXKMS	XML Key Management Specification
VXML	Voice Extensible Markup Language
W3C	World Wide Web Concortium
WAI	Web Accessibility Initiative
WAP	Wireless Application Protocol
WAV	Waveform audio format
WDDX	Web Distributed Data Exchange
WebApps	Web Applications
WebCGM	Web Computer Graphics Metafile
WebDAV	Web-based Distributed Authoring and Versioning
WebML	Web Modeling Language
WEP	Web Engineering Resources Portal
WER	Web Engineering Resources
WFA	Web Front-end Application
WHA	Web Hypermedia Application
WIA	Web Interactive Application
WIS	Web-based Information Systems
WML	Wireless Markup Language
WSDL	Web Services Description Language
WWW	World Wide Web
X3D	eXtensible 3D Graphics
XACML	Extensible Access Control Markup Language
XAML	Transaction Authority Markup Language
XBRL	Extensible Business Reporting Language
xCBL	XML Common Business Library
XDR	eXternal Data Representation
XHTML	eXtensible Hypertext Markup Language
XHTMLMOD	Modularization of XHTML
XLANG	Transaction Language
XMI	XML data Interchange
XML	eXtensible Markup Language
XMLNS	XML NameSpaces
XMPP	Extensible Messaging and Presence Protocol
XPATH	XML Path Language
XQuery	XML Query Language
XSD	XML Schema Definition
XSL	eXtensible Stylesheet Language
XSL/FO	XSL Formatting Objects
XSLT	eXtensible Stylesheet Language Transformation
XSP	eXtensible Server Pages
XUL	eXtensible User Interface Language

Section II

Web Application Development: Methodologies and Techniques

Chapter III

Web Application Development Methodologies[1]

Jim Q. Chen
St. Cloud State University, USA

Richard D. Heath
St. Cloud State University, USA

Abstract

Web-based application development represents some unique challenges to the developers. There is a growing need for better development methodologies. The traditional system development methods for non-Web applications can still be effective, but need to be adapted and enriched in the new development environment. This chapter discusses the challenges and proposes a Modified Prototyping Method (MPM) for Web application development. MPM views Web applications as organic systems that are continually adapting to their environments. MPM places more emphasis on architectural decision for system scalability and proactive system maintenance. It suggests not only a process but also a set of design techniques at each stage. The method provides a balanced view of technology and management requirements in the Web application development process.

Introduction

Web technology is transforming the way organizations conduct business and communicate with constituent groups. For application developers, Web technology represents a new world of software engineering with new techniques, new tools, and new design and deployment environment. The technology enables organizations to deliver Web applications easily and quickly and provides more efficient methods to do maintenance. As a result, organizations are more responsive to user needs and quicker to customize applications for specific users.

However, Web application development presents unique challenges to the developers. Among these challenges are usability design, content maintenance, high scalability, high security requirement, and increasing demand for fast system deployment by customers. In addition, the developers are faced with competing system architectures, platforms, and tools, most of which are still evolving.

Web application development lacks standards and structured methodologies. For many developers, building Web applications is a "mad science" (Callaway, 1997). The most common approach is "implement, test, and release." The resulting systems are often of low usability and very difficult to maintain (Powell, Jones, & Cutts, 1998; Nielsen, 2000; Nielsen & Tahir, 2002). Many organizations simply ignore the issue of software development processes altogether and depend on the talent, skills, and motivation of the development team (Yourdon, 2002). According to a study on the adoption of system development methodologies (Fitzgerald, 1998), 60 percent of the respondents reported not using any methodologies. Seventy-nine percent of those not using a methodology indicated that they did not intend to adopt one.

For simple projects of sufficient short duration and with experienced developers, not following a formal methodology may not be a problem. But for large projects of long duration and requiring more than one level of supervision, a methodology is highly recommended if organizations want to avoid anarchy within Web development teams (Yourdon, 2002).

This chapter discusses Web-based business applications and development methodologies. A Modified Prototype Method (MPM) for Web application development is presented. Among the major topics covered are Web applications components, the challenges facing Web application developers, client-side and server-side technologies, Web application architectures, Web design techniques, and comparisons between MPM and other similar methodologies. The chapter concludes with a summary and discussion on the advantages and disadvantages of deploying Web applications.

Web Applications

In recent literature, a Web application is defined as any application program that runs on the Internet or corporate intranets and extranets. The user of a Web application uses a Web browser on a client computer to run the program residing on the server. The entire processing is done on the server as if it were done at the user's local machine. In this chapter we use the term in a broader context to include any application that is Web browser based.

There are three types of Web applications: static Web documents, simple interactive Web applications, and complex Web-based database systems. Static Web applications do not interact or exchange information with their viewers. Their purpose is to share and distribute information to the public. Most personal Web sites can be classified as static. The next level of sophistication is the interactive Web applications where the visitors of the sites can exchange information with the Web owners. Many such Web sites use response forms to collect feedback or customer evaluation on their products or services. Complex Web applications handle sophisticated business transactions online, such as online banking, stock trading, and interactive database queries. They may be full-blown Java applications running on the client side but its code is automatically downloaded from the server, with multi-tiered client/server architecture. They could be applications based on .NET Framework technology and ASP.NET Web Forms that execute on both the client and on the server. Complex Web database are the cornerstone technology for e-commerce. This chapter is concerned with the development of such industrial strength Web applications.

A Web application is based on individual Web pages, whether they are static or dynamic. This enables the application to be divided into clearly demarcated sections, allowing or denying access as needed. For example, a company's human resource division might be allowed access to certain areas of the application when doing their human resource duties, while the sales department might want to look at inventory part of the application while placing a customer order.

As shown in Figure 1, each portion of the application can have its own Web page. Each page can include an appropriate user interface for gathering and displaying data to the user. Each page can include help right alongside the application's interface and can contain links to almost any other part of the application.

The application can be broken down as finely as the developer desires. Each page can do several functions or merely one. Special pages for specific users can be added and accessed based on the user's identity, which can easily be determined and managed by standard Hypertext Transfer Protocol (HTTP) and Web techniques such as authentication and the use of 'cookies.' New functionality can easily be added merely by adding additional Web pages and the appropriate links. Functionality can easily be updated or fixed by changing existing pages.

The use of Web-based technology means that the application can be managed from one central location. The developer can maintain total control over the content at the server rather than have to worry about delivering binary content to each individual user.

Figure 1. Layout of a Web application (each node represents a Web page)

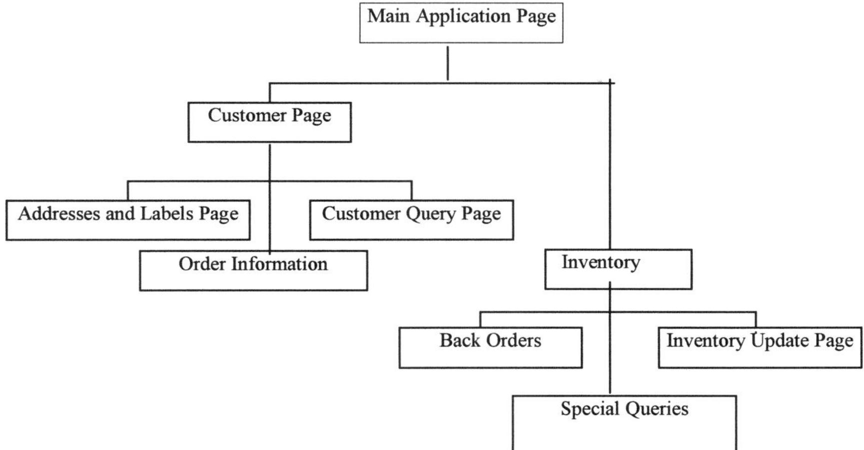

Web Application Components

An industrial strength Web database application may consist of five major components as shown in Figure 2. The Web server runs specialized Web server software that supports HTTP to handle multiple Web requests and is responsible for user authentication in case of intranet and extranet applications.

An application server performs most of the application processing logic and enforces business rules. It is also in charge of maintaining the state management and session control logic that are required for an online transactional system. The database server hosts Database Management System (DBMS) and provides data access and management capabilities. In a typical session, the Web server processes client requests and sends HTML pages back to the client. When needed, a Web server connects to application server to process business logic (e.g., credit authorization, checking inventory status). The database server performs database query and sends the result back to the Web server. Such multi-tier architecture provides high system scalability. When the system demand increases, workload can be distributed on additional application or database servers. However, this layout does not mean that there must be an application server for Web applications. Nor does it imply that the Web server and application server or database server cannot be located on the same machine. The decision on architectural components is affected by the requirements of the application, the business strategy, and the existing and future technology infrastructure.

Figure 2. Web database application components

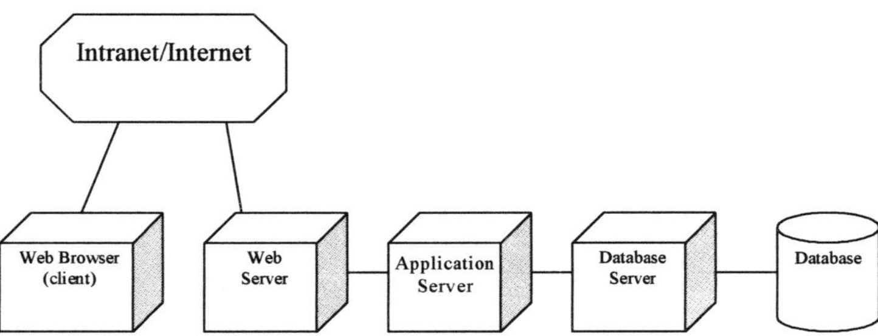

Client-Side Processing

Client-side processing has grown very popular in recent years because it improves the overall application's responsiveness and frees the Web server some resource for other tasks. Java applets and .NET Framework components are the two main technologies that allow developers to create and maintain code that runs on client workstations. The .NET Framework components and Java code reside on the server and are delivered to the client on demand. Both provide a means for automatically ensuring that the latest version of the code is available to the client. Version updating is done almost transparently, so that the user need not even know that any changes have been made. Both can be delivered to a user's browser via a simple Hyper-text Transfer Protocol (HTTP) request.

Java applets and .NET components are very similar in the means of execution. Both technologies require running of a runtime engine on the client machines. A runtime is a resident program that provides services to other programs during their execution. The .NET's runtime is known as the common language runtime (CLR). The .NET components are compiled Intermediate Language (IL) code. When the IL code arrives at the client machine, it will be translated into native machine code by the Just-In-Time compiler in CLR. The Java applets are compiled Java Bytecode and require the Java virtual machine (JVM) installed on the client machines.

The .NET Framework components can be created in Visual Basic.NET, Visual C++ .NET, or C# .NET. The .NET components currently require that the windows operating system be the client or that a special plugin be used in Netscape Navigator. Java code can be run on any machine that has a Java virtual machine installed, and thus is cross-platform in nature. Both .NET components and Java applets offer good security features, therefore, are better suited for open system such as the Internet. Other client side processing technologies include Javascript, Vbscript, Extensible Markup Language (XML), and Extensible Stylesheet Language (XSL).

Server-Side Processing

Any Web application will do at least some server-side processing. In its most strict form, applications that use server side processing do all of the application's processing on the server and then send only HTML back to the client. In the case of Web database applications, the Web browser sends a database request to the Web server. The Web server passes the request using Common Gateway Interface (CGI) or Internet Server Application Programming Interface (ISAPI) to the application server where the Web-to-database middleware may be located. The application server then uses a database middleware such as Open Database Connectivity (ODBC) to connect to the database. The application server receives the query result and creates the HTML-formatted page and sends the page back to the Web server, using the CGI or ISAPI transmission standard. The Web server sends the page to the browser. Server-side programming options include Java, ActiveServer Pages (ASP), ASP.NET, Java Active Pages (JSP), PHP, CGI-script (Perl, C, C++).

Challenges of Web Application Development

Web application development, no matter Internet-based or intranet- and extranet-based, presents unique challenges for developers. The major challenges include usability design, content-rich maintenance, security, integration with legacy systems, and fast application deployment. For Internet-based applications, there are additional two challenges — scalability and load balancing.

1. **Usability Design:** The usability of an e-commerce Web site, to a large extent, will determine the success or failure of the organization's Web presence. In traditional buyer-seller relationship, the users experience usability after they paid for the software. If a problem occurs, the users can always call the support center for help. However, on the Web, the users experience usability before they pay. Less usable Web design will turn users away because competitors are just one click away. E-commerce applications are designed for unknown users, unknown hardware platforms, and unknown software configurations at the users-side.
2. **Content-Rich:** Most Web applications are content-rich. Content-rich applications require frequent updates and maintenance. A less frequently updated Web site quickly cast doubt on its visitors' mind about its accuracy and usefulness. For Web applications, the notion of maintenance takes on a different meaning, where the lines between development and maintenance blur to the point where they are really the same thing.
3. **Scalability:** An Internet application runs in a different operating environment than a non-Internet based application does. Non-Internet based systems operate in a

well-defined environment. The system users and workload are well understood. Internet applications, however, run in an open environment where workload and user profiles are less understood and less predictable. Therefore, Internet applications can encounter highly variable and potentially huge transaction peak loads. The system must be designed to handle dramatic fluctuations of user demand and to have additional upgrades to boost the system performance and to support additional users.

4. **Load Balancing:** In a multi-server Internet application, unbalanced workload on servers reduces system performance, reliability, and availability. Balancing system's load requires careful selection from an array of tools and techniques. There is no single silver bullet that can be applied to all application systems. Some of the load balancing techniques includes application partitioning and service replication.
5. **Security:** Security is a major concern for Internet applications because of the open operating environment. Even for intranet and extranet applications, security should be a concern. No one product on the market can guarantee a secure application. Security needs to be designed into an application, and needs to be maintained in that application. Furthermore, organization-wide security policy and procedure must be in place. The following security issues must be addressed (Fournier, 1999):

- **Privacy:** How to ensure that confidential data are safeguarded.
- **Integrity:** How to ensure that data consistency and accuracy are maintained when they are traveling on the network.
- **Authentication:** How to verify the true identity of the parties involved in a business transaction.
- **Access Control:** How to allow authorized users to access only the information they are allowed to access. How to prevent unauthorized access.
- **Non-Repudiation:** How to prevent denial of transaction submissions, either from the sending or receiving ends of the communication process.

6. **Integrating Legacy Systems:** More and more organizations are linking their legacy systems, which may run on different computing platforms, to their Web applications. Many Web middleware solutions are available to bridge Web technology to relational databases or legacy systems. For example, Oracle Corporation, Informix Software, and Sybase Corporation offer Web database middleware; IBM's MQSeries and Talarian's SmartSockets are message-oriented middleware tools. The challenge is to find the proper tools that fit organization's needs.
7. **Fast Development:** A well-designed quality Web application can be a competitive advantage. Therefore, Web developers are under overwhelming pressure from management to develop the application very quickly.

Web Development Methodologies

The traditional system development methods such as the waterfall model and prototyping methods can still be effective, but need to be adapted and enriched in the new development environment to meet the challenges of Web applications.

Having observed many poorly designed Web sites by ad hoc processes, Powell, Jones, and Cutts (1998) advocated the need for formalized processes in Web development. They suggested a modified waterfall model with "whirlpools" for beginner Web application developers. The model consists of the same stages of waterfall model: problem definition, requirement analysis, design prototyping, implementation, integration/testing, and release/maintenance. However, the first two planning stages iterate a few times (forming "whirlpools") to develop a better understanding of users requirements. Yourdon (2002) expanded Web application development to include business strategy formulation and business process re-engineering. He recommended a lightweight process that includes five stages: developing e-business strategy, re-engineering business process, developing system requirements, design/code, and test. In a similar vein, Standing (2002) proposed an Internet commerce development methodology (ICDM), which starts with business environment analysis and process re-engineering. Both models focus on the management aspect of Web application development.

In the next section, we will present a modified prototyping method (MPM) for Web development. MPM differs from other methods in that it views Web applications as organic systems that are continually adapting to their environments. MPM places more emphasis on architectural decisions for system scalability and the important role of system maintenance. It suggests not only a process but also a set of design techniques at each stage. The method provides a balanced view of technology and management requirements in the Web application development process.

The Modified Prototype Method

The prototyping method was formally introduced to the Information Systems community in the early 1980s to combat the weakness of traditional waterfall model (Naumann and Jenkins, 1982). It is an iterative process of system development. Working closely with users, developers design and build a scaled-down functional model of a desired system. The developer demonstrates the working model to the user and then continues to develop the prototype based on the feedback received until the developer and the user agree that the prototype is "good enough." At that point, the developer either throws away the prototype and starts building the real system (throwaway prototype is used solely to understand user's requirements) or completes any remaining work on the prototype and releases the prototype as final product (evolutionary prototype). Figure 3 illustrates the evolutionary prototyping process. Please note that the maintenance phase begins only after the final system is formally deployed.

The prototyping method has gained its popularity because of its ability to capture user requirements in concrete form. In fact, the method is often used for designing decision

Figure 3. The evolutionary prototyping method (Adapted from McConnell, 1996)

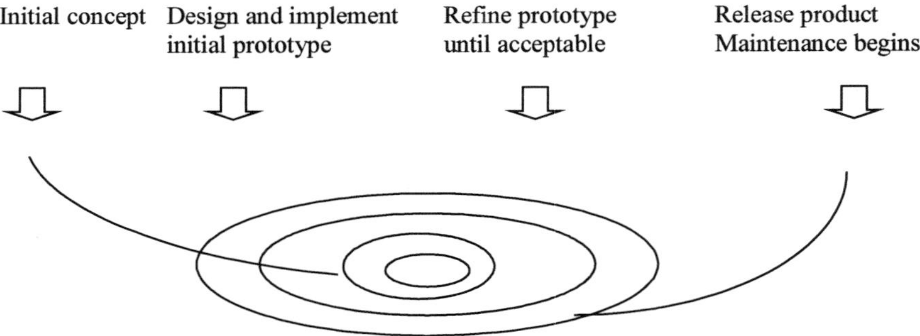

support systems when neither the decision maker nor the system designer understands information requirements well. It is often used along with traditional system development methods to speed up the system development process.

Another related method is the staged delivery in which the project is divided into several stages. Each stage consists of detailed design, code, debug, and delivery for a component of a desired system. Like evolutionary prototyping method, it has a distinctive boundary between development and maintenance.

These methods have been proven very successful when customized to specific development environments for non-Web-based applications development. They are also applicable to Web-based applications. In fact, prototyping methods are especially suitable for Web based applications because of the ease of system delivery and updates afforded by Web technology. However, the unique requirements of Web applications require the designers to take additional considerations when using these models.

Figure 4 outlines the modified prototype method (MPM) for Web application development. MPM allows for basic functionality of a desired system or a component of it to be formally deployed right away. The maintenance phase is set to begin right after the deployment. The method is flexible enough not to force an application to be based on the state of an organization at a given time. As the organization grows and environment changes the application changes with it rather than being frozen in place.

Basic System Analysis and Design

The basic system analysis and design involves studying general user requirements, the underlying data model, user interface, and architecture requirement. Understanding user requirements really means understanding requirements on two things: Web content and system behavior. Web content refers to information and its organization on your Web site. You need to decide what information to include, what level of details, and how it should be organized on your Web site. Traditional techniques such as survey and interview can still be used for Web content requirement analysis, especially for intranet/

Figure 4. The Web development methodology

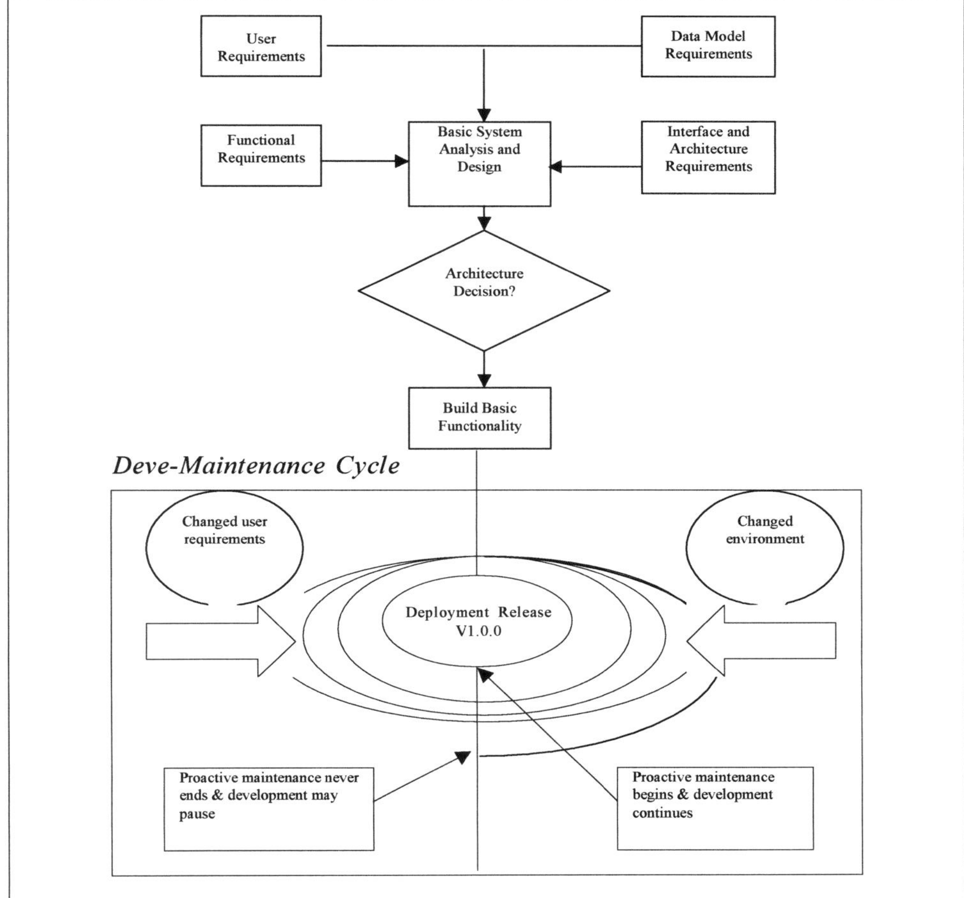

extranet applications. System behavior refers to the system's intended functionality. A powerful method to design system functionality is to develop use cases. A typical use case consists of a group of scenarios tied together by a common user goal. A scenario is a sequence of actions that a user or system component (called actor) performs within a system. Use cases serve as an easy-to-use communication tool to express the interactions and dialogs between system users and the system itself.

The data model is one of the most important parts of an application, and getting this right is crucial. While changes and additions can be made later, such changes are costly to make. There is no way to determine all of the data needs right at the beginning, but doing a good analysis and design on the data that is known will go a long way toward application success. The data model needs to be flexible enough to adapt to changing needs. By adhering to the strict database normalization rules should minimize the problems that might arise from the need to change the data model. Finally, basic interface and architectural decisions must be made based on the organization's existing technology infrastructure and user needs. Will there be server-side processing? Where will the data reside — Java or .NET component? Do sales people need access to the data while they are away? Will customers need access to the application? What part of the application will reside on the application server? Choosing a proper architecture has a long-lasting impact on the organization. It will determine how flexible technology-wise the organization can be in adapting to the constant changing business needs.

Architecture Decision

After a careful analysis of the system requirements and use cases, the decision on system architecture must be made. This decision must be made based on both the current needs and future development. For a simple static Web site, clients and Web server are the only two components you need to have. But for Web applications that are dynamic and process business logic, at least three significant architectural components are needed: clients, Web server, and application server. It is also very common for most Web applications to have a database server. There are many ways to layout a Web application architecturally. But there are three major models: (1) thin client, (2) fat client, and (3) distributed and component-based.

- **Thin Client:** Client has minimal computing power. All of the business logic and rules are processed at the server. The client is a standard Web browser. This model is mostly used for Internet-based and some extranet-based applications because control over the client's configuration is lacking. The model gives developer greater freedom in system deployment and maintenance. However, the application performance can be a bit slow due to the fact that all processes are done at the server side.
- **Fat Client:** In this model, a fair amount of business logic and rules are executed on the client machine. Fat clients typically use dynamic HTML, Java applets, or .NET Framework components. Fat clients are used for some intranet applications that must provide customized services to certain user group. For example, special reports tailored to top executives. System performance speed is expected to be faster, given the fact that some business logic is done locally.
- **Distributed and Component-Based:** Distributed and component-based architectures are used to support distributed object-oriented systems and Web services. In previous two models (thin and fat clients) a business system is deployed at one location. The business logic for the application is implemented in a tightly coupled proprietary system. A distributed object system or a Web service, however, allows parts of the system to be located on separate computers, possibly in many different locations. The object system itself is an assembly of reusable business software components. Business components are self-contained units of code designed to perform specific business functions. A major benefit of a distributed object system is its adaptability to changing environment. As a business's products, processes, and objectives evolve over time, new business software solutions can be easily

assembled using reusable business components. Another benefit is the elimination of vendor "lock-in" problem. There are three major competing distributed and component-based architectures for Web applications: The .NET Framework, Common Object Request Broker Architecture (CORBA), and Enterprise Javabean (EJB).

The .NET Framework is the core of Microsoft's .NET Initiative launched in 2000. The initiative is a bold vision to provide a technology platform to enable application development that is programming language independent, software and hardware independent. In other words, an application, either Web-based or non-Web-based, can be built in any programming language and is executable in any operating systems on any hardware platforms. The .NET Framework consists of two parts: the common language runtime (CLR) and the Framework Class Library (FCL).

The CLR is a multi-language execution environment, which provides services to executing programs. With CLR, programs written in a variety of languages are compiled into machine code in two steps. First, the program is compiled into Microsoft Intermediate Language (MSIL). Then, the Just-In-Time compiler in the CLR converts the MSIL into machine code for a particular platform. The FCL is a library of classes, interfaces, and value types that can be used by the .NET Framework applications. For .NET components development, Microsoft provides the developers with an integrated development environment called Visual Studio.NET, which houses Visual Basic.NET, Visual C++, and Visual C#. The disadvantage of using .NET Framework is the client requirement of running Windows.

The Common Object Request Broker Architecture (CORBA) is a set of standards that addresses the need for interoperability among the rapidly proliferating number of hardware and software products available today. CORBA model allows applications to communicate with one another no matter where they are stored. The Object Request Broker (ORB) is the middleware that establishes the client-server relationships between objects. Using an ORB, a client can transparently invoke a method on a server object, which can be on the same machine or across a network. The central protocol of the CORBA distributed component model is the Internet Interoperable ORB Protocol (IIOP). CORBA was proposed by Object Management Group (http://www.omg.org). CORBA is an important step on the road to object-oriented standardization and interoperability.

Enterprise JavaBeans model was defined by Sun Microsystems. It is an Application Programming Interface (API) specification for building scalable, distributed, component-based, multi-tier applications. EJB is different from original JavaBeans model. Original JavaBeans model provides standard specification for developing reusable, prefabricated Java components that are mainly used on client side of a business application. EJB, however, is defined as a server side model for component-based, transaction-oriented, distributed enterprise computing. The model defines four key components (1) the server, (2) the container, (3) the Remote Method Invocation (RMI), and (4) the interface to backend system and databases — Java Database Connectivity (JDBC).

The server provides a standard set of services for transaction management, security, and resource sharing. The container is where JavaBeans execute. The container provides life-cycle management (from object creation to destruction), persistence management, transparent distribution services. The Remote Method Invocation API allows JavaBeans components running on one machine to invoke methods on remote JavaBeans as if they were local. The JDBC API provides relational database connectivity for Java applications. JBE is an alternative or a complement to the .NET Framework and CORBA models. Major software vendors supporting EJB include IBM, SAP, HP, PeopleSoft, Oracle, and BEA.

The difference between CORBA and EJB or the .NET Framework is that CORBA is just a specification. It relies on individual vendors to provide implementations. CORBA and the EJB approaches are merging and are interoperable in some of today's implementations. The decision on which architecture to adopt rests on several factors (Fournier, 1999; Tate, Clark, Lee, & Linskey, 2003):

- The size, complexity, and level of scalability required by the application.
- The existing hardware/software.
- The level of compatibility of the different components that are assembled to create the application.
- The type of development tools available.
- The skills set and experience of the developer teams.

In general, for intranet applications, the organization should consider the mainstream software in use within the organization, if the organization is primarily windows-centric, the .NET Framework might be the choice. If the organization is Unix-based or if running under multi-platform environment, then OMG's CORBA might be a proper way to go. If the organization is committed to Java and plans to use it extensively in the future, the Sun's EJB may be the choice. For Internet applications, it is difficult to predict the client side environment; potential users may use any type of browsers in any version. The designers need to decide the targeted user groups and try to accommodate their needs first. In any case, developers need to understand their business problems and their team's experience and skills levels. They should choose the technologies that are most appropriate for solving their problems.

By the end of this step, the developer should have an idea of how the application will be structured, what each tier of the application will be doing, what the data model will look like, and what basic functions can first be deployed.

Building and Deploying Initial Version

This step begins with laying out the application as a series of connected Web pages, each page performing a specific function. Perhaps the initial version will provide nothing more than a collection of form and report pages that allow users to query, update, and report on customer address information. The developer might need to build only a few HTML pages and a few reports to be able to at least let users become aware of the application

Figure 5. Storyboards: Flow of Web page sketches

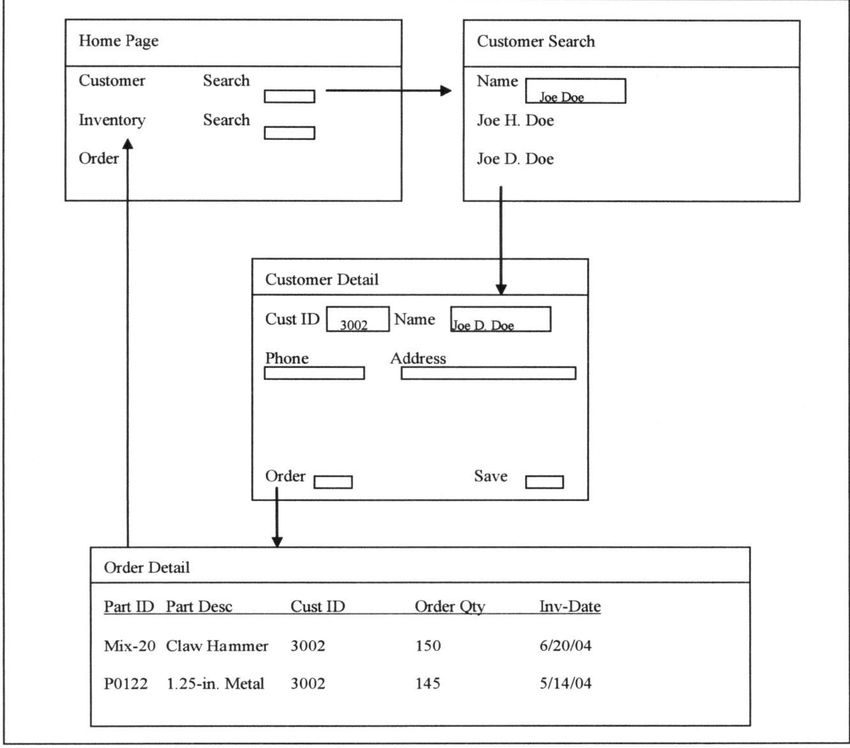

and get used to the basic functions provided. A helpful tool the developer may use to layout the user interface is storyboarding in which the developer use storyboards to capture Web pages and the flow among them (see Figure 5 for an example).

Deve-Maintenance Cycle

Once the initial version is deployed, a Deve-maintenance (Development and maintenance) cycle begins. This cycle is characterized by incremental enhancements and proactive maintenance.

- **Incremental Enhancement:** After a basic functionality is deployed, incremental enhancements can follow. Perhaps a section of the application that allows users to access inventory data can be added. This could be built and deployed without worrying about integrating it with customer order data. Once the customer and inventory data is deployed, the developer might build the part of the application that connects the two areas, allowing users to check orders against both customers and inventory. The really powerful part is that integrating the new functionality into the existing functionality might be as simple as adding HTML code to the existing pages in the customer and inventory sections. These changes, of course, will take effect immediately, as they are placed in the code base for the Web server. New functionality can be highlighted and explained right on each Web page. The application can easily direct users to help screens and point out new items and functions. Bug fixes can be transparently updated without a single change needing to be made on users' machines. New users who ask for specific reports can be given access to specific pages that meet their particular needs. All of this can be done with the code under the complete control of the development team, as all of the code will sit on the server, waiting to be accessed by the user.

- **Maintenance:** Maintenance takes on a different meaning for Web applications. The distinctive maintenance phase that we are familiar with in the traditional system development cycle no longer exists. The maintenance phase is interleaved into development phase. The application is constantly evolving and changing, with old features going away and new features being added. Thus, it is not really clear where maintenance begins and development ends. Maintenance may become bug fixing, and development means adding new features. However, there will no doubt be much overlap between the two, as new features are integrated into old portions of the application. Therefore, in the end, differentiating between a maintenance programmer and a development programmer may be difficult, at least in small IS departments.

The method also means that traditional reactive maintenance practices must be replaced by routine, systematic, and proactive maintenance. For intranet and extranet applications, it will be clear very quickly if the application is malfunctioning or contains outdated information because the developer's colleagues (intranet users) and business partners (extranet users) would love to point out a mistake. But for Internet applications, the general public is very unlikely to take the trouble to let the business know the problem. The easiest thing for them to do is to leave and go to the competition. Routine maintenance and frequent updates are essential for content-rich Web applications.

The method does not mean that testing is no longer needed. Developers can still test their changes and additions as much or as little as they do now, they simply do not deploy a new part of an application until they feel confident that it is ready for use by the users.

Nor does this mean that developers should be slaves to user requests or that the application should become a mishmash of different, special applications. Using good application management techniques will still be necessary. Developers will still need to apply sound configuration management and only build those new features that are thoroughly thought out and planned. The Web technology allows developers to seamlessly integrate the new features into the application. Often this will take nothing more than making a Web page accessible by updating a link on an existing page. Users will see the change the very next time they go to the application.

How MPM Differs from Traditional Prototyping

The differences between MPM and existing prototyping methods are more differences in emphasis and content than fundamental approach. First, MPM calls for the formal maintenance phase to begin right after the initial version is deployed, while in traditional prototyping methods, formal maintenance begins only after the final system is deployed.

Second, MPM maintenance activities are interleaved with development activities, while in traditional prototyping methods, there is a distinctive boundary between development and maintenance.

Third, there is no definite end to the system development process in MPM. At a certain point, the application may reach a stable state and development may pause. However, as the business grows and environment changes, development activities will resume. This may sound like that the application does not have a boundary or defined scope. In a sense, it is both true and false. It is true because Web technology affords us the platform of an open application design, which allows us to expand the scope of an application easily. In fact, distributed and component-based Web application designs have become a new trend. These new architectures offer Web applications great flexibility and adaptability to changes. It is also false because Web applications should be developed like any other systems. The developer must plan the project and define an initial scope of the system. As the business grows and practice changes, the scope of the application can be revised. The key, however, is to maintain a forward thinking and to adopt an open technology architecture. Finally, MPM calls for proactive maintenance to replace reactive bug fixing maintenance.

How MPM Differs from Extreme Programming

Extreme programming (XP) is one of the lightweight, human-powered agile methodologies which are claimed to be successful in reducing cost, meeting customer requirements, improving program quality, and increasing programming productivity.

XP is aimed for small-sized development teams working in problem domains whose requirements are less understood and are changing. It is based on four core values: communication, simplicity, feedback, and courage. *Communicate* effectively among team members, users, and management. Do not waste time on a complete system analysis and design. Design as you go. Keep it *simple*! Gain frequent *feedback* by coding in small iterations and working toward fast release cycles. Have *courage* to rewrite and improve code (refactor) when the code doesn't meet new requirements well.

The main tenets of XP methodology are a collection of programming practices that are practiced to extremes. Iterative planning, pair programming, collective code ownership, tests several times a day, continuous integration, 40 hour week, and on-site customer are some of the XP practices.

XP is not a solution for every project in every organization. It has its limitations. It works only for small teams (two to 10 members). The ideas of XP are nothing more than commonsense practices that are as old as there was program. The difficulty for successful adoptions of XP approach is not to learn the pieces but to put them together and keep them in balance. It is not an easy job to do. XP requires a new programming culture that may be at odds with most corporate cultures. For example, programming a large project without a complete system specification or analysis and design, writing testing code first, and working no more than 40 hours a week are likely to meet resistance from existing programming cultures. Furthermore, XP does not account for different personality types and work styles. Its success rests on the assumption that every player in the game has the necessary skills and will to do his or her best to be an unsung hero.

If XP is an extreme step away from traditional "heavyweight" software development methods, then MPM is a step in between the two extremes. MPM and XP share many common practices:

- Both methods seek maximum programming productivity, system reliability, and adaptability to changing business requirements.
- Both methods call for small iterations and short release cycles.
- Both methods advocate incremental changes. Start out with a minimal design and let the program expand in directions that provide the best business values.
- Both methods emphasize testing and customer involvement in the development process.

XP is a code-centric (or bottom-up), practice-oriented approach. It prescribes a set of precise practices that the development team members must follow. For example, if developers are doing everything except pair programming, they are not practicing XP. In contrast, MPM is a process-oriented and top-down approach. MPM places more emphasis on the overall process of application development and less emphasis on specific techniques. It requires little more formal up-front analysis than XP does.

Furthermore, MPM is proposed for Web application development. It addresses some of the issues specific to Web applications, such as maintenance, system scalability, and Web technology architectures.

Users Involvement

Some developers disdain users, believing that they do not know what they want, and are too ignorant to know a good application when they see one. Some developers are slaves to users and do whatever a user asks. Obviously, the correct path lies somewhere in between.

Figure 6. User and developer input

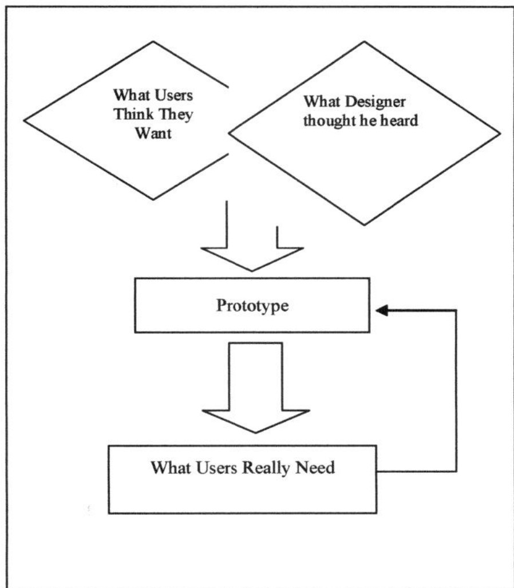

Figure 6 illustrates the important role played by users and the developer in the process. Users have unique knowledge that is crucial to meeting their needs. Developers have technical knowledge and skills that can bring new ideas and features to an application of which the users might never think. Each new feature requested by the user should be carefully evaluated. For example, when the user requests adding a new link from order page to catalog page in a Web application, the developer should analyze the impact of the new feature on the existing use cases. Would this change create additional scenarios to consider? Or is there a different solution to the user request? For Internet applications, getting user's involvement in the design process is difficult but not impossible. The prototyping method provides designers a unique way to collect user input. Once a prototype is deployed on the Web, its users' online actions can be monitored using your Web server's logging facilities. The subsequent analysis determines which parts of the application are being used the most and which are being used the least. This information can be used to plan future development priorities and add efficiency to the application development.

Beyond Methodologies

E-business represents very different approaches in terms of how business should be conducted. Organizations adopting an e-business strategy are advised to take a holistic approach to their systems development. Building a few Web applications will not necessarily make an organization more competitive unless the organization has formulated a clear e-business strategy and has re-engineered its business processes.

Business re-engineering is a fundamental rethinking and radical redesign of existing business processes. It may involve organizational restructuring, job redesign, and changes in management system, values, and even beliefs. Information technology (IT) should play a leading role in analyzing the business processes, recommending changes for improvements, and implementing technology solution to support re-engineered business processes. The challenging task of re-engineering business processes is to get top management support because IT project managers rarely, if ever, have the authority and responsibility to change the business processes.

The Advantages and Disadvantages

Advantages

Web based applications promise a number of advantages over traditional non-Web based applications.

1. **Control over Application:** As the Web application developer, you can control the application on the server side for all users. You can easily control the code base and access to any part of the application. The application can become truly dynamic, from the binary execution to the available help. You can provide instant updates and customization.
2. **Cross-Platform Capability:** An HTML solution gives you the ability to run an application on any web browser on any operating system. Having cross-platform capability relieves you from worrying about a client's configuration. If your client has a browser that can run Java code, you might not even need to know what operating system your users have. This can be a particular advantage if an organization wants to give its customers access to part of the application. Telling a Macintosh shop that they cannot get to your customer service application because they are not able to run your special client software is probably not good customer service. Giving the client a URL and a password that allow them access from almost any machine they have will build a lot more good will.
3. **Control over Versioning:** Instead of worrying about whether a particular user has the right version of a DLL, EXE or database file, you can control this at the server. You no longer need to get the latest version of any part of the application out to the user. You can always be sure that the client has the right code at the right time.
4. **User Input:** The prototyping method allows user inputs to be quickly and easy integrated into an existing application. Often it can be nothing more than a hyperlink to a new Web page. Users who need access to specific or limited areas of the application can be given access merely by being added to the password list, instead of having their client machines updated.

Disadvantages

Web applications are not the silver bullet that everyone has been dreaming about for so long. Depending on how a Web application is built and what technologies are chosen, some things must be given up.

1. **Speed Loss:** Web applications do not run as fast as those running on local machine because of the downloading time and network traffic. This may become less a problem as computer hardware and software improve.
2. **Data Presentation Limit:** If you choose to go with server-side Javascripting or a total HTML solution, such as is available via a tool like Intrabuilder, you may be limited to the interface defined by HTML. In other words, you may be unable to provide the users with the latest in the widgets and gadgets that the modern user interface can provide. For example, tools such as datagrids and their capabilities are currently not available. This may limit your ability to layout clearly an application and present data to the user. However, coming advances in HTML technology will reduce this limitation, as the HTML interface becomes more sophisticated.
3. **Security Vulnerability:** Web applications are inherently vulnerable to malicious Internet attacks. These attacks can be classified as vandalism and sabotage, breach of privacy, theft and fraud, violations of data integrity, and denial of service. As the e-commerce technologies become more sophisticated, these threats will be minimized.

Conclusion

Web applications are an essential element in e-commerce. They offer system developers many challenges and opportunities. The design and implementation of a successful Web application requires a disciplined approach that takes the organization's longterm development into consideration. The MPM method discussed here requires a new mindset. Instead of viewing an application as having a start and a finish, developers should treat Web applications as living entities, constantly adjusting to the changing business environment. This may mean a radical change not only in the development processes, but also in your management techniques, and even your hiring and training methods. You might no longer put your newest hires on maintenance to get them up to speed. Maintenance might not even exist anymore!

References

Callaway, E. (1997). Method from the madness. *PC Week, 14*, 99-100.

Chen, J. & Heath, R. (2001). Building Web applications: challenges, architectures, and methods. *Information Systems Management, 18*, 68-79.

Fitzgerald, B. (1998). An empirical investigation into the adoption of system development methodologies. *Information & Management, 34*, 317-328.

Fournier, R. (1999). *A methodology for client/server and Web application development.* Upper Saddle River, NJ: Yourdon Press Computing Series, Prentice Hall PTR.

Jubin, H. & Friedricks, J. (2000). *Enterprise JavaBeans by example.* Upper Saddle River, NJ: Prentice Hall PTR.

Kurata, D. (2002). *Doing Web development: client-side techniques.* Berkeley, CA: Apress.

McConnell, S. (1996). *Rapid development.* Redmond, WA: Microsoft Press.

Naumann, J. D. & Jenkins, A.M. (1980). Prototyping: The new paradigm for systems development. *MIS Quarterly, 6*, 29-44.

Neilsen, J. (2000). *Designing Web usability.* Indianapolis, IN: New Riders Publishing.

Nielsen, J. & Tahir, M. (2002). *Homepage usability: 50 Web sites deconstructed.* Indianapolis, IN: New Riders Publishing.

Powell, T., Jones, D. L., & Cutts, D. C. (1998). *Web site engineering: Beyond Web page design.* Upper Saddle River, NJ: Prentice Hall.

Standing, C. (2002). Methodologies for developing Web applications. *Information and Software Technology, 44*, 151-159.

Tate, B., Clark, M., Lee, B., & Linskey, P. (2003). *Bitter EJB.* Greenwich, CT: Manning Publications.

Yourdon, E. (2002). *Managing high-intensity Internet projects.* Upper Saddle River, NJ: Just Enough Series, Prentice Hall.

Endnote

[1] An earlier version of this work was published in Information Systems Management (Chen & Heath, 2001).

Chapter IV

Relationship Analysis: A Technique to Enhance Systems Analysis for Web Development

Joseph Catanio
LaSalle University, USA

Michael Bieber
New Jersey Institute of Technology, USA

Abstract

A significant aspect of systems analysis and design involves discovering and representing entities and their relationships. Neither structured nor object-oriented analysis techniques provide a formal process to identify relationships in a system being modeled. Existing techniques leave the relationship determination implicit; they are supposed to appear as a by-product of the other analysis activities. We present a comprehensive, systematic, domain-independent analysis technique, Relationship Analysis (RA), which focuses exclusively on a domain's relationship structure. RA serves three major purposes. First, it helps users, analysts, and designers develop a deeper understanding of the application domain through making the relationships explicit. It serves as an effective communication tool for the user and analyst to develop a shared understanding of the domain, and to work out differences in terminology, assumptions, and viewpoints. Second, the domains relationships are thoroughly documented utilizing an RA template and an RA diagram. Third, RA results in fuller and richer application analyses and designs. RA significantly enhances the systems analyst's effectiveness, especially in the area of relationship discovery and documentation, which will result in the development of higher quality software applications that consistently meet user needs.

Motivation

A significant aspect of systems analysis and design involves discovering and representing entities and their relationships. There are some informal guidelines (identify nouns, etc.) and tools (Use Cases, CRC cards, etc.) to help with identifying entities or objects. However, no defined processes or templates (for example, in the Unified Process) or diagrams (for example, in UML) exist to explicitly and systematically assist in eliciting relationships or documenting them in Class Diagrams or ER Diagrams (Beraha & Su, 1999). The existing techniques leave the relationship determination implicit; they are supposed to appear as a by-product of the other analysis activities.

As further evidence, a vital aspect of *hypermedia* system design is identifying relationships and implementing them as links (Fielding, Whitehead, Anderson, Bolcer, Oreizy, & Taylor, 1998). Yet even in hypermedia design methodologies (Christodoulou, Styliaras, & Papatheodourou, 1998; Isakowitz, Stohr, & Balasubramanian, 1995; Koufaris, 1998; Lange, 1994; Schwabe, Rossi, & Barbosa, 1996) where links (which represent relationships) explicitly are modeled as "first class objects" (as objects with a set of rich attributes), no technique exists for eliciting relationships/links explicitly during the analysis stage (Yoo & Bieber, 2000b).

A domain's relationships constitute a large part of its implicit structure. A deep understanding of the domain relies on knowing how all the entities or objects are interconnected. Relationships are a key component of vital design artifacts such as ER diagrams and object-class diagrams. These diagrams capture an important, but often rather limited subset of relationships, leaving much of the domain's structure out of the design and thus out of the model of the system. While analyses and models are meant to be a limited representation of a system, we believe the incomplete relationship specification is not by design, but rather from the lack of any methodology to determine them explicitly. Many analyses thus miss aspects of the systems they represent, and often do not convey all the useful information they could when passed on to the designers. It seems that formally and rigorously identifying relationships early on in the development process has not been a primary concern of software engineers in the past.

A rich plethora of relationships surround many objects in the real world. For example, a product may have several relationships to its customers, who can purchase it, recommend it to others, provide input for modifying it, make comments on it, transform it for other uses, dispose of it, trade it for other goods, etc. Often, a typical analysis would only capture the first of these. Figure 1 presents a subset of the relationships around a book, which one may wish to include, such as in a library support application. (The full set would be at least half again as large [Yoo & Bieber, 2000b].) Note the presence of multiple relationships among objects.

So, how does one go about discovering the relationships between objects/classes? Is it possible? And once discovered, how does one communicate this discovery to the designer in a formal manner? Relationship Analysis (RA) specifically addresses these concerns and offers solutions that we believe fill a vital gap in systems analysis.

RA provides systems analysts with a systematic and rigorous technique for determining the relationship structure of an application, helping them to discover all potentially useful relationships in application domains and to document them effectively.

RA enhances users', analysts' and system developers' understanding of application domains by broadening and deepening their conceptual model of the domain. Developers can then enhance their implementations by including additional links and other representations of the relationships.

Figure 1. A subset of the relationships around books found through the relationship questions in Table 2

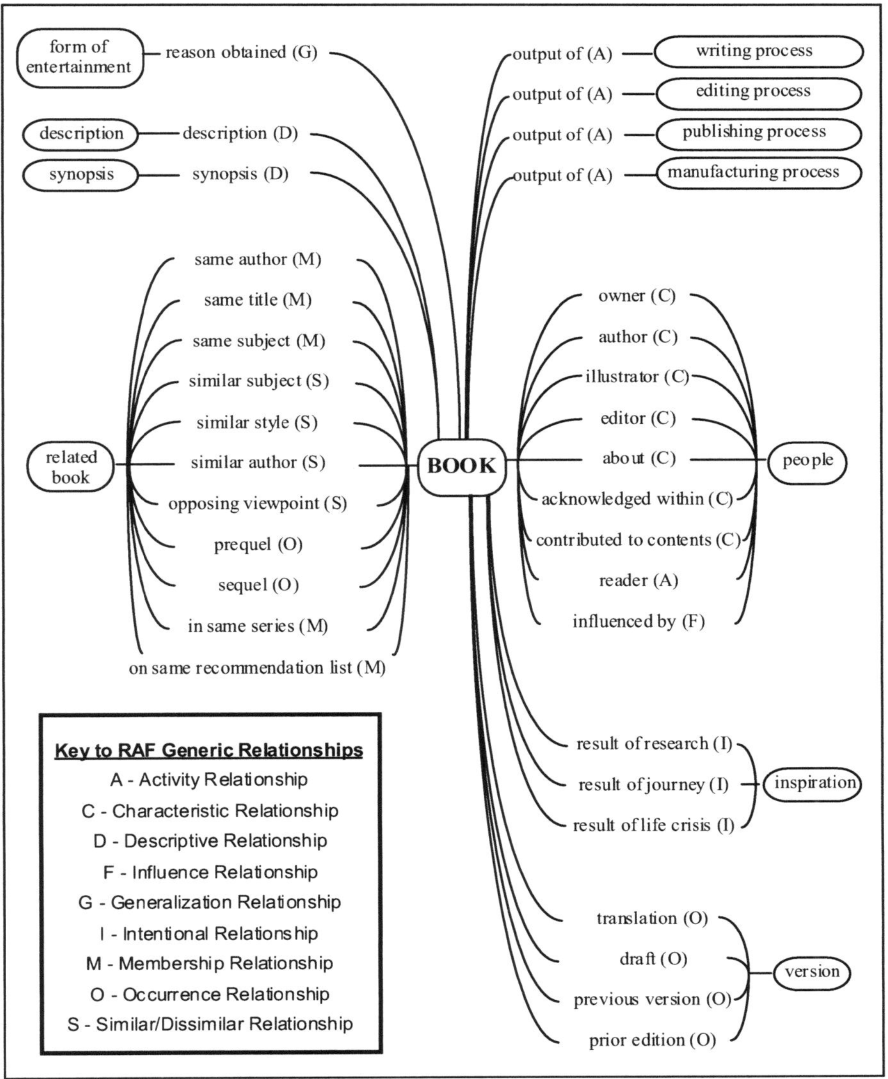

RA can be used either to thoroughly describe an existing application (or information domain) in terms of its relationships, or as part of a systems analysis to understand a new application being designed. It provides a comprehensive technique to perform a systematic analysis for identifying and modeling relationships in a generic domain.

Generic Relationship Taxonomy

These relationships of Figure 1 were discovered based on categories of a very extensive literature review (Yoo, 2000) and strenuous trial-and-adjustment prototyping. We believe it to be fairly complete. Yoo (2000) compares RA's taxonomy with 10 other domain-specific taxonomies in detail, with additional comparisons with over 20 others. RA's categories encompass all of these other taxonomies' relationships. This includes, for example, object-oriented analysis (Martin & Odell, 1995) (which provides RA's generalization/specialization, whole-part, classification/instantiation and association relationship classifications).

Generalization/specialization relationships concern the relationships between objects in a taxonomy (Borgida, Mylopoulos, & Wong, 1984; Brachman, 1983; Smith & Smith, 1977). Self relationships include characteristic, descriptive, and occurrence relationships.

Whole-part/composition relationships include configuration/aggregation relationships based on configuration aspect of the whole-part relationships, and membership/grouping relationships (Brodie, 1981; Motschnig-Pitrik & Storey, 1995) based on membership aspect of the whole-part relationships (Henderson-Sellers, 1997; Odell, 1994). Classification relationships connect an item of interest and its class or its instance.

Comparison relationships break down into similar/dissimilar and equivalence relationships, involving such relationships as in thesaurus or information retrieval (Belkin & Croft, 1987; Neelameghan & Maitra, 1978). Association/dependency relationships break down into ordering, activity, influence, intentional, socio-organizational, spatial, and temporal relationships. The term association and dependency could be used interchangeably, because every association involves some concept of dependency (Henderson-Sellers, 1998). Because association is defined as a relationship that is defined by users, there could be no fixed taxonomy for it. The association relationship taxonomy is fluid compared with other relationships. Current association relationship taxonomy is based on our observations, analyses, ontologies (Mylopoulos, 1998), and the existing classifications (Henderson-Sellers, 1998).

Ordering relationships involve some kind of sequence among items. Activity relationships are created by combining SADT activity diagrams (Mylopoulos, 1998) and case relationships (Fillmore, 1968) to deal with relationships associated with activities or actions abstractly. This relationship could cover any activities that involve input or output, and deal with agents and objects involved in the activities. Influence relationships exist when one item has some power over the other items. Intentional and socio-organizational relationships could be identified in intentional and social ontologies respectively. Temporal (Allen, 1983; Frank, 1998) and spatial (Cobb & Petry, 1998;

Egenhofer & Herring, 1990; Rodriguez, Egenhofer, & Rugg, 1999) relationships deal with temporal and spatial perspectives, respectively.

Each relationship category can be further broken down into lower levels of detail. Yoo (2000) details each of these and the literature from which each is derived.

Conducting a Relationship Analysis

RA begins with a stakeholder (role) analysis and "items of interest" (object or entity) analysis. (For the refined technique resulting from the proposed research, use cases will provide this and other contextual information.) For each item of interest identified by the domain expert or user, the analyst asks a series of questions to elicit the relationships around it, which actually often leads to discovering additional elements of interest these connect.

Table 1 gives a series of brainstorming questions that an analyst uses to elicit domain information from the user. Each set of questions is derived from the lower levels of detail for each relationship in the taxonomy, described in Yoo (2000). For the purposes of this chapter, the questions in Table 1 are rather condensed and highly generic and should

Table 1. Sample brainstorming questions emanating from RA's generic relationships

Generalization/ Specialization	Is there a broader term for this item of interest? Is there a narrower term for this item of interest?
Characteristic	What attributes and parameters does this item of interest have?
Descriptive	Does an item of interest have a description, definition, explanation, or a set of instructions or illustrations available within or external to the system?
Occurrence	Where else does this item of interest appear in the application domain? What are all uses of this item of interest?
Configuration/ Aggregation	Which components consist of this item? What materials are used to make this item? What is it a part of? What phases are in this whole activity?
Membership/ Grouping	Is this item a segment of the whole item? Is this item a member of a collection? Are these items dependent on each other in a group?
Classification/ Instantiation	Is this item of interest an example of a certain class? If a class, which instances exist for this element's class?
Equivalence	What is this item of interest equal or equivalent to in this domain?
Similar/ Dissimilar	Which other items are similar to this item of interest? Which others are opposite to it? What serves the same purposes as this item of interest?
Ordering	What prerequisites or preconditions exist for this item? What logically follows this item for a given user's purpose?
Activity	What are this item's inputs and outputs? What resources and mechanisms are required to execute this item?
Influence	What items (e.g., people) cause this item to be created, changed, or deleted? What items have control over this item?
Intentional	Which goals, issues, arguments involve this item of interest? What are the positions and statements on it? What are the comments and opinions on this item? What is the rationale for this decision?
Socio-organizational	What kinds of alliances are formed associated with this item of interest? Who is committed to it in the organizational structure? Who communicates with it or about it, under what authority and in which role?
Temporal	Does this item of interest occur before other items? Does this item occur while other items occur?
Spatial	Which items is this item of interest close to? Is this item of interest nearer to destination than other items? Does this item overlap with other items?

be tailored to each item of interest. For example, the descriptive relationship prompts analysts to ask whether an item of interest has "a definition, explanation, set of instructions or illustrations available within or external to the system." (These are all lower-level categories for the generic relationship "descriptive".) The analyst clearly should ask each of the questions individually, and in a way that makes the most sense

Experiment

We conducted an experiment to compare RA with other systems analysis techniques. Object-Oriented Analysis (OOA) by Coad and Yourdon was used as the traditional OOA method. The subjects were undergraduate students enrolled in four sections of a software engineering course. Each section served as one group: one control group, one with RA, one with OOA, and one with both techniques. After a training session, the subjects were asked to identify the objects and relationships for an online bookstore.

The number of modeling objects plus the number of relationships was used as one of the measures of the output quality. More objects and relationships would indicate deeper understanding of the application and richer representation of the model. Another measure for the quality of output was subjective 1-7 scale judgments by four expert judges. The criteria of the judgment were the extent to which the modeling was relevant to the task and whether the modeling included important entities in the domain. After the experiment the subjects filled out a questionnaire about the usability of the analysis techniques.

The data analysis showed that RA resulted in a significantly higher output quality in terms of number of entities and relationships. The usability score of RA was significantly higher than OOA, which implies that RA is easier to use. The information sufficiency and adequacy of RA was also significantly higher than that of OOA. The results of the experiment confirm that RA can be a powerful and easier to use systems analysis technique. Yoo (2000) describes the experiment, analysis and conclusions in detail.

RA Limitations

While RA was crafted from an extensive literature review, and trial and error revisions, it has no theoretical basis. This opens RA up to two criticisms. First, while we believe it can characterize systems thoroughly, we cannot claim categorically that its taxonomy is complete. Second, the taxonomy's categories are not distinct enough and relationships sometimes fall under more than one. In part, this is because the relationships themselves are interrelated (Yoo, 2000), especially within the lower levels. (For example, adjacent items found through the taxonomy's ordering relationship could also be found through the membership relationship if they are in the same group.) However, because RA is a brainstorming technique, it turns out not to matter whether the analyst or user discovers a particular relationship using questions from one category or another. What is important is that they found the relationship in the first place.

Another limitation is that while RA has a prescribed order and set of guidelines for conducting the analysis, it has no templates or other well-designed, user-friendly tools to assist in elicitation. All note-taking during the analysis is *ad hoc*. Similarly, no prescribed format exists for recording the results of an RA analysis, including no way to cluster, organize or present the relationships and new objects found. RA simply is not a fully-developed analysis technique. Yet analysts still have found it extremely useful!

Extending RA

In this section we describe our research agenda for extending RA. The proposed research will address the aforementioned limitations with RA and redevelop Relationship Analysis as a complete and fully usable analysis technique that can be integrated with the object oriented analysis methodology by developing the following four major components:

1. **Relationship Analysis Model (RAM):** A theory-guided taxonomy described below will generate the categories and brainstorming questions, which will help the analyst "discover" all the possible relationships among objects and classify these.
2. **Relational Analysis Template (RAT):** A form designed to capture elicited knowledge about the domain.
3. **Relationship Analysis Diagram (RAD):** A new design tool to help the analyst "formally" document all the discovered relationships and aid in communicating it to the designer who will, in turn, use it as the input to create the class diagram.
4. **Relationship Analysis Process (RAP):** A formal process to facilitate relationship discovery and documentation.

Relationship Analysis Model: Theoretical Basis

We intend to develop a new relationship taxonomy grounded in theory. We have preliminarily chosen Guilford's Structure of Intellect (SI) theory (Guilford 1956, 1967, 1971, 1982) as the basis of our taxonomy.

SI is a general theory of human intelligence. SI has formed the basis for comparing and classifying the complete range of tests for intellectual ability. Guilford designed SI with a focus on measuring creativity (Guilford, 1950), which is an integral aspect of the systems analysis and brainstorming activities in general. Because RA is a brainstorming elicitation technique, we believe that SI will help the analyst and user thoroughly explore a domain in a way that fits the way people conceptualize.

Figure 2. Guilford's structure of intellect model

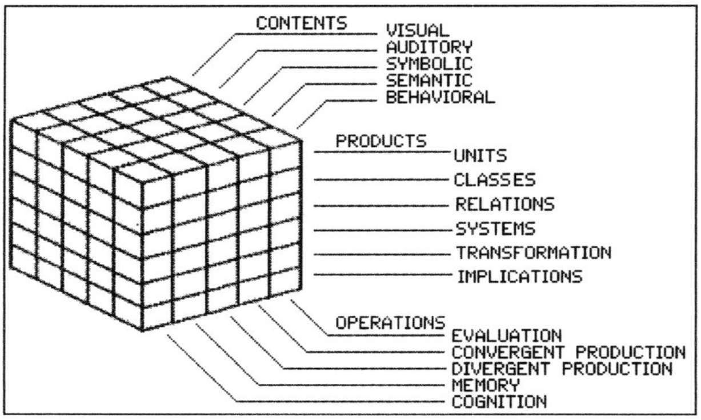

Thus we believe that a SI foundation will allow us to develop a complete taxonomy of relationships from a cognitive, human intellect viewpoint. Of course, not all relationships within a computer application domain have something to do with human intellect. But because SI is a complete taxonomy, we believe it will enable analysts to elicit as complete a set of relationships (and associated objects), as possible, within application domains.

The SI model classifies intellectual abilities into a cross-classification independent three-plane system comprised of contents, products, and operations (Guilford, 1956).

Figure 2 shows SI includes five kinds of contents, six kinds of products, and five kinds of operations. Due to the three independent planes, there are theoretically 150 different components of intelligence. The three dimensions of the model specify first, the operation, second, the content, and third, the product of a given kind of intellectual act. Every intellectual ability in the structure is characterized in terms of the type of operation employed, the content involved, and the sort of resulting product. The convention (Operations, Contents, Products) is used to specify each factor. For example, (Cognition, SeMantic, Unit) or (CMU) represents cognition of a semantic unit. In this way, the SI theory represents the major kinds of intellectual activities or processes as an interrelated three-dimensional model.

Turoff, Rao, and Hiltz (1991) apply SI to the computer application domain and argue that not all of the SI components are necessary for classifying computer application domains, they reduce it to two dimensions by classifying all SI types of content as one, namely semantic. The four SI contents — visual, auditory, symbolic, and behavioral — are useful in classifying tests of intellect, but are not necessary for classifying application domains. In addition, the SI operations, evaluation and memory are also not necessary for classifying application domains (Turoff et al., 1991).

Extending from these aforementioned models, the Relationship Analysis Model (RAM) approach in classifying relationships of computer application domains is to develop a semantic classification model. Therefore, the resulting model is a two-dimensional model, products vs. operations.

A product represents the organization that information takes in the analyst's processing of it (Guilford, 1967; Meeker, 1969).

- **Units:** Most basic item. Things to which nouns are normally applied. Described units of information.
- **Classes:** Sets of items of information grouped by virtue of their common properties.
- **Relations:** Connections between items of information based on variables or points of contact that apply to them.
- **Systems:** Organized or structured aggregates of items of information.
- **Transformations:** Changes, redefinition, shifts, or modifications of existing information or in its function.
- **Implications:** Extrapolations of information. Emphasizes expectancies, anticipations, and predictions.

Operations represent major kinds of intellectual activities or processes that analysts perform with information (Guilford, 1967; Meeker, 1969).

- **Cognition:** Discovery, awareness, or recognition of information by comprehension or understanding. Guilford views the cognition process as the classification of an object. Turoff et al. extend this concept to hypertext whereby cognition is represented by a node that classifies all the linked objects as related to a common concept or characteristic. Hypertext, at its core, concerns nodes (elements-of-interest) and links (relationships). These links or relationships among nodes are classified under convergent and divergent production properties. The RAM differentiates itself from the HMM in its application of cognition. The HMM represents cognition by a node and in hypertext terms: a node is an endpoint, and relationships exist among nodes or endpoints. In contrast, the relationships of each element-of-interest in the RAM represent by six cognitive focus perspectives.
- **Convergent Production:** Generation of information from the given information, where the emphasis is on achieving unique best outcomes. The given information fully determines the response. Guilford views convergent production as when the input information is sufficient to determine a unique answer. Turoff et al. (1991) extend this concept and a convergent link is a relationship that follows a major train of thought. This is referred to as a convergent relationship in the RAM.
- **Divergent Production:** Generation of information from the given information, where the emphasis is on variety and quality of output from the given information. Guilford views divergent production as fluency of thinking and flexibility of thinking. Turoff et al. (1991) extend this concept and a divergent link is a relationship that starts a new train of thought. This is referred to as a divergent relationship in the RAM.

Table 2. Relationship Analysis Model (RAM)

Cognition Focus	Convergent Relationship	Divergent Relationship
Unit	Specification	Elaboration
Collection	Membership	Aggregation
Comparison	Generalization/Specialization	Similar/Dissimilar
System	Structure	Occurrence
Transformation	Modify	Transpose
Implication	Influence	Extrapolate

The Relationship Analysis Model (RAM) applies these three operations to the six products defined in the previous section to categorize relationships (Catanio, 2004). Similar to Turoff's Hypertext Morphology Model (HMM), each cognitive product becomes a focus point that classifies all the linked relationships pertaining to the particular cognitive focus. Thus, relationships of an element of interest are described by six cognitive focal points. Relationships of each focal point are classified under convergent and divergent operation properties. Therefore it is possible to classify the relationships of an element of interest in terms of six products each of which has convergent and divergent relationships. Table 2 depicts the model.

Developing RA gave us the experience of developing brainstorming questions from relationship categories. We expect that the types of questions we shall develop using SI to be similar in spirit to those in Table 1. Turoff et al. (1999) provide several synonyms for each node and link category, which can form the basis of RA's corresponding set of questions. One difference is that the node synonyms could underlie additional brainstorming questions, whereas RA only had questions based on relationships. Node-based questions may pose a useful extension for RA.

Relationship Analysis Templates

Based on our experience with RA, several kinds of useful information come to light during the elicitation process. These include relationships, characteristics (metadata) about the relationships, new objects (at the other end of the relationships), characteristics about these new objects, characteristics of the object being focused upon for relationship elicitation, as well as general comments reflecting insight into context, terminology, assumptions, and viewpoints.

The Relationship Analysis Templates will have areas for recording each of these, as well as a place for recording comments. We may find it useful to provide another form for capturing the latter contextual information that arises from the focused communication between analyst and user, which RA provides.

Relationship Analysis Diagrams

We envision the Relationship Analysis Diagrams to look somewhat similar to Figure 1. Each diagram will show all the relationships, metadata and prioritizations around a single object-of-interest (or for complex cases, perhaps split a single object's relationships and metadata among several sub-diagrams). One issue is how busy the diagram may become. We may need to prototype several versions before determining the most useful format.

Relationship Analysis Diagrams are the final output from RA, and a primary input into the systems design phase. Through prototyping and revisions we will determine whether (and how) to include all metadata (and relevant comments) gathered on the templates with the diagrams. Perhaps a version of the templates should accompany each diagram for the subsequent design phase.

Relationship Analysis Process

We shall develop and refine a fully-usable Relationship Analysis Process (RAP) for conducting a Relationship Analysis. We believe it will encompass the following three stages, though these are open to refinement based on the evaluation described later.

- **Context Analysis:** The analyst starts with one or more use-cases. This provides the background (context, actions and functional requirements) as well as a starting set of objects.
- **Relationship Elicitation:** The analyst will work together with the users to elicit the domain relationships derived from the new Structure of Intellect-based taxonomy. The analysis will use the new Relationship Analysis Templates to ask appropriate brainstorming questions and record elicited information. The elicitation will produce a Relationship Analysis Diagram for each object showing all its relationships to other elements. We also need to develop accompanying full guidelines for conducting this analysis, completing the RA Templates and drawing the RA Diagrams.
- **Prioritization:** The analyst and users should feel cognitively unbounded during the Relationship Elicitation stage, in order to come up with a comprehensive map of the domain relationships (Gause & Weinberg, 1989). While very useful for understanding the domain fully, in practice the designer may need to prune the relationships in the subsequent systems design phase. Some relationships may be unnecessary to the final application; others may be too costly or difficult to implement. To help the designer in these decisions, the analyst and user work together to prioritize each element (relationship, object, metadatum) in the Relationship Analysis Diagram. To motivate the user to prioritize, he or she could be told that the designer may need to constrain the number of relationships (and objects) for budgetary reasons. They then assign each a ranking between one and five, where five is the most important and should be implemented if at all possible,

and one is the least important and can be left out of a final design with no detriment. This will provide important feedback to the designer as to the importance of each element in the diagram.

Discussion: Integration into Current Analysis Techniques

The research and solutions we propose here can be seamlessly integrated into both current object-oriented (OO) and structured analysis processes to fill the vital gap of identifying relationships.

Object-oriented analysis techniques like Unified Process (UP) and Unified Modeling Language (UML) certainly provide real benefits to the critical early stages of application development. A formal process and support to identify and document all relationships of interest in a domain, however, is not one of them. The UML depicts the interactions between the use-cases and the actors utilizing use-case diagrams. Subsequently, class diagrams are developed to depict the relationships between the classes that implement the use-cases. We believe that a step is missing and that the transition is too abrupt.

This also is the case with the structured analysis method. One of the most popular analysis tools used in structured analysis to capture relationships is the Entity Relationship (ER) diagram. Although an excellent technique for portraying the resulting relationships in a domain, just as with OO class diagrams, no formal techniques exist for identifying the relationships to include.

Thus, existing techniques leave the relationship determination implicit. Relationship analysis fills this void by providing a systematic technique to determine the relationship structure of an application. Relationship analysis (RA) is geared towards discovering and representing entities and their inter-relationships. The relationship analysis process (RAP) provides a relationship analysis diagram (RAD) that explicitly depicts these discovered relationships using the standard Unified Modeling Language (UML) notation. The RAP can be integrated into the UML technique between the use-case and class diagram identification steps. Thus, RA adds a step to the UML process but provides a technique to explicitly determine and depict the application's relationship structure, thereby enhancing the UML.

Conclusion

We begin this concluding section by summarizing some of the things that RA is not.

RA is not a design technique. Rather it is a method-independent analysis technique, which provides useful input to the systems design phase.

RA does not provide algorithms to generate relationships. RA is an elicitation technique embodied in a systematic procedure (RAP) to support the analysis phase. In follow-on research we hope to investigate automatic generation of design documents from the analysis documentation.

RA and the associated support tools presented here are intended to provide a high degree of support to the analyst and NOT to replace the analyst by totally automating the relationship discovery and documentation process. There can be no substitute to the quality and expertise provided by the human analyst. However, we believe that RA and the corresponding support mechanisms can significantly enhance the effectiveness of the human analyst.

Contributions and Potential Impact

This research addresses a major shortcoming in today's analysis techniques. Neither structured nor object-oriented analysis techniques provide a formal process to identify relationships in a system being modeled. RA is the only systematic, domain-independent analysis technique focusing exclusively on a domain's relationship structure. RA will provide a theoretically-based procedure and tools for conducting a systematic analysis.

RA serves three major purposes. First, it helps users, analysts and designers develop a deeper understanding of the application domain (through making the relationships explicit). Second, the domain relationships are thoroughly documented utilizing RA templates and diagrams. Third, RA results in fuller and richer application analyses and designs.

RA also provides the analyst with another tool for working with the user to better understand the application domain. Because of its brainstorming/elicitation approach, RA should serve as an effective communication tool for the user and analyst to develop a shared understanding of the domain, and to work out differences in terminology, assumptions and viewpoints. RA will provide a foundation for users and system analysts to communicate throughout systems analysis process.

We expect that RA will become an invaluable tool in the toolkit of the analyst irrespective of the software engineering approach taken during analysis. Since RA is methodology-independent, it should be equally effective in identifying relationships between entities when using the traditional structured approach to analysis and identifying relationships between objects using object-oriented methodologies. RA could very easily become a standard extension to the other tools and techniques currently available for analysis. While the analyst is working with the user in creating use-cases to understand the functionality required of the system, e.g., he or she also could be conducting RA and documenting it as part of the elicitation process.

Some object-oriented "gurus" hold that spending too much effort in trying to identify relationships is counterproductive. For example, while discussing guidelines to creating domain models, Larman (2002) states:

> *"Associations are important, but a common pitfall in creating domain models is to spend too much time during investigation trying to discover them... Too many associations tend to confuse a domain model rather than illuminate it. Their discovery can be time-consuming, with marginal benefit."*

We address these concerns by providing the tools and techniques to make an extensive relationship analysis useful and practical. We believe that using RA will produce a richer understanding of relationships in less time than the comparable informal processes currently followed. Further, our prototyping of the tools will address whether a plethora of relationships tends to confuse or enlighten. Finally, our evaluation should show that RA significantly improves the software development process.

One thing that became clear from using RA was that many applications (with and without Web interfaces) had many fewer links that users would find useful (Catanio et al., 2004). This occurs for several reasons (Bieber & Vitali, 1997; Bieber & Yoo, 1999). Few analysts explicitly think in great detail about their applications' interrelationships. In part, few existing applications have a rich link structure that could be an example for analysts and designers. In part, few tools exist that help system developers to think of an application in terms of its relationships (Bieber, 1998). Until the advent of recent World Wide Web standards such as XLINK, Web browsers did not support the easy display of multiple links from a single link anchor (e.g., underlined blue text in Netscape). With time, this now will become more commonplace. We believe that RA will provide the tools and help change the mindset of analysts and designers to include multi-headed links in applications.

RA will significantly enhance the systems analyst's effectiveness, especially in the area of relationship discovery and documentation, which will result in the development of higher quality software applications that consistently meet users' needs.

Acknowledgments

We gratefully acknowledge partial funding support for this research by the Alfred P. Sloan Foundation, the NASA JOVE faculty fellowship program, the United Parcel Service, the New Jersey Center for Multimedia Research, the National Center for Transportation and Industrial Productivity at the New Jersey Institute of Technology (NJIT), the New Jersey Department of Transportation, the New Jersey Commission of Science and Technology, the National Science Foundation under grants EISA-9818309, IIS-0135531, DUE-0226075, and DUE-0434581.

References

Allen, J. (1983). Maintaining knowledge about temporal intervals. *Communication of the ACM, 26*(11), 832-843.

Belkin, N. & Croft, W. (1987). Retrieval techniques. *Annual Review of Information Science and Technology (ARIST), 22*(1987), 109-131.

Beraha, S. & Su, J. (1999). Support for modeling relationships in object-oriented databases. *Data & Knowledge Engineering, 29*(3), 227-257.

Bieber, M. (1998). Hypertext and Web engineering. *Proceedings of the Ninth ACM Conference on Hypertext and Hypermedia* (pp. 277-278). ACM Press.

Bieber, M. (2001). *Supplementing applications with hypermedia.* Technical Report, IS Department, NJIT.

Bieber, M. & Vitali, F. (1997). Toward support for hypermedia on the World Wide Web. *IEEE Computer, 30*(1), 62-70.

Bieber, M. & Joonhee, Y. (1999). Hypermedia: A design philosophy. *ACM Computing Surveys, 31*(4es).

Booch, G., Rumbaugh J. & Jacobson, I. (1999). *The unified modeling language user guide.* MA: Addison-Wesley.

Borgida, A., Mylopoulos, J., & Wong, H. (1984). Generalization/specialization as a basis for software specification. In M. Brodie, J. Mylopoulos, & J. Schmidt (Eds.), *On conceptual modeling: Perspectives from artificial intelligence, databases, and programming languages* (pp. 87-117).

Brodie, M. (1981). Association: A database abstraction for semantic modelling. In P. P. Chen (Ed.), *Entity-relationship approach to information modeling and analysis* (pp. 583-608). ER Institute.

Brachman, R. (1983). What IS-A is and isn't: An analysis of taxonomic links in semantic networks. *IEEE Computer*, 30-36.

Catanio, J. (2004). Relationship analysis: Improving the systems analysis process. PhD Dissertation, New Jersey Institute of Technology.

Catanio, J., Nkechi, N., Zhang, L., Bieber, M., & Galnares, R. (2004). Ubiquitous metainformation and the WYWWYWI* Principle. *Journal of Digital Information, 5*(1). (*What you want, when you want it).

Christodoulou, S., Styliaras, G., & Papatheodourou, T. (1998). Evaluation of hypermedia application development and management systems. *Proceedings of ACM Hypertext '98 Conference*, Pittsburgh (pp. 1-10).

Coad, P. & Yourdon, E. (1991). *Object-oriented analysis.* Englewood Cliffs, NJ: Yourdon Press.

Cobb, M. & Petry, F. (1998). Modeling spatial relationships within a fuzzy framework. *Journal of the American Society for Information Science, 49*(3), 253-266.

Egenhofer, M. & Herring, J. (1990). Categorizing binary topological relations between regions, lines, and points in geographic databases. *Technical Report*, Department of Surveying Engineering, University of Maine.

Fielding, R., Whitehead, J.R., Anderson, K., Bolcer, G., Oreizy, P., & Taylor, R. (1998). Web-based development of complex information products. *Communications of the ACM, 41*(8), 84-92.

Fillmore, C.J. (1968). The case for case. In *Universals in Linguistic Theory*.

Fowler, M., & Scott, K. (2000). *UML distilled: A brief guide to the standard object modeling language*. MA: Addison-Wesley.

Frank, A. (1998). Different types of "Times" in GIS: Spatial and temporal reasoning. In M. Egenhofer & R. Golledge (Eds.), *Geographic Information Systems* (pp. 41-62).

Gause, D. C. & Weinberg, G. M. (1989). *Exploring requirements: Quality before design*. New York: Dorset House Publishing.

Guilford, J.P. (1950). Creativity. *American Psychologist, 5*, 444-454.

Guilford, J.P. (1956). The structure of intellect. *Psychological Bulletin, 53*(4), 267-293.

Guilford, J.P. (1967). *The nature of human intelligence*. New York: McGraw-Hill.

Guilford, J.P. (1982). Cognitive psychology's ambiguities: Some suggested remedies. *Psychological Review, 89*, 48-59.

Guilford, J.P. & Hoepfner, R. (1971). *The analysis of intelligence*. New York: McGraw-Hill.

Henderson-Sellers, B. (1997). OPEN relationships-compositions and containments. *Journal of Object-Oriented Programming,* 51-72.

Henderson-Sellers, B. (1998). OPEN relationships-associations, mappings, dependencies, and uses. *Journal of Object-Oriented Programming*, 49-57.

Isakowitz, T., Stohr, E. & Balasubramanian, P. (1995). RMM: A methodology for structuring hypermedia design. *Communications of the ACM, 38*(8), 34-44.

Jacobson, I., Booch G., & Rumbaugh, J. (1999). *The unified software development process*. MA: Addison-Wesley.

Jarvenpaa, S. L., Rao, V.S., & Huber, G.P. (1998). Computer support for meetings of groups working on unstructured problems: A field experiment. *MIS Quarterly*, 645-666.

Koufaris, M. (1998). Structured design of WWW and intranet applications. *The Seventh International WWW Conference Tutorial*.

Lam, S.S.K. (1997). The effects of GDSS and task structures on group communication and decision quality. *Journal of Management Information Systems, 13*(4), 193-215.

Lange, D. (1994). An object-oriented design method for hypermedia information systems. *Proceedings of the 27th Annual Hawaii International Conference on System Sciences* (pp. 366-375).

Larman, C. (2002). *Applying UML and patterns: An introduction to object oriented analysis and design and the unified process*. Englewood Cliffs, NJ: Prentice Hall.

Martin, J. & Odell, J. (1995). *Object-oriented methods: A foundation*. Englewood Cliffs, NJ: Prentice Hall.

Martin, J. & Odell, J. (1998). *Object-oriented methods: A foundation, UML Edition*. Englewood Cliffs, NJ: Prentice Hall.

McClave, J.T., & Benson, P.G. (1988). *Statistics for business and economics*. Dellen.

Motschnig-Pitrik, R. & Storey, V. (1995) Modelling of set membership: The notion and the issues. *Data & Knowledge Engineering, 16*(1995), 147-185.

Mylopoulos, J. (1998). Information modeling in the time of the revolution. *Information Systems, 23*(3/4), 127-155.

Neelameghan, A. & Maitra, R. (1978). Non-hierarchical associative relationships among concepts: Identification and typology. *Part A of FID/CR report No. 18*, Bangalore: FID/CR Secretariat Document Research and Training Center.

Ocker, R., Fjermestad, J., Hiltz, S.R., & Johnson, K. (1998). Effects of four modes of group communication on the outcomes of software requirements determination. *Journal of Management Information Systems*, Summer.

Odell, J. (1994). Six different kinds of composition. *Journal of Object-Oriented Programming,* January, 10-15.

Rao, U., & Turoff, M. (1990). Hypertext functionality: A theoretical framework. *International Journal of Human-Computer Interaction*, *4*(2), 333-358.

The Rational Unified Process online documentation (n.d.). Rational Corporation.

Rodriguez, M., Egenhofer, M. & Rugg, R. (1999). Assessing semantic similarities among geospatial feature class definitions. *Interop '99*, Zurich, Switzerland. In A. Vckovski (Ed.), *Lecture Notes in Computer Science,* New York.

Schwabe, D., Rossi, G., & Barbosa, S. (1996). Systematic hypermedia application design with OOHDM. *Proceedings of Hypertext '96*, Washington DC (pp. 116-128).

Shaft, T. M. & Vessey, I. (1998). The relevance of application domain knowledge: Characterizing the computer program comprehension process. *Journal of Management Information Systems*, *15*(1), 51-78.

Siau, K., Wand, Y., & Benbasat, I. (1997). The relative importance of structural constraints and surface semantics in information modeling. *Information Systems, 22*(2/3), 155-170.

Smith, J. & Smith, D. Database Abstractions: Aggregation and Generalization. *ACM Transactions on Database Systems, 2*(2), 105-133.

Straub, D.W. (1989). Validating instruments in MIS research. *MIS Quarterly*, June, 147-169.

Turoff, M., Rao, U. & Hiltz, S. R. (1991). Collaborative hypertext in computer mediated communications. *Proceedings of the 24th Annual Hawaii International Conference on System Sciences* (Vol. IV, pp. 357-366).

Yoo, J. (2000). Relationship analysis. *PhD Dissertation*, Rutgers University, 2000.

Yoo, J. & Bieber, M. (2000). Towards a relationship navigation analysis. *Proceedings of the 33rd Hawaii International Conference on System Sciences,* IEEE Press, Washington, DC.

Yoo, J. & Bieber, M. (2000b). A relationship-based analysis. *Hypertext 2000 Proceedings*, San Antonio, (June). ACM Press.

Chapter V

Engineering Location-Based Services in the Web

Silvia Gordillo
LIFIA, UNLP, Argentina

Javier Bazzocco
LIFIA, UNLP, Argentina

Gustavo Rossi
LIFIA, UNLP, Argentina,
and Conicet, Argentina

Robert Laurini
LIRIS, INSA-LYON, France

Abstract

In this chapter, we will present a modular approach for building evolvable location-based services in the context of Web applications. We first motivate our research by discussing the state of the art of location-based services; next we analyze which design problems we face while building this kind of application, stressing those problems related with the application's evolution. We present an object-oriented design approach for engineering location-based applications that effectively supports the evolution of these applications rather than their revolution and give a few examples of its use. We finally discuss some further research issues not explicitly addressed in this chapter.

Introduction

As communication and hardware technology are rapidly evolving, there is a growing interest in the development of mobile Web applications. The most important feature of these applications is their ability to react in different ways according to the user's context. Research issues related with mobile computing range from hardware (small memory devices, interface appliances) and communication networks (trustable connections, security, etc.) to software and data management aspects such as new interface metaphors, data models for mobile applications, continuous queries and transactions, adaptive applications, and information exchange between disparate applications. In this chapter, we focus on a particular kind of mobile application: those that adapt their behaviors to the user's location, the so-called Location-Based Services emphasizing which design issues are critical due to their evolution patterns.

Location-based services are a specific case of ubiquitous applications which "evolve organically. Even though they begin with a motivating application, it is often not clear up front the best way for the application to serve its intended user community" (Abowd, 1999). The main consequence of this fact is that the design structure of a location-based application should be thought to deal with evolution easily.

In this chapter, we analyze some design challenges that we face while building location-based services and discuss some micro-architectures that help solve these problems.

The structure of the chapter is as follows: we first present an example scenario to motivate the following discussion. We then survey the state of the art of location-based software, analyzing their evolution from monolithic GIS applications to lighter Internet services. Following the survey, we discuss the design challenges we have to face when applications evolve. Next, we outline our solution by presenting a set of design micro-architectures for building modular and adaptive location based services. We then present a simple example for integrating the mentioned architectures into the Web. Finally, we present some further work and concluding remarks.

An Example Scenario

Suppose, for example, a simple application to provide a foreign student with information when he moves in different places of his new place of residence. When he is traveling, he can be prompted with information about best routes to go somewhere and informed about tourist spots and services (such as gas stations). When he is in the city, he can find places of residence near the university, restaurants according his preferences, or shops. In our first application's release, we assume that we can obtain the user's location in terms of locators such as geographic coordinates or present address by using a cartography service such as NTV (2003) to inform him of what he needs. Existing state of the art technologies (Kraak, 2001) make these alternatives absolutely feasible.

Afterwards, and assuming that the first prototype was successful, we want to integrate it with a new component that helps the student move inside the campus and get information about courses. Using positioning artifacts like beacons (Pradham, 2002) or a wireless local network, we can know his actual position and tell him how to get where he wants (for example, to find a classroom). Notice that we now need to represent the location in a local reference-system (the campus) instead of using latitude/longitude. Eventually, we might have more specific information systems offering him some leisure or sport activities according to the time or day; once more, the location representation changes and the functionality needs to be extended.

When he enters a classroom, the problem has a new shift: he can download the material corresponding to the current course he is taking. There is no need to say that the application's structure might get rather complex, and evolution and maintenance may become a nightmare when we add new location classes and contexts for these kinds of queries. Further details will be presented later in this chapter.

While most technological requirements in this scenario can easily be fulfilled using current hardware and communication devices, there are many design and usability problems that need some further study. The aim of this chapter is to focus on a small set of these problems to show which kind of design structures we need to solve them.

The Evolution of GIS Software

Geographic Information Systems (GIS) are a special class of information system that keeps track not only of events, activities, and things, but also where these events, activities and things happen or exist (Longley, 2002).

GIS store geographic data, retrieve and combine these data to create new representations of geographic space, provide tools for spatial analysis, and perform simulations to help expert users organize their work in many areas, including transportation networks, public administration, and environmental information (Rigaux, 2002).

GIS manipulate information about phenomena occurring on the Earth's surface, and due to the complexity of the geographic world, it is necessary to carry out a careful process to determine *what* information will be taken into account and *how* this information will be represented. Spatial entities in the real world are by nature, multidimensional, voluminous, and often uncertain. Moreover, spatial relationships, rules, and laws have to be considered in order to represent geographic processes such as phenomena forecasting.

Considering the inherent complexity of geographic information, GIS provide facilities to represent and manipulate entities, such as specification of positions, reference systems to interpret these positions, definition of the entities' geometry, etc. They also provide specific operations to perform spatial analysis (topological operations, metric operations, etc.).

Locations are the base for the more common functionalities found in GIS; they allow map construction, calculation of distances, areas, and aggregation of spatial information, and provide the support to perform spatial queries.

These locations cannot be manipulated as simple attributes; they subsume a set of aspects that are needed to obtain the expected application's capabilities. For example, it is necessary to know the reference system in which locations should be interpreted; for example, the treatment of positional attributes expressed in latitude/longitude is different from those defined in the Cartesian system.

Locations should also be expressed depending on the individual aspects of the entity they represent: positions of entities whose geometry differ (points, lines, or polygons) are usually defined in a different way. Depending on the application, entities may be static (i.e. location does not change over time), and changes in their locations may be infrequent or their location may change, thus implying the manipulation of their evolution (and therefore handling additional concerns like time as an example).

Finally, locations (and as a consequence, spatial objects) are related to other application entities (spatial or not); these relationships should clearly reflect the domain model and should be designed carefully.

In order to manipulate locations, all GIS provide (at the digital representation level) different models to specify spatial objects. The most common are the vector and the raster model, which allow two different visions of data: one describing discrete objects appearing in the space (vector model) and the other one representing gridded regions with their characteristics (raster model).

GIS applications were originally monolithic and built using proprietary approaches. Only recently, they have evolved in order to support distributed data and processing (Peng, 2003). Corresponding modeling and software techniques have also evolved as discussed in Friis-Christensen (2001). Now, it is possible to link conventional software environments with GIS products using APIs, and there is a wide range of open software products that support typical GIS processing. Web cartography (Kraak, 2001) and cartographic Web services (Virrantaus, 2002) are now widely used due to the emergence of standards for interoperability such as GML (GML, 2000; Garmash, 2001).

As new technology and more complex applications have appeared, different ways of delivering geographic information and processing are needed. Many types of personal devices such as PDA's (Personal Digital Assistants) and cellular phones are originating a new generation of mobile applications for personal users, in which real-time geographic data must be handled in order to satisfy users' requirements (Laurini, 2001; Longley, 2002).

Location Based Services (LBS) represent the evolution of geographic applications in the context of mobility. These services are intended to give information to users considering a set of additional aspects like visualization concerns, communication aspects, memory consumption, and finally those spatio-temporal concerns that determine which information users might need according to their geographical context.

In Peng (2003), LBS are defined as "applications that have geospatial data-handling functions and the integration of georeferenced information with other types of data. For example, car navigation systems, realtor systems and pizza delivery are some representative location-based services."

LBS can be classified according to their functionalities (Virrantaus, 2002). Map services allow answering variations of well-known *where am I* questions. When maps are augmented with location information about points of interest, we can talk about mobile yellow pages; navigation services meanwhile provide information about the way to reach a place. LBSs can use the user's location to trigger some functionality instead of providing information, such as sending a taxi to the user's place.

Being LBS a particular case of ubiquitous software, they evolve "organically" as described in the introduction as new requirements appear in an unforeseen way. This kind of evolution gives rise to a new set of software design requirements that we discuss in the following sections.

Software Design Challenges

For the sake of conciseness, we do not review here the technological and usability problems we must face while building LBS. Technological problems involve network connections, quality and continuity of network service, and positioning devices. The reader can find useful information in Peng (2003); information on usability problems and some discussions on existing solutions can be found in Nielsen (2003).

As previously discussed LBSs can be seen as a special kind of ubiquitous (customized) software. For example, they usually need an adaptation capability to modify their behavior according to the user's position. In this sense, existing architectural solutions for the design of ubiquitous (Web) software can be used in this field with minor modifications. For example, we can use the approach described in Kappel (2003), in which three important architectural components are described (Figure 1):

- **Application Model:** Contains main application classes and functionalities; it must be constructed to be independent with respect to types of users and adaptation rules (in our first example, the campus and its components, the classrooms and the courses would be placed here).
- **User or Context Profile:** Contains information about the users' interests and preferences and the actual usage context; in particular, this module is responsible for maintaining the current user's location (in this component reside the preferences of the member, such as the courses he is taking, and also his mobile device capabilities).
- **Adaptation Model:** Encapsulates different kinds of rules, in order to adapt the application behavior to specific contexts or situations (for example, there might be a rule specifying to not play sounds upon delivery of system messages when the student is attending to a class or an exam).

When using this architectural strategy, domain model behaviors that need to be adapted (for example, those affected by the user's position) are mediated by the rule (adaptation) model which in turns collaborates with the corresponding user profile objects to decide how the behavior is affected. A clear separation between the adaptation model and the user profile, decoupling them from the application model, allows easier maintenance and

Figure 1. The architecture of ubiquitous applications

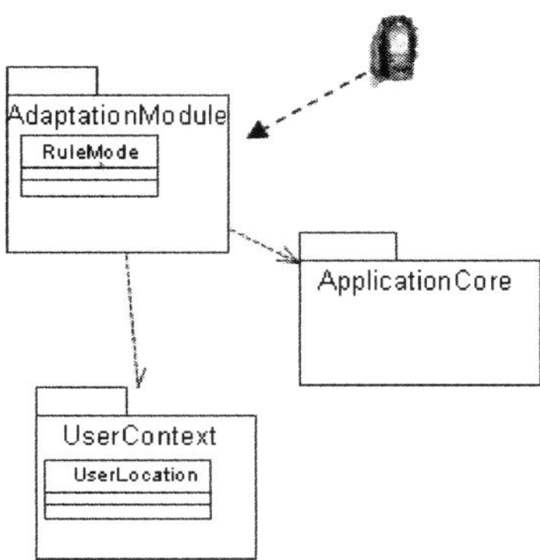

prevents the core functionality from being cluttered with conditional sentences regarding user's conditions and usage context. Besides, in many applications, adaptation rules can be easily transformed into database entries and thus edited without any programming effort (for example by final users, or by some administrators). The cost of this solution is that the rule model might become too complex with hundreds of rules that must be maintained and kept up to date. In Cappi (2002) we have discussed when adaptation rules should be replaced by polymorphic behaviors in order to simplify the adaptation model.

In this chapter, we will emphasize some design problems related with the very nature of location-based services, such as their dependency on the user position and the information objects/services that the user wants to explore. In particular, there are two problems that lie in the very heart of every LBS: representing location and integrating different kinds of location data and data models. In the context of the architecture in Figure 1, our discussion is centered in the interaction among the user context and the application model when locations are involved. We will also show that some adaptation rules can be replaced by class hierarchies of objects providing different services.

As LBSs evolve organically, it might happen that a particular representation of locations, such as latitude/longitude, is adequate for one service (e.g., suggesting the heading from the metro station to the campus) but not for a newer one such as informing our student about classroom activities. Even for the same service, we might find problems related with the interoperability between different sources of location-based data coming from different services providers. We next survey these two problems in separate subsections and then present a road map for solving them.

Dealing with Evolvable Location Representations and Services

The scenario presented previously clearly shows one of the problems that we face regarding the structure of classes that represent user locations, due to the evolution of the LBS. When we add new services, related for example with a new "type" of locations such as a specific building or classroom, we cannot tight to a specific location model such as latitude/longitude and we must use another one including more "semantics." Even though location models have been extensively studied in the literature, dealing with their evolution is not easy. In particular:

1. Object-representing locations might have different attributes according to the positional system we use. It may be not possible or reasonable to define new classes each time the application evolves.
2. The "granularity" of locations might change. For example, we want to see the residence of the student as a point in the campus or as a building with corridors or rooms.
3. The way in which we interpret the location's attributes varies with the context: for example *x, y* in a local Cartesian system or in a global positioning one, the name of the metro or train station, etc.
4. For each new kind of location, we might need new ways to calculate distances and trajectories; moreover, new services, previously unforeseen, may appear.

Integrating Different Location Information Sources

When an LBS uses data coming from different sources, we face new problems. One of them has to do with assuring continuity in the service of the LBS. Notice that when an LBS evolves and new services are added, this problem appears recurrently. Regarding continuity, we can deal with service and usage continuity. Service continuity is dedicated to low level layers ensuring that the signal arrives to the devices in whatever conditions such as mobility between cells; in other words, the service provider must guarantee no information loss (even when the device is suddenly disconnected). As previously mentioned, this chapter will not address this kind of problem. On the other hand, usage continuity is one aspect of usage interoperability dealing with spatial aspects. We can face the problem of usage continuity even though there is only one "connection" provider of the service that may be using data from different information providers. In Laurini (1998), a similar problem was addressed in GIS interoperability with the name of zone fragmentation or geographic partitioning.

Suppose, for example, that the LBS user is traversing a boundary, for instance city, county, province, or state, in which information providers are different but are providing the same kinds of services. How do we guarantee seamless usage of this service?

For instance, it is well known that if one cuts the same country out of two different paper maps with scissors, the maps do not match for several reasons — essentially due to scale and quality of surveying measures. Even if the two paper maps have the same scale, when matching their boundaries, holes and overlaps will occur. We can distinguish three different kinds of usage continuity: cartographic, topological, and semantic.

Cartographic Continuity

By cartographic continuity, we mean that maps must look good, for example, that matching is correct for lines. For instance, let us consider streets which are artificially cut in two databases. The streets in one database must then be aligned with the streets in a second database. In order to ensure alignment, a correction swath can be defined in which a rubber sheeting technique can be launched, possibly with constraints. This technique is also known as elastic transformation. For a LBS user, it means that the map in his device is transparent from providers.

Topological Continuity

Topological continuity implies that at the boundary, nodes are created such that corresponding graphs are connected. Without connection, path algorithms cannot run astride different zones. In other words, it is not possible to find a path from one place in zone A to another place in zone B (supposing zone information is provided by different providers). The theoretical solution is to find nodes located at the boundaries, and for each one, look for its counterpart. When those nodes are found, a supplementary edge (or arc) is drawn with zero length. Doing so, the initially unconnected graphs become connected. Usually those zero-length edges must be installed in both databases. An additional problem is to ensure that path algorithms can easily handled those edges and are able to refer to nodes in other sites.

Semantic Continuity

Semantic continuity deals with the continuity of object identifiers. Usually within a database, each object is associated a unique Oid in order to manipulate it. In our case, the same object, for instance a river, is artificially cut in several databases with possible different Oid's, and possibly with different usage name. In Europe, for example, generally a river bears several names, for instance Rhine (English), Rhein (German), Rhin (France), Reno (Italian).

The role of semantic continuity is double:

- First, allowing different Oid's to refer to different pieces of the same object; perhaps a global Oid can be defined and referring to those local Oid's; and
- Second, ensuring that object names, for instance in different languages, refer to the same global and local Oid's.

From the previous subsections, it is clear that a specific layer should be designed to deal with the continuity inconsistencies as stated above. This layer should be constructed on top of the existing solutions rather that altering them, so that we can minimize the changes in those systems.

Figure 2. Different types of usage continuity to face, cartographic, topologic and semantic

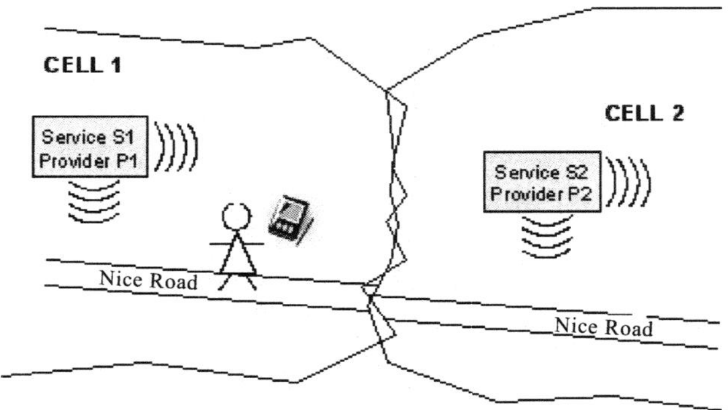

Building Adaptive Location-Based Software

In this section ,we explain how we solve those design problems arising from the evolvable nature of LBS that were discussed in the previous section.

Dealing with Evolvable Location Types

The first key issue that must be addressed when modeling adaptive location models is how to represent locations of distinguished entities both in the user model and in the application model. As we explained earlier, new types of locations might have to be defined when the LBS evolves.

If we consider that each location could be expressed in a different reference system, a first, naïve solution is to create a class hierarchy of location types. The problem with this solution (based on heavy inheritance and sub-classing) is that these different types of locations do not differ in their behavior, but mainly in their structure. Besides, with this approach we can end up with dozens of similar classes.

A better approach would be to use a generalization of the Type Object Pattern, named "Adaptive Object Model" in Yoder (2000), replacing different location classes with a generic class *LocationType* whose instances are different types of locations as shown in Figure 3. Each LocationType defines a set of property types, having a name and a type (class *PropertyType*). Instances of *Location* contain a set of properties (instances of class *Property*) each one referring to one property type. Using the "square" in Figure 3, we can manage the "meta" (or knowledge) level by creating new instances of the "type side" (at the right) and the concrete level by creating new instances of classes in the left.

By this means, adding new types of locations is not restricted by the "code, compile and deploy" process (which is still error prone in languages such as Java), that is known to

Figure 3. Adaptive model for locations and their properties

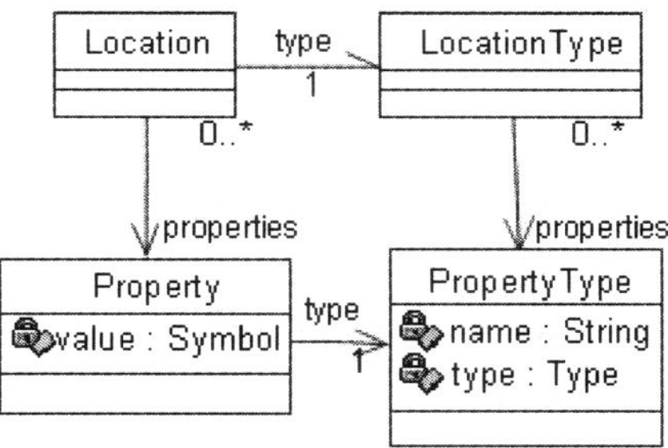

be a very static solution. By using the previous approach, the definition of a new kind of location can be easily made by arranging the required properties instances as needed (each one of them belonging to a particular type of property). The static definition of the structure imposed by the classes approach is changed in favor of the more dynamic alternative presented by the "square" solution presented above. Note that as a consequence of this approach, new types of location types can be defined by the users themselves when the application is running to better represent their needs.

Defining Location Contexts

While location types allow us to represent information about specific locations, we need to add more "application semantics" by relating them to the context in which they are going to be interpreted. In "conventional" GIS applications, location contexts are called reference systems (Gordillo, 1999). A reference system provides the basic operations for dealing with locations (such as distance calculations). In the context of our work, a location context might also provide higher level operations such as path finding (for example, how to go from a building to another in the campus example). In Figure 4, we show the relationship between the location square and its location context. Notice that location contexts belong to the application model in Figure 1.

Figure 4. Introducing location contexts

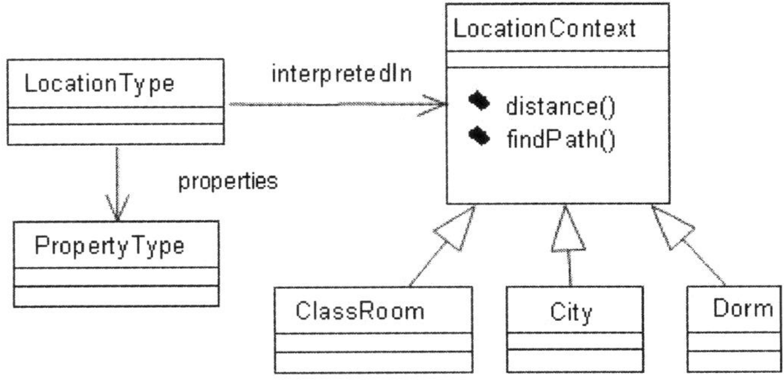

As mentioned before, the core of any LBS (that is the set of functions that can be requested by the mobile user) should support the addition of new functionality as an "evolution" rather than a "revolution."

The Command Design Pattern (Gamma, 1995) presents a solution to this matter that is clearly better than adding methods to the corresponding location context class. According to this pattern, each new functionality is modeled as an instance pertaining to a specific class. It is in this class where the new functionality is coded. As a consequence, the whole system becomes more evolvable and robust, since the addition of new functionality does not imply changes to the actual system, but only coding and deploying the new command class. The system also remains robust, since the addition of a new functionality does not introduce new errors in the current services (if there is a bug, it is easily located and isolated by the new command class). Moreover, as most services might imply complex application interactions, decoupling services into objects allows us to reduce the complexity of the corresponding class. In Figure 5 we show the command hierarchy.

It must be pointed out that being able to easily add new functionality is just a part of the solution, since the new added functionality has to be published to the mobile user. We briefly present here two different approaches that can be applied to solve this situation:

- **Push-based approach:** Under this schema, a hypothetical server (dealing with information about the different contexts) would be responsible for notifying events to all clients. The clients register their interest in a particular set of events, and then wait for a notification to come. This approach can be seen as a special implementation of the Observer Pattern (Gamma, 1995) in which we have distributed parties.

  An important benefit that comes out of this approach is the low bandwidth usage, since the mobile applications do not have to use the network in a regular basis, but receive the notification once an interesting event has occurred. Notice that special care should be taken considering the complexities of mobile transactions, which are a very important part of the whole system.

- **Pull-based approach:** for those devices that cannot be addressed directly by our hypothetical server (i.e., due to the lack of an IP address), this approach is the only

Figure 5. The command hierarchy

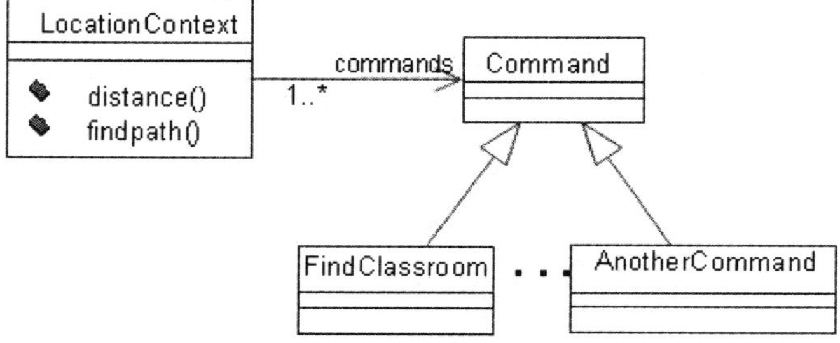

alternative. Every certain period of time, the application connects itself to the server to download relevant information. Under this approach, the usage of the available bandwidth increases, since the clients must connect to the server, perhaps just to find out that no relevant events or information haves been generated since the last connection. Nevertheless, this approach is the preferred one nowadays.

Notice that the location contexts solution moves some behavior that is usually implemented as rules (for example in UWA [Kappel, 2003]) to polymorphic methods in the location context hierarchy. This solution is rather more elegant and certainly more evolvable than the rules approach.

Dealing with Multiple Data Sources

As stated in the previous section, multiple data sources may cause different kinds of continuity problems. Consider for example a mobile user who is using an LBS to safely sail in a given river. Once the user crosses the border line between two countries, the user is still conceptually in the same river, so the LBS must reflect this fact, instead of displaying a message that the service is no longer available.

An elegant approach to deal with multiple data sources is to use the idea of mediators (Wiederhold, 1999) by defining an adaptors layer (as will be detailed in the following section). Mediators "smooth" the inconsistencies between different information providers without the need to change that information in the source itself. For example, instead of adding a new node (see the section titled "Integrating different location information sources"), we wrap the corresponding database by adding the node and providing the relationship with nodes in the other source. In this way we not only solve technical but also political problems (no data source owner is willing to introduce new information just because of integration problems with other providers). Under this new context, the adapter layer could be extended to interact with several "integration strategies;" each one of them representing a different manner of integrating two or more different data sources.

Engineering Location Models in the Web: An Example

In this section we present a comprehensive example in which we show how we map all previously discussed abstractions onto a concrete Web architecture.

Let us consider again the example scenario presented earlier in this chapter. We have a mobile user traveling across the state or province to arrive to his new city of residence. During this travel, the user is considered to be moving in a context relative to the province as a whole. This context has some recognizable entities such as cities and rivers; the locations of these entities are expressed using the WGS84 (Leick, 1990) positional system (which uses latitude and longitude attributes).

Once the mobile user enters the destination city, we need to change the context to reflect the fact that now the information presented to him should only be related to the city (not the province). At this point, information about the state becomes useless (although "useless" does not necessarily mean it is deleted).

Earlier we assumed that this new student does not know the campus, so when dinner time is approaching, he may decide to query the campus online service to find out the restaurants available in the surrounding areas. The service that provides the list of restaurants was "published" to the mobile user at the exact moment the user entered the corresponding context (the campus). This service considers some relevant information about the current situation of the user (primarily its location and the time of the day) to filter the list of available destinations (those whose can be reached from the location of the user before they close). This is the typical example of a location based service, which is augmented by the addition of another types of information (the time of the day) to provide a more meaningful service to the final user.

When the user arrives at the selected destination and enters the restaurant, once again his context is changed in favor of a more detailed context (the one corresponding to the restaurant itself) to present the important information to the user (smokers area, menu, shows presenting that day and so on).

To provide the previous service, an LBS server must perform some of these critical actions:

- Publish the available services to users entering its context. Such publication could be done in one of the manners previously described (pull based vs. push based approaches).
- Adapt (transform) the input from clients to a standard form. Since each device may have its own way of determining the location, it must be transformed to a well known form.
- Find the corresponding command (at this point we can see a command as a mediator between the information sources and the LBS itself since each command object encapsulates the required interactions). In this case, each possible service is implemented as a command object, responsible of carrying out the necessary logic to fulfill the user's request.
- Interact with the information systems involved in the query (possibly adapting each input from the different sources of information) by executing the command. Here, multiple possible sources of information must be "glued" to obtain more meaningful information. The issue of mixing different sources of information can be addressed applying the Strategy Design Pattern to implement various approaches.
- Format the results according to the resources of the device of the mobile user and the network. Each device has its own set of capabilities and restrictions, imposed

Figure 6. Conceptual architecture

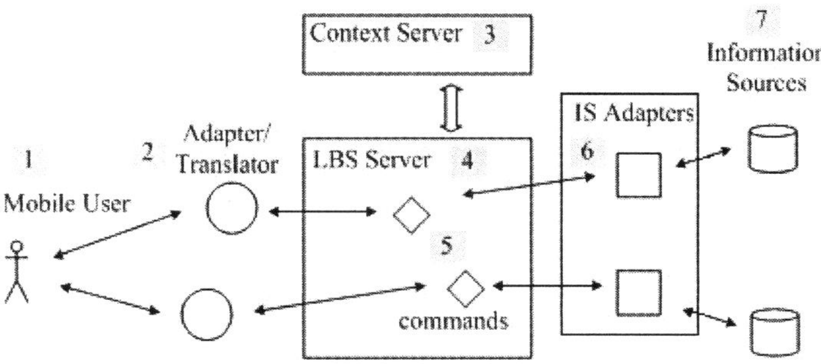

primarily by the network interface and computation power; these capabilities and restrictions ought to be considered to provide a value added service to the user.

In Figure 6 we show a simplified architecture to support the described functionality. We next describe each relevant actor/component in detail:

1. Mobile users communicate with the LBS server by means of a portable device such as a Palm Pilot. Their requests are intercepted by the translation layer. Context objects that hold important information about the environment are created in the mobile device. These context objects are then sent to the LBS server when requesting a service.
2. Each one of the adapters/translators is designed to *translate* the request from the users to an appropriate representation so the LBS server can deal with the information sent.

   Once the request has been fulfilled, the adapters/translators are used again to adapt the results to a form that can be efficiently transmitted and handled by the user's device. To achieve this, we can use a rule-based approach (see Figure 1) to customize the way in which the information is delivered and presented to the mobile user.
3. The context server is responsible of dealing with important information about the current environment of the user which is relevant to the execution of the requested services. This server is primarily responsible for managing the various contexts provided by the mobile users, and their corresponding changes.
4. The LBS server holds the definitions of the available services and executes them by demand using information about the context and information obtained from different information sources (IS). It is in this server where the command solution presented in previous sections should be used as a means of providing an extensible set of services.

5. Each command instance specifies the application logic that must be executed to fulfill a user's request. To make the commands as independent as possible from the representation of the location, we suggest the utilization of the "Location Square." Each command gets the necessary information to perform its operation from one or more "IS Adapters."
6. These adapters help to provide a uniform interface to the set of commands of the server. Each adapter is responsible of adapting the data pertaining to a specific source of information, and performing the necessary computation to deal with information inconsistencies. To cope with the second responsibility, these layers could be augmented with the addition of different strategies (see Pattern Strategy [Gamma, 1995]) to deal with the different ways a inconsistency problem may be solved.
7. Repositories of different kinds of information (or even owners), that have to be adapted in order to be used by the commands residing in the LBS server.

Further Work and Concluding Remarks

In this chapter, we have addressed some issues related with the construction of location-based services on the World Wide Web. We have shown that, when introducing geographic locations in software applications, we have to face many different and certainly new problems. In this chapter, we focused on those problems related with the evolution of LBS, in particular the need to add new location types, contexts, and services. We have also discussed those problems related with integrating different data sources. In the core of this chapter we have presented some simple micro-architectures for solving the preceding problems and have shown how these micro-architectures play together in a simple Web scenario.

We are now working in three different directions. First, we are researching the evolution of an object-oriented framework for (conventional) GIS applications into a platform for developing LBS. For this to be possible we need to study how to be able to adapt geographic objects to the user location context, for example, we need to change the topology of these objects as the user moves (the metro station is a point in the map of Paris but later it might need to be managed as a 2D or 3D object).

We are also pursuing research related to middleware support for building location-aware applications. In this sense we are studying how to adapt the well-known Model-View-Controller metaphor to make it more sensitive to the user location and location contexts.

Finally, we are also studying how to publish new location based services, considering mobile users running thick clients.

References

Abowd, G. (1999). Software engineering issues for ubiquitous computing. *Proceedings of the International Conference on Software Engineering (ICSE '99)* (pp. 75-84). ACM Press.

Banavar G., & Bernstein, A. (2002). Software Infrastructure and design challenge for ubiquitous applications. *Communications of the ACM, 45*(12), 92-96.

Cappi, J., Rossi, G., & Fortier, A. (2002). Customization policies need more than rule objects. *Proceedings of OOIS 2002, Springer Verlag, Lectures Notes in Computer Science* (pp. 117-123).

Friis-Christensen, A., Tryfona, N., & Jensen, C. (2001). Requirements and research Issues in geographic data modeling. *ACM-GIS 2001*, 2-8

Gamma, E., Helm, R., Johnson, J., & Vlissides, J. (1995). Design patterns. *Elements of reusable object-oriented software*. Addison Wesley.

Garmash, A. (2001). A Geographic XML-based Format for the Mobile Environment. *Proceedings of the 34th Hawaii International Conference on System Sciences*. IEEE Press.

GML (2000). Geographical mark-up language. In *www.opengis.org/techno/specs/00-029/GML.html*

Gordillo, S., Balaguer, F., Mostaccio, C., & Das Neves, F. (1999). Developing GIS applications with objects: A design pattern approach. *GeoInformatica*. Kluwer Academic Publishers, *1*(3), 7-32.

Hjelm, J. (2002). *Creating location services for the wireless Web: Professional developer's guide*. John Wiley.

Kappel, G., Proll, B., & Retschitzegger, W. (2003). Customization of ubiquitous Web applications. A comparison of approaches. *International Journal of Web Engineering and Technology*, 79-111

Kraak, M., & Brown, A. (2001). *Web cartography: Development and prospects*. Taylor and Francis.

Laurini, R. (1998). Spatial Multidatabase Topological Continuity and Indexing: a Step towards Seamless GIS Data Interoperability. *International Journal of Geographical Information Sciences, 12*(4), 373-402.

Laurini, R. (2001). Real Time Spatio-Temporal Databases. In *Transactions on Geographic Information Systems*, Guest Editorial, *5*(2), 87-98.

Laurini, R., & Thompson, D. (1993). *Fundamental of Spatial Information Systems*. Academic Press.

Leick, A. (1990). *GPS Satellite Surveying*. Department of Surveying Engineering University of Maine. Editorial John Wiley & Sons.

Longley, P., Goodchild, M., Maguire, D., & Rhind, D. (2002). *Geographical Information Systems and Science*. Wiley.

NTV (2003). Navigation Technologies Corporation. Online *www.navtech.com*

Nielsen, J. (2003). Mobile Devices: One generation from useful. AletBox. In *http://www.useit.com/alertbox/20030818.html*

OpenSource (2003). Open Source GIS. In *www.opensourcegis.org*

Peng, Z., & Tsou, M. (2003). *Internet GIS. Distributed Geographic Information Services for the Internet and Wireless Networks.* John Wiley.

Pradham, S. (2002). Semantic location. *Personal and Ubiquitous Computing,* (6), 213-216.

Rigaux, P., Scholl, M., & Voisard, A. (2002). *Spatial databases with applications to GIS.* Morgan Kaufmann Publishers.

Virrantaus., K., Veijalainen, J., & Markkula, J. (2002). Developing GIS-supported location-based services. *Proceedings of the Second International Conference on Web Information Systems Engineering (WISE'02).*

Wiederhold, G. (1999). Mediation to deal with heterogeneous data sources. *Proc. Interop'99: Interoperating Geographic Information Systems 2nd Conf.* (pp. 1-16). Springer-Verlag.

Yoder, J., & Razavi, R. (2000). Metadata and Adaptive Object-Models. ECOOP 2000 Workshops. In *www.adaptiveobjectmodel.com*

Section III

Web Metrics and Quality:
Models and Methods

Chapter VI

Architectural Metrics for E-Commerce: A Balance between Rigor and Relevance

Jinwoo Kim
Yonsei University, Korea

Abstract

Metrics for the architectural quality of Internet businesses are essential in measuring the success and failure of e-commerce. This chapter *proposes six dimensions of architectural metrics for Internet businesses: internal stability, external security, information gathering, order processing, system interface, and communication interface. For each of the six metrics, we have constructed questionnaires to measure the perceived level of architectural quality and identified feature lists that might be closely related to the perceived quality level. Large-scale empirical studies were conducted both to validate the proposed metrics and to explore their relevance across four Internet business domains. The results indicate that metrics have high validities and reliabilities in three different domains. The relevance of the metrics was also proved by the meaningful relations between design features and customer loyalty. This chapter ends with the implications and limitations of the study results.*

Introduction

As the Internet has rapidly spread throughout our society, so has electronic commerce, which is defined as any commercial activity made over the Internet (Kalakota & Whinston, 1996). Similarly, a sharp increase has been observed in the number of Internet businesses involved in electronic commerce (The Yankee Group, 2001). Internet businesses, such as E*trade and Amazon, are defined as individual entities that perform commercial activities on the Internet (Adam, Awerbuch, Slonim, Wegner, & Yesha, 1997; Margherio, Henry, Cooke, & Montes, 1998; Kim, 1999). As the number of Internet businesses has increased, so has the variety of individual businesses. At the beginning of the digital economy era, most Internet businesses were created to announce on the Web the existence of traditional companies (Sullivan, 1999). Nowadays Internet businesses include those that trade physical and digital goods (Chircu & Kauffman, 2000; Chau, Au, & Tam, 2000), cyber communities (Wilde & Swatman, 1997; Kodama, 1999), and even online network games (Mulligan, 1998).

As the variety of Internet businesses increases, we need diverse kinds of metrics to measure the current state of individual businesses comprehensively. For example, financial metrics such as total sales and revenue are important to measure the financial performance of individual businesses selling products and services (Bell & Tang, 1998). Similarly, behavioral metrics such as total number of visitors or average time per visit are important measuring the behavioral performance of portal businesses trying to entice as many people as possible in order to generate revenue from business partners and advertising (Day, 1997; Kodama, 1999). Even though these financial and behavioral metrics inform us of the final outcomes of individual businesses, they are hardpressed to explain why the businesses are successful or failing. In order to answer this question, we need additional metrics that can evaluate the architectural quality of Internet businesses.

This chapter proposes that metrics for architectural quality can be used to evaluate the quality of individual Internet businesses. Architecture is related to the understanding and conveying of the big picture of an Internet business (Rosenfeld & Morville, 1998; Bauer & Scharl, 2000; Park & Kim, 2000). It consists of individual features that include not only various system characteristics such as link structures and screen layout (Kim & Yoo, 2000), but also important managerial characteristics such as the amount of provided information and security policies (Huizingh, 2000). Metrics for architectural quality are especially important because one of the ultimate goal of an Internet business is to provide the optimal experience to its customers (Hoffman & Novak, 1996; Kim & Moon, 1998; Nel, Niekerk, Berthon, & Davies, 1999). Financial or behavioral metrics do not consider the visitor's experience and, therefore, cannot provide concrete guidelines to achieve a business's goals. In other words, they only measure the results of the provided level of experience, but do not suggest how to enhance customer experience. Architectural metrics, on the other hand, can provide direct recommendations on how to enhance the quality of the customer experience because they are closely related to Web site development. This is because most Internet businesses are eventually implemented through Web sites[1].

Many architectural metrics have been proposed in the course of development and evaluation of Internet businesses (Smith, 1997; Selz & Schubert, 1998; Webby Awards, 2001; Webobjectives Research, 2001). However, these metrics have problems in four aspects. First, these metrics generally lack a strong theoretical background, suggesting several measures based on existing practices with no explicit theoretical constructs (Webby Awards, 2001; Gomez, 2001). Others suggest a lot of measures without any justification of why they are needed. Therefore, we cannot be sure if they are comprehensive or missing any important aspects of the architectural quality of Internet business. Second, some prior studies simply proposed architectural metrics without any empirical tests of construct validities and reliabilities (e.g., Selz & Schubert, 1997). We cannot, therefore, be sure they are reliably measuring what they are supposed to measure, which is the architectural quality of the Internet business (Straub, 1989; Boudreau, Geren, & Straub, 2001). It is even harder to find empirical tests across multiple domains. Some metrics, for example, are domain-specific and applicable to virtual malls but not to portal businesses (Bell & Tang, 1998; Perry & Bodkin, 2000). Finally, the metrics proposed by some prior studies lack managerial or technical relevance to Internet businesses (Smith, 1997). Therefore, even if we are sure about the rigor of the metrics validation, we cannot be sure either that they are related to important managerial factors in Internet business or that they can be applied to various technical features involved in Internet system developments (Davenport & Markus, 1999; Benbasat & Zmud, 1999).

This study proposes a set of architectural metrics that are based on a conceptual framework, which has been used in architecture for over a thousand years (Britannica, 2001; Giedion, 1941). It can provide comprehensive constructs to cover the important architectural qualities of Internet business. This study also involved a large-scale survey to test empirically the construct validity and reliability of the proposed metrics. In terms of the construct validity, this study conducted a factor analysis to test the convergent and discriminate validity. In terms of the reliability, this study provides the Cronbach alpha coefficient for the six measures. Once the validities of the six measures have been confirmed empirically, their relevance to the managerial and technical aspects of Internet business has also been explored in two ways. In terms of the technical relevance, regression analyses were conducted to identify important objective features that were closely related to the perceived quality of Internet business. In terms of the managerial relevance, LISREL analyses were conducted to test the causal relations among three constructs measured by the six measures, user satisfaction and customer loyalty, which have been regarded as important managerial goals in Internet business.

Finally, the proposed metrics have been applied to four different domains of Internet businesses. These domains were selected to test whether the proposed architectural metrics can be applied to a wide variety of Internet businesses.

The next section will explain the conceptual framework of architecture that has been applied to the development of architectural metrics for Internet business. Section 3 describes subjective questionnaire and objective feature lists. Section 4 explains the processes of the main study in four different domains of Internet businesses. Section 5 provides explanations of the study results of the construct validity and reliability, as well as the managerial and technical relevance of the proposed metrics to the four Internet business domains. This chapter then ends with the implications and limitations of study results.

Architectural Metrics

Analogy between Businesses and Buildings

The analogy of a software system as a building has been used frequently in system design (Kapor, 1996; Winograd & Tabor, 1996; Mitchell, 1995). Just as the building is a typical artifact that people construct in the real space, so is the Internet business a typical artifact that people build in cyber-space. Internet businesses can be regarded as buildings in cyber space for two reasons. First, Internet businesses and buildings serve similar objectives. Buildings offer physical living space in the real world and Internet businesses can be considered to offer a virtual living space in the cyber world. In other words, buildings such as marketplaces, schools, post offices, and libraries in the real world can be compared to Internet businesses such as virtual malls, education sites, e-mail sites, and portal sites in the cyber world (Mitchell, 1995). Second, users' perspectives are important both for Internet businesses and for buildings because one of the ultimate goal of the two is to provide appropriate experiences for users (Gonzales, Fernandez, & Cameselle, 1997; Liao & Cheung, 2001). Therefore, the architecture of Internet businesses and buildings emphasizes the quality of users' experiences. For example, stability, convenient functions, and visual aspects are important factors for both Internet business customers and building residents. The architectural quality of Internet businesses may be similar to that of buildings, therefore, from the user experience perspective.

One of the advantages of using the building metaphor is that we can learn from the conceptual framework of architectural quality that has been used to measure the quality of buildings for over a thousand years (Giedion, 1941). Buildings have been usually appraised from three interrelated perspectives based on the works of the famous Roman architecture critic Vitruvius: firmitas, utilitas, and venustas (Rasmussen, 1959). These three perspectives have been elaborated later in the domain of POE (Post Occupancy Evaluation), which is the process of evaluating buildings in a systematic and rigorous manner after they have been built and occupied for some time (Zimring, 1980; Preiser, Rabinowitz, & White, 1988; Gonzales, Fernandez, & Cameselle, 1997).

Firmitas refers to the structural firmness of architecture (Giedion, 1941). A building has to be firm enough to protect inhabitants from all external threats such as cold winds and snow. It also has to stand firm through internal erosions in order to avoid collapsing. Utilitas means the appropriate spatial accommodation of architecture. A building should provide spaces suitable for the purposes for which it is intended (Giedion, 1941). Finally, venustas represents the representational delight of architecture (Rasmussen, 1959). A building should have a pleasant appearance to arouse pleasurable emotions. In summary, in order to be evaluated as a good building, it has to provide structural firmness, functional convenience, and representational delight. The conceptual framework of architectural quality is used in this study as a useful tool to organize numerous quality metrics of Internet business into a systematic evaluation framework.

Six Dimensions of Architectural Metrics

We propose that the three architectural perspectives be used in the process of evaluating Internet businesses in the same systematic and rigorous manner as the process of evaluating architecture. Based on the three architectural perspectives, we propose six architectural measures for Internet business: internal stability and external security based on the structural firmness perspective, information gathering and order processing based on the functional convenience perspective, and system interface and communication interface from the representational delight perspective (Kapor, 1996; Winograd & Tabor, 1996).

Structural Firmness (firmitas)

From the structural perspective, a building should be firm enough to withstand expected and unexpected forces of nature. This dimension in POE includes such factors as fire safety, electrical systems, sanitation and ventilation, exterior walls, and roofs (Preiser, Rabinowitz, & White, 1988).

The structural firmness in the Internet business can be defined as the solidity of the system structure in overcoming all expected and unexpected threats. We hypothesize that structural firmness is an important construct of the architectural quality for Internet business that may affect customer satisfaction and loyalty. This is because customers want to feel safe and secure before they initiate any transactional activities. For example, a survey conducted by the European Messaging Association revealed that the vast majority of respondents demand structural firmness before they conducted any electronic marketing activities on the Web (Shankar, 1996). It is also noted in a recent study that structural firmness on the Internet has received considerable attention both directly in the form of safe and secure transfer of money and indirectly in the form of transaction risks (National Computer Board, 1997).

We believe that the firmness dimension of Internet business can be measured by two measures according to the source of threats: internal stability vs. external security. The *internal stability* metric denotes the safety of Internet business from internal bugs (Huang & Wang, 1999). We hypothesize that internal stability is important for the structural firmness of Internet business because unstable systems frustrate customers and diminish the consumption experience. For example, it was found that online shopping adoption depends on the perceived stability of customer's experience (Liang & Huang, 1998). Similarly, it was argued that the most important obstacle to online shopping is the lack of system stability (Salkin, 1999). Internal stability of Internet business can be measured by such factors as rapid access, quick error recovery, and correct operation and computation (Bhimani, 1996).

The *external security* metric represents the safety of Internet business from external threats (Zona Research, 2000). We believe that the external security is important for the structural firmness of Internet business because an electronic market that is not considered a safe place would not attract customers (Liu, Arnettt, Calella, & Beatty,

1997). Lack of security has been found to be one of the main factors inhibiting customers from engaging in online transactions (Forrester Research, 1999). A recent study in e-commerce also found that perceived risks of security exert significant effect on the willingness to be involved in transaction activities (Liao & Cheung, 2001). The external security of Internet businesses can be measured by such factors as the quality of firewalls and privacy policies (Panurach, 1996).

Functional Convenience (utilitas)

From the functional perspective, a building should be appropriate for its usage (Britannica, 2001). A building that is good for an office may not necessarily be suitable for residential purposes. This dimension in POE includes such factors as storage, workflow, human factors, and flexibility (Preiser, Rabinowitz, & White, 1987).

Functional convenience of Internet business is defined as the provision of convenient functions for the customers' process of transaction activities. Therefore, this perspective ensures that our metrics are specific to Internet businesses rather than any personal and non-commercial entities on the Internet. We hypothesize that providing convenient functions for the customers to complete their intended business activities is an important architectural construct because the customers should be provided with convenient functions to accomplish their goals in Internet business. For example, it was found that usefulness and ease of use are the most important factors for customer satisfaction (Davis, 1989).

The convenience dimension can be measured by two metrics relating to the phases of transaction process: information gathering vs. order processing (Lohse & Spiller, 1998; Schmid, 1995; Selz & Schubert, 1998; Kim, 1997; Huizingh, 2000; O'Keefe & McEachern, 1998). The *information-gathering* phase refers to the activities that customers conduct in collecting relevant information about the products and services (Perry & Bodkin, 2000; Huang & Yang, 1999). We hypothesize that convenient functions for customers to obtain all the information they need to make a purchase decision are important for the functional convenience of Internet businesses. A recent study revealed that an informative strategy highlighting key product information was essential to the success of online businesses (Miles, Howes, & Davies, 2000). It has also been argued that information quality is important for the success of general information systems (Huang & Yang, 1999). The convenience of information gathering can be measured by such features as accurate product lists or comprehensive information about specific products.

The *order-processing* phase includes all the activities of purchasing and after-purchasing (Selz and Schubert, 1998). We hypothesize that a convenient order-processing phase is an important aspect of the functional convenience in Internet business because it is in this phase that the revenue for the business is realized. A recent study found that consumers with online purchasing experience believed that the Internet business supported the order-processing phase efficiently (Rhee & Riggins, 1999).

The convenience of the order-processing phase can be measured by such functions as confirming the completion of the order process and tracking the ordered products in delivery (Lucas, 1996).

Representational Delight (venustas)

From the representational perspective, a building should be enjoyable enough to provide a pleasant feeling to the inhabitants. This dimension includes such factors as image, graphics, and environmental perception (Preiser, Rabinowitz, & White, 1988).

Representational delight in Internet business refers to the interface aspects of the Web site with which the user comes into contact. Interface is the representational aspect that users actually see and hear from computer systems (Moran, 1981). We hypothesize that representational delight is an important architectural construct of Internet business because it enhances a customer's pleasant experience as they learn to browse and to find relevant information (Benjamin, 1995). A recent study found that interfaces between customers and businesses, as well as among customers, were important variables for the success of Internet businesses (Liu & Arnett, 2000).

The delight dimension can be measured by two metrics according to the target of the interface: interface to system vs. interface to human. This classification is based on the fact that interaction in Internet business can either be with the system or with those using the same system. The *system interface* refers to the measure of the pleasantness of the interface between human and computers (Lohse & Spiller, 1998). We believe that providing a pleasant system interface is an important measure for representational delight. This is because customers would return to the Internet business if it provided an interesting and entertaining interface (Rice, 1997). It has been found that homepage presentation is a major antecedent of consumer satisfaction in Internet business (Ho & Wu, 1999). It was also found that system interface features were important in determining if the customer decided to make a repeated visit to the Web sites (Rice, 1997). The delightfulness of system interface can be measured by such design features as screen and navigation (Kim & Yoo, 2000; Park & Kim, 2000).

The *communication interface* refers to the measures of the pleasantness of the interface between humans. These are mostly implemented by communication systems (Wilson, Morrison, & Napier, 1997; Daft & Lengel, 1986). We hypothesize that providing pleasant communication interfaces among customers are important because communicating with other people in a community is the heart of Internet businesses (Armstrong & Hagel, 1996). For example, it was found that providing a pleasant peer review feedback section is one of the best ways to increase customer satisfaction (Kim, 1999). It is also noted that most Internet businesses allow buyers and sellers to interact through the electronic medium (Liu, Arnett, Calella, & Beatty, 1997). The communication interface can be measured by such factors as bulletin boards and chatting rooms.

In summary, the architectural quality of an Internet business can be measured using the six metrics. From the structural perspective, it should be stable internally and secure externally. From the functional perspective, it should be convenient in both the information gathering and order processing phases. Finally, from the representational perspective, it should provide enjoyable interfaces both to the system and to other people who are using the same system.

Relevance of Architectural Metrics to Internet Business

In order for the proposed metrics to be useful, we should not only rigorously test the validities of the metrics but also to explore their relevance with the technical or managerial aspects of Internet business (Davenport & Markus, 1999; Benbasat & Zmun, 1999). We have investigated two types of relations in order to explore the relevance of the proposed metrics with important aspects of Internet business.

Relations between Subjective Questionnaires and Objective Feature Lists

For each of the six dimensions, a set of questionnaires measuring subjective architectural quality and a set of objective feature lists are constructed based on related studies. An example of the questionnaires and feature lists is provided later in Section 3. We believe that there exist close relations between the subjective architectural quality and feature lists. In other words, the objective features in a dimension should be closely related to the subjective perception in the same dimension of the architectural quality. For example, users may perceive a high level of internal safety if the Internet business provides appropriate features related to the safety of the Internet business systems. As another example, certain features of Internet business sites such as search engines or shopping carts may be closely related to the subjective feeling of convenience. This relation is important if the metrics are to provide technical suggestions to the developers of Internet business sites. This research, therefore, identifies important features that are closely related to the subjective level of the architectural quality for each of the six measures.

Relations between the Six Metrics and Latent Constructs

We believe that the architectural quality of Internet businesses has impacts on the level of user satisfactions and, in turn, on the level of customer loyalty. In other words, an Internet business with a high architectural quality may provide a higher level of user satisfaction, which then provides a higher level of customer loyalty. User satisfaction is a subjective evaluation of the consequences of using the Internet business on a pleasant-unpleasant continuum (Seddon, 1997; Lewis, 1995). User satisfaction is one of the most frequently used measures of system success because the success of a system is usually related to what its users say they like (DeLong & McLean, 1992). It is also clearly related to customer loyalty, which is the customer's intention to visit the Internet business site again based on their previous experiences as well as future expectations (Czepiel & Gilmore, 1987; Berry, 1995).

It is especially important for Internet businesses to ensure that customers visit their sites repeatedly because their value is determined mostly by the number of loyal customers (Rose, Khoo, & Straub, 1999). If none of the customers is willing to visit the site again its business value becomes worthless despite its technical or managerial assets. A recent study on Internet shoppers provides some concrete evidence of the economic value of

Figure 1. Overall model of architectural metrics

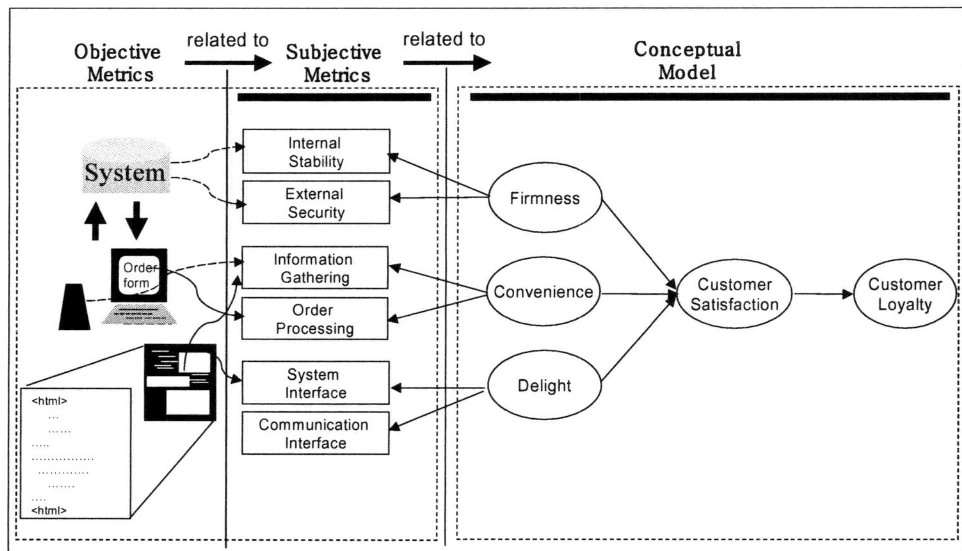

customer loyalty, such as the expenditure of loyal customers is almost twice as much as that of new users (Nielsen, 1997). This is because loyal customers conduct hefty transactions only with those sites proven reliable after several trial purchases with relatively small amounts. Therefore, we selected customer loyalty as the final dependent variable in our causal model. The overall model with the architectural metrics is shown in Figure 1.

Subjective Questionnaires and Objective Features

The full set of questions for the virtual mall domain is presented in Table 1. The first column of Table 1 presents the three perspectives in architecture, the second column indicates the corresponding six architectural metrics and the actual questions used in the empirical study.

The full set of the objective system-feature list for the virtual mall domain is presented in Table 2. The first column of Table 2 shows the three perspectives in architecture and the second column indicates six architectural metrics. The third column denotes the high-level objective feature and the fourth column indicates the objective features at a more detailed level with the actual coding scheme for each of the objective features.

Table 1. Questionnaire of the six architectural metrics for the virtual mall domain

Architectural Concepts	Architectural metrics: Questionnaires	
Structural	**Internal Stability**	
Firmness	IS-1	It is reliable.
	IS-2	It does not take long time to load the front page of the site.
	IS-3	It provides a fast loading speed when it is used for Internet business.
	External Security	
	ES-1	It protects users' personal information completely.
	ES-2	It manages and maintains the personal account records.
	ES-3	It provides a thorough protection preventing any invasion from outsiders.
	ES-4	I can rely on this business whenever I want to purchase important products.
	ES-5	I will use this business always to do shopping in any urgent situations.
Functional	**Information Gathering**	
Convenience	IG-1	It provides various kinds of information about goods and services.
	IG-2	Information related to goods and services offered in this business is
	IG-3	accurate.
	IG-4	The latest information related to goods and services is adequately provided.
		Information provided is easy to understand.
	Order Processing	
	OP-1	In comparison to other virtual malls, the price of the goods and services (including postage handling) are reasonable.
	OP-2	Processes of ordering goods and services are convenient.
	OP-3	It provides adequate information to check the ordered items and its location during the process of ordering the items.
	OP-4	It maintains my personal information, so I can make orders repeatedly more conveniently.
	OP-5	Ordered items are delivered right on the promised time.
	OP-6	There is no difference between the ordered items and the delivered items.
	OP-7	It is convenient to make claims when there are problems in the delivered goods and services.
	OP-8	It is convenient to get exchange and refund for the purchased goods and services.

Main Study

In order to test the construct validity and reliability of the proposed metrics, as well as to explore their managerial and technical relevance, empirical studies were conducted in four different business domains: virtual malls, online stock brokerage, search portal, and online network games.

Table 1. Questionnaire of the six architectural metrics for the virtual mall domain (cont.)

Architectural Concepts	Architectural metrics: Questionnaires	
Representational Delight	**System Interface**	
	SI-1	It is pleasant to follow the overall flow.
	SI-2	It is delight to recognize where I am and what I am doing in the business.
	SI-3	It is easy to learn the steps on how to use the system.
	SI-4	It is pleasant to follow and use the menu structure.
	SI-5	It is easy to remember the business address (URL: Domain Address)
	SI-6	The images and typographies used in the sites are stylish.
	SI-7	Overall atmosphere and screen displays of the sites are well coordinated.
	SI-8	It is pleasant to see the provided information on each screen in this site.
	SI-9	Information provided in this site is consistent through out the whole presented in the same format to keep the flow of consistency.
	Communication Interface	
	CI-1	It is easy to share individual information with others.
	CI-2	Well-coordinated community has been formed among the users of this site.
	CI-3	It offers various ways to communicate between the customer and the company.
	CI-4	It provides fast and accurate answers to the customers' inquires (Q &A)
	CI-5	It offers custom-made communication services to individual users.

A large-scale survey was conducted in the third quarter of the year 2000 with the help of an online research company (www.bzeye.com). Respondents to the survey were recruited through banner advertisement on several popular domestic Web sites. Among those who applied, only those who had used one of the selected Internet-businesses sites more than twice during the one-week prior to the survey were solicited with monetary compensation. First, respondents were asked to answer demographic questions (e.g., age, gender, occupations). Then, for the target Internet businesses, they answered questions about customer loyalty and user satisfaction, which were borrowed from Czeipiel and Gilmore (1987) and Lewis (1995), respectively. Finally, they answered the questionnaires for architectural qualities, such as shown in Table 1 for virtual malls, using a seven point Likert scale. Only those respondents who answered all the questions faithfully were retained for further analysis. Table 3 presents the number of effective respondents after user verification and the number of respondents included in the final data set for the four business domains, with the gender and age ratio.

Objective features of architectural quality have been measured for each of the selected Internet business sites. In order to code the objective features of selected Internet

Table 2. Objective features lists of the six metrics for the virtual mall domain

Architectural Metrics		
	Constructs	Detailed level
Firmness	Internal Stability	
	Link check	# of bad links
	HTML check and repair	# of html errors
	Browser compatibility	# of problems (browse version errors)
	Loading time check	Loading time of first page according to network lines(28kb, 56kb, ISDN line)
	External Stability	
	Protection of personal information	Whether it provides explicit policy on personal information protection (yes/no)
		Whether it provides rights to modify the customer's personal information (yes/no)
		Whether it asks for the customer's consent to the process of joining membership (yes/no)
	Completeness of transaction condition	According to transaction condition of the Fair Trade Commission (yes/no)
	Completeness of system security	Whether it provides explicit policy for system security (yes/no)
	Completeness of company profile	Whether it provides information on company address, contact phone number, manufacturer registration number and CEO name (yes/no)

businesses, a total of 30 people were recruited by advertisement on campus. The selected Internet businesses were then randomly assigned to a team of two coders. The two coders in a team investigated the objective features of the selected businesses independently. After both of them coded an Internet business, they were asked to reconcile their coding if there existed any inconsistency between the two.

Results

The study results are explained in terms of the construct validity and reliability of the proposed metrics, followed by their relevance to technical and managerial aspects of Internet business.

Instrument Validation

In order to assess the discriminate and convergent validity of the six architectural measures in our questionnaires, we performed the confirmatory factor analysis with the six measures toward the three constructs across the four business domains. The results are summarized in Table 4.

Table 2. Objective features lists of the six metrics for the virtual mall domain (cont.)

Architectural Metrics		
	Constructs	**Detailed level**
Convenience	**Information Gathering**	
	Completeness of basic help information	Whether it provides enough information about the order process and claim process (yes/no)
		Whether it provides advice on payment way (yes/no)
		Whether it provides advice on delivery charge, region and period of time (yes/no)
		Whether it provides advice on exchange/refund condition, scope and method (yes/no)
		Whether it provides advice on joining membership, modification withdraw and loss of password (yes/no)
	Completeness of additional help information (related extra service)	Whether it provides advice on the product search (yes/no)
	Completeness of basic information on product	Whether it provides information on Item name, brand, price, item pictures (in the product info page) (yes/no)
	Completeness of extra information on product	Whether it provides information on detailed description, renewal data, buyer, review information, price comparison, and suggested goods (in the goods info page) (yes/no)
		Whether it provides information on goods name, manufacturer, price, and mileage information (in the goods list page) (yes/no)
	Order Processing	
	Convenience of order Process	Whether it provides explanation on each level of order process
		Whether it use of existing customer's personal information (address, phone #...) in order process (yes/no)
	Customization of order	Whether it provides tool to modify recipients message, postage related message (yes/no)
		Whether it provides tool to choose delivering package, delivering at the appointed date (yes/no)
	Completeness of Information in shopping cart	Whether it provide information, on manufactures name, name of an item, price, the total amount,, item code, mileage and postage handling fee (yes/no)
	Convenience of detailed function in shopping cart	Whether it provides function on deleting items, remove the entire items, continue shopping, make payment, and changing its quality (yes/no)
	Variety of searching method for items	Whether it provides the function of keywords search, source selection search, search from the results, brand name search, search on other shopping mall sties (yes/no)
	Completeness of search result information	Whether it provides a search engine that present information on item name, price, accuracy, manufactured place, picture of an item, and explanation on the item goods in the search result (yes/no)

Table 2. Objective features lists of the six metrics for the virtual mall domain (cont.)

Convenience	Order Processing	
	Convenience of product list view	Whether it provides the function of comparing goods and services in various aspects other than price (yes/no)
		Whether it provides the function of list sorting by name, price (yes/no)
	Convenience of order confirmation	Whether it provides the function of order confirmation (yes/no)
		Whether it provides information on order data, order quality, delivery place, payment (yes/no)
	Variety of payment method and its convenience	Whether it provides variety of payment method (online remittance, credit card etc.) (yes/no)
	Variety of delivery method and its convenience	Whether it provides variety of delivery method (quick service, mail, fedex etc.) (yes/no)
		Whether it provides the function to delivery tracking (yes/no)
	Variety of settlement method to customer's complaint	Whether it provides variety of solution window to customer's complaint (e-mail, call-center etc.) (yes/no)
	System Interface	
	Completeness of user location information	Whether it provides information on its location check
	Convenience of navigation tool	Whether it provides variety of navigation tools (home button in each level page, number of available navigation links in each level, back button in the end product page, shortcut navigation link and sitemap etc.) (yes/no)
	Communication Interface	
	Convenience and its variety of communication tool	Whether it provides communication tools between the customer and the company (yes/no)
		Whether it provides communication tools between the customer and the customer (providing chatting room, message system) (yes/no)
		Whether it provides notice board (yes/no)

As we can see in Table 4, the six measures (internal stability, external security, information gathering, order processing, system interface, communication interface) converge well into the three corresponding constructs (structural firmness, functional commodity, representational delightfulness) across the four different domains (virtual malls, online stock brokerages, search portal, and network games). Also the several indices of goodness of fit are found to be within acceptable limits across the four business domains. Therefore, we may conclude that the six architectural metrics are to have appropriate construct validity across the four business domains.

The reliability tests the accuracy of metrics mostly using Cronbach alphas (Straub, 1989). Table 5 presents the Cronbach alphas of the six sets of questionnaires for architectural

Table 3. Number of effective respondents and final respondents

Respondents \ Domain		Virtual mall	Stock brokering	Search Portal	Online Game
Total respondents		4644	6582	3462	1991
Sex (%)	Male	64.9	88.6	57.0	82.7
	Female	35.1	11.4	43.0	17.3
Age (%)	10 age	11.6	-	13.5	43.5
	20 age	51.1	19.8	60.9	46.0
	30 age	29.7	56.8	22.6	9.7
	40 age	7.6	23.6	3.0	0.8

metrics in the four Internet business domains. The first column of Table 5 indicates the three dimensions of architecture, the second column shows the six architectural metrics, and the following four columns show the Cronbach alpha coefficient for virtual malls, stock brokerage, search portals, and online network games, respectively.

As you can see in Table 5, most coefficients are well above 70 percent, which means that the questionnaires shown in Table 1 reliably represent the six dimensions of metrics. The exceptions occurred only in the online network game domain in which questions for the internal stability, system interface, and communication interface dimension fail to meet the appropriate significance level.

Relevance of the Proposed Metrics to Internet Business

For each of the four selected Internet business domains, two types of analyses have been conducted to explore the relevance of the proposed metrics. First, LISREL models were evaluated to test the causal relations among the three constructs measured by the six metrics, user satisfaction, and customer loyalty. Second, regression analyses were conducted to identify the relations between the objective features and subjective questionnaires. These analyses were expected to provide concrete suggestions for improving user satisfaction and customer loyalty.

Evaluation of Structural Equation Models

Using structural equation modeling analysis, the hypothesized sequence of relationships of the models was tested as a set. The units of the analyses were the individual respondents who participated in the main survey study. The left half of Table 6 summarizes the results of four LISREL analyses. The first group of columns presents the

Table 4. Results of confirmatory factor analysis with the six measures across four domains

		Firmness	Delight	Convenience	Goodness of Fit Statistics
Virtual Mall	Internal Stability	0.78 *			DF=6
	External Security	0.86 *			Chi-square=132.84
	Information Gathering		0.78 *		RMSEA=0.067
	Order Processing		0.85 *		RMR=0.015
	System Interface			0.86 *	GFI=0.990
	Communication Interface			0.71 *	AGFI=0.970
Stock Brokerage	Internal Stability	0.83 *			DF=6
	External Security	0.87 *			Chi-square=231.23
	Information Gathering		0.76 *		RMSEA=0.104
	Order Processing		0.87 *		RMR=0.027
	System Interface			0.76 *	GFI=0.980
	Communication Interface			0.69 *	AGFI=0.920
Search Portal	Internal Stability	0.76 *			DF=6
	External Security	0.76 *			Chi-square=61.36
	Information Gathering		0.86 *		RMSEA=0.037
	Order Processing		0.83 *		RMR=0.008
	System Interface			0.86 *	GFI=1.00
	Communication Interface			0.69 *	AGFI=0.99
Online Game	Internal Stability	0.66 *			DF=6
	External Security	0.78 *			Chi-square=10.90
	Information Gathering		0.65 *		RMSEA=0.017
	Order Processing		0.82 *		RMR=0.008
	System Interface			0.70 *	GFI=0.100
	Communication Interface			0.66 *	AGFI=0.100

** $p<0.05$; DF: Degree of Freedom; Chi-square: Normal Theory Weighted Least Squares Chi-Square; RMSEA: Root Mean Square Error of Approximation; RMR: Root Mean Square Residual; GFI: Goodness of Fit Index*

four domains and the second group presents four indicators expressing the goodness of the fit for the LISREL models for each of the four domains. The results indicate that the conceptual model of the architectural metrics holds across four different domains. Therefore, all four LISREL models clearly indicate that the proposed three architectural constructs measured by the six metrics faithfully represent the architectural quality,

Table 5. Cronbach alpha coefficients of questionnaires in the four domains

		Virtual mall	Stock brokerage	Search Portal	Online Game
Firmness	Internal Stability	0.847223	0.920375	0.837615	0.415851
	External Security	0.906328	0.933072	0.878519	0.841827
Convenience	Information Gathering	0.846980	0.904822	0.800552	0.764672
	Order Processing	0.868906	0.839539	0.845602	0.755971
Delight	System Interface	0.910620	0.936622	0.909486	0.627121
	Communication Interface	0.880288	0.885936	0.878395	0.696328

which is stably related to user satisfaction and customer loyalty across the four Internet business domains.

Regression Analysis with Objective Features

The regression analysis was conducted for each of the six measures for each of the four Internet business domains. Therefore, the regression analysis was conducted 24 (6 x 4) times in total. The dependent variable of each regression analysis is the average of subjective answers from the survey respondents for one of the six measures in one of the four domains. The independent variables of each regression analysis are the objective for the corresponding measure for each Internet business sites. For example, in terms of the internal stability dimension of the virtual mall domain, the average of responses from the respondents to the three questions related to internal stability (as shown in Table 1) for one business was used as dependent variables, whereas the four objective features related to internal stability (as shown in Table 2) for the same business were used as independent variables. The units of the analysis are individual businesses because the independent variables (objective features) should be coded at the Internet business level, not at the individual respondent level. Therefore, we averaged the questionnaire responses for an Internet business in order to move from the individual respondent level to the Internet business level.

The third group of columns in Table 6 shows the significance of regression models for each of the metrics that have been found to be important. The results indicate that the objective features explain significant portions of variances among the subjective quality level in all four domains except the system interface of the search portal. Therefore, we may conclude that the proposed metrics and constructs can be applied to different business domains fairly well.

Virtual Mall Domain

The more detailed results of the regression analyses for the virtual mall domain are shown in Table 7. The adjust R square of the regression model is 0.6156 ($F=15.32, p<0.01$) for

Table 6. Summary for LISREL and regression analyses

Domains	LISREL				Regression			
	Chi-square	RMR	RMSEA	GFI (AGFI)		Metrics	F	Prob.> F
Virtual Mall	247.03	0.019	0.056	0.99 (0.97)	F	Internal stability	6.41	0.04
						External Security	19.47	0.00
					C	Information gathering	10.78	0.01
						Order Processing	12.69	0.03
					D	System Interface	7.28	0.02
						Communication Interface	6.01	0.03
Stock Brokerage	231.67	0.015	0.045	0.99 (0.98)	F	Internal stability	4.63	0.02
						External Security	7.91	0.01
					C	Information gathering	8.42	0.00
						Order Processing	17.08	0.00
					D	System Interface	6.54	0.01
						Communication Interface	6.34	0.00
Search Portal	338.49	0.029	0.076	0.99 (0.98)	F	Internal stability	6.31	0.04
						External Security	17.38	0.02
					C	Information gathering	7.60	0.04
						Order Processing	12.69	0.03
					D	System Interface	-	-
						Communication Interface	19.06	0.01
Online Game	66.94	0.014	0.034	0.99 (0.98)	F	Internal stability	4.64	0.04
						External Security	5.69	0.02
					C	Information gathering	14.19	0.00
						Order Processing	4.23	0.04
					D	System Interface	5.74	0.03
						Communication Interface	19.06	0.01

internal stability, 0.7956 (F=19.47, $p<0.00$) for external security, 0.6425(F=10.78, $p<0.01$) for information gathering, 0.8088 (F=12.69, $p<0.05$) for order processing, 0.4764 (F=7.28, $p<0.02$) for system interface, and 0.4291 (F=6.01, $p<0.05$) for communication interface. The significance of the regression model for the six dimensions indicates that objective features explain a significant portion of the variance in the subjective responses for all the six measures. -In each of the six measures, one objective feature was found to be closely related to the average of subjective responses. -For example, the protection of personal information was found to be an important site feature that is closely related to the average response of perceived external security (t=19.47, $p<0.05$).

Table 7. Results of the regression analyses for the virtual mall domain

Architectural Dimensions	Model		Adjusted R^2 & Standardized Estimate (β)	F value	Prob.> F
Firmness					
Internal Stability	Adjusted R square of Model (R^2)		0.6156	6.41	0.04 *
	Var.	Page loading time check	0.0330 (β)	6.41	0.04 *
External Security	Adjusted R square of Model (R^2)		0.7956	19.47	0.00 **
	Var.	Protection of personal information	0.0231 (β)	19.47	0.00 **
Convenience					
Information Gathering	Adjusted R square of Model (R^2)		0.6425	10.78	0.01 *
	Var.	Amount of information provided for the product list	0.0886 (β)	10.78	0.01 *
Order Processing	Adjusted R square of Model (R^2)		0.8088	12.69	0.03 *
	Var.	Function of order confirmation	0.1686 (β)	12.69	0.03 *
Delight					
System Interface	Adjusted R square of Model (R^2)		0.4764	7.28	0.02 *
	Var.	Function to present its current location	0.0702 (β)	7.28	0.02 *
Communication Interface	Adjusted R square of Model (R^2)		0.4291	6.01	0.03 *
	Var.	Variety of proposed communication channels	0.0275 (β)	6.01	0.03 *

** $p<0.01$, * $p<0.05$

Online Stock Brokerage Domain

The results of the regression analyses in the stock brokerage domain in Table 8 show that objective features explain significant portions of the variance in the subjective responses to all the six measures; internal stability (F=4.63, $p<0.05$), external security (F=7.91, $p<0.01$), information gathering (F=8.42, $p<0.01$), order processing (F=17.08, $p<0.01$), system interface (F=6.54, $p<0.01$) and communication interface (F=6.34, $p<0.01$). In terms of internal stability, the number of bad links and HTML errors is found to be important (t=14.33, $p<0.01$), while the provision of an explicit policy for system security is found to be important for the external security dimension (t=15.32, $p<0.01$).

Two objectives features are seen to be closely related to the internal stability, information gathering, and communication interface, whereas one objective feature is found to be closely related to the external security, order processing and system interface.

Table 8. Results of the regression analyses for the online stock brokerage domain

Architectural Dimensions	Model		Adjusted R^2 & Standardized Estimate (β)	F value	Prob.> F
Firmness					
Internal Stability	Adjusted R square of Model (R^2)		0.3819	4.63	0.02 *
	Var.	Link (bad link) check	0.3788 (β)	7.30	0.01 *
		Browser (MS explorer, Netscape) compatibility	-0.0448	3.04	0.10
External Security	Adjusted R square of Model (R^2)		0.3307 (β)	7.91	0.01 *
	Var.	Transaction Security level (128/56/4bits)	0.0563	7.91	0.01 *
Convenience					
Information Gathering	Adjusted R square of Model (R^2)		0.4122	8.42	0.00 **
	Var.	Provision of past stock analysis information	0.0280 (β)	7.65	0.01 *
		Provision of web site help information	0.0326 (β)	7.49	0.01 *
Order Processing	Adjusted R square of Model (R^2)		0.5323	17.08	0.00 **
	Var.	Variety of searching method for stock code	0.0635 (β)	17.08	0.00 **
Delight					
System Interface	Adjusted R square of Model (R^2)		0.2665	6.54	0.01 *
	Var.	Balance of screen layout	0.0260 (β)	6.54	0.01 *
Communication Interface	Adjusted R square of Model (R^2)		0.3116	6.34	0.00 **
	Var.	Provision of communication channels to customer's complaint	0.0569 (β)	4.46	0.04 *
		Function of customization	0.0658 (β)	3.56	0.06

** $p<0.01$, * $p<0.05$

Search Portal Domain

In the search portal domain, Table 9 shows that objective features are found to explain significant portions of the variations of the subjective responses for most measures except the system interface measure; internal stability (F=6.31, $p<0.05$), external security (F=17.38, $p<0.05$), information gathering (F=7.60, $p < 0.05$), order processing (F=12.69, $p<0.05$), system interface (*n.s.*) and communication interface (F=19.06, $p<0.01$). -This

Table 9. Results of the regression analyses for the search portal domain

Architectural Dimensions	Model		Adjusted R^2 & Standardized Estimate (β)	F value	Prob.> F
Firmness					
Internal Stability	Adjusted R square of Model (R^2)		0.5895	6.31	0.04 *
	Var.	Html error check	0.0021 (β)	6.31	0.04 *
External Security	Adjusted R square of Model (R^2)		0.8528	17.38	0.02 *
	Var.	Provision of transaction stipulation	0.0558 (β)	17.38	0.02 *
Convenience					
Information Gathering	Adjusted R square of Model (R^2)		0.7916	7.60	0.04 *
	Var.	Provision of financial information (e.g. securities, insurance...)	-0.0754 (β)	6.91	0.06
		Provision of commercial information (e.g. shopping, auction...)	0.0395 (β)	15.15	0.01 *
Order Processing	Adjusted R square of Model (R^2)		0.8088	12.69	0.03 *
	Var.	Provision of search function on extra service (e.g. phone number, map search...)	0.1686 (β)	12.69	0.03 *
Delight					
System Interface	Adjusted R square of Model (R^2)		-	-	-
	Var.	-	-	-	-
Communication Interface	Adjusted R square of Model (R^2)		0.8265	19.06	0.01 *
	Var.	Provision of customization function (e.g. individual address book, schedule organizer...)	0.0432 (β)	19.06	0.01 *

** $p<0.01$, * $p<0.05$

means that none of the objective features that we selected from the pretest for system interface are closely related to the average of subjective responses from the users. For the rest of the five dimensions, we are able to identify one or two important objective features. For example, the check for HTML errors turns out to be an important factor to the internal stability of search portals.

Online Network Game Domain

Finally, the results shown in Table 10 indicate that objective features in online network games are found to explain significant portions of the variance of the subjective responses in all six dimensions: internal stability (F=4.64, $p<0.05$), external security (F=5.69, $p<0.05$), information gathering (F=6.46, $p < 0.01$), order processing (F=4.23, $p<0.05$), system interface (F=5.74, $p<0.05$) and communication interface (F=15.32, $p<0.00$). Two objective features are found to be closely related to the subjective responses for the internal stability, two features for external security, four features for information gathering, two features for order processing, one feature for system interface, and finally two features for communication interface.

In summary, all regression analyses in the four domains clearly indicate that we can identify as least one objective feature that is closely related to the subjective quality measured by questionnaires except only one case (the system interface for the search portal domain). The results imply that the relation between the objective features and subjective questionnaires is maintained in each Internet business domain.

Conclusions and Discussion

In order to measure the architectural quality of Internet business, this study has proposed new metrics based on the three perspectives in the real world buildings. The metrics consist of six dimensions: internal stability, external security, information gathering, order processing, system interface and communication interface. Large-scale surveys in the four different domains have been conducted in order to test the construct validity and reliability of the proposed metrics, as well as to explore the technical and managerial relevance of the metrics to Internet business. In terms of the construct validity, the results of confirmatory factor analysis indicate that the six measures have a high level of convergent and discriminate validity. In terms of the reliability, the Cronbach alphas for each of the six measures for each of the four business domains indicate that the reliability is relatively high except for the internal stability, system interface, and communication interface measures in the online network games. In terms of the technical relevance, the results from the regression analysis show that we can identify several important features that are closely related to the six dimensions of architectural quality. Finally, in terms of the managerial relevance, the results from LISREL analysis show that there are strong causal relations among the three architectural constructs, user satisfaction, and customer loyalty. Therefore, we may conclude both that the six measures turn out to achieve content validity, construct validity, and reliability and that they are relevant to important technical and managerial aspects of Internet business.

The study results have several implications from the theoretical and practical perspectives. From the theoretical perspective, this study first provides a comprehensive framework of architectural quality of Internet business. This is possible because we used

Table 10. Results of the regression analyses for online network games

Architectural Dimensions	Model		Adjusted R^2 & Standardized Estimate (β)	F value	Prob.> F
Firmness					
Internal Stability	Adjusted R square of Model (R^2)		0.5369	4.64	0.04 *
	Var.	Backup of personal game information	0.2757 (β)	9.27	0.01 *
		Provision of monitoring group to analyze game error	0.0532	3.32	0.10
External Security	Adjusted R square of Model (R^2)		0.5585 (β)	5.69	0.02 *
	Var.	Provision of stipulation on personal information protection	0.0718 (β)	7.27	0.02 *
		Provision of transaction stipulation	-0.0562	4.64	0.06
Convenience					
Information Gathering	Adjusted R square of Model (R^2)		0.7636	6.46	0.01 *
	Var.	Provision of information on game rules	0.1080 (β)	14.19	0.00 **
		Provision of help information on command	0.0912 (β)	6.50	0.03 *
		Provision of game scenario related information	0.1375 (β)	16.17	0.00 **
		Provision of character related information	-0.0305 (β)	3.13	0.11
Order Processing	Adjusted R square of Model (R^2)		0.4136	4.23	0.04 *
	Var.	Variety of game tool (e.g. short distance weapon, defense weapons...)	0.0727 (β)	7.35	0.01 *
		Provision of game preview	0.0697	4.86	0.04 *

** $p<0.01$, * $p<0.05$

the conceptual model of architectural quality for buildings as an organizational guidance. The comprehensive framework leads us to include important dimensions that had not been dealt in previous studies. Representational delightfulness, for example, has not been used as an evaluation measure for the quality of Internet businesses previously (Liu & Arnett, 2000). Second, this study aims at both the rigor of the metrics validation and the relevance of the metrics to the technical and managerial aspects of Internet business.

Table 10. Results of the regression analyses for online network games (cont.)

Architectural Dimensions	Model		Adjusted R^2 & Standardized Estimate (β)	F value	Prob.> F
Delight					
System Interface	Adjusted R square of Model (R^2)		0.3235	5.74	0.03 *
	Var.	Variety of view perspective (e.g. quarter view, top view, side view...)	0.0507 (β)	5.74	0.03 *
Communication Interface	Adjusted R square of Model (R^2)		0.8140	15.32	0.00 **
	Var.	Function to create initial Identity (e.g. character, gender...)	0.1645 (β)	27.36	0.00 **
		Variety of communication channels among game users	-0.0352 (β)	2.96	0.12

** $p<0.01$, * $p<0.05$

In terms of the rigor, the construct validity was confirmed by the two-step factor analysis, and the reliability was tested by the Cronbach alphas. In terms of the relevance, the technical aspects were explored through the regression analysis identifying the relations between subjective measures and objective features, and the managerial aspects were explored through the LISREL analysis testing the causal relations among the latent constructs. Achieving both rigor and relevance of the proposed metrics significantly increases the usefulness of the proposed metrics (Davenport & Markus, 1999; Benbasat & Zmud, 1999). Finally, a large-scale survey, which had hardly been made in architectural quality metrics previously, was conducted in four different domains. The results indicate that the six measures are faithfully measuring the three constructs, which turned out to be important in increasing the satisfaction and loyalty of customers.

From the practical perspective, the metrics can be used to diagnose the current architectural quality of Internet business. The generalizability of the metrics allows us to use the metrics safely in various types of Internet business. The metrics are currently being used by the Internet Business Research Center in producing consumer reports for various Internet businesses (ibiz.re.kr), as well as by a major news company in evaluating contest entrants for the best Internet business awards (www.chosun.com).

Second, the metrics can be used to provide guidelines of how the architectural quality of Internet business can be enhanced. The relevance of the metrics enables us to provide concrete suggestions in terms of system features, which have close relations to user satisfaction and customer loyalty. A professional Web consulting company is currently using the metrics for commercial purposes. Finally, the metrics may allow Internet businesses to benchmark themselves against their own past performance.

Acknowledgments

The author appreciates the supports from members of Human Computer Interaction Lab and the Internet Business Research Center at Yonsei University. The research is funded by the Korean Research Foundation (KRF-2002-005-H20002).

References

Adam, N., Awerbuch, B., Slonim, J., Wegner, P. & Yesha, Y. (1997). Globalizing business, education, culture through the Internet. *Communications of ACM, 40*(2), 115-121.

Bauer, C., & Scharl, A. (2000). Quantitative evaluation of Web site content and structure. *Internet Research: Electronic Networking Applications and Policy, 10*(1), 31-43.

Bell, H., & Tang, N. (1998). The effectiveness of commercial Internet Web sites: A user's perspective. *Internet Research: Electronic Networking Applications and Policy, 8*(3), 219-228.

Benbasat, I., & Zmud, R. (1999). Empirical research in information systems: The practice of relevance. *MIS Quarterly, 23* (1), 3-16.

Benjamin, R. I. (1995). Electronic markets and virtual chains on the information superhighway. *Sloan Management Review, 36*(1), 62-72.

Berry, L. (1995). Relationship marketing of services: Growing Interest, emerging perspectives. *Journal of the Academy of Marketing Science, 23*(4), 236-245.

Bhimani, A. (1996). Securing the commercial Internet. *Communication of ACM, 39*(6), 29-35.

Boudreau, M., Gefen, D., & Straub, D. (2001). Validation in IS research: A state-of-the-art assessment. *MIS Quarterly, 25*(1), 1-24.

Britannica (2001). Commodity, firmness, and delight: The ultimate synthesis. Online *Encyclopedia Britannica* article. Available: *http://www.britannica.com/eb/article?eu=119280*

Chau, P. Y. K., Au, G., & Tam, K. Y. (2000). Impact of information presentation modes on online shopping: An empirical evaluation of a broadband interactive shopping service. *Journal of Organizational Computing and Electronic Commerce, 10*(1), 1-22.

Czepiel, J. A., & Gilmore, R. (1987). Exploring the concept of loyalty in services. In J.A. Czepiel, C. A. Congram, & J. Shanahan (Eds.), *The services challenge: Integrating for competitive advantage* (pp. 91-94). Chicago, IL: American Marketing Association.

Daft, R., & Lengel, R. (1986). Organizational information requirements, media richness and structural design. *Management Science, 32*(5), 554-571.

Davenport, T., & Markus, L. (1999). Rigor vs. relevance revisited: Response to Benbasat and Zmud. *MIS Quarterly, 23* (1), 19-23.

Davis, F.D. (1989). Perceived usefulness, perceived ease of use, and user acceptance of information technology. *MIS Quarterly, 13*(3), 319-340.

Day, A. (1997). A model for monitoring web site effectiveness. *Internet Research: Electronic Networking Applications and Policy, 7*(2), 109-115.

Forrester Research, *Forrester Research*, 25/04/99.

Giedion, S. (1941). *Space, time, and architecture: The growth of a new tradition.* Cambridge, MA: Harvard University Press.

Gomez. (2001). Consumer evaluation. Available: *www.gomezpro.com*

Gonzales, M., Fernandez, C., & Cameselle, J. (1997). Empirical validation of a model of user satisfaction with buildings and their environments as workplaces. *Journal of Environmental Psychology, 17*, 69-74.

Ho, C. F., & Wu, W. H. (1999). Antecedents of customer satisfaction on the Internet: An empirical study of online shopping. *Proceeding of the 32nd Hawaii International Conference on System Sciences* (pp. 1-9).

Hoffman, D. L., & Novak, P. T (1996). Marketing in hypermedia computer-mediated environments: Conceptual foundations. *Journal of Marketing, 60*(July), 50-68.

Huang, K. T., & Yang, W.-E. (1999). *Quality information and knowledge.* Upper Saddle River, NJ: Prentice Hall.

Huizingh, E. (2000). The content and design of Web sites: An empirical study. *Information and Management, 37*(3), 123-134.

Kalakota, R., & Whinston, A. (1996). *Frontiers of electronic commerce.* MA: Addison Wesley.

Kapor, M. (1996). A software design manifesto. In T. Winograd, J. Bennett, L. De Young, P. S. Gordon, & B. Hartfield (Eds.), *Bringing design to software* (pp. 1-9). Reading, MA: Addison-Wesley.

Kim, J. (1997). Toward the construction of customer interfaces for cyber shopping malls. HCI Research for the electronic commerce. *International Journal of Electronic Commerce and Business Media, 7*(2), 12-15.

Kim, J. (1999). *Internet Business.com.* Seoul, Korea: YoungJin Publishing.

Kim, J., Kim, J., Lee, H., & Suh, G. (2000). *Suggestions and strategies for the expansion of Korean EC markets: An analysis of factors affecting customer oriented EC success.* Seoul, Korea: National Computerization Agency.

Kim, J., & Moon, J. (1998). Designing towards emotional usability in customer interface: Trustworthiness of cyber-banking system interfaces. *Interacting with Computers, 10*, 1-29.

Kim, J., & Yoo, B. (2000). Toward the optimal link structure of the cyber shopping mall. *International Journal of Human Computer Studies, 52*(3), 531-551.

Kodama, M. (1999). Strategic business applications and new virtual knowledge-based businesses through community-based information networks. *Information Management & Computer Security, 7*(4), 186-199.

Lewis, J. R. (1995). IBM computer usability satisfaction questionnaires: Psychometric evaluation and instructions for use. *International Journal of Human-Computer Interaction, 7*(1), 57-78.

Liang, T. P., & Huang, J. S. (1998). An empirical study on consumer acceptance products in electronic markets: A transaction cost model. *Decision Support System, 24*(1), 29-43.

Liao, Z., & Cheung, M. T. (2001). Internet-based e-shopping and consumer attitudes: An empirical study. *Information & Management, 38*, 299-306.

Liu, C., & Arnett, K. P. (2000). Exploring the factors associated with web site success in the context of electronic commerce. *Information & Management*, 38(1), 23-33.

Liu, C., Arnett, K.P., Calella, L., & Beatty, B. (1997). Web sites of the Fortune 500 companies: Facing customer through home pages. *Information and Management, 31*(1), 335-345.

Lohse, G. L., & Spiller, P. (1998). Electronic shopping: The effect of customer interfaces on traffic and sales. *Communications of the ACM, 41*(7), 81-88.

Lucas, A. (1996). What in the world is electronic commerce. *Sales and Marketing Management, 148*(6), 24-29.

Margherio, L., Henry, D., Cooke, S., & Montes, S. (1998). The emerging digital economy. U.S. Dept. of Commerce, Washington, DC. Available: *http://www.ecommerce.gov/emerging.htm*

Miles, G. E., Howes, A., & Davies, A. (2000). A framework for understanding human factors in Web-based electronic commerce. *International Journal of Human-Computer Studies, 52*, 131-163.

Mitchell, T. (1995). *City of bits: Space, place, and the Infobahn.* Cambridge, MA: MIT Press.

Moran, T. P. (1981). The command language grammar: A representation for the user interface of interactive systems. *International Journal of Man-Machine Studies, 15*(1), 3-50.

Mulligan, J. (1998). Online gaming: Why won't they come? *Gamasutra*, 2. Available: *http://www.gamasutra.com/features/*

National Computer Board (1997). Internet Web site launched for secure electronic commerce project, Singapore National Computer Board Corporate Publication, Singapore.

Nel, D., Niekerk, R. V., Berthon, J., & Davies, T. (1999). Going with the flow: Web sites and customer involvement. *Internet Research: Electronic Networking Applications and Policy, 9*(2), 09-116.

Nielsen, J. (1997). Loyalty on the web. Alertbox, useit.com. Available: *http://www.useit.com/alertbox/9708a.html*

O'Keefe, R. M., & McEachern, T. (1998). Web-based customer decision support systems. *Communication of ACM, 41*(3), 71-78.

Panurach, P. (1996). Money in electronic commerce: Digital cash, electronic fund transfer, and e-cash. *Communication of ACM, 39*(6), 45-50.

Park, J. & Kim, J. (2000). Contextual navigation aids for two World Wide Web systems. *Internation Journal of Human Computer Interaction, 12*(2), 193-217.

Perry, M., & Bodkin, C. (2000). Content analysis of Fortune 100 company Web sites. *Corporate Communications, 5*(2), 87-96.

Preiser, W., Rabinowitz, H., & White, E. (1988). *Post-occupancy evaluation.* New York: Van Nostrand Reinhold.

Rasmussen, S. (1959). *Experiencing architecture.* Cambridge, MA: MIT Press.

Rhee, S., & Riggins, F. (1999). *Internet user's perception of World Wide Web vendors and their support of consumer mercantile activities.* In Center for electronic commerce at the Dupree college of Management at Georgia Tech.

Rice, M. (1997). What makes users revisit a Web site? *Marketing News, 31*(6), 12.

Rose, G., Khoo, J., & Straub, D. W. (1999). Current technological ipediments to business-to-consumer electronic commerce. *Communications of the AIS, 1*(16), 1-74.

Rosenfeld, L., & Morville, P. (1998). *Information architecture for the World Wide Web.* Cambridge, MA: O'Reilly.

Salkin, S. (1999). Fear of buying. *Logistics Management and Distribution Report, 38*(5), 101-102.

Schmid, B. (1995). *Electronic mall: Banking and shopping in Globalen Netzen.* Stuttgart: Teubner.

Seddon, P. (1997). A respecification and extension of the DeLone and McLean model of IS success. *Information Systems Research, 8*(3), 240-253.

Selz, D., & Schubert, P. (1998). Web assessment – A model for the evaluation and the assessment of successful electronic commerce applications. *Proceedings of Thirty-First Annual Hawaii International Conference on System Sciences* (Vol. 4, pp. 222-223).

Shankar, B. (1996). Electronic commerce will be a big business. *Telecommunications, 30*(7), 24.

Smith, A.G. (1997). Testing the surf: Criteria for evaluating Internet information resources. *The Public Access Computer Systems Review, 8*(3), 5-23.

Straub, D.W. (1989). Validating instruments in MIS research. *MIS Quarterly, 13*(2), 147-169.

Sullivan, J. (1999). What are the functions of corporate home pages? *Journal of World Business, 34*(2).

The Yankee Group. (2001). The Yankee Group 2001 Predictions- Updated January 5, 2001. Available: *http://www.yankeegroup.com/*

Web objectives research. How Web site evaluation works. Available: *http://www.surveysite.com/newsite/docs/howork.htm*

Webby Awards (2001). Judging criteria. Available: *http://www.webbyawards.com/judging/criteria.html*

Wilde, W., & Swatman, P. (1997). Toward virtual communities in rural Australia. *International Journal of Electronic Commerce, 2*(1), 43-60.

Wilson, E., Morrison, J., & Napier, A. (1997). Perceived effectiveness of computer mediated communications and face-to-face communications in student software development teams. *Journal of Computer Information Systems, 48*, 484-495.

Winograd, T., & Tabor, P. (1996). Software design and architecture. In T. Winograd, J. Bennett, L. De Young, P. S. Gordon, & B. Hartfield (Eds.), *Bringing design to software* (pp. 10-16). Reading, MA: Addison-Wesley.

Zimring, C. M., & Reizenstein, J. (1980). Post-occupancy evaluation: An overview. *Environment and Behavior, 12*(4), 429-450.

Zona Research Inc. (2000). Web robustness measurement: The future may be now. *Zona Market Report*, Issue 37.

Chapter VII

The eQual Approach to the Assessment of E-Commerce Quality: A Longitudinal Study of Internet Bookstores

Stuart J. Barnes
Victoria University of Wellington, New Zealand

Richard Vidgen
University of Bath, UK

Abstract

Understanding the customer is a key aspect of developing any e-commerce offering. In doing so, organizations can improve their offerings over time and benchmark against competitors and best practice in any industry. eQual is a method for assessing the quality of Web sites. The eQual instrument has evolved via a process of iterative refinement in different e-commerce domains. Two of the studies conducted have examined online bookshops as a domain for e-commerce quality evaluation, one based on eQual 2.0 and the other on eQual 4.0. In this chapter we aim to examine these studies, and, as a result, to evaluate the use of the instrument and the benchmarking of the bookshops on two separate occasions. Of particular note are whether the findings are consistent across the two studies and the implications of the findings for e-commerce practice. Finally, the paper rounds off with some conclusions and directions for further research.

Introduction

Adapting to the needs of the consumer is an important part of commercial activity on the Internet; where competitors are just one click away, building and maintaining a relationship requires continuous innovation and investment. Moreover, the level of innovation and transformation far exceeds that of the traditional business world, with one year of "Internet time" estimated to be equivalent to five years in mainstream business. In such a dynamic environment, pragmatic methods are needed to assess the extent to which Web sites meet customer needs.

This chapter utilizes the eQual method (previously called WebQual) to assess Web quality in a specific domain: online bookshops. The eQual instrument has been under development since the early part of 1998 and has evolved via a process of iterative refinement in different Web domains. Previous applications of eQual include UK business school Web sites (Barnes & Vidgen, 2000), Internet bookshops (Barnes & Vidgen, 2001a, 2002), small companies (Barnes & Vidgen, 2001b), online auction houses (Barnes & Vidgen, 2001c), and national or international government organizations (Barnes & Vidgen, 2003a, 2003b, 2003c). The method turns qualitative customer assessments into quantitative metrics that are useful for management decision-making. Typically, the tool allows comparisons to be made between organizations in the same industry or for the same organization over time.

The structure of the chapter is as follows. Next, we give the rationale and background to the development of eQual. Then, the research design is described, including a review of the domain in which eQual is deployed in this chapter — Internet bookshops. The following sections report the data analysis and preliminary findings, which are discussed and interpreted. Finally, the chapter provides a summary and makes recommendations for future work.

The Provenance of eQual

This section describes the development of the eQual instrument and method, from versions 1.0 through 4.0, and its application in a number of domains.

eQual 1.0

The first version of the eQual instrument was developed in the domain of UK business schools (Barnes & Vidgen, 2000). The development methodology for the instrument was to use quality function deployment (QFD), which is a "structured and disciplined process that provides a means to identify and carry the voice of the customer through each stage of product and or service development and implementation" (Slabey, 1990). The starting point for QFD is to articulate the "voice of the customer" and to this end we ran a quality workshop in August 1998 with six master's students. Bossert (1991) recommends a three-stage process for a quality workshop: establish a single issue for discussion; collect quality requirements and functions using post-it notes; and, use affinity grouping to gather requirements into categories that make sense to the customer.

The single issue for discussion was: "What are the qualities of an excellent business school Web site?" Delegates worked individually writing out their ideas onto post-it notes and were encouraged to put down a brief phrase together with a longer sentence to explain the rationale for the proposed quality. The delegates were then allocated to two teams and asked to combine their qualities into affinity groups (a tree-structured list), initially working in silence to move the post-its around and creating headings as they felt appropriate. Finally, the two teams were brought back together to produce a single consolidated list of demanded qualities. By the end of the session we had collected 54 raw qualities which were structured hierarchically into affinity groupings.

From the raw qualities a pilot questionnaire with 35 questions was developed. This was completed by the six attendees of the workshop and used to refine the questions. One outcome of the pilot was a recognition that the questionnaire was too long — to answer 35 questions for each of four business school Web sites involves the respondent in 140 assessments, plus a further 35 assessments of the importance of each quality. Using the literature on information quality, particularly Bailey and Pearson (1983), Delone and McLean (1992), Strong, Lee, and Wang (1997), and looking carefully for overlap of qualities the questionnaire was reduced to a more manageable 24 questions. Wherever possible, we removed questions that referred too directly to characteristics, functions, or parts of the Web site, since these represent the supplier perspective rather than the subjective user experience.

eQual 2.0

In applying eQual to B2C Web sites it became clear that the interaction perspective of quality was largely missing from eQual 1.0. Bitner, Brown, and Meuter (1990, p. 72) adopt Shostack's (1985) definition of a service encounter as "a period of time during which a consumer directly interacts with a *service*" and note that these interactions need not be interpersonal — a service encounter can occur without a human interaction element. Bitner et al. (1990) also recognize that "many times that interaction *is* the service from the customer's point of view" (p. 71). We suggest that interaction quality is equally important to the success of e-businesses as it is to "bricks and mortar" organizations (and possibly more so given the removal of the interpersonal dimension). In eQual 2.0 we therefore extended the interaction aspects by adapting and applying the work on service quality, chiefly SERVQUAL (Parasuraman, 1995; Parasuraman, Zeithaml, & Berry, 1988, 1991, 1995; Zeithaml, Parasuraman, & Berry, 1990, 1993) and IS SERVQUAL (Pitt, Watson, & Kavan, 1995, 1997; Kettinger & Lee, 1997; Van Dyke, Kappelman, & Prybutok, 1997), to a Web site evaluation of online bookshops. As with eQual 1.0, quality workshops were conducted to elicit customer requirements, this time in the domain of Internet bookshops (see Barnes & Vidgen, 2001a, for a full account).

eQual 3.0

While eQual 1.0 was strong on information quality, it was less strong on service interaction. Similarly, where eQual 2.0 emphasized interaction quality it lost some of the information quality richness of eQual 1.0. Both instruments contained a range of qualities concerned with the Web site as a software artifact. In reviewing the instruments we found that all of the qualities could be categorized into three distinct areas: site quality, information quality, and service interaction quality. This new version of eQual (3.0) was tested in the domain of online auctions (Barnes & Vidgen, 2001c).

eQual 4.0

Analysis of the results of eQual 3.0 led to the identification of three dimensions of e-commerce Web site quality: usability, information quality, and service interaction quality. The core qualities of eQual 4.0 are shown in Table 1, along with literature support. This instrument has been applied in a number of studies (Barnes & Vidgen, 2002, 2003a, 2003b, 2003c). Usability has replaced site quality in eQual version 4.0 because it keeps the emphasis on the user and their perceptions rather than on the designer and the site as simply a context-free software artifact. The term usability also reflects better on the level of abstraction of the other two dimensions of eQual — information and service interaction. In eQual 4.0, the usability dimension draws from literature in the field of human computer interaction (Davis, 1989, 1993, Nielsen, 1993) and more latterly Web usability (Nielsen, 1999, 2000a; Spool, Scanlon, Schroeder, Snyder, & DeAngelo, 1999). Usability is concerned with the pragmatics of how a user perceives and interacts with a Web site: is it easy to navigate? Is the design appropriate to the type of site? It is not, in the first instance, concerned with design principles such as the use of frames or the percentage of white space, although these are concerns for the Web site designer who is charged with improving usability.

Thus, eQual has evolved using quality workshops, factor analysis to identify question groupings, and literature from three core research areas: information quality from mainstream IS research; service interaction quality from marketing (as well as some IS and e-commerce sources); and usability from human-computer interaction. We ran quality workshops at every stage of eQual's development to ensure that the qualities were relevant, particularly where they relate to pre-Internet literature and new industries. We also found some items that are not adequately captured in the extant research — in particular, those questions in Table 1 that do not have a primary source. In this case, emphasis was placed on providing secondary literature support for these qualities.

Table 1. Provenance of eQual

Category	*eQual 4.0 Questions*	*eQual 2.0 Questions*	*Illustrative Support for Questions*
Usability	1. I find the site easy to learn to operate		Bailey & Pearson 1983; Davis et al., 1989; Davis, 1989, 1993
	2. My interaction with the site is clear and understandable	{Has things where you expect to find them (Q13)} {Is easy to find your way around (Q12)} {Has fast navigation to information (Q8)}	Davis et al., 1989; Davis, 1989, 1993
	3. I find the site easy to navigate		Nielsen, 1999, 2000a; Spool, 1999
	4. I find the site easy to use		Davis et al., 1989; Davis, 1989, 1993; Nielsen, 1993, 1999, 2000a
	5. The site has an attractive appearance	Has an attractive appearance (Q1)	Nielsen, 2000a; Parasuraman et al., 1988, 1991; Pitt et al., 1995, 1997
	6. The design is appropriate to the type of site	Has an appropriate style of design for site type (Q2)	From eQual workshops; tangential to research on customer expectations of appearance, e.g., Zeithaml et al., 1990
	7. The site conveys a sense of competency	Gives a professional and competent image (Q9) Can process transactions competently (Q9)	Parasuraman et al., 1988, 1991; Pitt et al., 1995, 1997; Zeithaml et al., 1990, 1993
	8. The site creates a positive experience for me	Creates an audio-visual experience (Q3)	Moon & Kim, 2001; Nielsen 2000a
Information	9. Provides accurate information	Provides information which is free from errors (Q5)	Bailey & Pearson, 1983; Strong et al., 1997; Wang, 1998
	10. Provides believable information	-	Strong et al., 1997; Wang, 1998
	11. Provides timely information	Provides up-to-date information (Q6)	Bailey & Pearson, 1983; Strong et al., 1997; Wang, 1998
	12. Provides relevant information	-	Bailey & Pearson, 1983; Strong et al., 1997; Wang, 1998
	13. Provides easy to understand information	Provides information content that is easy to understand (Q19)	Bailey & Pearson, 1983; Strong et al., 1997; Wang, 1998
	14. Provides information at the right level of detail	Provides information at an appropriate level of detail (Q20)	Bailey & Pearson, 1983; Strong et al., 1997; Wang, 1998
	15. Presents the information in an appropriate format	Communicates information in an appropriate format (Q21)	Bailey & Pearson. 1983; DeLone & McLean, 1992; Wang, 1998
Service Interaction	16. Has a good reputation	Is a site with a good reputation (Q14)	Aaker & Joachimsthaler, 2000; Nielsen 1999; Zeithaml et al., 1990, 1993
	17 It feels safe to complete transactions	Feels safe to complete transactions (Q16)	Parasuraman et al., 1988, 1991; Pitt et al., 1995, 1997; Zeithaml et al., 1990, 1993
	18. My personal information feels secure	-	Hoffman et al., 1999; Wang, 1998
	19. Creates a sense of personalization	Provides content tailored to the individual (Q22) Can customize products or prices (Q23)	McKenna, 2000; Parasuraman et al., 1988, 1991; Pitt et al., 1995, 1997; Zeithaml et al., 1988, 1990, 1993
	20. Conveys a sense of community	Conveys a sense of community appropriate to the user (Q24)	Chang et al., 1998; Hagel & Armstrong, 1997
	21. Makes it easy to communicate with the organization	Makes it easy to give feedback or contact the organization (Q18)	Bitner et al., 2000; Jarvenpaa et al., 2000; Hoffman et al., 1999; Nielsen 2000a
	22. I feel confident that goods/services will be delivered as promised	Gives confidence that it will deliver products or services (Q17) Gives a time of delivery for products or services (Q7) Guarantees services or products offered (Q15) Can be depended on to provide whatever is promised (Q4)	Parasuraman et al., 1988, 1991; Pitt et al., 1995, 1997; Zeithaml et al., 1990, 1993
-	-	Is easy to find and to return to (Q11)	From eQual workshops

Research Methodology and Research Domain

Both eQual 2.0 and eQual 4.0 were applied to the domain of Internet bookstores. This gives us a common basis for longitudinal comparison. This section describes in more detail the domain of research and the specifics of the methodology used.

Internet Bookstores Evaluated

In each application of eQual to Internet bookstores, three Web sites were examined. Buying books over the Internet is one of the early applications of B2C e-commerce and has matured to become relatively stable, at least in Internet terms, with 5.4 percent of total global book sales in 1999 (Mintel, 2000). Further, the growth of online bookstores and the role of players such as Amazon — with more than half of the online book market — is well documented (Chircu & Kauffman, 2001; Kalakota & Robinson, 1999).

For the most recent version of eQual (version 4.0), the bookshops chosen for the research were Amazon, Bertelsmann Online (BOL) and the Internet Bookshop (IBS). These are currently considered the largest players in the UK Internet bookstore market (Mintel, 2000). The application of eQual 2.0 focused on Amazon, IBS and Blackwells. Therefore, two major Internet bookstores were common to the studies, and the four bookshops examined were:

- **Amazon.** Amazon.com was launched in July 1995. However, although Amazon.com is accessible from all over the world, in the last few years the company has also established a localized presence in other international markets — including the UK, Germany, France, and Japan — to comply with publishers' territorial rights while minimizing shipping costs. Amazon established a UK presence in 1998, amazon.co.uk, with headquarters in Slough, a town 25 miles west of London. It had an estimated annual turnover of £45 million during 1999 — 4.1 percent of the UK book market (Publishing News, 2000).
- **BOL.** Owned by the media conglomerate Bertlesmann AG, BOL (Bertelsmann Online) is the newest of the sites examined — launched in 1999. The launch of BOL follows Bertelsmann's acquisition of a 50 percent share in US-based Barnes and Noble's online book retailing subsidiary BarnesandNoble.com for $200 million in October 1998 (Mintel, 2000). Barnes and Noble is one of the world's largest booksellers with around 1000 bookstores.
- **IBS.** The Internet Bookshop was established in 1993, making it one of the UK's longest-established Internet bookstores. The owner of the IBS Web site, WH Smith, is a traditional UK high-street business, selling newspapers, books, music and stationery. WH Smith have an estimated £330 million (19.4 percent) of the UK book market (Publishing News, 2000) and is estimated to be second for Internet

sales behind Amazon.co.uk (Mintel, 2000), although there are no accurate figures for its Web operations.

- **Blackwells.** Blackwells was founded in 1879 and is the leading academic bookstore in the UK with 80 stores. Blackwells have been in the mail order business for 100 years, delivering books worldwide. Their online presence was established in 1995. By contrast with Amazon and the Internet Bookshop, Blackwells have targeted a niche market — academic books — where they have built a strong reputation and identity (Blackwells also offer a full range of non-academic books). This market positioning and identity are reflected well in their online offering.

Research Design

General Aspects of the Research Design

There are a number of ways of evaluating the quality of a Web site, including competitive analysis, scenarios, inspection, log analysis, and online questionnaires (Cunliffe, 2000). The eQual approach is to use an online questionnaire targeted at real users of an e-commerce offering. The use of students as experimental subjects can lead to results that are artificial, particularly where students are asked to perform a task of which they have little experience. However, in the case of Internet bookstores the students and staff of a university make excellent subjects given that both groups buy books as a matter of course and have considerable experience of this area of e-commerce. We were therefore comfortable that the target population would be representative of online bookstore customers and constitute a valuable market segment for book retailers.

In each study, the questionnaires were administered online. For eQual 4.0, the URL of the survey was posted on the University's home page and promoted through a mixture of posters on notice boards, e-mail, and announcements at lectures. For eQual 2.0, a smaller subset of MIS students was targeted locally. In each case, respondents were directed to the start page for the survey, where they could read a set of brief instructions and then click the "start" button. This button opened a second window that was used to collect questionnaire data (Figure 1). By clicking on the question number the user could see a dictionary entry for that item — a paragraph of text expanding on the quality and giving examples as appropriate. Questionnaires were checked online prior to submission to ensure that valid responses had been entered for all questions (an option "not applicable" was included to ensure that responses were not forced). To ensure a deeper level of commitment to the evaluation of the site the respondents were asked to find a book on the site that they would like as a prize. Respondents were asked to supply the title, price, and delivery cost. Using the terminology of Spool et al. (1999), these are "facts" that the respondent is asked to determine, which made it more likely that a respondent would engage in searching and navigating the site. Furthermore, in setting a task we aimed to maintain a more "natural" and representative flow of interaction between the user and the Web site.

Figure 1. eQual 4.0 interface

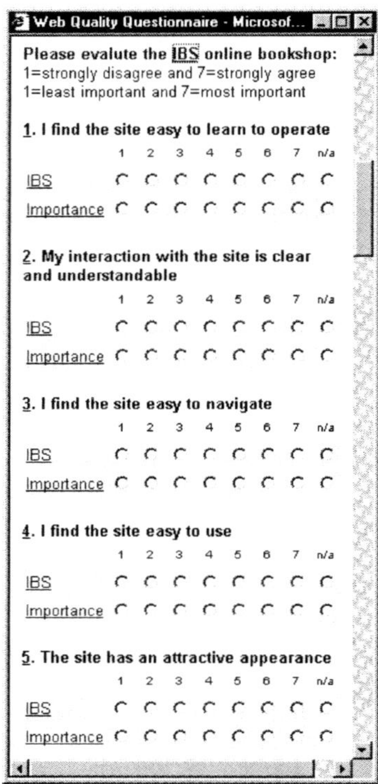

Respondents were asked to evaluate each of the sites using a Likert scale. For eQual 4.0, a 7-point scale was used (as in SERVQUAL; see Zeithaml et al., 1990) where the anchors are 1 = "strongly disagree" and 7 = "strongly agree." The importance scale was anchored with 1 = "least important" and 7 = "most important" (as recommended in the QFD literature; see King, 1989). For eQual 2.0, the mechanism was identical, except that a 5-point scale was used. The online questionnaire responses were written directly to a file, filtered to check for duplicates, and converted into a form usable in SPSS (a statistical software package) and Microsoft Excel.

In the eQual 2.0 survey we received 54 completed questionnaires from students — each of which evaluated all three Web sites. In the eQual 4.0 survey we received 376 usable responses. The latter survey involved a first prize of 250, in addition to the four book prizes. In this study we tried to address the possibility of ordering or comparison bias and each respondent evaluated only one site (selected randomly). Overall, we received 143 responses for Amazon, 117 for BOL, and 116 for the Internet Bookshop.

Data Analysis

This section reports on the results of the survey, using a variety of statistical methods for data analysis. These provide an analysis of the particular areas of strengths and weaknesses for the Web sites.

Information on the Sample

In each survey, we collected data on the book buying habits of the respondents. In each case the majority of the sample was experienced in online book purchasing. The sample is also very experienced in Internet use with a high intensity of use; more than three-quarters of the sample have used the Internet for in excess of two years with two-thirds using it more than once per day. Of the different bookstores evaluated, the market leader — Amazon.co.uk — was the most familiar for previous purchases and the tendency to buy while evaluating was greater for Amazon. In order to verify that book buying did not bias the responses, we conducted Levene's test for equality of variances and a t-test for means.

Summary of Questionnaire Data

In terms of the importance ratings for the individual questions, there were some interesting groupings for the two surveys. For eQual 2.0, those questions considered most important by the respondents — as indicated by means above the upper quartile — concern assurance and reliability regarding completion of transactions and receipt of goods, as well as ease of navigation. For eQual 4.0, the pattern was similar, with security and reliability regarding completion of transactions, receipt of goods and personal information, accuracy of content, as well as ease of site use and navigation. Conversely, when examining those items considered least important for eQual 2.0 — below the lower quartile — we find empathy with the user (customization, community), as well as aesthetics, reputation, and information format. For eQual 4.0, we find a similar pattern: empathy with the user (communication, community, and personalization), as well as site design issues (site experience, appropriateness of design, and aesthetics).

The results suggest that there are a number of priorities demanded from online bookshops by Web site users. In particular, customers are most concerned with ease of site use, finding accurate information, and being able to reliably transact and receive goods. Intuitively, these are the features one would expect as critical to an e-commerce Web site. In relative terms, there seems to be much less emphasis placed upon technical issues, which appears to be a general trend (Dutta & Segev, 2001). Interestingly though, softer qualities such as community, personalization and site experience rate quite low in importance. This is likely to be due, in part, to slow adoption and acceptance of some of these ideas in this commercial domain (Chang, Kannan, & Whinston, 1998).

There were some differences in the standard deviations of ratings for particular questions and sites, although overall, the patterns were quite similar. For example, the respondents appeared more certain about harder service interaction qualities (questions 1 to 4 in eQual 4.0) and information qualities (questions 9 to 10 and 12 to 15 in eQual 4.0), than about softer qualities such as reputation (question 16 in eQual 4.0) and empathy (questions 19 to 21 in eQual 4.0). The standard deviations and errors for the Amazon site appear lower overall than the other sites.

eQual Index

To obtain weighted scores, each respondent's site rating for a question is multiplied by the importance attached to it by the individual. Tables 2 and 3 display the average of weighted scores for each site for eQual 2.0 and 4.0. In each case, Amazon appears to rank highest, with some competition among the other players. The total weighted scores give some indication of this.

However, the weighted scores make it difficult to give an overall benchmark for the sites. One way to achieve this is to index the total weighted score for a site against the total possible score. The highest possible score that a site can achieve is the mean importance multiplied by 5 or 7, for eQual 2.0 and 4.0 respectively, the maximum rating for a question (the maximum score column in Tables 2 and 3). In Table 3, BOL, for example, achieves a

Table 2. Weighted scores and the eQual Index (EQI) for eQual 2.0 (n=54)

No.	Description	Max. Score	Amazon Wgt. Score	Amazon EQI	Blackwells Wgt. Score	Blackwells EQI	IBS Wgt. Score	IBS EQI
1	Has an attractive appearance	18.52	14.41	0.78	11.39	0.62	11.43	0.62
2	Has an appropriate style of design for site type	17.69	13.50	0.76	11.80	0.67	11.44	0.65
3	Creates an audio-visual experience	15.56	10.04	0.65	8.31	0.53	8.39	0.54
4	Can be depended on to provide whatever is promised	20.56	17.43	0.85	14.80	0.72	5.50	0.27
5	Provides information which is free from errors	20.56	16.15	0.79	15.13	0.74	14.50	0.71
6	Provides up-to-date information	20.46	16.54	0.81	14.54	0.71	14.89	0.73
7	Gives a time of delivery for products or services	19.81	17.09	0.86	14.02	0.71	14.39	0.73
8	Has fast navigation to information	20.83	17.81	0.86	15.35	0.74	15.39	0.74
9	Gives a professional and competent image	19.91	16.76	0.84	14.43	0.72	13.61	0.68
10	Can process transactions competently	20.83	18.96	0.91	18.60	0.89	6.50	0.31
11	Is easy to find and to return to	19.54	17.41	0.89	14.00	0.72	13.06	0.67
12	Is easy to find your way around	20.74	18.04	0.87	14.30	0.69	15.02	0.72
13	Has things where you expect to find them	18.89	15.76	0.83	12.98	0.69	12.78	0.68
14	Is a site with a good reputation	17.96	16.70	0.93	11.98	0.67	10.44	0.58
15	Guarantees services or products offered	20.09	16.35	0.81	14.78	0.74	13.96	0.69
16	Feels safe to complete transactions	21.67	18.50	0.85	16.13	0.74	15.31	0.71
17	Gives confidence that it will deliver products or services	21.67	18.83	0.87	16.07	0.74	15.28	0.71
18	Makes it easy to give feedback or contact the organization	18.61	14.93	0.80	13.04	0.70	13.59	0.73
19	Provides information content that is easy to understand	18.61	15.61	0.84	13.54	0.73	14.17	0.76
20	Provides information at an appropriate level of detail	18.80	15.04	0.80	13.02	0.69	13.17	0.70
21	Communicates information in an appropriate format	18.06	14.09	0.78	12.70	0.70	13.43	0.74
22	Provides content tailored to the individual	16.57	12.20	0.74	10.57	0.64	10.98	0.66
23	Can customize products or prices	16.76	10.30	0.61	9.69	0.58	9.76	0.58
24	Conveys a sense of community appropriate to the user	15.65	11.35	0.73	10.26	0.66	9.96	0.64
	TOTALS:	***458.33***	373.80	***0.82***	321.42	***0.70***	296.94	***0.65***

score of 565.00 of a maximum possible 832.91, giving it an eQual Index (EQI) of 0.68, or 68 percent. Tables 2 and 3 also show the EQI for the individual questions. Overall, Amazon is benchmarked well above the other two cyber-bookstores, with an overall EQI of 0.82 for both studies. In the first study, Blackwells follows with an EQI of 0.70, whilst IBS is close behind at 0.65. In the second study, IBS follows with an EQI of 0.70, whilst BOL is close behind at 0.68.

Table 3. Weighted scores and the eQual Index (EQI) for eQual 4.0 (n=376)

No.	Description	Max. Score	Amazon		BOL		IBS	
			Wgt. Score	*EQI*	*Wgt. Score*	*EQI*	*Wgt. Score*	*EQI*
1	I find the site easy to learn to operate	41.74	35.57	0.85	32.44	0.78	33.84	0.81
2	My interaction with the site is clear and understandable	40.73	33.29	0.82	30.62	0.75	31.99	0.79
3	I find the site easy to navigate	42.45	35.10	0.83	32.53	0.77	33.25	0.78
4	I find the site easy to use	42.22	36.20	0.86	33.27	0.79	33.61	0.80
5	The site has an attractive appearance	31.85	23.08	0.72	20.85	0.65	21.85	0.69
6	The design is appropriate to the type of site	33.21	27.31	0.82	24.67	0.74	23.08	0.69
7	The site conveys a sense of competency	37.42	32.39	0.87	27.95	0.75	28.03	0.75
8	The site creates a positive experience for me	32.08	25.15	0.78	21.32	0.66	21.02	0.66
9	Provides accurate information	43.49	36.62	0.84	31.41	0.72	33.73	0.78
10	Provides believable information	39.97	35.30	0.88	30.07	0.75	31.28	0.78
11	Provides timely information	36.30	30.38	0.84	23.78	0.65	27.77	0.76
12	Provides relevant information	40.12	33.46	0.83	29.06	0.72	31.29	0.78
13	Provides easy to understand information	40.44	34.17	0.84	31.59	0.78	33.29	0.82
14	Provides information at the right level of detail	39.64	31.16	0.79	25.84	0.65	28.95	0.73
15	Presents the information in an appropriate format	38.33	30.74	0.80	28.68	0.75	29.13	0.76
16	Has a good reputation	36.88	36.73	1.00	17.16	0.47	15.19	0.41
17	It feels safe to complete transactions	43.47	36.47	0.84	23.63	0.54	23.07	0.53
18	My personal information feels secure	42.93	34.28	0.80	22.54	0.52	23.86	0.56
19	Creates a sense of personalization	29.79	23.64	0.79	16.10	0.54	16.59	0.56
20	Conveys a sense of community	22.04	13.17	0.60	12.17	0.55	10.27	0.47
21	Makes it easy to communicate with the organization	34.59	23.88	0.69	20.33	0.59	23.28	0.67
22	I feel confident that goods/services will be delivered as promised	43.21	37.24	0.86	28.98	0.67	29.82	0.69
	TOTALS:	*832.91*	*685.32*	*0.82*	*565.00*	*0.68*	*584.21*	*0.70*

Perhaps more interesting is some conceptual assessment of how the Web sites differ in quality. For this, we need to move beyond the scores and indices of individual questions towards a set of meaningful and reliable sub-groupings. To this end, the next subsection derives a set of subcategories that are the applied to the analysis.

Scale Validity and Reliability

To better facilitate comparison between the Web sites, the research attempted to establish a number of question subgroupings. In this sense, the generation of subcategories is relatively similar to the work associated with SERVQUAL (Zeithaml et al., 1990). As a starting point, and to establish that the qualities can be disentangled and are not part of a single scale, a factor analysis was conducted on the data. The sample in eQual 2.0 was too small for factor analysis, so here we concentrate on the data for eQual 4.0. In particular, we were interested in testing the construct validity of the usability, information quality and service interaction quality groupings from earlier studies.

Factor analysis was conducted on the set of 376 cases. The Varimax factor rotation converged in 8 iterations and a relatively simple factor structure emerged. Five factors are shown quite clearly in the principal components analysis — as given in Table 4. Factor loadings in excess of 0.7 can be considered "excellent" (Comrey, 1973). The eQual groupings from Table 1 are confirmed in the data and demonstrate nomological and discriminant validity. Specifically, all the information qualities load as a single factor, whilst usability and service interaction qualities both load as two sets of factors. Usability quality consists of "usability" (questions 1 to 4) and "design" (questions 5 to 8). Service interaction quality is made up of "trust" (questions 16, 17, 18 and 22) and "empathy" (questions 19 to 21). The usability and service interaction constructs each

Table 4. Exploratory factor analysis – eQual 4.0

(Principal Components Method with Varimax Rotation; Loadings ≥ 0.55*)

	Component				
	1	2	3	4	5
Q1		.780			
Q2		.789			
Q3		.794			
Q4		.777			
Q5				.713	
Q6				.726	
Q7					
Q8				.576	
Q9	.702				
Q10	.711				
Q11	.756				
Q12	.706				
Q13	.599				
Q14	.608				
Q15	.594				
Q16			.607		
Q17			.887		
Q18			.862		
Q19					.688
Q20					.882
Q21					
Q22			.684		

* *The cutoff point for loadings is .01 significance, which is determined by calculating 2.58/√n, where n is the number of items in the questionnaire (Pitt et al., 1995)*

miss one quality — questions 7 and 16 have factor loadings less than the 0.55 cutoff point. However, the factor loadings for both questions can be considered near misses (and still significant at the 5 percent level) and consequently we have retained them in the analysis and presentation of results. These questions have loaded in other tests of eQual.

Based on the emerging factor structure, Cronbach's alpha (Cronbach, 1970) was computed to assess reliabilities of all scales and subscales. Table 5 shows the alpha reliability statistics for each scale as computed from the data, both for each site and as a mean of site scores. All of the alpha scores for the three constructs are in the range of acceptability (Nunnally, 1978). Moreover, the alpha scores of all subcategories are also acceptable — with one exception; "empathy" falls below the 0.7 mark on the IBS data set.

To summarize, there appear to be five factors in the eQual instrument. These factors can be grouped into three main components that confirm earlier research:

- **Usability.** Qualities associated with "site design" and "usability;" for example, appearance, ease of use and navigation, and the image conveyed to the user.
- **Information quality.** The quality of the content of the site: the suitability of the information for the user's purposes, for example, accuracy, format, and relevancy.
- **Service interaction quality.** The quality of the service interaction experienced by users as they delve deeper into the site, embodied by "trust" and "empathy;" for example, issues of transaction and information security, product delivery, personalization, and communication with the site owner.

As we shall see in the next section, these provide some useful insight into the company data.

Table 5. Reliability analysis for constructs – eQual 4.0

Scale	Questions	Amazon α	BOL α	IBS α	Average α
Usability	***1 to 8***	***0.88***	***0.88***	***0.87***	***0.88***
Usability	1 to 4	0.88	0.89	0.93	0.90
Design	5 to 8	0.78	0.76	0.72	0.75
Information quality	***9 to 15***	***0.89***	***0.88***	***0.90***	***0.89***
Information	9 to 15	0.89	0.88	0.90	0.89
Service Interaction quality	***16 to 22***	***0.82***	***0.85***	***0.76***	***0.81***
Trust	16 to18 and 22	0.83	0.83	0.75	0.80
Empathy	19 to 21	0.72	0.74	0.64	0.70
OVERALL	***1 to 22***	***0.93***	***0.93***	***0.92***	***0.93***

Site Analysis Using Question Subcategories

By utilizing a framework of categories, we are able to build a profile of the qualities of an individual Web site that makes it easy to compare with its rivals. Thus, we may examine why some sites fared better than others on the eQual Index. In this section we use the categories from the last section on the eQual 4.0 data, along with the eQual 2.0 categories derived from SERVQUAL.

Figure 2. Radar chart of subcategories for eQual 2.0 and eQual 4.0

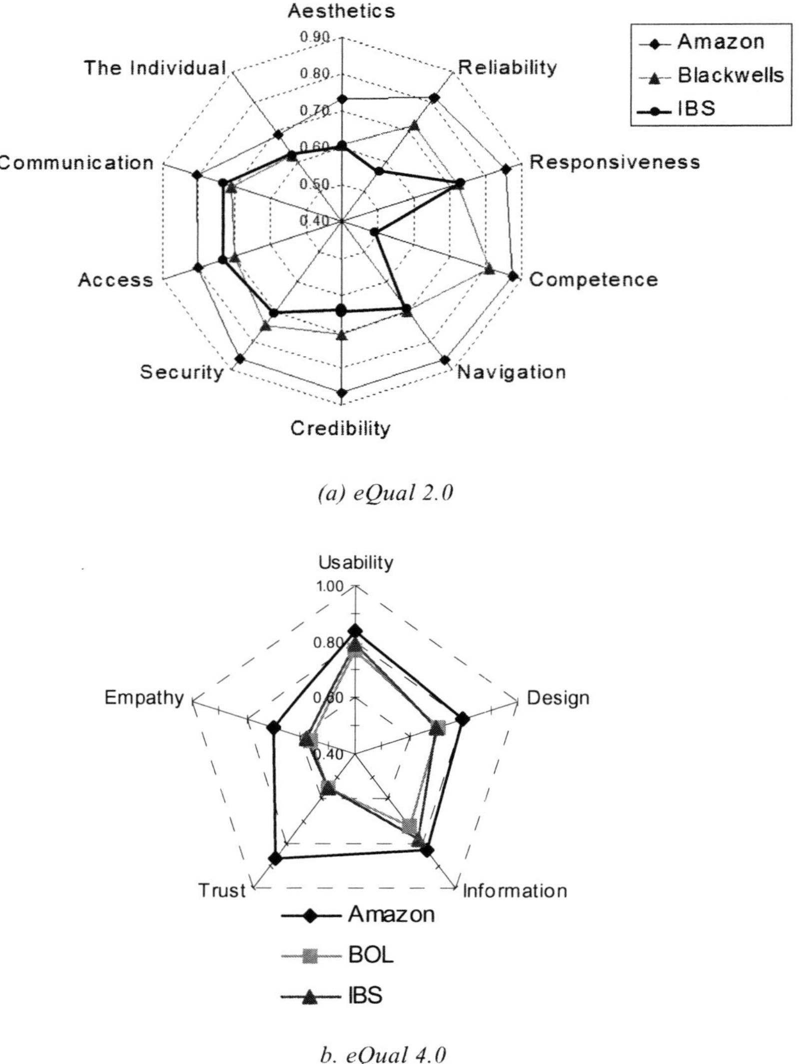

(a) eQual 2.0

b. eQual 4.0

As a starting point, the data was summarized around the five questionnaire subcategories for eQual 4.0 and 10 subcategories for eQual 2.0. Then, and similarly to the eQual Index in Table 3, the total score for each category was indexed against the maximum score (based on the importance ratings for questions multiplied by 5 or 7, for eQual 2.0 and 4.0 respectively). Figure 2 is the result, which rates the three Web sites for each study using these criteria. Note that the scale has been restricted to values between 0.4 and 0.9 (for eQual 2.0) and 0.4 and 1.0 (eQual 4.0) to allow for clearer comparison.

Figure 2 demonstrates very clearly that the Amazon UK site stands "head and shoulders" above the two rivals in both studies. The indices for the Amazon subcategories make a clear circle around the other two sites. For eQual 2.0, responsiveness, competence, navigation, credibility, and security rate particularly well. Other areas are less strong, in relative terms, although still ahead of other sites. In particular, aesthetics and understanding the individual ranked lowest for Amazon, with other categories somewhere in between. For eQual 4.0, trust rates particularly well — more than 30 points in excess of the two competitors. Other areas are less strong, in relative terms, although still four to 12 points ahead of the nearest rival. Empathy had the lowest EQI for Amazon (although still 12 points above IBS), with other categories somewhere in between. Some explanations for these results are discussed in the next section.

Of the two other sites for eQual 2.0, Blackwells appears to be the stronger, with a consistent set of rankings that combine to create a rectangle on the radar chart. Overall, the scores are around the 0.7 mark, but scoring particularly well for competence and less well for aesthetics and understanding the individual. The former is likely to be a function of the customers' experiences with the bricks-and-mortar side of the business. In contrast, the EC-only Internet Bookshop has some very discontinuous indices. Although mirroring some of the scores of Blackwells, edging ahead or just slightly behind for seven of the subcategories, IBS falls down on competence, reliability, and credibility. Apparently, this competitor is having more difficulty convincing customers that it is a trustworthy, knowledgeable, capable, and reliable alternative to the other players in the cyber-bookstore market.

The scores of the two other bookshops for eQual 4.0 are very close, with IBS edging only slightly ahead of BOL for three of the subcategories. Information quality presents the largest discrepancy — a lead of five points for IBS — with empathy and usability both two points ahead. The remaining categories contain almost equal scores.

Discussion

eQual is a useful diagnostic tool for assessing the perceived quality of an organization's e-commerce operation. The iterative process of development and integration of the literature has helped to build a degree of external validity in the instrument. It is particularly powerful when used to provide a benchmark against competitor organizations and can also be applied longitudinally to evaluate the impact of e-commerce development activities. However, despite providing a valuable profile of e-commerce quality, eQual does not provide prescriptive advice concerning how an organization might improve its e-commerce offering. In this section we consider the implications of the results of the eQual survey.

Ease of use and navigation rated high in importance for both surveys. With regard to design and navigation, the difference is more marked in both surveys, indicating that the design of the Amazon site is preferred, although this may be due in part to respondents being more likely to be familiar with the Amazon site. It is a relatively straightforward task for an organization to benchmark the usability of its Web site, for example by holding a usability workshop (Nielsen, 1993; Spool et al., 1999). Indeed, Nielsen (2000b) goes as far as to argue that five users are enough to evaluate the usability of a site.

Respondents rated "accurate information" as the most important item in the eQual 4.0 instrument. This suggests that e-commerce businesses need to pay attention to the content of their Web sites. Lack of control over content is evident when, for example, organizations do not remove special offers that have expired (a Web content management system should remove documents automatically based on an expiry date). However, managing information quality is likely to be rather more difficult than improving Web usability. Web content management is becoming a major issue for organizations; Ovum (2000) predict that the market for Web content management tools will grow from the 1999 level of $475 million to $5.3 billion by 2004. Web content management is concerned with the life cycle of Web documents, from creation through Web publishing to destruction. Whereas usability can be evaluated quickly, information quality is likely to require an enterprise-wide approach that addresses all the sources of content, encompassing authors, existing systems and databases.

Whereas usability/design and information quality might be addressed largely through internal changes, service interaction quality requires a stronger external perspective. The greatest differentiator of the sites is "trust," where Amazon is a long way ahead of its competitors. Security and trust rated high in importance for both surveys. Indeed, "trust" appears to be a key aspect of competition in e-commerce (Gefen, 2000; Jarvenpaa, Tractinsky, & Vitale, 2000).

Notwithstanding, the concept of "trust" has a degree of ambiguity; research has discovered a variety of definitions of trust, including those related to benevolence, integrity, competence, and predictability, amongst others (McKnight & Chervany, 2001). However, these ideas surface comfortably through the questionnaire items. Of the four questions that comprise "trust," three of the questions were rated as second, third, and fourth most important by respondents for eQual 4.0. For eQual 2.0, the top two questions relate to security/trust.

It is unlikely that excellent Web site design and judicious use of new technology will increase the perception of trust by customers, since trust is affected by external factors, such as the strength of the brand, the customer's previous experiences, and the whole range of communications generated by the brand-owner, the media, and word-of-mouth (Aaker & Joachimsthaler, 2000; McKenna, 2000). There are Web site design implications for "trust," such as making sure that the privacy policy is visible, and displaying the logo of a third party for accreditation of security mechanisms (Hoffman, Novak, & Peralta, 1999). However, given Amazon's first-mover advantage and the switching costs incurred by customers in moving to a competitor, other players need to go further than Web site design considerations and offer something that distinguishes them from Amazon. In the case of the Internet Bookshop and Blackwells this might involve integration of online activity with the physical high-street network of WH Smith and Blackwells respectively, and for BOL with its partner Barnes and Noble (Chircu & Kauffmann, 2001).

To improve service interaction quality an organization will need to both integrate its front office operations — Web-based or otherwise — with its back office systems (Zeithaml et al., 1988), and integrate e-marketing with traditional marketing and customer relationship management activities. Consequently, established organizations with successful e-commerce offerings may tend to be mature users who have embraced the Internet wholeheartedly rather than as a bolt-on addition to their current organizational form, for example, they pursue advanced levels of process integration. For example, the loss of traditional interpersonal elements in the move to cyberspace has implications for the removal of physical surroundings (Bitner, 1990) and service employees (Hartline & Ferrell, 1996), while virtual environments and intelligent agents can present interesting alternatives (Maes, Guttman, & Moukas, 1999).

Summary and Conclusions

eQual is a method for assessing the quality of an organization's e-commerce offering. The eQual Index gives an overall rating of an e-commerce Web site that is based on customer perceptions of quality weighted by importance. This chapter has reported two applications of different versions of eQual, versions 2.0 and 4.0, to online bookshops. The application in two separate occasions has provided some interesting insights into the similarities of perceptions of the Web sites studied.

The most recent version of eQual has three dimensions, mapped from five factors: usability (usability and design), information quality (information), and service interaction quality (trust and empathy). Organizations can address these three dimensions of Web site quality through Web site design, Web content management, and process integration respectively. Three Internet bookstores were evaluated in two surveys — Amazon and two competitors — and analysis of the survey showed Amazon to be perceived as better in all three dimensions, and particularly so with regard to "trust," which is part of service interaction quality. Given that "trust" was the most highly rated factor in terms of customer importance, this has considerable implications for the presentation and communication of e-commerce offerings — both online and via traditional channels; a considerable body of extant research suggests that "trust" is likely to be a key differentiator of future "winners" and "losers" in e-commerce (Jarvenpaa et al., 2000; McKnight, Cummings, & Chervany, 1998) and "trust building" has become a major focus for concern (Aaker & Joachimsthaler, 2000; Hoffman et al., 1999).

Future development of the eQual approach includes longitudinal studies, Web site design characteristics, and testing in further domains. The eQual 4.0 instrument was designed to ensure that all the questions could be answered without having completed the entire purchasing process. Although this approach gives an indication of user perceptions, it does not take into account lifecycle aspects of service quality. We therefore intend to follow up the eQual survey with a longitudinal study of respondents who have made purchases from online bookstores in order to make a fuller assessment of service quality. This will involve a questionnaire that looks at the delivery, after-sales service, and customer relationship management aspects of each of the bookshop's e-commerce offerings. Further work with eQual will consider how to use the results of the survey from the perspective of the supplier. For example, with regard to usability this will involve looking at design characteristics of Web sites (Nielsen, 2000a). Finally, we recognize that eQual needs to be tested in different domains, such as the public sector and e-Government, and on applications with higher degrees of complexity (e.g., online tax filing) for it to be validated as a more general assessment of Web quality.

References

Aaker, D.A., & Joachimsthaler, E. (2000). *Brand leadership.* New York: Harvard Business School Press.

Bailey, J.E., & Pearson, S.W. (1983). Development of a tool measuring and analyzing computer user satisfaction. *Management Science, 29*(5), 530-544.

Barnes, S.J., & Vidgen, R.T. (2000). WebQual: An Exploration of Web Site Quality. *Proceedings of the Eighth European Conference on Information Systems*, Vienna (July 3-5).

Barnes, S.J., & Vidgen, R.T. (2001a). An evaluation of cyber-bookshops: The WebQual method. *International Journal of Electronic Commerce, 6*, 6-25.

Barnes, S.J., & Vidgen, R.T. (2001b). Assessing the effect of a Web site redesign initiative: An SME case study. *International Journal of Management Literature, 1*(1), 113-126.

Barnes, S.J., & Vidgen, R.T. (2001c). Assessing the quality of auction Web sites. *Proceedings of the Hawaii International Conference on Systems Sciences*, Maui, Hawaii, January 4-6.

Barnes, S.J., & Vidgen, R.T. (2002). Assessing e-commerce quality with WebQual: An evaluation of the usability, information quality, and interaction quality of Internet bookstores. *Journal of Electronic Commerce Research, 3*(3), 114-127.

Barnes, S.J., & Vidgen, R.T. (2003a). Interactive e-government: Evaluating the Web site of the UK Inland Revenue. *Journal of Electronic Commerce in Organizations, 2*(1), 42-63.

Barnes, S.J., & Vidgen, R.T. (2003b). Measuring Web site quality improvements: A case study of the forum on strategic management knowledge exchange. *Industrial Management and Data Systems, 103*(5), 297-309.

Barnes, S.J., & Vidgen, R.T. (2003c). Evaluating alcohol advice Web sites: A cross-country perspective. *International Journal of Management Literature, 2*(2), 51-64.

Bitner, M. (1990). Evaluating service encounters: The effects of physical surroundings and employee responses. *Journal of Marketing*, April, 69-82.

Bitner, M.J., Brown S.W., & Meuter, M.L. (2000). Technology infusion in service encounters. *Academy of Marketing Science, 28*(1), 138-149.

Bossert, J.L. (1991). *Quality function deployment: A practitioner's approach.* WI: ASQC Quality Press.

Chang, A.M., Kannan, P.K., & Whinston, A.B. (1998). Marketing information on the I-way. *Communications of the ACM, 41*, 35-43.

Chircu, A.M., & Kauffman, R.J. (2001). Digital intermediation in electronic commerce – the eBay model. In S.J. Barnes & B.N. Hunt (Eds.), *Electronic commerce and virtual business*. Oxford: Butterworth-Heinemann.

Comrey, A. (1973). *A first course in factor analysis*. New York: Academic Press.

Cronbach, L. (1970). *Essentials of psychology testing*. New York: Harper and Row.

Cunliffe, D. (2000). Developing usable Web sites - A review and model. *Internet Research, 10*, 295-308.

Davis, F.D. (1989). Perceived usefulness, perceived ease of use, and user acceptance of information technology. *MIS Quarterly, 13*(3), 391-340.

Davis, F.D. (1993). User acceptance of information technology: System characteristics, user perceptions, and behavioral impacts. *International Journal of Man-Machine Studies, 3*, 475-487.

Davis, F.D., Bagozzi, R.P., & Warshaw, P.R. (1989). User acceptance of computer technology: A comparison of two theoretical models. *Management Science, 35*(8), 982-1003.

DeLone, W.H., & McLean, E.R. (1992). Information systems success: The quest for the dependent variable. *Information Systems Research, 3*(1), 60-95.

Dutta, S., & Segev, A. (2001). Business transformation on the Internet. In S.J. Barnes & B.N. Hunt (Eds.), *Electronic commerce and virtual business*. Oxford: Butterworth-Heinemann.

Gefen, D. (2000). E-Commerce: The role of familiarity and trust. *Omega, 28*(6), 725-737.

Hagel, J., & Armstrong, A. (1997). *Net gain: Expanding markets through virtual communities*. Boston: Harvard Business School Press.

Hartline, M., & Ferrell, O. (1996). The management of customer-contact service employees: An empirical investigation. *Journal of Marketing, 60*, 52-70.

Hoffman, D.L., Novak, T.P., & Peralta, M. (1999). Building consumer trust online. *Communications of the ACM* (4), 80-84.

Jarvenpaa, S.L., Tractinsky, N., & Vitale, M. (2000). Consumer trust in an Internet store. *Information Technology and Management, 1*(1), 45-71.

Kalakota, R., & Robinson, M. (1999). *E-business: Roadmap for success*. Berkeley: Addison Wesley.

Kettinger, W., & Lee, C. (1997). Pragmatic perspectives on the measurement of information systems service quality. *MIS Quarterly*, June, 223-240.

King, R. (1989). *Better designs in half the time: Implementing QFD*. Methuen, MA: GOAL/QPC.

Kline, P. (1994). *An easy guide to factor analysis*. London: Routledge.

Maes, P., Guttman, R., & Moukas, A. (1999). Agents that buy and sell. *Communications of the ACM, 42*(3), 81-91.

McKenna, R. (2000). Marketing in an Age of Diversity. In J.H. Gilmore & B.J. Pine (Eds.), *Markets of one*. Boston: Free Press.

McKnight, D.H., & Chervany, N.L. (2001). Conceptualizing trust: A typology and e-commerce customer relationships model. *Proceedings of the Hawaii International Conference on System Sciences*, Maui, Hawaii.

McKnight, D.H., Cummings, L.L., & Chervany, N.L. (1998). Initial trust formation in new organizational relationships. *Academy of Management Review, 23*, 473-490.

Mintel (2000). *Internet retailers*. London: Mintel International Group Limited.

Moon, J. W., & Kim, Y. G. (2001). Extending the TAM for a World-Wide-Web context. *Information and Management, 38*, 217-230.

Nielsen, J. (1993). *Usability engineering*. San Francisco: Morgan Kaufmann.

Nielsen, J. (1999). User interface directions for the Web. *Communications of the ACM, 42*(1), 65-72.

Nielsen, J. (2000a). *Designing Web usability*. IN: New Riders Publishing.

Nielsen, J. (2000b). Why you only need to test with five users. Accessed May 19, 2001: *http://www.useit.com/alertbox/20000319.html*

Nunnally, G. (1978). *Psychometric theory*. New York: McGraw-Hill.

Ovum (2000). *Web content management*. London: Ovum Ltd.

Parasuraman, A. (1995). Measuring and monitoring service quality. In W. Glynn & J. Barnes (Eds.), *Understanding services management*. Chichester, UK: Wiley.

Parasuraman, A., Zeithaml, V.A., & Berry, L. (1985). A conceptual model of service quality and its implications for future research. *Journal of Marketing, 49*, 41-50.

Parasuraman, A., Zeithaml, V.A., & Berry, L. (1988). SERVQUAL: A multiple-item scale for measuring consumer perceptions of service quality. *Journal of Retailing, 64*(1), 12-40.

Parasuraman, A., Zeithaml, V.A., & Berry, L. (1991). Refinement and reassessment of the SERVQUAL scale. *Journal of Retailing, 67*(4), 420-450.

Pitt, L., Watson, R., & Kavan, C. (1995). Service quality: A measure of information systems effectiveness. *MIS Quarterly*, June, 173-187.

Pitt, L., Watson, R., & Kavan, C. (1997). Measuring information systems service quality: Concerns for a complete canvas. *MIS Quarterly*, June, 209-221.

Publishing News (2000). UK book market. *Booksellers Association Report Library*, February. Accessed May 19, 2001: *http://www.booksellers.org.uk/newlibrary/statistics/UK%20Book%20Market%201995%2D1999%2Edoc*

Shostack, G. (1985). Planning the service encounter. In J. Czepiel, M. Solomon, & C. Surprenant (Eds.), *The service encounter*. Lexington MA: Lexington Books.

Slabey, R. (1990). QFD: A basic primer. Excerpts from the implementation manual for the three day QFD workshop. *Transactions from the Second Symposium on Quality Function Deployment*, Novi, Michigan, June 18-19.

Spool, J., Scanlon, T., Schroeder, W., Snyder, C., & DeAngelo, T. (1999). *Web site usability: A designer's guide*. San Francisco: Morgan Kaufmann.

Strong, R., Lee, Y., & Wang, R. (1997). Data quality in context. *Communications of the ACM, 40*(5), 103-110.

Van Dyke, T., Kappelman, L., & Prybutok, V. (1997). Measuring information systems service quality: Concerns on the use of the SERVQUAL questionnaire. *MIS Quarterly*, June, 195-208.

Wang, R.Y. (1998). A product perspective on total data quality management. *Communications of the ACM, 41*(2), 58-65.

Zeithaml, V.A., Berry, L., & Parasuraman, A. (1993). The nature and determinants of customer expectations of service. *Journal of the Academy of Marketing Science, 21*(1), 1-12.

Zeithaml, V.A., Parasuraman, A., & Berry, L. (1990). *Delivering quality service: Balancing customer perceptions and expectations*. New York: The Free Press.

Chapter VIII

Web Cost Estimation: An Introduction

Emilia Mendes
University of Auckland, New Zealand

Nile Mosley
MetriQ (NZ) Limited, New Zealand

Abstract

Despite the diversity of Web application types, technologies employed, and the number of free templates available on the Web, we still have a considerable amount of Web companies bidding and competing for as many Web projects as they can accommodate. Bidding and winning a proposal does not mean that the project will be developed within time and budget. Cost estimation can help managers manage projects adequately and bid for projects based on realistic and feasible costs and deadlines. The objective of this chapter is to briefly introduce cost estimation principles, followed by a literature review of Web cost estimation. Then we compare this literature according to set criteria.

Introduction

One of the top current Web search engines claims over 3 billion pages on its index[1]. In December 2001, the number of Web sites on the Internet was 36,276,25 [2]. This just gives a glimpse about the vastness of data available throughout the Web. The Web is being used as the delivery platform for numerous types of applications, ranging from e-commerce solutions with backend databases to personal static Web pages and even mystical Web sites where you can have an instant tarot reading!

The Standish Group's Chaos report published in 2003 shows that out of the more than 40,000 completed IT projects they considered only 34 percent finished on time and within budget, with required features and functions (Morris 2003). The report suggests a set of success factors, including reliable effort estimates[3]. According to the report: "If the measurement for success is based on cost and time, then having accurate estimates is essential to improving success rates."

This chapter's objective is to introduce Web cost estimation and to present previous work in the area, followed by a discussion of Web size measures, conclusions, and suggestions for future work.

Web Cost Estimation

Introduction to Cost Estimation

Several techniques for cost and effort estimation have been proposed over the last 30 years in software engineering, falling into three general categories (Shepperd, Schofield, & Kitchenham, 1996):

1. **Expert Opinion:** Expert opinion has been widely used. However, the means of deriving an estimate are not explicit and therefore not repeatable. Expert opinion, although always difficult to quantify, can be an effective estimating tool on its own or as an adjusting factor for algorithmic models (Gray, MacDonell, & Shepperd, 1999).
2. **Algorithmic Models:** Algorithmic models, to date the most popular in the literature, attempt to represent the relationship between effort and one or more project characteristics. The main "cost driver" used in such a model is usually taken to be some notion of software size (such as the number of lines of source code, number of pages, number of links). Algorithmic models need calibration or adjustment to local circumstances. Examples of algorithmic models are the COCOMO model (Boehm, 1981) and the SLIM model (Putnam, 1978).
3. **Machine Learning:** Machine learning techniques have in the last decade been used as a complement or alternative to the previous two categories. Examples include fuzzy logic models (Kumar, Krishna, & Satsangi, 1994), regression trees (Selby and Porter, 1998), neural networks (Srinivasan and Fisher, 1995), and case-based reasoning (Shepperd et al., 1996). A useful summary of these techniques is presented in Gray and MacDonell (1997b).

An advantage of algorithmic models over machine learning and expert opinion is that it allows users to see how a model derives its conclusions, an important factor for verification as well as theory building and understanding of the process being modelled (Gray and MacDonell, 1997b). Algorithmic models need to be calibrated relative to the local environment in which they are used, considered by some to be an advantage (Kok, Kitchenham, & Kirakowski, 1990; DeMarco, 1982).

Over the past 15 years, numerous comparisons have been made in software engineering between the three categories of prediction techniques aforementioned, based on their prediction power (Gray and MacDonell, 1997a; Gray and MacDonell, 1997b; Briand, El-Emam, Surmann, Wieczorek, & Maxwell, 1999; Briand, Langley, & Wieczorek, 2000; Jeffery, Ruhe, & Wieczorek, 2000; Jeffery, Ruhe, & Wieczorek, 2001; Myrtveit and Stensrud, 1999; Shepperd et al., 1996; Shepperd and Schofield, 1997; Kadoda, Cartwright, Chen, & Shepperd, 2001; Shepperd and Kadoda, 2001; Kemerer, 1987; Angelis and Stamelos, 2000; Finnie, Wittig, & Desharnais, 1997; Schofield, 1998; Hughes, 1997). However, as the datasets employed had differing characteristics (outliers, collinearity, number of features, number of cases, etc.) and engaged different comparative designs, it is of little surprise that no convergence has been obtained to date.

In addition, Shepperd and Kadoda (2001) suggest that there is a strong relationship between the success of a particular technique and training set size, nature of the "cost" function and characteristics of the dataset (outliers, collinearity, number of features, number of cases, etc.), concluding that the "best" prediction technique that can work on any type of dataset may be impossible to obtain.

Introduction to Web Cost Estimation

Over the last four years, researchers have proposed and compared cost estimation techniques for Web applications using industrial and student-based datasets (Morisio, Stamelos, Spahos, & Romano, 1999; Mendes, Counsell, & Mosley, 2000; Mendes, Mosley, & Counsell, 2001; Fewster and Mendes 2001; Mendes, Mosley, & Counsell, 2002a; Mendes, Watson, Triggs, Mosley, & Counsell, 2002b; Mendes, Mosley, & Counsell, 2003; Baresi, Morasca, & Paolini, 2002; Baresi, Morasca, & Paolini, 2003; Ruhe, Jeffery, & Wieczorek, 2003). The techniques employed to date to generate Web cost models have been case-based reasoning (CBR), linear and stepwise regressions and classification and regression trees. A detailed explanation of each of these techniques is presented in Mendes et al. (2002b).

Finally, the most common approaches to date to assess the predictive power of effort prediction models have been:

- The Magniture of Relative Error (MRE) (Kemerer, 1987)
- The Mean Magnitude of Relative Error (MMRE) (Shepperd et al., 1996)
- The Median Magnitude of Relative Error (MdMRE) (Myrtveit & Stensrud, 1999)
- The Prediction at level n (Pred[n]) (Shepperd & Schofield, 1997)

MRE is the basis for calculating MMRE and MdMRE, and defined as:

$$MRE = \frac{|e - \hat{e}|}{e} \tag{1}$$

where e represents actual effort and $\hat{e}$ estimated effort.

The mean of all MREs is the MMRE, which is calculated as:

$$MMRE = \frac{1}{n}\sum_{i=1}^{i=n}\frac{|e_i - \hat{e}_i|}{e_i} \tag{2}$$

The mean takes into account the numerical value of every observation in the data distribution, and is sensitive to individual predictions with large MREs.

An alternative to the mean is the median, which also represents a measure of central tendency, however, it is less sensitive to extreme values. The median of MRE values for the number *i* of observations is called the MdMRE.

Another indicator which is commonly used is the Prediction at level *l,* also known as Pred(*l*). It measures the percentage of estimates that are within l percent of the actual values. Suggestions have been made (Conte, Dunsmore, & Shen, 1986) that *l* should be set at 25 percent and that a good prediction system should offer this accuracy level 75 percent of the time.

Although MMRE, MdMRE, and Pred(l) have emerged as the de facto standard evaluation criteria to assess the accuracy of cost estimation models (Stensrud, Foss, Kitchenham, & Myrtveit, 2002), recent work by Kitchenham, Pickard, MacDonnell, & Shepperd (2001) shows that MMRE and Pred(l) are respectively measures of the spread and kurtosis of z, where ($z = \frac{\hat{e}}{e}$). They suggest boxplots of z and boxplots of the residuals ($e - \hat{e}$) (Pickard, Kitchenham, & Linkman, 1999) as useful alternatives to simple summary measures since they can give a good indication of the distribution of residuals and z and can help explain summary statistics such as MMRE and Pred(25) (Kitchenham et al., 2001). Finally, researchers have also employed the EMRE (Magnitude of Relative Error relative to the Estimate) (Kitchenham et al., 2001). This measure, unlike MRE, uses the estimate as the divisor, and is defined as:

$$\boldsymbol{EMRE} = \frac{|e - \hat{e}|}{\hat{e}} \tag{3}$$

Survey of Web Cost Estimation Models

This section presents a survey of Web cost estimation models proposed in the literature. Each work is described and finally summarised in Tables 16-17.

First Study: Measuring Functionality and Productivity in Web-Based Applications: A Case Study (Morisio et al., 1999)

The aim of this study (Morisio et al. 1999) was to build cost estimation models to help Web development companies predict and track development costs when new technologies are employed. This work gathered data on five Web applications developed using an object-oriented framework. Their cost estimation model takes into account the learning factor associated with writing new code that uses a framework, when this framework is used for the first time. They considered different types of reuse and the size measures employed were object-oriented function points and lines of code. Their cost models were generated using linear regression.

Their results showed that the cost of writing new code, represented by calls to components provided by the framework, is reduced as developers are more experienced in using the framework.

Second Study: Measurement and Effort Prediction for Web Applications (Mendes et al., 2000)

Mendes et al. (2000) investigated the use of case-based reasoning, linear regression, and stepwise regression techniques to estimate development effort for Web applications developed by experienced or inexperienced students. The case-based reasoning estimations were generated using a freeware tool called ANGEL developed at the University of Bournemouth, UK. The most similar Web projects were retrieved using the unweighted Euclidean distance using the "leave one out" cross-validation. Estimated effort was generated using either the closest analogue or the mean of two or three analogues. The two datasets (HEL and LEL) employed had data on Web applications developed by second-year computer science students and had 29 and 41 data points respectively. HEL represented data from students with high experience in Web development, whereas LEL had data from inexperienced students. The size measures collected were page count (total number of HTML pages created from scratch), reused page count (total number of reused HTML pages), connectivity (total number of links in the application), compactness (Botafogo, Rivlin, & Shneiderman, 1992) (scale from one to five indicating the level of inter-connectedness in the application. One represents no connections and five represented a totally connected application), Stratum (Botafogo et al. 1992), (scale from zero to one indicating how "linear" the application is. One represents no sequential navigation and five represents totally sequential navigation) and structure (topology of the application's backbone, being either sequential, hierarchical or network). Prediction accuracy was measured using MMRE and MdMRE. Results for the HEL group were statistically significantly better than those for the LEL group. In addition, case-based reasoning showed the best results overall.

Third Study: Web development: Estimating Quick-to-Market Software (Reifer, 2000)

Reifer (2000) proposed a Web cost estimation model, WEBMO, which is an extension of the COCOMO II model. The WEBMO model has nine cost drivers and a fixed effort power law, instead of seven cost drivers and variable effort power law as used in the COCOMO II model. Size is measured in Web objects, which are calculated by applying Halstead's formula for volume. They are based on sub-components such as: number of building blocks (Active X, DCOM, OLE, etc.), number of COTS components (includes any wrapper code), number of multimedia files, except graphics files (text, video, sound, etc.), number of object or application points (Cowderoy, 2000) or others proposed (number server data tables, number client data tables etc.), number of xml, sgml, html and query language lines (number lines including links to data attributes), number of Web components (applets, agents, etc.), number of graphics files (templates, images, pictures, etc.), number of scripts (visual language, audio, motion, etc.) and any other measures that companies find suitable. Reifer allegedly used data on 46 finished industrial Web projects and obtained predictions which are "repeatable and robust." However, no information is given regarding the data collection nor any summary statistics for the data.

Fourth Study: Web Metrics - Estimating Design and Authoring Effort (Mendes et al., 2001)

Mendes et al. (2001) investigated the prediction accuracy of top-down and bottom-up Web cost estimation models, generated using linear and stepwise multiple regression models. They employed one dataset with data on 37 Web applications developed by honours and postgraduate computer science students. Gathered measures were organised into five categories: length size, reusability, complexity size, effort, and confounding factors (factors that, if not controlled, could influence the validity of the evaluation), and are associated to one of the following entities: application, page, media and program. Measures for each category are presented in Tables 1-5. Prediction models were generated for each entity and prediction accuracy was measured using the MMRE metric. Results showed that the best predictions were obtained for the entity program, based on non-reused program measures (code length and code comment length).

Table 1. Size metrics

Entity Type	Metric	Description
Application	*Page Count*	Number of html or shtml files used in the Web application. *
	Media Count	Number of media files used in the application.*
	Program Count	Number of cgi scripts, Javascript files, Java applets used in the application.
	Total Page Allocation	Total space (Mbytes) allocated for all the html or shtml pages used in the application. *
	Total Media Allocation	Total space (Mbytes) allocated for all the media files used in the application. *
	Total Code Length	Total number of lines of code for all the programs used by an application.
Page	*Page Allocation*	Size of a html or shtml file, in Kbytes. *
Media	*Media Duration*	The duration (in minutes) of the media. Only applies to audio, video and animation.
	Media Allocation	Size of a media file, in Kbytes. *
Program	*Code Length*	Number of lines of code that a program has.
	Code Comment Length	Number of comment lines that a program has.
* The metric is only useful for static Web applications, where the number of dynamically generated links and/or pages is absent.		

Table 2. Reusability metrics

Entity Type	Metric	Description
Application	*Reused Media Count*	Number of reused/modified media files. *
	Reused Program Count	Number of reused/modified programs.
	Total Reused Media Allocation	Total space (Mbytes) allocated for all the reused media files used in the application. *
	Total Reused Code Length	Total number of lines of code for all the programs reused by an application.
Program	*Reused Code Length*	Number of reused lines of code.
	Reused Comment Length	Number of reused comment lines.
* The metric is only useful for static Web applications, where the number of dynamically generated links and/or pages is absent.		

Table 3. Complexity metrics

Entity Type	Metric	Description
Application	*Connectivity*	Total number of internal links[1]. We do not include dynamically generated links. *
	Connectivity Density	*Connectivity* divided by *Page Count*. *
	Total Page Complexity	$\sum_{1}^{PageCount} PageComplexity \Big/ PageCount$ *
	Cyclomatic Complexity	(*Connectivity* - *Page Count*) + 2. *
	Structure[2]	Measures how the main structure (backbone) of the application is organised: sequence, hierarchy, or network. *
Page	*Page Linking Complexity*	Number of links per page. *
	Page Complexity	Number of different types of media used on a page. Does not include text. *
	Graphic Complexity	Number of graphics media used in the page. *
	Audio Complexity	Number of audio media used in the page. *
	Video Complexity	Number of video media used in the page. *
	Animation Complexity	Number of animations used in the page. *
	Scanned Image Complexity	Number of scanned images used in the page. *
* The metric is only useful for static Web applications, where the number of dynamically generated links and/or pages is absent.		

Table 4. Effort metrics

Entity Type	Metric	Description
Application authoring and designing Tasks	*Total Effort*	*Structuring Effort + InterLinking Effort + Interface Planning + Interface Building + Link Testing Effort + Media Testing Effort*
	Structuring Effort	Estimated elapsed time (number of hours) it took a subject to structure an application.
	InterLinking Effort	Estimated elapsed time (number of hours) it took a subject to inter-link the pages in order to build the application's structure. *
	Interface Planning	Estimated elapsed time (number of hours) it took a subject to plan the application's interface.
	Interface Building	Estimated elapsed time (number of hours) it took a subject to implement the application's interface.
	Link Testing Effort	Estimated elapsed time (number of hours) it took a subject to test all the links on an application. *
	Media Testing Effort	Estimated elapsed time (number of hours) it took a subject to test all the media on an application. *
Page Authoring Task	*Total Page Effort*	*Text Effort + Page Linking Effort + Page Structuring Effort*
	Text Effort	Estimated elapsed time (number of hours) it took a subject to author or reuse text in a page.*
	Page Linking Effort	Estimated elapsed time (number of hours) it took a subject to author the links in a page.*
	Page Structuring Effort	Estimated elapsed time (number of hours) it took a subject to structure a page.
Media Authoring Task	*Media Effort*	Estimated elapsed time (number of hours) it took a subject to author or reuse a media file.
	Media Digitise Effort	Estimated elapsed time (number of hours) it took a subject to digitise a media.
	Total Media Effort	*Media Effort + Media Digitise Effort*
Program Authoring Task	*Program Effort*	Estimated elapsed time (number of hours) it took a subject to author or reuse a program.
* The metric is only useful for static Web applications, where the number of dynamically generated links and/or pages is absent.		

Table 5. Confounding factors

Entity Type	Metric	Description
Developer	*Experience*	Measures the authoring/design experience of a subject using a scale from 0 (no experience) to 4 (very good experience).
Tool	*Type*	Measures the type of tool used to author/design the Web pages: WYSIWYG, semi-WYSIWYG[1] or text-based.

Fifth Study: Measurement, Prediction, and Risk Analysis for Web Applications (Fewster & Mendes, 2001)

Fester and Mendes (2001) investigated the used of proposed a generalised linear model (GLM) for Web cost estimation. Generalised linear models provide a flexible regression framework for predictive modeling of effort. The models allow non-linear relationships between response and predictor variables, and they allow for a wide range of choices for the distribution of the response variable (e.g., effort).

Fester and Mendes (2001) employed the same dataset used in Mendes et al. (2001), however they reduced the number of size measures targeting at only the entity type application. These measures were organised into five categories: effort metrics, structure metrics, complexity metrics, reuse metrics and size metrics (see Tables 6-10).

In addition to proposing a prediction model, they also investigate the use of the GLM model as a framework for risk management. They did not measure prediction accuracy but relied on the model fit produced for the model. However a model with a good fit to the data is not the same as a good prediction model.

Table 6. Size metrics

Entity Type	Metric	Description
Application	*Page Count*	Number of html or shtml files used in the Web application. *
	Media Count	Number of media files used in the application.*
	Program Count	Number of cgi scripts, Javascript files, Java applets used in the application.
	Total Page Allocation	Total space (Mbytes) allocated for all the html or shtml pages used in the application. *
	Total Media Allocation	Total space (Mbytes) allocated for all the media files used in the application. *
	Total Code Length	Total number of lines of code for all the programs used by an application.

Table 7. Reusability metrics

Entity Type	Metric	Description
Application	*Reused Media Count*	Number of reused/modified media files. *
	Reused Program Count	Number of reused/modified programs.
	Total Reused Media Allocation	Total space (Mbytes) allocated for all the reused media files used in the application. *
	Total Reused Code Length	Total number of lines of code for all the programs reused by an application.

Table 8. Complexity metrics

Entity Type	Metric	Description
Application	*Connectivity*	Total number of internal links[1]. We do not include dynamically generated links. *
	Connectivity Density	*Connectivity* divided by *Page Count*. *
	Total Page Complexity	$\sum_{1}^{PageCount} \text{Numb. diff. types media in a page} / \text{PageCount}$ *
	Cyclomatic Complexity	(*Connectivity* - *Page Count*) + 2. *
	Structure[2]	Measures how the main structure (backbone) of the application is organised. *

Table 9. Effort metrics

Entity Type	Metric	Description
Application authoring and designing Tasks	*Total Effort*	*Structuring Effort* + *InterLinking Effort* + *Interface Planning* + *Interface Building* + *Link Testing Effort* + *Media Testing Effort* *
	Structuring Effort	Estimated elapsed time (number of hours) it took a subject to structure an application.
	InterLinking Effort	Estimated elapsed time (number of hours) it took a subject to inter-link the pages in order to build the application's structure. *
	Interface Planning	Estimated elapsed time (number of hours) it took a subject to plan the application's interface.
	Interface Building	Estimated elapsed time (number of hours) it took a subject to implement the application's interface.
	Link Testing Effort	Estimated elapsed time (number of hours) it took a subject to test all the links on an application. *
	Media Testing Effort	Estimated elapsed time (number of hours) it took a subject to test all the media on an application. *

Table 10. Confounding factors

Entity Type	Metric	Description
Developer	*Experience*	Measures the authoring/design experience of a subject using a scale from 0 (no experience) to 4 (very good experience).
Tool	*Type*	Measures the type of tool used to author/design the Web pages: WYSIWYG, semi-WYSIWYG or text-based.

Sixth Study: The Application of Case-Based Reasoning to Early Web Project Cost Estimation (Mendes et al., 2002a)

Most work on Web cost estimation proposes models based on late product size measures, such as number of HTML pages, number of images etc. However, for the successful management of software/Web projects, estimates are necessary throughout the whole development life cycle. Preliminary (early) effort estimates in particular are essential when bidding for a contract or when determining a project's feasibility in terms of cost-benefit analysis. Mendes et al. (2002a) focus on the harvesting of size measures at different points in the Web development life cycle, to estimate development effort, and

Table 11. Requirements and design measures

Metric	Description
Use Case Count (UCC)	Total number of use cases in the use case diagram.
Entity Count (EC)	Total number of entities in the entity-relationship diagram.
Attribute Count (AC)	Total number of attributes in the Entity-relationship diagram.
Node Count (NC)	Total number of nodes in the Navigation diagram.
Anchor Count (AnC)	Total number of anchors in the Navigation diagram.
Design Effort (DE)	Effort in person hours to design the application.

Table 12. Application measures

Metric	Description
Page Count (PaC)	Total number of html files.
Media Count (MeC)	Total number of original media files.
Program Length (PRL)	Total number of statements used in either Javascript or Cascading Style Sheets.
Connectivity Density (COD)	Average number of links, internal or external, per page.
Total Page Complexity (TPC)	Average number of different types of media per page.
Total Effort (TE)	Effort in person hours to design and implement the application.

their comparison based on several prediction accuracy indicators. Their aim was to investigate how different cost predictors are, and if there are any statistically significant differences between them. Their effort estimation models were generated using case-based reasoning, where several different parameters were used: similarity measure; scaling; number of closest analogues; analogy adaptation; and feature subset selection. Their study was based on data from 25 Web applications developed by pairs of postgraduate computer science students. The size measures employed are presented in Tables 11-12. The measures of prediction accuracy employed were the MMRE, MdMRE, Pred(25) and Boxplots of residuals.

Seventh Study: A Comparison of Development Effort Estimation Techniques for Web Hypermedia Applications (Mendes et al., 2002b)

An in depth comparison of Web cost estimation models is presented in Mendes et al. (2002b), where they: (1) compare the prediction accuracy of three CBR techniques to estimate the effort to develop Web applications and (2) compare the prediction accuracy of the best CBR technique, according to our findings, against three commonly used prediction models, namely multiple linear regression, stepwise regression, and regression trees. They employed one dataset of 37 Web applications developed by honours and postgraduate computer science students and the measures used are: page count (number of html or shtml files used in the application), media count (number of media files used in the application), program count (number of JavaScript files and Java applets used in the application), reused media count (number of reused/modified media files), reused program count (number of reused/modified programs), connectivity density (total number of internal links[3] divided by page count), total page complexity (average number of different types of media per page) and total effort (effort in person hours to design and author the application).

Regarding the use of case-based reasoning, they employed several parameters, as follows: three similarity measures (unweighted Euclidean, weighted Euclidean, and maximum), three choices for the number of analogies (1, 2, and 3), three choices for the analogy adaptation (mean, inverse rank weighted mean, and median) and two alternatives regarding the standardisation of the attributes ("Yes" for standardised and "No" for not standardised). Prediction accuracy was measured using MMRE, MdMRE, Pred(25) and boxplots of residuals. Their results showed that different measures of prediction accuracy gave different results. MMRE and MdMRE showed better prediction accuracy for Multiple regression models whereas boxplots showed better accuracy for CBR.

Eighth Study: An Empirical Study on the Design Effort of Web Applications (Baresi et al., 2002)

Baresi et al. (2002) conduct an exploratory study, where, using an experiment, several hypotheses are tested. Amongst these, the study investigates whether estimated effort provided by students can be used to estimate actual effort. Their results show that it is possible to use the estimated values as predictors for the actual ones, however other variables, such as size, also need to be incorporated to the model to make it more realistic and meaningful. The dataset they used had data on 39 Web applications developed by computer science students.

Ninth Study: Cost Estimation for Web Applications (Ruhe et al., 2003)

The aim of Ruhe et al.'s study (2003) was to assess whether the COBRA™[4] (Cost Estimation Benchmarking and Risk Analysis) method was adequate for estimating Web development effort accurately using data from a small Web company. COBRA is a method that aims to develop an understandable cost estimation model based on a company-specific dataset. It uses expert opinion and data on past projects to estimate development effort and risks for a new project. The size measure employed was Web objects (Reifer 2000), measured for each one of the 12 finished Web applications used in this study. The prediction accuracy obtained using COBRA was compared to those attained employing expert opinion and linear regression, all measured using MMRE and Pred(25), giving COBRA the most accurate results.

Tenth Study: Do Adaptation Rules Improve Web Cost Estimation? (Mendes et al., 2003)

This study (Mendes et al. 2003a) compared several methods of CBR-based effort estimation, investigating the use of adaptation rules as a contributing factor for better estimation accuracy. They used two datasets, where the difference between these datasets was the level of "messiness" each had. "Messiness" was evaluated by the number of outliers and the amount of collinearity (Shepperd & Kadoda, 2001). The dataset which was less "messy" than the other presented a continuous "cost" function,

Table 13. Size and complexity measures for less "messy" dataset

Measure	Description
Page Count (PaC)	Total number of html or shtml files
Media Count (MeC)	Total number of original media files
Program Count (PRC)	Total number of JavaScript files and Java applets
Reused Media Count (RMC)	Total number of reused/modified media files.
Reused Program Count (RPC)	Total number of reused/modified programs.
Connectivity Density (COD)	Average number of internal links per page.
Total Page Complexity (TPC)	Average number of different types of media per page.
Total Effort (TE)	Effort in person hours to design and author the application

Table 14. Size and complexity measures for "messier" dataset

Measure	Description
Page Count (PaC)	Total number of html files.
Media Count (MeC)	Total number of original media files.
Program Length (PRL)	Total number of statements used in either Javascript or Cascading Style Sheets.
Connectivity Density (COD)	Average number of links, internal or external, per page.
Total Page Complexity (TPC)	Average number of different types of media per page.
Total Effort (TE)	Effort in person hours to design and author the application

translated as a strong linear relationship between size and effort. The "messiest" dataset, on the other hand, presented a discontinuous "cost" function, where there was no linear or log-linear relationship between size and effort. Both datasets represented data on Web applications developed by students. Two types of adaptation were used, one with weights and another without weights (Mendes et al. 2003). None of the adaptation rules gave better predictions for the "messier" dataset, however for the less "messy" dataset one type of adaptation rule (no weights) gave good prediction accuracy. Prediction accuracy was measured using MMRE, Pred(25) and boxplots of absolute residuals. The measures for both datasets are presented in Tables 13-14.

Eleventh Study: Estimating the Design Effort of Web Applications (Baresi et al., 2003)

Baresi et al. (2003) investigated the relationship between a number of size measures obtained from W2000 design artifacts and the total effort needed to design web applications. Their size measures were organised in categories and presented in detail in Table 15. The categories employed were information model, navigation model and presentation model. They identified a few attributes that may be related to the total design effort. In addition, they also carried out a finer-grain analysis, studying which of the used measures have an impact on the design effort when using W2000. Their dataset comprised 30 Web applications developed by students.

Table 15. Measures for design model

Measure	Description
	Information model
entities	number of entities in the model
components	number of components in the model
infoSlots	number of slots in the model
slotsSACenter	average number of slots per semantic association center
slotsCollCenter	average number of slots per collection center in the model
componentsEntity	average number of components per entity
slotsComponent	average number of slots per component
SAssociations	number of semantic associations in the model
SACenters	number of semantic association centers in the model
segments	number of segments in the model
	Navigation model
nodes	number of nodes in the model
navSlots	number of slots in the model
nodesCluster	average number of nodes per cluster
slotsNode	average number of slots per node
navLinks	number of links in the model
clusters	number of clusters in the model
	Presentation model
pages	number of pages in the model
pUnits	number of publishing units in the model
prLnks	number of links in the model
sections	number of sections in the model

Table 16 summarises the studies presented previously and show a few trends such as: the prediction technique used the most is linear regression; the measures of prediction accuracy employed the most are MMRE and Pred(25); the size of the datasets employed is small and not greater than 46 data points; and size measures were not constant throughout studies, which indicates the lack of standards to sizing Web applications.

Another perspective in which we can look at previous work is determining what type of Web applications were used in the empirical studies, since they can be classified as Web hypermedia applications or Web software applications (Christodoulou, Zafiris, & Papatheodorou, 2000). A Web hypermedia application is a non-conventional application characterised by the authoring of information using nodes (chunks of information), links (relations between nodes), anchors, access structures (for navigation) and its delivery over the Web. Technologies commonly used for developing such applications are HTML, JavaScript, and multimedia. In addition, typical developers are writers, artists, and organisations that wish to publish information on the Web and/or CD-ROMs without the need to use programming languages such as Java.

Conversely, a Web software application represents conventional software applications that depend on the Web or use the Web's infrastructure for execution. Typical applications include legacy information systems such as databases, booking systems, and knowledge bases. Many e-commerce applications fall into this category. Typically they employ technology such as components off-the-shelf, like DCOM, OLE, ActiveX, XML, PHP, dynamic HTML, databases, and development solutions such as J2EE. Developers are young programmers fresh from a computer science or software engineering degree,

Table 16. Summary of literature in Web cost estimation

Study	Type (case study, experiment, survey	# datasets - (#datapoints)	Subjects (students, professionals)	Size Measures	Prediction techniques	Best technique(s)	Measure Prediction Accuracy
1st	experiment	1 - (5)	Not mentioned	Object-oriented Function Points, Lines of code	Linear regression	-	-
2nd	Case study	2 - (29 and 41)	2nd year Computer Science students	Page Count, Reused Page Count, Connectivity, Compactness, Stratum, Structure	Case based reasoning	Case based reasoning for high experience group	MMRE
3rd	Case study	1 - (46)	professionals	Web objects	WEBMO (parameters generated using linear regression)	-	Pred(n)
4th	Case study	1 - (37)	Honours and postgraduate Computer Science students	Length size, Reusability, Complexity, Size	Linear regression Stepwise regression	Linear Regression	MMRE
5th	Case study	1 - (37)	Honours and postgraduate Computer Science students	Structure metrics, Complexity metrics, Reuse metrics, Size metrics	Generalised Linear Model	-	Goodness of fit
6th	Case study	1 - (25)	Honours and postgraduate Computer Science students	Requirements and Design measures, Application measures	Case-based reasoning		MMRE, MdMRE, Pred(25), Boxplots of residuals
7th	Case study	1 - (37)	Honours and postgraduate Computer Science students	Page Count, Media Count, Program Count, Reused Media Count, Reused Program Count, Connectivity Density, Total Page Complexity	Case-based reasoning, Linear regression, Stepwise regression, Classification and Regression Trees	Linear/ stepwise regression or case-based reasoning (depends on the measure of accuracy employed)	MMRE, MdMRE, Pred(25), Boxplots of residuals
8th	experiment	1 - (39)	Computer Science students	Estimated effort	Linear regression	-	-
9th	Case study	1 - (12)	professionals	Web Objects	COBRA, Expert opinion, Linear regression	COBRA	MMRE, Pred(25), Boxplots of residuals
10th	Case study	2 - (37 and 25)	Honours and postgraduate CS students	Page Count, Media Count, Program Count, Reused Media Count (only one dataset) Reused Program Count (only one dataset), Connectivity Density, Total Page Complexity	Case-based reasoning	-	MMRE, Pred(25), Boxplots of absolute residuals
11th	experiment	1 - (30)	Computer Science students	Information model measures, Navigation model measures, Presentation model measures	Linear regression	-	-

Table 17. Types of Web applications used in Web cost estimation studies

Study	Type of Web application: Web hypermedia or Web software application
1st	Web software applications
2nd	Web hypermedia applications
3rd	Not documented
4th	Web hypermedia applications
5th	Web hypermedia applications
6th	Web hypermedia applications
7th	Web hypermedia applications
8th	Web software applications
9th	Web software applications
10th	Web software applications
11th	Web hypermedia applications

managed by more senior staff. Table 17 presents the classification, indicating that six (55 percent), out of the 11 papers referenced in this section, have used datasets of Web hypermedia applications, and another four (36 percent), out of 11 papers, have used Web software applications.

Conclusion

Software practitioners recognise the importance of realistic estimates of effort to the successful management of software projects, the Web being no exception. Having realistic estimates at an early stage in a project's life cycle allow project managers and development organisations to manage resources effectively.

In the context of Web development, cost estimation is also crucial, and very challenging given that:

- Web projects have short schedules and a fluidic scope (Pressman, 2000).
- There is no standard to sizing Web applications since they can be created using diverse technologies such as several varieties of Java (Java, servlets, Enterprise java Beans, applets, and Java Server Pages), HTML, JavaScript, XML, XSL, and so on.
- Web development differs substantially from traditional approaches (Reifer, 2002).
- A Web project's primary goal is to bring quality applications to market as quickly as possible, varying from a few weeks (Pressman, 2000) to six months (Reifer, 2002).
- People involved in Web development are represented by less experienced programmers, users as developers, graphic designers and new hires straight from university (Reifer, 2002).

- Typical project size is small, using three to seven team members (Reifer, 2002).
- Processes employed are in general ad hoc, although some organisations are starting to look into the use of agile methods (Ambler, 2002).

This chapter has presented a survey of previous work in Web cost estimation and has summarised their findings. This helps organise the body of knowledge in Web cost estimation and also helps those who wish to research or to know more about the field. One of the trends found was that different size measures were employed by the different studies, suggesting the need for a standard size measure such that we can better compare and contrast results.

Another important point is the use of automated tools for automating data collection. None of the surveyed papers employed automated tools for measuring size, which also points to the need for automated tools to be developed such that we can reduce the errors inherent in data collection.

Finally, we have also shown that most studies were based on case studies rather than formal experiments. Although case studies are important and sometimes are the only way of obtaining not only data but also volunteers for the study, it is important to remember that their results only apply to the scope of the study, for example, their results cannot be generalised beyond the scope of the study. Therefore we urge the Web engineering community to also plan and run formal experiments as these will allow the building of a wider body of knowledge where findings can be generalised to a wider context.

References

Ambler, S.W. (2002). Lessons in agility from Internet-based development. *IEEE Software*, Mar-Apr, 66-73.

Angelis, L., & Stamelos, I. (2000). A simulation tool for efficient analogy based cost estimation. *Empirical Software Engineering, 5*, 35-68.

Baresi, L., Morasca, S., & Paolini, P. (2002). An empirical study on the design effort for Web applications. *Proceedings of WISE 2002* (pp. 345-354).

Baresi, L., Morasca, S., & Paolini, P. (2003). Estimating the design effort for Web applications. *Proceedings of Metrics 2003* (pp. 62-72).

Boehm, B. (1981). *Software engineering economics*. Englewood Cliffs, NJ: Prentice-Hall.

Botafogo, R., Rivlin, A.E., & Shneiderman, B. (1992). Structural analysis of hypertexts: Identifying hierarchies and useful metrics. *ACM TOIS, 10*(2), 143-179.

Briand, L.C., El-Emam, K., Surmann, D., Wieczorek, I., & Maxwell, K.D. (1999). An assessment and comparison of common cost estimation modelling techniques. *Proceedings ICSE 1999*, Los Angeles, (pp. 313-322).

Briand, L.C., Langley, T., & Wieczorek, I. (2000). A replicated assessment and comparison of common software cost modelling techniques. *Proceedings ICSE 2000*, Limerick, Ireland (pp. 377-386).

Christodoulou, S. P., Zafiris, P. A., & Papatheodorou, T. S. (2000). WWW 2000: The developers' view and practitioner's approach to Web engineering. *Proceedings of the 2nd ICSE Workshop Web Eng.* (pp. 75-92).

Conte, S., Dunsmore, H., & Shen, V. (1986). *Software engineering metrics and models*. Menlo Park, CA: Benjamin/Cummings.

Cowderoy, A.J.C. (2000). Measures of size and complexity for Web site content. *Proceedings Combined 11th ESCOM Conference and the 3rd SCOPE conference on Software Product Quality*, Munich, Germany (pp. 423-431).

DeMarco, T. (1982). *Controlling software projects: Management, measurement and estimation*. New York: Yourdon.

Fewster, R., & Mendes, E. (2001). Measurement, prediction and risk analysis for Web applications. *Proceedings of Metrics '01*, London (pp. 338-348).

Finnie, G.R., Wittig, G.E., & Desharnais, J.M. (1997). A comparison of software effort estimation techniques: Using function points with neural networks, case-based reasoning and regression models. *Journal of Systems and Software*, *39*, 281-289.

Gray, A., & MacDonell, S. (1997a). Applications of fuzzy logic to software metric models for development effort estimation. *Proc. Annual Meeting of the North American Fuzzy Information Processing Society - NAFIPS*, Syracuse, New York (pp. 394-399). IEEE.

Gray, A.R., & MacDonell, S.G. (1997b). A comparison of model building techniques to develop predictive equations for software metrics. *Information and Software Technology*, *39*, 425-437.

Gray, R., MacDonell, S. G., & Shepperd, M. J. (1999). Factors systematically associated with errors in subjective estimates of software development effort: the stability of expert judgement. *Proceedings IEEE 6th Metrics Symposium* (pp. 216-225).

Hughes, R.T. (1997). An empirical investigation into the estimation of software development effort. PhD thesis, Dept. of Computing, the University of Brighton, UK.

Jeffery, R., Ruhe, M., & Wieczorek, I. (2000). A comparative study of two software development cost modelling techniques using multi-organizational and company-specific data. *Information and Software Technology*, *42*, 1009-1016.

Jeffery, R., Ruhe, M., & Wieczorek, I. (2001). Using public domain metrics to estimate software development effort. *Proceedings of IEEE 7th Metrics Symposium*, London (pp. 16-27).

Kadoda, G., Cartwright, M., Chen, L., & Shepperd, M.J. (2000). Experiences using case-based reasoning to predict software project effort. *Proceedings EASE 2000 Conference*, Keele, UK.

Kemerer, C.F. (1987). An empirical validation of software cost estimation models. *CACM*, *30*(5), 416-429.

Kitchenham, B.A., Pickard, L.M., MacDonell, S.G., & Shepperd, M.J. (2001). What accuracy statistics really measure. *IEE Proceedings of Software Engineering, 148*(3), 81-85.

Kok, P., Kitchenham, B. A., & Kirakowski, J. (1990). The MERMAID approach to software cost estimation. *ESPRIT Annual Conference*, Brussels (pp. 296-314).

Kumar, S., Krishna, B.A., & Satsangi, P.S. (1994). Fuzzy systems and neural networks in software engineering project management. *Journal of Applied Intelligence, 4*, 31-52.

Mendes, E., Counsell, S., & Mosley, N. (2000). Measurement and effort prediction of Web applications. *Proceedings of the 2nd ICSE Workshop on Web Engineering*, June, Limerick, Ireland (pp. 57-74).

Mendes, E., Mosley, N., & Counsell, S. (2001). Web metrics – Estimating design and authoring effort. *IEEE Multimedia, Special Issue on Web Engineering*, Jan-Mar, (pp. 50-57).

Mendes, E., Mosley, N., & Counsell, S. (2002a). The application of case-based reasoning to early Web project cost estimation. *Proceedings COMPSAC 2002* (pp. 173-183).

Mendes, E., Mosley, N., & Counsell, S. (2003). Do adaptation rules improve Web cost estimation? *Proceedings ACM Hypertext Conference* (pp. 173-183).

Mendes, E., Watson, I., Triggs, C., Mosley, N., & Counsell, S. (2002b). A comparison of development effort estimation techniques for Web hypermedia applications. *Proceedings Metrics 2002* (pp. 131-140).

Morisio, M., Stamelos, I., Spahos, V., & Romano, D. (1999). Measuring functionality and productivity in Web-based applications: A case study. *Proceedings of the Sixth International Software Metrics Symposium* (pp. 111-118).

Morris, P. (2003). Metrics based project governance. *Keynote, Metrics'03*.

Myrtveit, I. & Stensrud, E. (1999). A controlled experiment to assess the benefits of estimating with analogy and regression models. *IEEE Trans. on Software Engineering, 25*(4), 510-525.

Pickard, L.M., Kitchenham, B.A., & Linkman, S.J. (1999). An investigation of analysis techniques for software datasets. *Proceedings of the 6th International Symposium on Software Metrics*. IEEE Computer Society Press, Los Alamitos, CA (pp. 130-140).

Pressman, R.S. (2000). What a tangled Web we weave. *IEEE Software*, Jan.-Feb., 18-21.

Putnam, L. H. (1978). A general empirical solution to the macro sizing and estimating problem. *IEEE Trans. on Software Engineering, SE-4*(4), 345-361.

Reifer, D.J. (2000). Web development: Estimating quick-to-market software. *IEEE Software*, Nov -Dec, 57-64.

Reifer, D.J. (2002). Ten deadly risks in Internet and intranet software development. *IEEE Software*, Mar-Apr, 12-14.

Ruhe, M., Jeffery, R., & Wieczorek, I. (2003). Cost estimation for Web applications. *Proceedings ICSE 2003* (pp. 285-294).

Schofield, C. (1998). *An empirical investigation into software estimation by analogy.* PhD thesis, Dept. of Computing, Bournemouth Univ., UK.

Selby, R.W., & Porter, A.A. (1998). Learning from examples: generation and evaluation of decision trees for software resource analysis. *IEEE Trans. on Software Engineering, 14*, 1743-1757.

Shepperd, M.J., & Kadoda, G. (2001). Using simulation to evaluate prediction techniques. *Proceedings IEEE 7th International Software Metrics Symposium*, London (pp. 349-358).

Shepperd, M.J., & Schofield, C. (1997). Estimating software project effort using analogies. *IEEE Trans. on Software Engineering, 23*(11), 736-743.

Shepperd, M.J., Schofield, C., & Kitchenham B. (1996). Effort estimation using analogy. *Proceedings of ICSE-18*, Berlin (pp. 170-178).

Srinivasan, K., & Fisher, D. (1995). Machine learning approaches to estimating software development effort. *IEEE Trans. on Software Engineering, 21*, 126-137.

Stensrud, E., Foss, T., Kitchenham, B.A., & Myrtveit, I. (2002). An empirical validation of the relationship between the magnitude of relative error and project size. *Proceedings of IEEE 8th Metrics Symposium* (pp. 3-12).

Endnotes

* The metric is only useful for static Web applications, where the number of dynamically generated links and/or pages is absent.

1 Subjects did not use external links to other Web sites. All the links pointed to pages within the application only.

2 The structure can be a sequence, hierarchy or network. A sequential structure corresponds to documents linearly linked; a hierarchical structure denotes documents linked in a tree shape and a network structure for documents linked in a net shape [19].

3 Subjects did not use external links to other Web hypermedia applications. All the links pointed to pages within the original application only.

4 COBRA is a registered trademark of the Fraunhofer Institute for Experimental Software Engineering (IESE), Germany.

Section IV

Web Resource Management: Models and Techniques

Chapter IX

Ontology-Supported Web Content Management

Geun-Sik Jo
Inha University, Korea

Jason J. Jung
Inha University, Korea

Abstract

This chapter introduces the ontology-supported Web content management. Since the Web was regarded as one of the most important tools for searching relevant information, many studies have been attempting to develop efficient and accurate management of Web content and resources. We have been focusing on how to exploit the ontology to support semantic conceptualization of information on the Web. Especially, the emergence of semantic Web emphasizes the importance of the ontological processes. In this chapter, we will mention content management systems on the semantic Web, and then, we will introduce two applications from viewpoints of personalized content and electronic commerce as case studies.

Introduction

With the emergence of the World Wide Web, it has become easier to access its information reservoir. However, each user has difficulties in managing the content material he or she has acquired from the WWW. People have to carefully consider their information space to be well organized. Not only personal problems on the client-side but also the relationships between suppliers and customers on the business-side have changed. The US Department of Commerce estimates that online sales in the US for the year 2000 were around 1 percent of the overall sales figures. Even though this was only a small fraction of the overall business figures, the continued fast growth of onlines sales appears likely given the fact that the number of Internet users grew from 100 to 300 million between 1997 and 2000. Similar estimates are done for the business-to-business (B2B) area.

In order to handle these problems, much research has been introduced, such as the automatic content management system. Content management has evolved into one of the most important streams of management research, affecting organizations of all types at many different levels. The challenges of content management span everything from content identification and representation to the impact of content management systems on organizational culture and to the significant integration and cost issues being faced by human resources, MIS/IT, and production departments. Content management theories, models, systems, and applications abound — each dealing with some aspect of an increasingly complex field spanning organizational theory, strategic management, and information technology. These issues can be noted as follows:

- How to organize and structure contents
- How to analyze and conceptualize contents
- How to retrieve, reuse, and share contents

With an emerging semantic Web, meanwhile, ontology has become a major focal point. The concept of a semantic Web has excited researchers in areas ranging from distributed information systems to artificial intelligence. With the aspect of managing content on the Web, ontology can be regarded as one of the most effective methods to support the conceptualization of arbitrary contents.

In this chapter, we describe how to exploit ontology to manage Web contents and resources. We introduce two case studies that we have conducted on ontology-based resource management on the Web: personalization from user-specific content (Jung, 2002) and the comparison shopping mall system in electronic commerce (Lee, Ghose, Yu, & Jo, 2003).

Ontological Approaches to Manage Web Content and Resources

While ontology is philosophically defined as the study of what exists and what we must assume to exist in order to achieve a cogent description of reality, knowledge engineers have considered that ontology is a formal and explicit specification of a shared conceptualization (Gruber, 1993). This means that ontology plays a role in facilitating the construction of a domain model in knowledge engineering, by providing vocabulary terms and relationships with which to model the domain. So far, several classic ontologies such as *CYC*, *#Skin*, *MIKROKOSMOS*, *GALEN*, and *ENTERPRISE* have been introduced. These have mainly been applied to linguistic approaches like machine translation and background (common sense) knowledge.

Many researchers, however, have been trying to develop and seek out the most proper ontology on the Web. Especially the semantic Web, mentioned by Tim Berners-Lee (Berners-Lee, Hendler, & Lassila, 2001), is emphasizing the importance of ontology in bringing structure to the meaningful content of Web resources. Basically, ontology on the Web is represented as XML (eXtensible Markup Language) syntax. The Web Ontology Language (OWL)[1], DAML+OIL[2], and RDFS[3] are the representative languages for expressing ontology on the Web. As an example, we have generated ontology for cameras by DAML+OIL, which is as follows:

```
<daml:Ontology rdf:about="Camera">
    <rdfs:comment>
        DAML-OIL-Based Ontology
    </rdfs:comment>
    <daml:imports rdf:resource="http://www.daml.org/2001/03/daml+oil"/>
</daml:Ontology>

<daml:Class rdf:ID="SLR">
    <daml:intersectionOf rdf:parseType="Collection">
        <daml:Class rdf:about="#Camera"/>
        <daml:Restriction>
            <daml:onProperty rdf:resource="#viewFinder"/>
            <daml:hasValue rdf:resource="#ThroughTheLens"/>
        </daml:Restriction>
    </daml:intersectionOf>
</daml:Class>
```

After ontology is well established, we have to consider how to exploit this ontology to manage Web contents and resources, to provide content chosen by users with semantic information. In other words, we have to make an agreement among users, embodied in terms of ontological commitment and knowledge sharing through shared use of ontology. For example, in our first case study we tried using ODP (Open Directory Project), which is the most comprehensive, human-edited directory on the Web. Each Web site that users are accessing can be conceptualized according to the ODP. This means that these users can be assumed to be trying to find information related to the concepts included in that Web site.

Semantic interoperability between businesses is another problem that has to be solved by ontology-based content management. Several tools such as *Dublin Core*, *RossettaNet*, *ecl@ss*, *Common Business Library* (*CBL*), and *Commerce XML* (*cXML*) have been introduced to describe local content and common understanding. In our second case study, we used semantic Web technology DAML+OIL. By using this, we made ontology for each shopping mall, defined the concept and the structure, made DAML markup instance data, and then extracted the semantic factors by using DAMLJessKB. We have also used these extracted semantic factors for the Jess inference engine, in order to make it possible to provide reasoning to Web data structures. Our approach allows inference to be carried out when a query is requested. Thereby, we have implemented a working prototype based on, and then used by the above semantic Web inference system.

We think the following two case studies are the best examples describing ontology-based Web resource management systems with respect to personalization and e-commerce.

Case Studies

Web Directory-Based Bookmark Management and Collaborative Browsing

Introduction

Many kinds of information filtering methods have appeared in order to handle information-overload problems (Maes, 1994). Personalization, which is tailoring the presentation of content to a specific group or individual based on characteristics of that group or individual, has been a major focal point. For example, the e-mail filtering systems *Ringo* and *WebHound* can be called personalized information filtering systems (Sheth & Maes, 1993; Pazzani, Nguyen, & Mantik, 1995; Shardanand & Maes, 1995; Lashkari, 1995). Therefore, user preference (or interest) is information that should be extracted first in order to increase the performance of filtering systems. While the sparsity of information on users and dynamic characteristics of the Web environment have caused difficulties in the acquisition of user preference, there are many kinds of information that make user preferences inferable, such as footprints on navigation, viewing (or accessing) time of Web pages, and site access frequency.

In this study, a bookmark, which is stored for revisiting a particular site and memorizing the URL information, is regarded as one of the most important pieces of evidence for discovering user interests. According to GVU's 10th WWW User Surveys (October 1998), approximately 68 percent of all respondents use more than 50 bookmarks[4]. There is an information filtering system to which bookmarks are applied. *BISAgent* (Bookmark Information Sharing Agent) is a collaborative Web browsing system based on a modified *TF-IDF* scheme without considering user preference (Jung, Yoon, & Jo, 2000; Salton & Lesk, 1988).

Nowadays Web directory services like Yahoo[5] are offering users much more relevant answers than any other general keyword-searching engines, even though the Web coverage provided by directories is very low (Baeza-Yates & Ribeiro-Neto, 1999). Web directories, also called "categories," "yellow pages," or sometimes "subject directories," are hierarchical taxonomies that classify human knowledge or a general class of ideas, terms, or things that mark divisions or coordinations within a conceptual scheme. Not only Yahoo but also digital libraries, UseNet, and *DMOZ* (the open directory project)[6] have served as a category service (Pelillo, Siddiqi, & Zucker, 1999).

This study assumes that the most important role of a category is so that the bookmarks of the users can be conceptualized for extracting user preferences. Because hierarchically tree structured categories are mutually dependent, influences between them have to be considered. As hierarchical influences propagate based on a Bayesian network, all user preferences can be detected as well as the fact that the favorite categories of each user can be extracted. Thus, preference maps of each user can be established as more than one disjointed tree, called a clique (Horowitz & Sahni, 1994). Approximate tree matching is a method used in molecular biology to compare vast amounts of RNA structures, natural language processing, or pattern recognition (Wang, Zhang, Jeong, & Shasha, 1994). We can make queries to inquire about the user group interested in each category. Then the similarities between users are calculated for clustering like-minded users by approximate tree matching. Through user clustering, we can apply this result to recommend and distribute relevant information adaptively to each user on collaborative browsing.

Characteristics of a Web Directory

A bookmark contains URL information saved in order to revisit a Web site. Even though users may not want to access that page again, they put it in their bookmark storage if the Web site is interesting to them. Hence, these saved bookmarks imply that a user is looking for information related to a given topic. However, a bookmark may have more than one kind of content, which is an obstacle to automatically discovering the user's interest.

Web directories such as Yahoo and Cora are hierarchical taxonomies that classify human knowledge (Baeza-Yates & Ribeiro-Neto, 1999). These directories are hierarchically organized in a tree-like structure. The causality between categories, however, makes their hierarchical structure more complicated. Different paths of a category and semantically identical categories also cause this kind of problem. For example, a bookmark for the category "*Computer science : Artificial Intelligence : Constraint Satisfaction : Laboratory*" can also be in the category "*Education : Universities : Korea : Inha University : Laboratory*". In most cases, a category contains the same information as other categories. In practice, most companies are forced to manage a non-generic tree structure in order to avoid a waste of memory space caused by redundant information (Salton & Lesk, 1988). In brief, the problems with a bookmark and a Web directory as ontology are the following:

- **The multi-attributes of a bookmark.** A bookmark may be included in more than one category, as shown in Figure 1. The bookmark can be in two black categories.

Figure 1. The multi-attributes of a bookmark

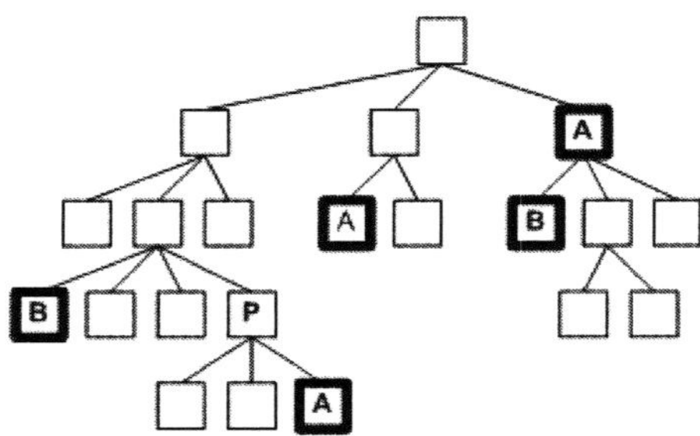

- **The relationship between categories.** This means that all nodes do not connect only with their root node. In other words, one category can be pointed to by another category on a totally different path. More specifically, we note the two kinds of relationships between both categories.
    - Redundancy between semantically identical categories
    - Subordination between semantically dependent categories

First, redundancy can occur because of semantically identical categories. This means Web site information in a particular category can be exactly the same as that of the other category. Second, relationship is subordination. As shown in Figure 2, category C can be one of the subcategories of more than a single other category (e.g., P).

Web Directory-Based Conceptualization of Bookmarks

A Web directory functioning as ontology can conceptualize bookmarks. The bookmark set of a user can be replaced with the category set of that user by referring to the ontology, as shown in Figure 3.

Figure 2. A subordinate relationship between two categories

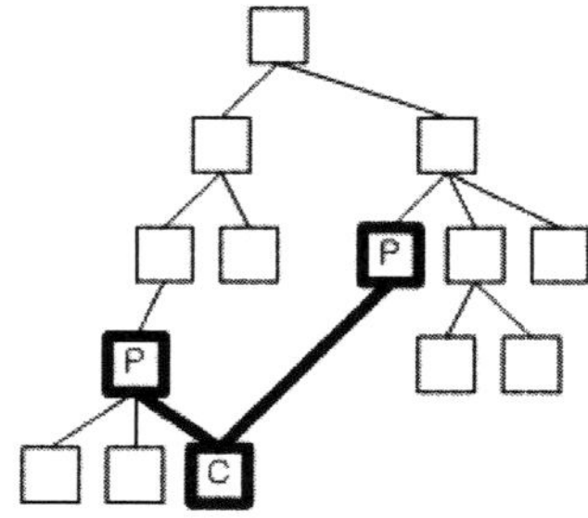

Figure 3. Pseudo code for categorizing bookmarks

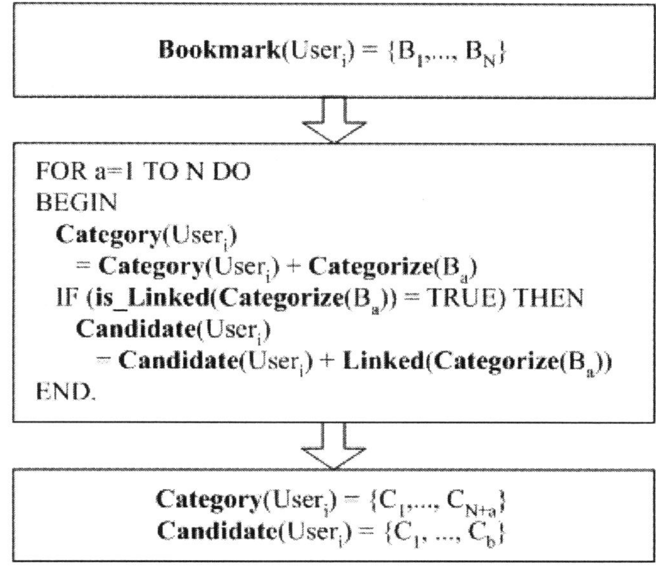

```
Bookmark(User_i) = {B_1,..., B_N}

FOR a=1 TO N DO
BEGIN
  Category(User_i)
    = Category(User_i) + Categorize(B_a)
  IF (is_Linked(Categorize(B_a)) = TRUE) THEN
    Candidate(User_i)
      = Candidate(User_i) + Linked(Categorize(B_a))
END.

Category(User_i) = {C_1,..., C_N+a}
Candidate(User_i) = {C_1, ..., C_b}
```

The subscripts "a" and "b" in this flowchart represent meaning the increased values caused by Web directory problems, as mentioned in the previous section. The function *Categorize* looks up the ontology for matching bookmarks to proper categories. In addition, the function *is_Linked* can check whether a category, as an input parameter, is connected to more than one other category or not. Finally, the function *Linked* retrieves the other categories connected to them. As a result, the size of each user's category set becomes larger than that of his bookmark set because of the incomplete properties of the category structure mentioned in the previous section. Therefore, we have supplemented with a candidate category set. The candidate category set improves the coverage of user preferences. This means that potential preferences can be detected as well.

Extracting and Modeling User Preferences Based on a Bayesian Network

Even though categorizing bookmarks makes the inference of user interests much easier, the real preferences of a user can be different from the ones that we have guessed. More importantly, however, is that the probability that the real one is geometrically close to the estimated one is very high. Support propagation between mutually linked categories on Bayesian networks can solve this problem (Jung, 2002). With this propagation, we can extract the categories a particular user is most interested in. In other words, every category can be sorted by the degree of interest.

Support Propagation on Bayesian Networks

Bayesian networks are basically probabilistic models that allow the structured representation of a cognitive or decision process and are commonly used for decision tree analysis in business and the social sciences (Pearl, 1988; Giarratano & Riley, 1994). The following is used to measure conditional probability. The strengths of causal influences between categories are expressed by these conditional probabilities (Baeza-Yates & Ribeiro-Neto, 1999). This is how categories reflect their causal relationship on parent nodes. The degree of user preference for the node parent is the summation of the evidential supports of the node children linked to the node parent.

$$P(parent, children) = \sum_i P(parent \mid children(i)) \times P(children(i)) \qquad (1)$$

We assume that every category is assigned a *VOP*, the degree of user preference. The *VOP* is denoted by the function "propagate," the number of bookmarks of children categories and their *VOP*'s, recursively.

$$VOP(c) = \sum \left(propagate[VOP(child(c))] \times VOP(child(c))\right) \qquad (2)$$

The following axioms define the rules used to assign the VOP's to each category.

Axiom 1. The initial VOP is equal to the number of times categorized to a proper category by bookmarks.

$$\forall Category_i,\ VOP(Category_i) = \text{the number of times categorized by bookmarks}$$

Axiom 2. As the number of times a given category found in the user's bookmarks increases, it can be inferred that the user is more interested in this category that the bookmark is included in. This means that the degree of user interest for this field is in linear proportion to these numbers.

$$\text{the number of times categorized} \propto VOP(Category_i)$$

Axiom 3. Hierarchically, a lower category is more causally influential in deciding user preferences than a higher one. The causal influence propagation from child nodes to their parent node is exponentially decreased as the distance between nodes increases.

Axiom 4. As the number of subcategories of a node increases, each subcategory has less influence on that node. This is why user interests disperse.

Axiom 5. The category set candidate has the same level of influence as the normal one does.

Axiom 6. All categories' supports are propagated up to the vertex node.

Axiom 7. After a normalization step, categories whose VOP's are over the threshold value can be represented as user preferences. The threshold value controls how many categories will be extracted.

The function *propagate* based on Axioms 3 and 4 is defined as a logarithm function in the following equation.

$$propagate[VOP(C)] = \frac{\log_k (VOP(C)+1)}{N}$$
$$k = \text{Variance}(VOP(\text{subcategories})) + 2 = \sigma^2 + 2 \qquad (3)$$
$$N = \text{The number of subcategories of a parent category}$$

In addition, the *VOP*'s of categories in Figure 4 can be measured based on Axiom 4.

$$VOP(C_3) = propagate[VOP(C_1)]\ \text{s\%}\ VOP(C_1) \qquad (4)$$
$$VOP(C_4) = propagate[VOP(C_3)] + propagate[VOP(C_2)]\ \text{s\%}\ VOP(C_2)$$

As a result, the *VOP*'s of the categories C_3 and C_4 are not zero. In other words, despite the fact that there are no bookmarks in the categories C_3 and C_4, they have evidential supports (possibilities) derived from other categories. In the process of normalization, the average *VOP*'s of all categories and the portions of each category are calculated. The categories whose portions are over the threshold value are regarded as the representative categories of user preference.

Figure 4. Support propagation on Bayesian network

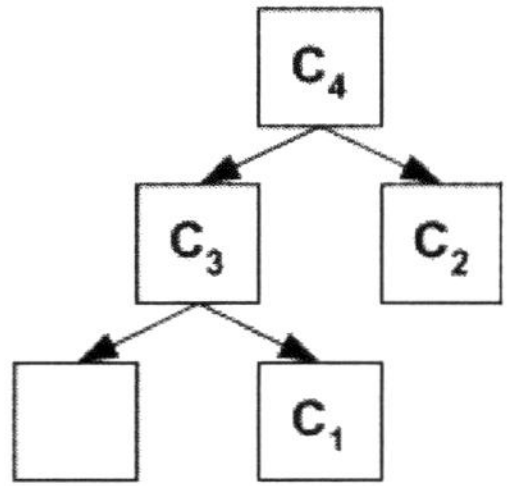

Figure 5. An example of the categorized bookmarks of a user

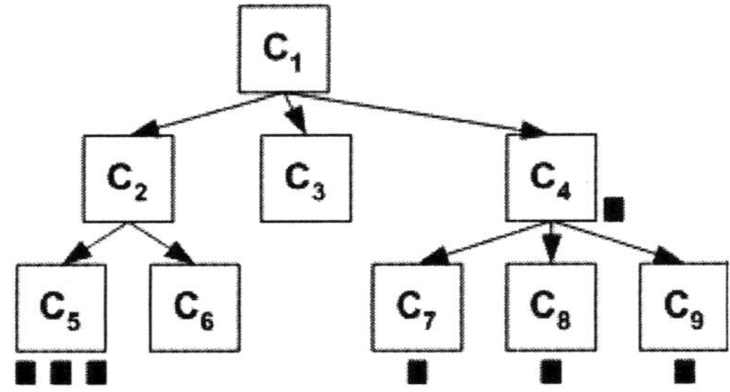

An Example of How The User Preference Map Is Obtained

In Figure 5, the black boxes express the user's bookmarks located in proper categories. The candidate category information is ignored. The initial states are represented in the equations that follow.

$$Bookmark(U) = \{B_1, ..., B_7\}$$
$$Category(U) = \{C_4, C_5, C_5, C_5, C_7, C_8, C_9\}$$

$$VOP(C_4) = 1, VOP(C_5) = 3, VOP(C_6) = 0, VOP(C_7) = 1, VOP(C_8) = 1, VOP(C_9) = 1$$

For means and variances of the *VOP*'s of the categories,

$$\mu(\{VOP(C_5), VOP(C_6)\} = 1.5$$
$$\mu(\{VOP(C_7), VOP(C_8), VOP(C_9)\} = 1$$

$$\sigma^2(\{VOP(C_5), VOP(C_6)\} = 4.5$$
$$\sigma^2(\{VOP(C_7), VOP(C_8), VOP(C_9)\} = 0$$

Therefore, the *VOP*'s of C_2 and C_4 are as follows:

$$VOP(C_2) = \sum_{k-1}^{2} Propagate[VOP(C_k)] \times VOP(C_k) = \frac{\log_{6.5}(VOP(C_5)+1)}{2} \times VOP(C_5) = 1.11$$

$$VOP(C_4) = 1 + \left(\frac{\log_2 2}{3} \times 1 \right) \times 3 = 1 + 1 = 2$$

Figure 6. User preferences map representing the high ranked categories

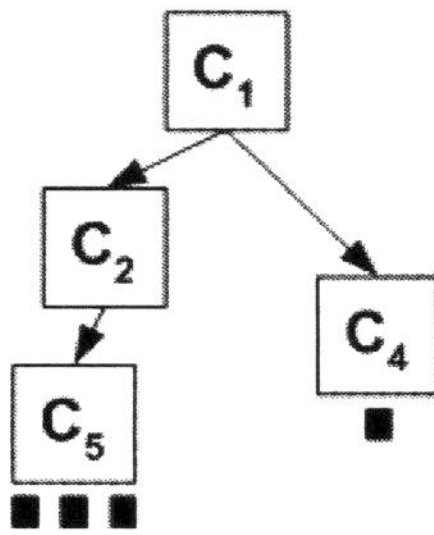

In the same way, we can calculate the *VOP* of C_1.

$$VOP(C_1) = \left(\frac{\log_{2.93}(1.11+1)}{3} \times 1.11 \right) + \left(\frac{\log_{2.93}(2+1)}{3} \times 2 \right) = 0.94$$

The mean of all *VOP*'s is 1.44 and the *VOP* of every category is assigned after normalization. If the threshold value is 0.2, only C_4 and C_5 are extracted as the categories most interested in by the user.

In Figure 6, the tree represents the user's preference map (*PM*). Each user can obtain his *PM*, and every time he inserts his bookmark, this *PM* will be updated.

Collaborative Browsing by Sharing User Preferences

Comparing preferences between users is a simple task for users who are interested in only one field. However, ordinary users are generally interested in more than one. The similarities (or distances) between users' *PM*'s have to be measured in order to determine how similar both sets of users' preferences are. Many algorithms have been developed and studied for an exact tree comparison. This study is based on the approximate tree matching algorithms presented in (Wang et al., 1994; Apostolico & Galil, 1997). The edit operations give rise to a *mapping* that is a geographical specification of which edit operations apply to each node in the two trees in order to determine the editing distance between sequences (Boyer & Moore, 1977). In this study, as the two PM's of both users simply overlapped, a *mapping* between users was conducted, and a query processing with respect to each category could be efficiently executed in order to investigate the user group interested in a particular category. When the *PM*'s of $User_1$ and $User_2$ overlapped, we were able to make queries. For example, a query such as "Who is interested in the category home > computer > database>?" was available. Moreover, for this query, it was possible that not only users in the category but also users in its subcategories were replied to. Next, the distance between the two *PM*'s was expressed as the following equation

$$\begin{aligned}&Similarity(User_1, User_2)\\&= threshold - \sum_i \sum_j \min[dist(Category(User_1), Category(User_2))]\end{aligned}$$

where the variables i and j meant the sizes of the high ranked category sets of $User_1$ and $User_2$ respectively. Also, the variable i had to be equal to or larger than j. If the distance among sibling nodes was equal to k, the distance to the parent node was $k/2$, which was a depth difference. We were then able to calibrate the variable threshold and k to establish the threshold value as the standard and to control the number of user clusters.

Experiments and Results

We made a hierarchical tree structure as a test bed for "*Home : Science : Computer Science*" from Yahoo (http://www.yahoo.com). This sampled tree consisted of about 1300 categories and the maximum depth was eight. For gathering bookmarks, 30 users explored Yahoo directory pages for about 50 hours (two hours for 25 days) using this system. Whenever they found a site related to their own preference, they stored that URL information. As a result, 2,718 bookmarks were collected. After 8.1 days, 80 percent of the total bookmarks were stored. We used these testing data to evaluate the performance of information filtering according to user preference. The evaluation measures *recall* and *precisions* were utilized in order to present quantitative comparison between both cases. After resetting the bookmark sets of all users, these users began to gather bookmarks again upon getting the system's recommendations according to their own preferences.

During this time, users were being recommended information retrieved from Yahoo based on user preference extracted up to that moment. As a result, 80 percent of the total bookmarks were collected in 3.8 days. As shown in Figure 7, 53.1 percent of the total time could be saved according to *recall*.

The measure *precision* was determined by the rate of the inserted bookmarks among the recommended information set. In other words, this was the measurement of the accuracy of predictability. As time passed, the user preferences changed according to the inserted bookmarks. At the beginning, the precision was especially low because the user preferences were not yet set up. While user preferences were being extracted in the first six days, the *precision* of recommended information tracked to that of the testing data quickly, as shown in Figure 8.

For the final 15 days, it maintained the same level as that of the testing data. Web browsing to search for relevant information is not only a difficult but also a boring task. Hence, collaborative Web browsing through which users can share helpful information to increase the performance of information searching is used in digital libraries and, particularly, for guiding beginning users. Such systems are "*Let's Browse*" (Lieberman, Dyke, & Vivacqua, 1999) and "ARIADNE" (Twidale & Nichols, 1996). All bookmarks are patched into the server in order to infer the preferences of each user. The user-clustering module is used for computing the similarities between users. Both query generators for user information and category information can search the user information repository and the global category set in a Web directory service.

Figure 7. Evaluating with according to recall

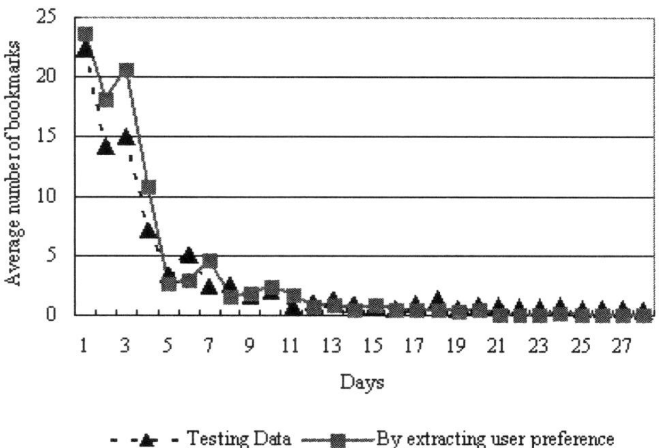

Figure 8. Evaluating with according to precision

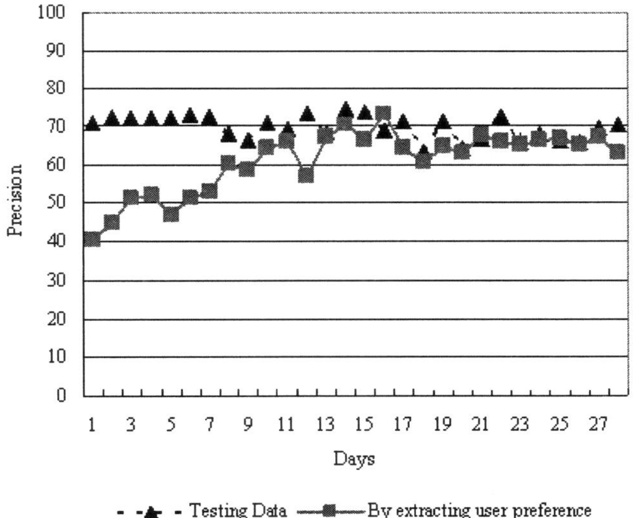

Comparison Shopping Malls on the Semantic Web

Introduction

The Web is enormous and it is growing at a staggering rate. This growth has made it increasingly difficult for humans and software to quickly and accurately access Web information and services. In particular, the existing shopping malls have their own codes for formatting their products and managing content databases. These codes can be regarded as metadata such as product categories and descriptions. It is hard for such shopping malls built on local metadata to offer good searching performance, compared with simple text searching. It causes irrelevant search results to shown up, thereby annoying most clients. It is, however, possible to deal with these problems by providing the conceptual information of each product and its contents. An ontology, which is the global specification of concepts, can structure knowledge from the formatted, defined local specifications of the contents in order to efficiently share information between shopping malls. When doing this, we can obtain similar advantages with comparison systems for buyers such as Cost, Finin, Joshi, Peng, Nicholas, Soboroff, Chen, Kagal, Perich, Zou, and Tolia (2002) and Dukle (2003). More importantly, this system can be easily evolved to the semantic Web.

System Architecture

Our comparison shopping system architecture based on the Semantic Web is shown in Figure. 9. Each domain generates an ontology based on DAML+OIL for its products, and an instance is being made from this ontology by a DAML document. When integrating information to a semantic Web based comparative shopping system, an ontology mapper of the system is used so that ontology from various domains can be mapped. By doing this, the system can obtain a merged ontology (Merged DAML+OIL) that defines the relations among products from various domains. The buyer can search any product that interests him by using this user interface. All queries generated by a buyer are sent to each domain, then it is inputted as a fact for Jess through Merged DAML+OIL and DAMLJessKB and the inference is being made based on DAML+OIL rules/domain rules. Last, DAMLJessKB transforms the result to a DAML format. The Semantic Web Search system accepts user queries by means of a Graphical User Interface (GUI). On initialization, the GUI loads the default ontology and displays the ontology classes and their respective property values. We utilized a Jena toolkit[7] for this purpose. The toolkit includes an ARP (Another RDF Parser) to parse the RDF documents. It also contains a DAML API with classes to manipulate DAML ontology and extract information from them. The Jena toolkit dynamically reads the ontology and obtains the class-property information. This ensures that the application is domain neutral.

The final result, which is processed from various domains, is sent to the final buyer by the result display module on the system.

Figure 9. System architecture

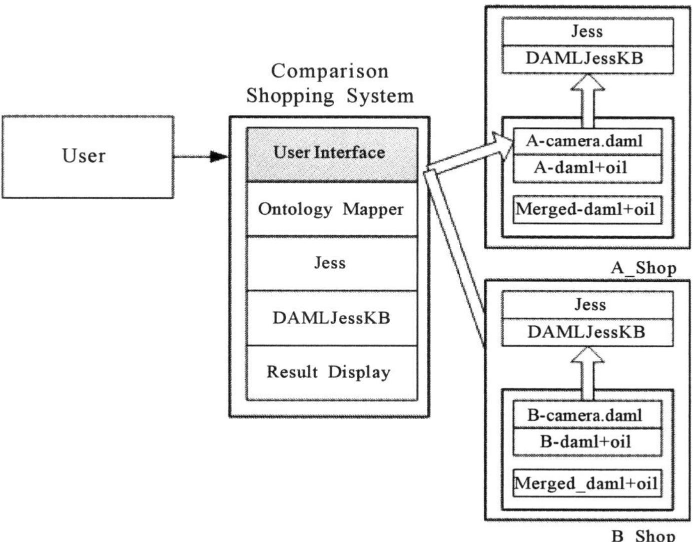

User Interface. The user interacts with the system by means of the user interface that allows the user to make appropriate selections for classes, their properties, and properties of object properties within the domain. The buyer usually inputs detailed search information as well as the purchasing item and the search item through the user interface of the Web or application. The queries are made and executed at the Jess Query, and the result is then provided to the buyer.

Creation of the Ontology and Metadata. The ontology based on DAML+OIL of a camera as a comparison-purchasing domain is provided in this study. For example, the SLR is defined as a subclass of "camera." The SLR class is a search object when the camera class is selected at the query. Therefore, a subclass of the camera search as a digital large-format can be selected at the time of searching for the SLR. While all cameras have a

Figure 10. Jess reasoning process through DAMLJessKB

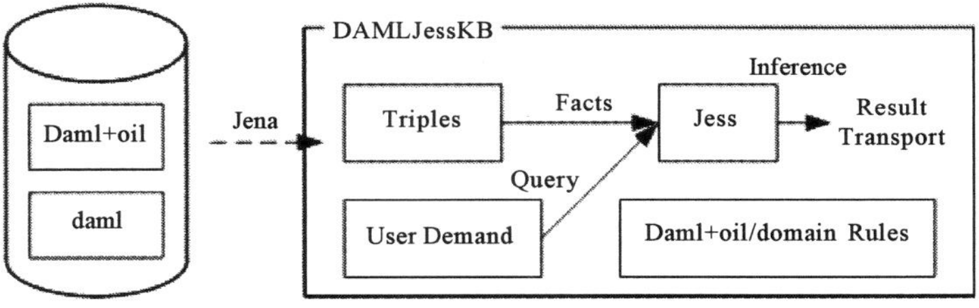

viewfinder, a SLR has a viewfinder whose value is restricted to "Through the Lens." DAML instance metadata is made based on the concept structure of the ontology.

```
<daml:Class rdf:ID="SLR">
    <daml:intersectionOf rdf:parseType="Collection">
        <daml:Class rdf:about="#Camera"/>
        <daml:Restriction>
            <daml:onProperty rdf:resource="#viewFinder"/>
            <daml:hasValue rdf:resource="#ThroughTheLens"/>
        </daml:Restriction>
    </daml:intersectionOf>
</daml:Class>
```

Ontology Metadata. The mapping of the relationship concept among domain ontology is needed to protect a conflict of terminology when content unification is done in each domain. A terminology relationship between the domains is made by using the KAON (The Karlsruhe Ontology and Semantic Web Tool Suite) Ontology Mapper (Guttman & Maes, 1998). For instance, let us assume that "size" is used for the property as the size of the camera lens in domain A and at the same time, we can assume that "focal-length" is used for the same meaning in domain B. These two properties must then be considered as the same concept by the Jess inference process. The "focal-length" and "size" relationship equality is represented by using "samePropertyAS" in the DAML+OIL specification.

```
<daml:DatatypeProperty rdf:ID="focal-length">
<daml:samePropertyAs rdf:resource="#size"/>
    <rdfs:domain rdf:resource="#Lens"/>
    <rdfs:range rdf:resource="&xsd;#string"/>
</daml:DatatypeProperty>
<daml:DatatypeProperty rdf:ID="f-stop">
    <daml:samePropertyAs rdf:resource="#aperture"/>
    <rdfs:domain rdf:resource="#Lens"/>
    <rdfs:range rdf:resource="&xsd;#string"/>
</daml:DatatypeProperty>
```

DAMLJessKB. Jess must be converted into a rule through DAMLJessKB because it does not understand the DAML+OIL syntax declaration. DAMLJessKB provides Jess with the meaning of the ontology compared to daml+oil in the form of facts. The information can be achieved by a *defquery* of Jess based on facts and rules. For example, the Jess Query, as shown in the following box, includes the camera body in the list of cameras with a price of over 2,000,000 Korean won.

```
(defquery search2 (declare (max-background-rules 100))
(PropertyValue &rdf;type ?n &machi;Body)
(PropertyValue &machi;cost ?n ?res)
(PropertyValue &rdf;value ?res
   ?s&:(or (integerp ?s) (floatp ?s))&:(>= (float ?s) 200000)))
```

Experiments and Implementation

To date, through the implemented system the user can query with some specifications for purchasing a camera.

The user starts by entering several search terms to specify what he or she is looking for. Figure 12 is the resulting set of a particular relevant query entered by the user at the query interface shown in Figure 11.

The relevant information of a product is shown in a tree structure in the right window upon selection of the particular product type from the left window. The interface produced a meaningful and intuitive display of search results in a hierarchically displayed output. To give a precise difference in meaning between a concept and its sub-concept in the

Figure 11. Query interface

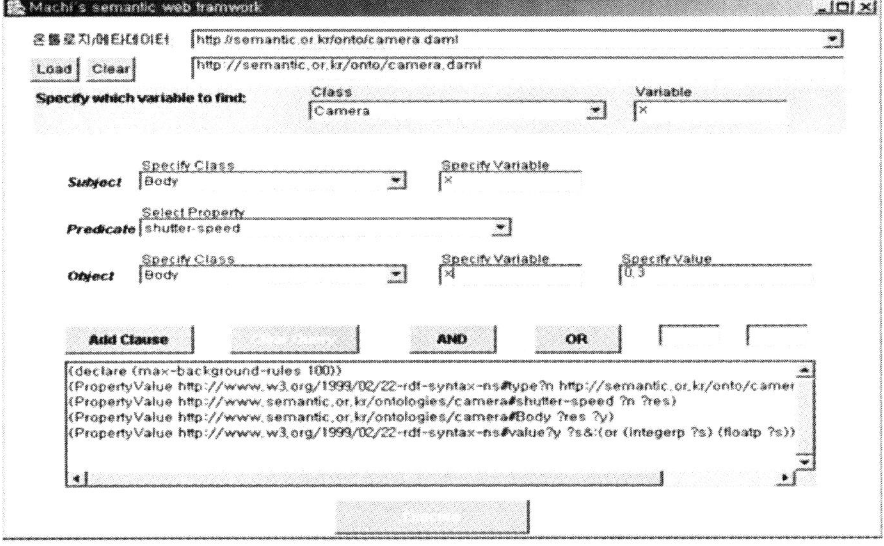

Figure 12. Resulting display for Query interface

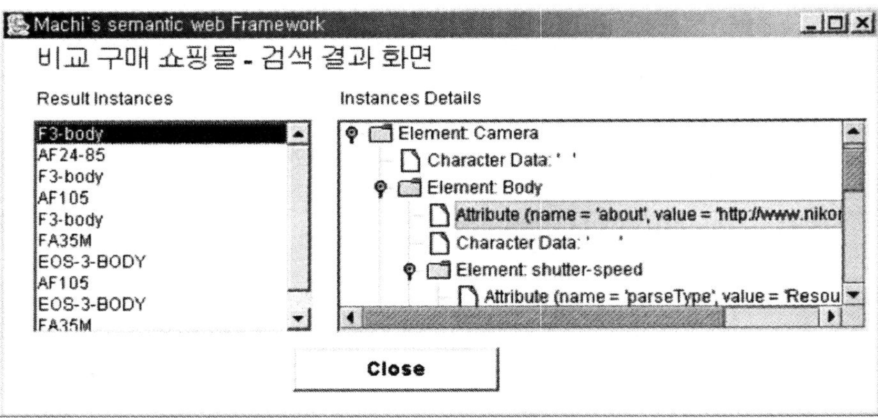

concept hierarchy, our solution lies in producing a meaningful display of search results by moving away from the traditional ranked list of relevant documents and to generate instead a hierarchically displayed output. This output visualizes the query results with numbers attached to the relevant fragments of the concept hierarchy. Each number indicates the importance of the camera component level of a particular product type with respect to the particular component concept it is attached to.

The system was evaluated based on recall and precision, widely used metrics in information retrieval. We examined the camera data, which consisted of three types, to make a comparison of them. Type A was based on the semantic Web, type B was RDBMS databased on individual shopping malls, and type C was the metadata that was gathered by integrating each piece of RDBMS data. We categorized each of 500 camera lenses and bodies into three types — A, B, C — and distributed them to three severs. Using this data set, we measured the average recall and precision for the results of 50 queries in the following way:

> *"Find cameras which are priced under 1,500,000, zoom lens is 75~300mm, shutter-speed is 1/500 sec~1.0 sec, and with the brand name is SAMSUNG"*

Our experimental results have shown that the recall and precision of our system A improved by 66 percent and 54 percent over those of B and 5 percent and 22 percent over those of C. Moreover, we can clearly see that system *A,* based on the Semantic Web, is more effective than the others which are not based on the Semantic Web.

Conclusion

With the advent of the semantic Web, ontology has emerged as the most important ways for managing and sharing Web resources. We have introduced two kinds of applications for Web content management based on ontology, one being client-based and the other business-based.

First, we investigated ODP, one of the most well known Web directory projects, as ontology for semantically enriching a URL chosen by users. Thereby, user behaviors on the Web were analyzed in order to extract what the user was interested in. User interests were applied to adaptive responses. As a result of this study, we have assumed that categorized bookmarks give us information that is more evidentially supportable than any other to extract user preferences. Incompleteness of practical directory services can be driven by this system. By propagating the influences on Bayesian networks, all possible and potential preferences of the user were covered and extracted. With this system 74 percent of the users were able to find the field that they were potentially interested in. The influence propagation proposed in this case study is confirmed to be reasonable. Additionally, the evaluation measures *recall* and *precisions* were acquired. Moreover, the *recall* results showed high-level values, which means that this system is covering as many user preferences as possible. In the beginning, the *precision* results were low-level because of a deficient adaptation. However, by the end of the experiment period, the *precision* value quickly converged to as stable a level as that of the testing data quickly. This means instantly updating user preferences as accumulated information. Finally, information filtering based on influence propagation allows users to retrieve highly relevant information. To approach a practical system, collaborative Web browsing was applied to this method and user clustering by using approximate matching, and we have verified high performances of information retrieval. Furthermore, we could find the possibility of navigation.

In the second case study, we described an ontological approach to a price-comparable, shopping mall system. The goal of this system was to demonstrate an e-commerce application enabled by semantic Web techniques and to support purchase decisions by simplifying price comparisons. Thereby, we used DAML metadata, DAML+OIL ontology and a reasoning engine with Jess and DAMLJessKB. The main idea is to mark up shopping Web pages with Semantic Web languages and, based on their list prices, compare the real end prices by applying various business rules. Because of the machine's ability to understand and relate to a concept, we can express the specific details of a product using reasoning with DAML+OIL. This system can be used to answer queries about explicit and implicit knowledge specified by the ontology and thus provide a query answering facility that performs deductive retrieval from knowledge represented in DAML+OIL.

We can expect these processes to be applied to Customer Relationships Management (CRM) in e-business, Web usage mining, and Web content prefetching of Web caching. Moreover, on the semantic Web, contents in the existing shopping malls should be semantically analyzed and then efficiently shared with other contents. Not only price information for customers but also specification information for various products can be useful to B2B (business to business).

References

Apostolico, A., & Galil, Z. (1997). *Pattern matching algorithms - Approximate tree pattern matching*. Oxford University Press.

Baeza-Yates, R., & Ribeiro-Neto, B. (1999). *Modern information retrieval.* Addison-Wesley Publishing.

Berners-Lee, T., Hendler, J,. & Lassila, O. (2001). *The Semantic Web: A new form of Web content that is meaningful to computers will unleash a revolution of new possibilities.* Scientific American.

Boyer, R.S., & Moore, J.S. (1977). A fast string matching algorithm. *Communication of ACM, 20*(10), 762-772.

Cost, R.S., Finin, T., Joshi, A., Peng, Y., Nicholas, C., Soboroff, I., Chen, H., Kagal, L., Perich, F., Zou, Y., & Tolia, S. (2002). ITTALKS: A Case Study in the Semantic Web and DAML+OIL. *IEEE Intelligent Systems, 17*(1), 40-47.

Dukle, K.R. (2003). A Prototype Query-Answering Engine Using Semantic Reasoning. Master's Thesis, University of South Carolina.

Giarratano, J., & Riley, G. (1994). *Expert systems principles and programming*. PWS publishing company.

Gruber, T.R. (1993). A translation approach to portable ontology specifications. *Knowledge Acquisition, 5*, 199-220.

Guttman, R.H., & Maes, P. (1998). Agent-mediated integrative negotiation for retail electronic commerce. In P. Noriega & C. Sierra (Eds.), *Lecture Notes in Computer Science, Vol. 1571*, Springer-Verlag, pp. 70-90, First International Workshop on Agent Mediated Electronic Trading (AMET-98).

Horowitz, E., & Sahni, S. (1994). *Fundamentals of data structures in Pascal.* Computer Science Press.

Jung, J.J. (2002). Collaborative Web browsing system based on sharing bookmarks. Master's Thesis, Inha University, Korea.

Jung, J.J., Yoon, J.S., & Jo, G.S. (2000). BISAgent: Collaborative Web browsing through sharing of bookmark information. *Proceeding of the 16th IFIP World Computer Congress 2000 (IIP).*

Lashkari, Y. (1995). Webhound. Master's thesis, MIT Media Laboratory.

Lee, H.K., Yu, Y.H., Ghose, S., & Jo, G.S. (2003). Comparison shopping systems based on semantic Web – A case study of purchasing cameras. In M. Li, X.-H. Sun, Q. Deng, & J. Ni (Eds.), *Lecture Notes in Computer Science, Vol. 3032*, Springer-Verlag, pp. 139-146, Grid and Cooperative Computing, Second International Workshop (GCC 2003).

Lieberman, H., Dyke, N., & Vivacqua, A. (1999). Let's browse: A collaborative Web browsing agent. *Proceedings of the 1999 International Conference on Intelligent User Interfaces* (pp. 65-68).

Maes, P. (1994). Agents that reduce work and information overload. *Communications of the ACM, 37*(7), 31-41.

Pazzani, M., Nguyen, L., & Mantik, S. (1995). Learning from hotlists and coldlists: Towards a WWW information filtering and seeking agent. *Proceedings of the 7th International Conference on Tools with Artificial Intelligence* (pp. 492-493).

Pearl, J. (1988). *Probabilistic reasoning in intelligent systems.* Morgan Kauffman Publisher.

Pelillo, M., Siddiqi, K., & Zucker, S.W. (1999). Matching hierarchical structures using association graphs. *IEEE Transactions on Pattern Analysis and Machine Intelligence, 21*(11), 1105-1120.

Salton, G., & Lesk, M.E. (1988). Term-weighting approaches in automatic retrieval. *Information Processing & Management, 24*(5), 513-523.

Shardanand, U., & Maes, P. (1995). Social information filtering: Algorithms for automating word of mouth. *Proceedings of ACM CHI Conference on Human Factors in Computing Systems* (pp. 210-217).

Sheth, B., & Maes. P. (1993). Evolving agents for personalized information filtering. *Proceedings of the 9th IEEE Conference on Artificial Intelligence for Applications*, (pp. 345-352).

Twidale, M., & Nichols, D. (1996). Collaborative browsing and visualization of the search process. *Electronic Library and Visual Information Research Conference (ELVIRA-96).*

Wang, J., Zhang, J.K., Jeong, K., & Shasha, D. (1994). A System for Approximate Tree Matching. *IEEE Transaction on Knowledge and Data Engineering, 6*(4), 559-570.

Endnotes

1 The Web Ontology Language (OWL), http://www.w3.org/TR/2002/WD-owl-guide-20021104

2 DAML+OIL, http://www.daml.org/

3 RDFS, http://www.w3.org/TR/rdf-schema/

4 GVU's 10th WWW User Surveys, http://www.gvu.gatech.edu/user_surveys/survey- 1998-10/

5 Yahoo, http://www.yahoo.com

6 DMOZ, http://dmoz.org/

7 Jena toolkit, http://jena.sourceforge.net/

Chapter X

Design Principles and Applications of XRML

Jae Kyu Lee
Korea Advanced Institute of Science and Technology, Korea

Mye M. Sohn
Sungkyunkwan University, Korea

Abstract

XML has become the standard platform for structured data exchange on the Web. The next concern of the Semantic Web is the exchange and process of rules in markup language form. The rules should be represented in such a way as to allow software agents to process and browse them for human comprehension. For this purpose, we propose a language **eXtensible Rule Markup Language (XRML)**. *XRML is composed of rule identification, rule structure, and rule triggering markup languages. In XRML, a critical concern is how to extract the structured rules from the Web pages and keep consistency between the two. By using the XRML, the Web-based Knowledge Management Systems (KMS) can be integrated with rule-based expert systems. The advanced architecture with XRML can extend the application of KMS to automated form processing, preventive auditing, rule exchange and integration, and agent-based e-commerce.*

Introduction

The Hypertext Markup Language (HTML) makes Web technology possible by giving users the ability to browse. However, software agents cannot understand HTML files because their general-purpose natural language processing capability is not totally reliable or efficient. To overcome this limitation, the Extensible Markup Language (XML) explicates the implicitly embedded data in a formal structure with mutually agreed-on semantic definitions. A large number of industrial standard initiatives using the XML are under way, including ebXML (Electronic Business XML Initiative). Other XML initiatives include OTP (Open Trading Protocol), OBI (Open Business on the Internet), CBL (Common Business Language), RosettaNet, eBis-XML, BizTalk, XCBL, and others (Cover, 2004). Some of these are expected to make up the standards of message exchanges for Business-to-Business (B2B) EC. Knowledge representation for software agent communication has also adopted the XML platform (Grosof, 2001).

The Semantic Web community is concerned about processing the rules implicitly embedded in Web pages that cannot be processed with XML. The implicit rules must be represented in such a way as to allow software agents to process and browse the original Web pages for human comprehension. We have now developed a language — the eXtensible Rule Markup Language (XRML) — for this purpose; Figure 1 contrasts the topology of XRML with XML and HTML (Lee & Sohn, 2003). Pages written in XRML should be transformable into XML and eventually into HTML; an early version of XRML was presented in Lee (2000) and Sohn (2001).

The remainder of this chapter is organized as follows: we first identify components and objectives of XRML. Next, we review the relevant researches in XRML. The next section explains the syntax of Rule Identification Markup Language (RIML), Rule Structure Markup Language (RSML) and Rule Triggering Markup Language (RTML). Potential application areas and challenges of XRML are then identified. Finally, we conclude with a summary and the potential contributions.

Figure 1. Topology of XRML

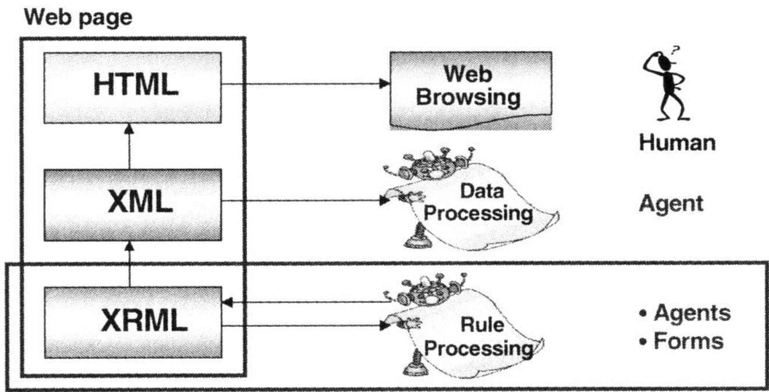

Components and Objectives of XRML

Components of XRML

In order to achieve these goals, XRML has three components (Lee & Sohn, 2003):

1. **Rule Identification Markup Language (RIML).** The meta-knowledge expressed in RIML should be able to identify the existence of implicit rules in the hypertexts on the Web; the formal association with the explicitly represented structured rules should also be identified.
2. **Rule Structure Markup Language (RSML).** The rules in knowledge-based systems (KBSs) must be represented in a formal structure so they can be processed with inference engines. The identified implicit rules are transformed into the formal rule structure of RSML. However, since there is no clue for linking two representations directly, we need an intermediate representation — RSML. The rules represented in RSML should be transformed automatically into structured rules, while RSML needs the support of generation and maintenance from RIML in hypertext.
3. **Rule Triggering Markup Language (RTML).** RTML defines the conditions that trigger certain rules. RTML is embedded in KBSs, as well as in software agents (such as the forms in workflow management systems).

Figure 2 outlines an architecture we designed to apply XRML to workflow management (Lee & Sohn, 2003). In this application, the RTML embedded in forms can trigger the inference engine to use the rules generated from RSML. Note that humans can read hypertext on the browser that XML statements are transformed to the database, and that RSML statements are transformed to rules in the rule base. The inference engine in the knowledge-based system calls rules and data and returns the inference results back to the inquiring software agents (workflow management system in this case). A challenging issue here is how to assist the extraction of RSML from hypertexts while maintaining consistency with RIML.

Design Criteria of XRML

As we designed XRML, we pursued six main goals (Lee & Sohn, 2003):

1. **Expressional Completeness.** RSML should be completely transformable into a canonical syntax of structured rules;
2. **Relevance Linkability.** Linkages of the relevance between hypertexts with RIML, as well as rules in RSML syntax (called RSML rules), should be expressed completely;

Figure 2. An illustrative architecture of XRML

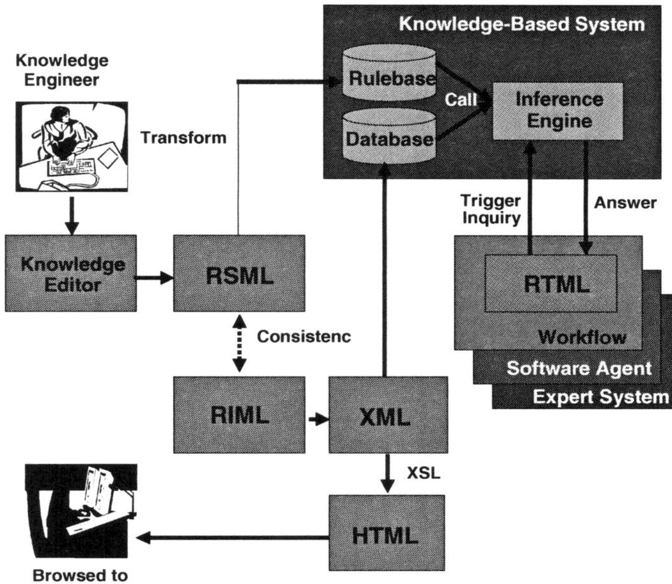

3. **Polymorphous Consistency.** Consistency should be maintained for knowledge expressed in various types of expressions (such as RSML rules and hypertext with RIML);
4. **Applicative Universality**. The rule expressions in RSML should be able to support multiple applications embedding RTML in the domain universe;
5. **Knowledge Integratability.** Structured rules collected from multiple sources, including those from RSML, should be integrated uniformly; and
6. **Interoperability.** Rules in RSML should be exchangeable and sharable among multiple commercial solutions.

Literature Review

KBSs and Knowledge Management Systems (KMSs)

To explain XRML's inherent practical value as a Semantic Web, consider two relevant disciplines — KBSs and KMSs — which, despite having similar names, have evolved from different research roots (see Table 1).

Table 1. Knowledge-based systems and knowledge management systems

System Title	KBS	KMS
Knowledge Processor	Inference Engine	Human
Inference	Forward/Backward Chaining, Approximate Reasoning	HyperLink, Keyword Search
Knowledge Representation	Rule, Predicate Calculus, Object (Frames)	HTML, XML, VRML
Scope of Knowledge	Specific Knowledge Base	Global Knowledge Portal Corporate Portal
Tools	Domain Specific	General Purpose
Popularity	Limited to the Application Users	Everybody, Everyday

Knowledge Based Systems

Stemming from research in artificial intelligence in the early 1980s (Liebowitz, 2001), a KBS's main goal is the automatic inference of coded knowledge. Natural language understanding is a key part of knowledge processing, but success in real-world applications has been limited. Therefore, for knowledge processing, practical KBSs use only structured knowledge representations (such as rules, predicate calculus, objects, and tailored inference engines). In light of its limited capability in commonsense reasoning, applications are developed for specific domains (such as diagnosis, configuration, manufacturing planning, and managerial decision making). Knowledge acquisition and maintenance have been hurdles for justifying implementation. The KBS application domain was recently expanded to include intelligent e-mail interpretation and classification, smart advisories about products for customer service and training, online configurations, and help desks providing technical support (Firepond, 2001). Knowledge acquisition from Web pages is being explored (Gaines & Shaw, 1997), as is a tool that automatically generates the hypertext structure (Song & Lee, 2000).

Knowledge Management Systems

On the contrary, the KMS has started with Web technology that supports powerful search engines over the vast knowledge on the Internet, intranet or extranet. The primary targeted users of KMS are not software agents, but human who desire comprehension with interactive search. Technically speaking, any knowledge on the Web (or any other storage structures such as a database) can be within the scope of a KMS application. The application area of KMS is thus very general, and can be used widely. So far knowledge management research has exploited the issues of knowledge sharing and reusing mainly from the managerial and motivational point of view.

Corporate portal, under a bright spotlight nowadays, is a new trial to accomplish knowledge sharing and reusing. Corporate portal makes it possible for inner and outer users of corporation to search, manipulate and share electronic resources including documents, enterprise application, e-business services and information from the Internet, stored in the corporate database.

Convergence of KBS and KMS with XRML

Commercial-scale KBS/KMS convergence is inevitable because knowledge should be sharable by humans and software agents (Liebowitz, 2000; O'Leary, 1998) and is precisely the goal XRML researchers pursue today. The necessity of maintaining consistency between the hypertext knowledge in KMS and the structured rules in KBS is a key research issue in XRML development. XRML is thus a framework for integrating KBSs and KMSs.

Generating RSML rules from hypertext can be regarded as a process of knowledge extraction; generating meta-knowledge of the relationships between hypertext and RSML rules (regarding which hypertext is related to which RSML rules and vice versa) is a process of meta-knowledge extraction. Knowledge acquisition from a variety of sources is generally very expensive, but knowledge extraction from existing hypertexts is less a social issue than a technical issue and thus can be cost-effective.

A sea of hypertext knowledge is already coded in markup language form on the Internet, so the cost of XRML applications is readily justified while yielding enormous benefit. XRML is not only the next step for KBSs and KMSs but also the direction rule markup language researchers worldwide are pursuing for the Semantic Web (Berners-Lee, Hendler, & Lassila, 2001; Boley, Tabet & Wagner, 2001).

Rule Markup Language Research

The emerging research in rule markup languages covers a range of issues; for example, RuleML was described in (Boley & Tabet, 2004). Although most of it focuses on the representation of rules, objects, cases, and functions in XML format, they do not cover the knowledge association and consistency issues found in XRML (Lee & Sohn, 2003):

1. **Business Rules Markup Language:** Specifies a common rule structure to exchange rules between heterogeneous rule-based systems;
2. **Agent-Object-Relationship Markup Language:** Describes the business rules to be processed with software agents, including the business process, interaction process, sequence of events, actions, activities, and control;

3. **Universal Rule Markup Language:** Represents the input/output data of AI applications in XML for reducing conversion effort and time;
4. **Artificial Intelligence Markup Language:** Is the XML specification for the Artificial Linguistic Internet Computer Entity (ALICE) using a simple pattern-matching technique;
5. **Case-Based Markup Language:** Is an XML-based case-representation language for achieving interoperability and flexibility of case reuse; and
6. **Relational-Functional Markup Language:** Is an XML version of Relfun, a logic programming language using call-by-value expressions.

XRML can be applied to a spectrum of Web-based KBSs and make KMSs more intelligent.

Syntax of RIML, RSML, and RTML

Consider the syntax of RIML, RSML, and RTML; see Sohn (2001) for the full XRML 1.0 syntax, along with an example application involving research fund account management.

Rule Identification Markup Language

Suppose two paragraphs in HTML describe the regulations about a research budget's expenditures:

```
<HTML>
<p>A research account can be spent only within the limit of the contract budget, according to the following restrictions.</p>
<p>If the budgetary source is the type-P research fund, the spendable items are limited to on student's salary and expenses for data collection.</p>
</HTML>
```

The second paragraph includes an implicit rule that can be explicitly expressed as:

```
Rule Title: Restriction of Type-P Research Fund Expenditure
IF          ((budgetary source IS type-P research fund)
   AND      ((spendable item IS student's salary)
        OR (spendable item IS expense for data collection)))
THEN        expenditure IS permitted
```

Even though the two types of expression imply the same regulation, the relationship between them is not clear. So we need to add meta-knowledge on how the text relates to the structured rule, as outlined in the following example:

<HTML>

<p>A research account can be spent only within the limit of the contract budget, according to the restrictions.</p>

<RIML>

<Rule>

<RuleTitle> Restriction of Type-P Research Fund Expenditure **</RuleTitle>**

<p>If the **<variable1>**budgetary source**<variable1>** is the **<value1>**type-P research fund**</value1>**, the**<variable2>**spendable items**</variable2>** are limited to on **<value2>**student's salary**</value2>** and **<value2>**expenses for data collection**</value2>.**</p>

</Rule>

</RIML>

</HTML>

Here, the section related to the structured rules is delineated by *<RIML> ... </RIML>*. The rule and its title are identified by *<Rule> ... </Rule>* and *<RuleTitle> ... </RuleTitle>*. The tags *<variable#>* and *<value#>* identify the variables and values used in the structured rule. The same numbers in the tags imply a particular association between a variable and a value. The HTML/RIML can be transformed into the original HTML file by eliminating RIML statements. The transformation process can become increasingly complex as more RIML commands are employed for arithmetical functions.

In XRML 2.0, the tag set of RIML is extended by adding the algebraic operators, functions, and rule tables which extract rules from tables (Kang & Lee, 2003). For instance, the sentence of RIML in XRML 2.0 is represented as follows:

<variable1> items </variable1> <operator1 type="GT"> greater than </operator1> <value1>2</value1>

The HTML/RIML editor should support the process of editing the hypertext as well as its meta-knowledge.

Rule Structure Markup Language

The fragments of a rule that is identified RIML should be transformed to a structured rule that can be readily associated with RIML. Note that the variables are transformed into tags in XML syntax with their values within the paired tags. Rules in this syntax can be directly matched with the data in the XML file — a big advantage of RSML.

```
<RSML>
<Rule>
<RuleTitle> Restriction of Type-P Research Fund Expenditure </RuleTitle>
<IF>
    <AND>
        <budgetary source>type-P research fund</budgetary source>
    <OR>
        <spendable item>student's salary</spendable item>
        <spendable item>expense for data collection</spendable item>
    </OR>
    </AND>
</IF>
<THEN>
    <Result Action="Add_Value">
        <expenditure>permitted</expenditure>
    </Result>
</THEN>
</Rule>
</RSML>
```

Note that the variables and values in RSML are the same as the words identified in RIML. Using the definitions in RIML, the RSML editor generates a crude version of the rules by assigning the key words to corresponding slots of variables and values. The tag set of RSML is extended as RIML did. In XRML 2.0, the consistency between multiple Web pages and a rule base is maintained with the assistance of cross-checking meta-knowledge (Kang & Lee, 2003). A thesaurus of synonyms and the plausibility of associations between a variable and the other(s), and between a variable and relevant value(s) in the domains can assist the knowledge editing and maintenance making the processes easier and more accurate. Developing the aids for consistent maintenance in the context of ontology is an interesting research issue worth exploring.

RSML statements can be transformed into canonical rules by matching the reserved words of RSML. To improve the automated editing of RSML, knowledge engineers need to specify more meta-knowledge during the RIML stage; for instance, if the association's knowledge concerning a variable and a value is specified in RIML, a statement with the variable and the value can be generated automatically, as mentioned earlier. Thus, the total effort needed for knowledge management is determined by how RIML and RSML are generated and maintained.

RTML

RTML is a language embedded in such applications as forms in workflow management and in software agents. Therefore, RTML has to define a set of standard statements about when to trigger the inference, as well as which rules to use and how to use the obtained result. RTML tags are useful for identifying the relevant tags in RIML and RSML and the data files in the XML format.

The following example of RTML syntax shows that when a requisition using *Type-P* research funds is requested, the rule-based inference is triggered to derive the permission decision:

```
<RTML>
<WhenTrigger>
<AND>
    <requisition>on</requisition>
    <budgetary source>type-P research fund </budgetary source>
</AND>
</WhenTrigger>
<Bring>
    <RuleTitle>Restriction of Type-P Research Fund Expenditure</RuleTitle>
    <DataFile>Research Fund Accounts</DataFile>
</Bring>
<Result>
    <expenditure>permitted</expenditure >
</Result>
</RTML>
```

The tag *<WhenTrigger>* specifies the condition of rule triggering; *<Bring>* brings the relevant rules and data to the inference engine; and *<Result>* returns the inference result as the value of the tag. The application program, probably written in Java, can call up the returned results.

Applicative Examples of XRML

We have touched on the outline of XRML application in the workflow environment above. In this section, we will demonstrate the advantages of XRML with form processing which is related to the process of expenditure in the KAIST P-type research account.

Rule Identification Procedure

To generate the structured rules, we should identify the fragments of the rule which is implicit in the HTML document. So we had developed the XRML editor in order to support the rule identification process. Enriched tag sets of RIML in XRML 2.0 have summarized Table 2.

These RIML tags should be added to the HTML document. Identification steps are summarized in Kang and Lee (2004) in detail.

Table 2. Meaning of tags in RIML 2.0

Element - Attributes	Description
RIML - version	Root element of RIML and it's version number
RuleGroup	The element "RuleGroup" envelops the body of rule group.
URL – RSML	It is the Uniform Resource Locator (URL) that the RSML rule is extracted from.
RuleTable	It envelopes a table that can be converted to the structured rule.
Rule - id	The element "Rule" envelops the body of rule. The presence of this element indicates that at least one variable, value, and operator will be defined within the rule.
IF/THEN	It matches of condition and action part of structured rule.
AND/OR/NOT	AND and OR are connectives between terms, while NOT is a prefix.
variable – id, name, standard	This represents a variable name, and its attribute "id" shows its sequential order generated.
value – id, name, standard	This represents a value name, and its attribute "id" shows its sequential order generated.

Rule Structuring Procedure

The RIML rule should be transformed to a structured rule named RSML. Such transformation is accomplished by the addition of omitted variables, values, and operators. An illustrative statement of RSML is depicted in Figure 3.

The XRML editor can partially support the rule structuring procedure. The knowledge engineer must make the rule complete by an IF and THEN part. In other words, it should be performed to remove incompleteness and inconsistency of the rule in the refinement process (Liebowitz, 2001; Nguyen, Perkins & Walton, 1987; Torsun, 1995).

Automated Form Processing

To pay a student's salary, a project manager, for instance Mr. Lee, will want to draft a payment requisition form. To do so, a project manager should upload the digital payment requisition form from the Workflow Management System in KAIST as shown in Figure 4. After a project manager inputs appropriate values in each item such as recipient, reference, sender, unit, rank, and ID number, RTML is activated. RTML sends an inquiry to the KBS in order to check whether the payment is appropriate. KBS derives the answer from the rule-based inference and returns the inference result to the payment requisition form. Form process may proceed to next step or return to previous step as inference result.

Figure 3. An illustrative RSML-type rule

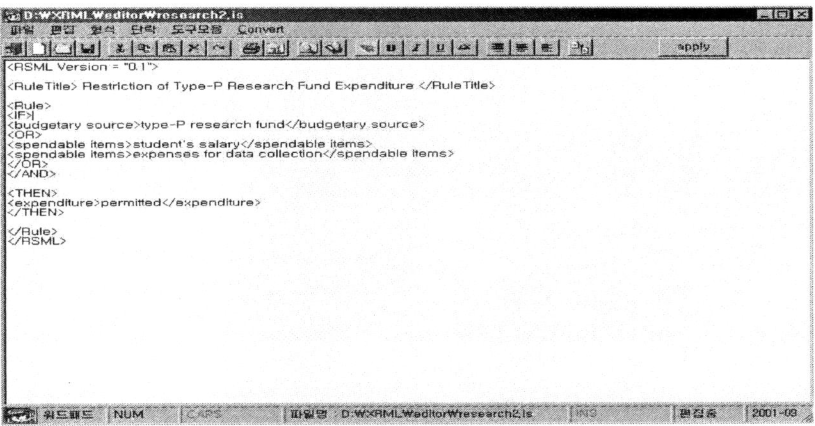

Figure 4. Payment requisition form of ICEC

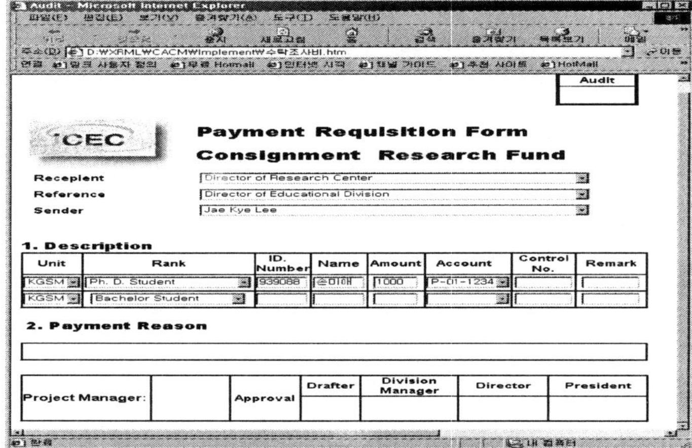

Audit

ICEC

Payment Requisition Form

Consignment Research Fund

Recepient: Director of Research Center
Reference: Director of Educational Division
Sender: Jae Kye Lee

1. Description

Unit	Rank	ID. Number	Name	Amount	Account	Control No.	Remark
KGSM	Ph. D. Student	939088	손미애	1000	P-01-1234		
KGSM	Bachelor Student						

2. Payment Reason

Project Manager:		Approval	Drafter	Division Manager	Director	President

Other applicative areas of XRML are as follows:

- **Automated Form Processing.** Object-oriented forms equipped with RTML can trigger inquiries for automated approval of routine and frequent tasks (such as business travel reimbursement and petty acquisitions). This function is effectively integrated with desktop purchases in which the requisitioner bypasses both the approval process and the procurement department (Lee & Efraim, 2001). The hypertext used in forms can also be visualized for the requisitioners via the Web.
- **Preventive Auditing.** Certain activities need to be audited. Audit knowledge implemented in XRML can be displayed for the inquirers and automatically stamp the auditors' approval. Auditors can focus on knowledge maintenance instead of on audit transactions.
- **Knowledge Exchange and Integration:** The rules in different organizations can be shared by exchanging the XRML rules. The transmitted rules can be displayed to receivers, integrated with the existing rules in the receiver's site, and processed by the receiver's agents. Regulations by government and corporate could be integrated in this architecture as depicted in Figure 5 (Lee, 2003).
- **Agent-Based Intra- and Inter-Organizational E-Commerce.** During B2B transactions and collaboration, software agents can request knowledge about products and services, as well as about contract terms and conditions. XRML is particularly useful in call centers because human agents are often not expert enough to address the inquiries. In this case, they may use the relevant KBS and share it with customers. Synchronized Web browsers for both human agents and customers would improve their communication.

Figure 5. Inter-organizational knowledge sharing with XRML

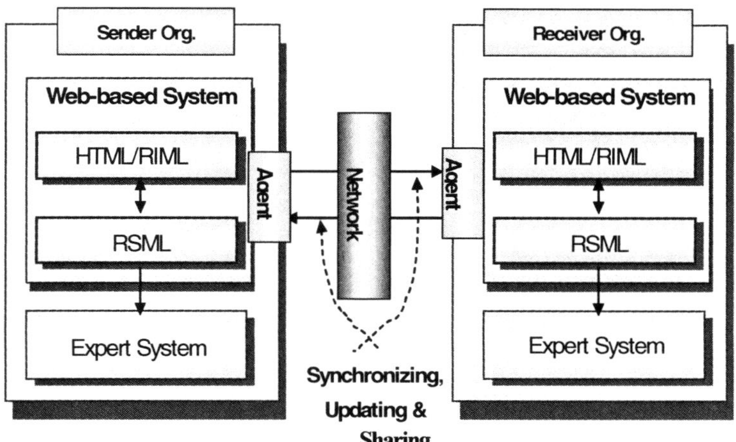

Challenges – The Opportunity

The technical challenges involved in implementing XRML in real-world applications should be viewed more as an opportunity than a hurdle:

- **Consistent Maintenance of Polymorphic Knowledge Representations.** The same data and rules may exist in a relational database, in HTML and XML files, in RSML, and in the rulebase. So when one type of knowledge or data changes, consistency must be maintained. Consistency in XRML among HTML/RIML, RSML, and XML is especially important. Meta-knowledge supports the process.
- **Domain-Specific Thesaurus.** RIML can start with a natural language-independent syntax. Understanding the syntax of a particular natural language (such as English and Korean) is, however, helpful for identifying the relationships among variables and values. Moreover, to support the frequently used domains, including online customer support for electronic products, knowledge engineers can a priori define the relationship among vocabulary items.
- **Multi-URL-Based Inference.** In the earlier example concerning the research fund account, a single Web page was used to infer a certain issue. However, an inference may require more than one Web page. Therefore, because the RSML rules need to maintain the information about the URL, as well as the rules in each URL, the tags in XRML also have to be extended.
- **Integration of Rules from RSML and other Sources.** When inquiries by RTML require knowledge from RSML, as well as from other sources, RTML should be able to identify the rules from all necessary sources. If all types of rules are transformed

into a canonical structure in advance, then no matter what the initial form had been, the problems at execution time can be avoided. However, this approach increases the integration effort during knowledge maintenance.

The current research topics of the XRML working group are the following:

- **Knowledge Acquisition Methodology from Web pages:** Rules can be acquired more effectively from Web pages by RIML. In order to achieve the enhanced rule acquisition, we design a RIML editor that supports the rule identification. To enrich the target representation of Web pages, RIML is identified not only from the natural texts, but also the tables and implicit numeric functions. The performance of using RIML is experimented by acquiring rules about delivery service from Amazon.com, and we found that 90 percent of rule completeness could be obtained.
- **XRML Ontology:** Ontology can be used in building XRML documents. By using the ontology, an intelligent rule editor can automatically recommend identification of variable and value during the identification step. At the same time, an intelligent rule editor can detect and recommend specialization and generalization operation to modify the existing rules according to the new rules. Ontology can also be used to check incompleteness and inconsistency in the rule base.
- **XRML-S:** To integrate the XRML and the Web services, we are conducting the research about XRML-S. In XRML-S architecture, the application programs equipped with RTML statement does not have to know their interaction objects previously. Instead, when the application program is necessary to interact with another application program, XRML-S goes through "search-decision-interaction" process. Automatic processing between software agents on the Web can be enabled because of the advent of XRML-S. As XRML adopt the *de-facto* standards of Web services, it will become more popular.

Concluding Remarks

During the past two years, we designed the XRML version 2.0 and developed its prototype, called Form/XRML an automated form processing platforms, making knowledge management and e-commerce more intelligent. Since many research groups and vendors are investigating these issues, we expect to see XRML in commercial products within a few years. Meanwhile, mature XRML applications may change the way information and knowledge systems are designed and used.

Acknowledgment

An earlier version of this chapter was published in the *Communications of the ACM*, in May 2003.

References

Berners-Lee, T. Hendler, J., & Lassila, O. (2001). *The Semantic Web*. Scientific American.

Boley, H., & Tabet, S. (2001). Rule Markup Language. See *http://www.dfki.uni-kl.de/ruleml*

Boley, H., Tabet, S., & Wagner G. (2001). Design rationale of RuleML: A markup language for semantic Web rules. *Proceedings of the International Semantic Web Working Symposium.* See *www.semanticweb.org/swws/ program/full/paper20.pdf*

Cover, R. (2004). The XML Cover Pages–XML Articles and Papers, *http://xml.coverpages.org/XMLArticles.html*

Firepond, Inc. (2001). E-ServicePerformer Concierge. See *www.firepond.com/SPconcierge.pdf*

Gaines, R. & Shaw, L. (1997). Knowledge acquisition, modeling, and inference through the World Wide Web. Center for Person-Computer Studies, Knowledge Science Institute, University of Calgary, Canada.

Grosof, N. (2001) Standardizing XML rules: Rules for e-business on the Semantic Web (invited talk). *Workshop on E-business and the Intelligent Web at the International Joint Conference on Artificial Intelligence.*

Kang, J., & J. Lee (2003). Extraction of structured rules from Web pages and maintenance of mutual consistency: XRML approach. *Second International Workshop, RuleML 2003.8.*

Lee, J. (2000). Artificial intelligence in electronic commerce. *Plenary speech at the Pacific Rim International Conference on Artificial Intelligence.* See *www.icec.net*

Lee, J. (2003). Sematic Web with XRML. *The Second International Human Society@ Internet Conference*, 10.

Lee, J. & Efraim, T. Planning B2B e-procurement marketplaces. In P. Lowry, J. Cherrington, & R. Watson (Eds.), *Handbook of electronic commerce in business and society.* CRC Press LLC.

Lee, J., Song, Y.U., Kwon, S.B., Kim, W.J., & Kim, M.Y. (1996). Rule Syntax of UNIK-BWD. Development of Expert System with UNIK, Bup Young, Ltd.

Lee, J. K., & Sohn, M. (2003). The extensible rule markup language *Communications of the ACM, 46*(5), 59-64.

Liebowitz, J. (2001). *Knowledge management: Learning from knowledge engineering.* CRC Press LLC.

Nguyen, T., Perkins, A. & Walton, A. (1987). Knowledge base verification. *AI Magazine*, *8*(2), 69-75.

O'Leary, E. (1998). Using AI in knowledge management: Knowledge management and ontologies. *IEEE Intelligent System*, *13*(3), 34-39.

Sohn, M. (2001). XRML, Version 1.0. Korea Advanced Institute of Science and Technology, Seoul; see *xrml.kaist.ac.kr*

Song, Y. & Lee, J. (2000). Automatic generation of Web-based expert systems. *J. Intelligent Information System*, *6*(1), 1-16 (in Korean).

Torsun, I.S. (1995). *Foundations of intelligent knowledge-based systems*. Academic Press.

Section V

Web Maintenance and Evolution:

Techniques and Methodologies

Chapter XI

Program Transformations for Web Application Restructuring

Filippo Ricca
ITC-irst, Italy

Paolo Tonella
ITC-irst, Italy

Abstract

This chapter aims at providing a presentation of the principles and techniques involved in the (semi-)automatic transformation of Web applications, in several different restructuring contexts. The necessary background knowledge is provided to the reader in the sections about the syntax of the multiple languages involved in Web application development and about the role of restructuring in a highly dynamic and rapidly evolving development environment. Then, specific examples of Web restructuring are described in detail. In the presentation of the transformations required for restructuring, as well as in the description of the grammar for the involved languages, TXL (Cordy, Dean, Malton & Schneider, 2002) and its programming language is adopted as a unifying element. The chapter is organized into the following sections: in the section following the Introduction, *the problems associated with the analysis of the multiple languages used with Web applications are discussed. Then, the process of Web application restructuring is considered. Three examples of Web restructuring are described in more detail in the next three sections (design restructuring, migration of a static Web site to a dynamic Web application, consistency among monolingual portions of a multilingual Web site). Related works and concluding remarks are at the end of the chapter.*

Introduction

All known problems that characterize the evolution of software systems are exacerbated in the case of Web applications, because their typical life cycle is much shorter and their development iterations are executed faster and more frequently. In fact, Web applications must accommodate continuing changing requirements, since the user's needs evolve rapidly over time. Moreover, the infrastructure technology is itself subject to continuous updates. New technologies emerge at a high rate, replacing the existing ones. A strong pressure for change comes also from the market, where it is fundamental to be up to date with the new services and paradigms.

The consequences of a high evolution rate are often very negative for the internal quality of the Web applications. The initial architecture is subject to a drift, so that the original assignment of responsibilities to components is violated and the dependencies among components tend to resemble a fully connected graph. Code fragments may be duplicated, thus making the related functionality delocalized, and consequently difficult to maintain and reuse. While in the beginning such negative effects may be invisible to the end user, after some time the application becomes unmanageable. New requirements are difficult to accommodate, nobody has a sufficient understanding of the architecture to allow for major changes, and defects tend to be inserted with the modifications, due to unexpected ripple effects.

The evolution scenario described above is more complicated with Web applications than with traditional software, because of the technologies underlying their development. In fact, Web applications involve a basic client-server architecture, with the browser as the client and the Web server on the other side, upon which higher level functionalities are built. Since multiple users can connect concurrently, user sessions must be handled over time. However, this is not supported by the HTTP protocol in use, which is stateless and connectionless. When transactions are executed inside user sessions, the problem is even harder. Security is another central concern. The support technologies used to solve these problems are based on multiple standards and programming languages. Consequently, the resulting Web application is composed of a heterogeneous set of components written in different languages and based on different standards. Portability across environments and browsers is another factor that complicates the internal organization of the Web applications.

When the evolution of a Web application makes its source code difficult to maintain, the typical action that is undertaken consists of rewriting the entire application from scratch in the new setting. In this chapter, a different approach is considered. It is based on the notion of continuous restructuring, and it assumes that preventive interventions can be made to avoid the progressive degradation that accompanies software evolution. Restructuring is an expensive activity for which a budget is rarely available in a highly competitive market such as that of Web applications. However, the possibility to (partially) automate restructuring can make it cost-effective. Its adoption would involve periodic interventions of preventive maintenance that precede the actual implementation of the required changes.

Web Application Languages

Web applications are typically developed in multiple programming languages. Browsers are able to interpret HTML, so that this is the language that every Web application must include. However, any non trivial Web application involves some processing that occurs on the server side and produces a part of the displayed information. Moreover, the interactive facilities offered by purely HTML pages are often too poor and more advanced navigation modes are achieved by inserting code that runs on the client side. Thus, a typical Web application is written in at least three languages: HTML, a server side language (e.g., PHP) and a client side language (e.g., Javascript). Additional languages may be involved in the server side computation. For example, database access is typically achieved using SQL.

This section deals with the problems specific to each programming language used in Web development. The HTML language has features that are challenging from the point of view of its analysis and manipulation. Moreover, the coexistence of multiple languages in a single source file poses additional problems. A grammar of the HTML+PHP+Javascript languages is sketched in order to indicate possible solutions to the highlighted problems. The TXL language is used for grammar specification. In the next section, the most important TXL constructs, used in the following sections, are summarized, for convenience of the readers who are not familiar with this transformation language.

TXL

TXL (Cordy, Dean, Malton & Schneider, 2002) is a programming language designed to support the transformation of source code represented as a tree. A TXL program consists mainly of a context-free grammar and a set of transformation functions and rules. Given a grammar of the language under analysis, the parse tree of the source code is first, automatically, built, and TXL functions/rules are applied to it.

In a TXL grammar specification, each *"define"* statement contains the productions for each nonterminal. The vertical bar | is used to separate the alternatives. Nonterminals appearing in the body of a *define* statement are enclosed in square brackets, while symbols not enclosed in brackets are terminals. Conventionally, the nonterminal *program* is the goal symbol, that is, the root of the parse tree being built.

Any nonterminal enclosed in square brackets may be modified by a nonterminal modifier. An example is the modifier *repeat.* If a nonterminal is preceded by *repeat,* zero or more repetitions of such a nonterminal are admitted. For example, the following *define* statement specifies that the nonterminal *program* derives into a repetition of zero or more *element* nonterminals:

```
define program
    [repeat element]
end define
```

Transformation of the source code is specified as a set of transformation functions and rules. Each function (rule) contains a *pattern* and a *replacement*. The former is the pattern that the function's (rule's) argument tree must match in order for the function (rule) to be applicable, while the latter is the result of the function (rule) application. A rule has the same syntax as a function (except for the keyword *function*, replaced by *rule*), but its semantics are quite different: a rule repeatedly searches the scope tree where it is applicable and replaces every such match, while a function is applied just once to its argument tree. The TXL syntax for the specification of a pattern and its replacement is the following:

```
replace [type]
    pattern
by
    replacement
```

where *type* is the subtree root type (nonterminal), and *pattern* must comply with such a type (i.e., it has to be derivable from the nonterminal). Of course, *replacement* must also be of the same type.

Rules and functions may contain constructors (keyword *construct*) and deconstructors (keyword *deconstruct*). Constructors allow building intermediate subtrees for later use, while deconstructors allow breaking tree variables into smaller pieces (subtrees), by means of a more refined pattern. When a deconstructor pattern does not match, the whole function/rule is considered to have not matched its pattern at all. The following examples deconstruct/construct a list into/out of head and tail:

```
deconstruct list
    head [element] tail [repeat element]
```

```
construct list [repeat element]
    head tail
```

Searching deconstructors (keyword *deconstruct* *) are a specialization of deconstructors. They allow searching and taking a subtree of the deconstructed tree. A searching deconstructor has the following form:

```
deconstruct * tree
    pattern
```

The semantics of this construct is: searching the tree bound to variable tree for the first subtree that matches the *pattern* and binding the pattern variables accordingly.

HTML

Parsing HTML may seem an easy task at first sight, since HTML is defined precisely by its DTD (Document Type Definition, see www.w3c.org). Unfortunately, only a few real world Web pages are compliant with it: HTML pages with missing end tags, overlapped tags, or tags in the wrong context with respect to the DTD are quite common in existing Web sites and are not rejected by many of the available HTML browsers. For this reason, our grammar (see Figure 1) does not enforce the DTD, being more general. The parse tree that is built out of this grammar is pretty simple, consisting just of a sequence of elements: tags (nonterminal *Tag*), end tags (*endTag*) and texts (*htmlText*). The usage of the nonterminal *TagBlock* is clarified below.

In Figure 1, *special* includes all punctuation marks and special symbols; *value* represents strings (possibly double or single quoted); *id* indicates an identifier.

The HTML parser works into two steps. First, a flat sequence of *element* subtrees is appended to the parse tree, ignoring the nesting structure of the HTML tags. Then, nesting is taken into account and the initial parse tree is modified to properly represent it.

In the first step, the parser does not attempt to match start tags with corresponding end tags. This is done more easily after the parsing phase (second step) by a set of transformation rules (not shown here) that build *TagBlock* elements. A *TagBlock* is a composite element (see Figure 1) consisting of a tag (first *id*), a matching end tag (second *id*), and a sequence of elements (*repeat element*) in between. Each time a pair of matching

Figure 1. HTML grammar specified in TXL

```
define program
    [repeat element]
end define
define element
    [htmlText] | [TagBlock] | [Tag] | [endTag]
end define
define htmlText
    [repeat idORspecial]
end define
define idORspecial
    [id] | [special]
end define
define TagBlock
    Block([id][opt attrs] [repeat element])[id] | [empty]
end define
define Tag
    <[id] [opt attrs]>
end define
define attrs
    [repeat attr]
end define
define attr
    [id] = [value] | [id]
end define
define endTag
    </[id]>
end define
```

open and closed tags is found in the initial parse tree, a *TagBlock* subtree is constructed which replaces the original pair of tags and the enclosed *element* sequence.

The main advantage of this approach to HTML parsing is that documents that do not comply with the standard HTML DTD are not rejected. A parse tree can always be constructed for any HTML input, with start tags and matching end tags transformed into *TagBlocks* whenever possible. Such a transformation reproduces the structure of the HTML document in the parse tree when the HTML DTD is respected, while maintaining a flat sequence of elements when the HTML DTD is violated. Having *TagBlocks* in the parse tree is essential in the process of restructuring by means of transformation rules, because typical transformation patterns include the specification of a nesting structure to be matched.

Multiple Programming Languages

Another important aspect to consider in the parsing phase is that a Web page may contain several different languages: HTML, scripting languages (e.g., Javascript), style sheet languages (e.g., CSS) and server side languages (e.g., PHP). In the following, HTML, Javascript and PHP are considered. A solution to this problem is working concurrently with multiple languages. TXL permits defining grammars for the different languages that may appear in a same source file and allows working with "mixed trees" (see Figure 2).

In order to admit multiple subtree types inside the resulting parse tree, the HTML grammar given in Figure 1 has to be extended, by redefining the nonterminal *element* in the following way:

```
redefine element
   ... | php_code | javascript_code
end redefine
```

Figure 2. Mixed parse tree, containing a Javascript subtree

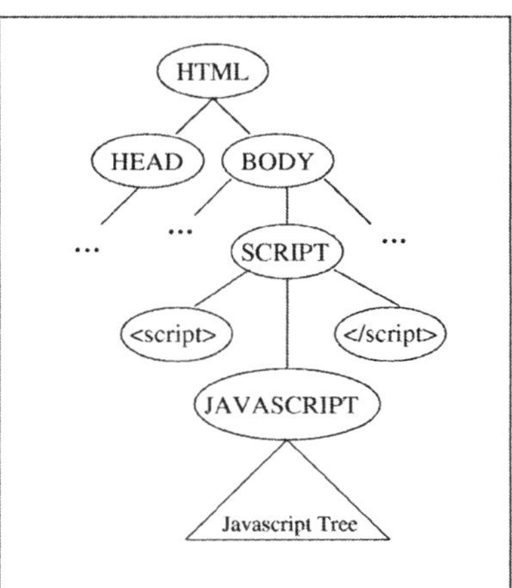

In addition to the previous productions (indicated by the ellipsis), *element* can now derive into a PHP or a Javascript subtree. The following new productions for the PHP and Javascript subtrees are added:

```
define php_code
  [start_php] [sequence_php] [end_php]
end define
define javascript_code
  [start_javascript] [sequence_javascript] [end_javascript]
end define
```

The nonterminals *start_php* and *end_php* are the alternative tags that can be used to insert portions of PHP inside HTML code (for example <? and ?>), while *sequence_php* is a repetition of PHP statements, PHP declarations, and PHP expressions, such as the actual body of the PHP code fragment. The same holds for Javascript code portions.

Web Application Restructuring

The life cycle that characterizes Web application development is extremely short and the user requirements are very volatile, so that the evolution of a Web application is particularly hard. Radical changes in the adopted technologies, user interface, data access and format, and presentation modes, are quite common, and may result in a progressive degradation of the Web application architecture, if not addressed properly. Continuous restructuring, as prescribed in the Extreme Programming development process (Jeffries, Anderson, & Hendrickson, 2000), is the key to manage the complexity resulting from a high evolution rate.

Process

In Figure 3, the role of restructuring in the whole Web engineering process is highlighted. During Web site evolution, a modification of the source code is triggered by a change request. The origin of the change request may vary, ranging from a new user requirement to the availability of new technologies, but it is always reflected into a source code change.

When no restructuring practice is in use, the process of source code change involves four main steps. First, the code portion to be changed is located. Such a task is mainly a program comprehension task, which might be quite difficult if the Web application has a large size and is not well documented. Then, the direct and indirect effects associated with the located change are assessed (impact analysis), to determine the actual amount of code to be updated. The next step is the implementation of the change, followed by

Figure 3. Role of restructuring in the process of Web site evolution

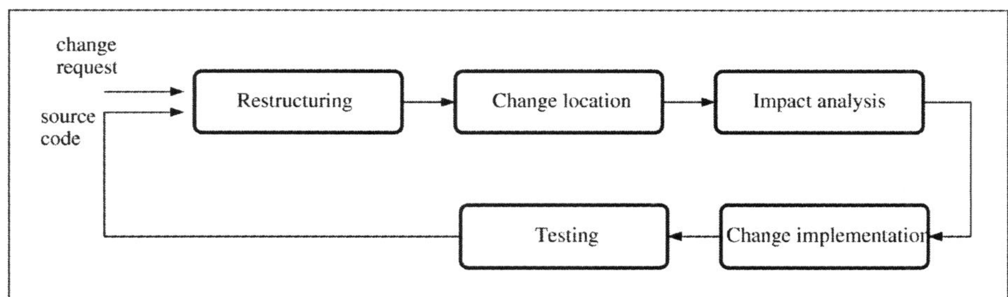

a testing phase where the functionalities expected by the application are verified. In the context of Web applications, which are subject to a tremendous pressure for change, the cycle depicted in Figure 3 is repeated several times, with very close deadlines for its completion.

The consequence of a fast and repeated execution of the four rightmost steps in Figure 3 is typically a degradation of the initial architecture of the Web application and an increasing difficulty in managing the complexity of the software and its evolution. These negative effects can be contrasted by introducing a fifth step, which precedes the other four ones, and is focused on a preventive reorganization of the Web application, aimed at improving its internal structure, thus simplifying and anticipating future changes. If supported by automated tools, the introduction of a restructuring step may be cost-effective even in a rapidly evolving environment with a very short life cycle, such as that of Web engineering.

Preventive restructuring ensures that location of the change will be easier, since functionalities are properly assigned to software components. The impact of the change will be much more limited, thanks to a lower coupling among components. Implementation of the change will be straightforward, and testing will also be limited to the test cases that exercise the (small) code portion that was changed.

Restructuring Categories

The main kinds of restructuring interventions that are specific to Web applications are the following:

- **Syntax Update**
- **Internal Page Improvement**
- **Design Restructuring**
- **Separation of Style/Presentation from Content**
- **Dynamic Page Construction**

Syntax Update

The W3C consortium defines the standard version of the HTML language. However, popular browsers are often tolerant to syntax errors and non compliances with the standard, and they succeed rendering a given HTML page even if it is not syntactically correct. Moreover, the tools that support the creation of Web pages often introduce syntax errors in the HTML code they automatically produce. As a consequence, several existing HTML pages do not follow the standard.

To further complicate the matter, the standard itself which defines the syntax of HTML changes over time. Old documents should therefore be updated to the new versions of the standard. However, browsers are often tolerant also in this respect, accepting documents that follow the old standard, as well as those that follow the new one.

The main disadvantage of a Web site that contains pages with syntax errors or pages not compliant with the current standard is that its correct visualization depends on the ability of the browsers to recover from syntax errors in a reasonable way. Such a feature may vary from browser to browser, so that there is no warranty of portability across browsers. Moreover, new versions of the same browser may handle syntax errors differently. For these reasons, it is advisable to update the syntax of the HTML pages in a Web site, making them compliant with the standard. One of the tools available for such a purpose is *Tidy* (see the W3C Web site, www.w3c.org).

Internal Page Improvement

Restructuring interventions, in the *internal page improvement* category, aim at supporting easier-to-follow and shorter navigation paths. Moreover, they operate on the mechanisms used to inter-connect documents and objects.

For example, the transformation of absolute URLs into relative URLs (by means of the tag *BASE*) is an internal improvement of a navigation mechanism that makes the references to other resources independent from the base directory containing them and from the server hosting the site. The addition of a *NOFRAMES* section in the HTML code allows a correct navigation also in browsers which do not handle frames. The addition of a description for non loaded objects (such as applets and movies) makes the Web site useful also for users who disable such object loading.

Design Restructuring

Restructuring of the design refers to the overall architecture of the Web application. It affects the decomposition of the software into components and the mechanisms used to make components communicate with each other. The quality of the architecture is one of the main factors that influence the maintainability and evolvability of the Web application. Thus, these restructuring interventions are essential to preserve and increase the internal quality of the source code.

Examples of design restructuring are the reorganization into frames of pages containing hard-coded menus, the migration of part of the content to a database (see also below), the separation of different concerns (such as security, style, etc.) and their assignment to different components, the factorization of replicated functionalities into shared library components.

Separation of Style/Presentation from Content

Separation of style/presentation from content can be achieved by resorting to style sheets, such as CSS, to control layout and presentation, so that formatting tags can be removed from the pages. Moreover, Content Management Systems (CMS) can be employed to reach an even higher degree of separation between the content, not necessarily written in HTML, and its HTML version, that is published on the Web.

Dynamic Page Construction

Dynamic page construction is useful each time the actual HTML page transmitted to the browser depends on some user-specific parameters. If all possible combinations of parameters are accounted for by a static set of HTML pages, the number of such pages tend to explode, making the site impossible to manage. A parametric dynamic generation of these pages may solve the problem.

An example where dynamic generation might be convenient is the presence of several pages with a same structure (template), filled in with variable parts. Instead of replicating the structure for all possible variants, a same template is dynamically filled in with information extracted from a database. Another example is a Web site that provides the same information in multiple languages (e.g., English and Italian). Instead of replicating the pages for all supported languages, a shared page structure can be filled in with a monolingual content selected dynamically.

In the following sections, three of the restructuring examples sketched above are considered in more detail: design restructuring, migration to dynamic sites, where data and presentation are stored separately, and support to the automatic consistency among Web site portions written in different languages.

Design Restructuring

An example of design restructuring is the *automatic reorganization into frames*. This transformation allows separating menu and content in a Web application where the menu is inserted and replicated in all pages.

When a menu is embedded in Web pages, usually a portion of HTML code is devoted to it. For example, the HTML construct *TABLE* may be exploited to format the list of URL references in the menu. Such a construct is replicated in all pages that share the same menu. A limited number of programming patterns, similar to the usage of the *TABLE* tag described above, is typically used to insert a menu into a Web page. Thus, matching such patterns on the parse tree of the pages under analysis can be an effective way to discover the presence of a menu in a page.

A reorganization of the pages into frames simplifies the navigation and improves the maintainability of the Web site. In fact, if the menu is displayed in a separate frame, it remains always accessible during the navigation, and it does not have to be replicated in all pages that share it. When some menu item changes, a single HTML file has to be updated if frames are used, while all pages sharing the same menus need an update otherwise. An example of such a transformation is depicted in Figure 4.

In the initial Web site, all four pages *home, page 1, page 2, page 3*, are linked with each other through the menu represented as *h-1-2-3* (see Figure 4, left). After the transformation a new main page (*index*) is introduced. This page consists of two frames, with identifiers *L* and *R* (see Figure 4, right). Page *menu* is loaded into frame *L*, while page *home* is the initial page of the frame *R*. The dashed edges labeled *R* indicate that the pages reachable through the hyperlinks in page *menu* are loaded into the frame *R;* in other words, the page *menu* is used as a menu to force the loading of pages into the frame *R*.

Figure 4. Reorganization of menus into a frame

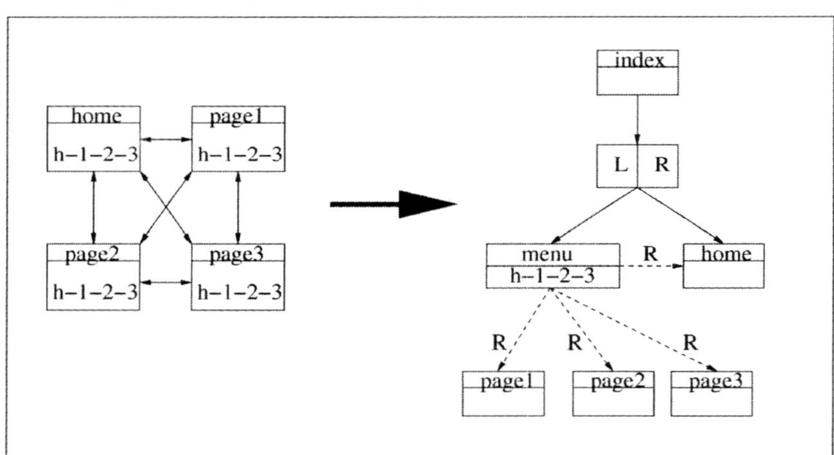

Figure 5. Main steps of the reorganization into frames

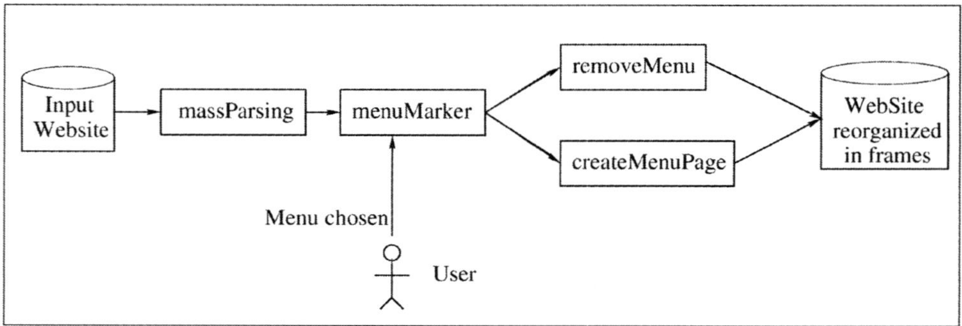

The reorganization into frames requires the TXL functions/rules depicted in Figure 5, as well as some (limited) intervention of the user, who has to choose which menu to migrate into the frame *L*. The rest of the process is totally automatic.

The TXL function *massParsing* parses the list of Web pages in the input Web site and builds a set of Parse Trees (PTs), one for each page. The function *menuMarker* applies the rule *markWithTagMenu* to each PT. For each page, this rule marks the identified menus by inserting them between *<MENU>* and *</MENU>* tags. A semi-automatic procedure devoted to the identification of potential menus inside a Web site was proposed in (Ricca, Tonella, & Baxter, 2002). The user chooses one of such menus for restructuring. The selected menu is then removed from each page containing it, being replaced by a single menu page to be loaded into the frame *L*.

The following rule, named *removeMenu*, is applied to each page of the initial Web site to remove the selected menu.

```
rule removeMenu
    replace [element]
      el [element]
     deconstruct el
      Block('MENU attrs [opt attrs] inBlock [repeat element] )'MENU
      by
        _
end rule
```

This rule searches an element that matches the pattern *"Block('MENU attrs [opt attrs] inBlock [repeat element]) "MENU"*. If this element is in the Web page under analysis, it is deleted from the page. The replacement in the rule above is the underscore, indicating a subtree built according to the default constructor (in this case, an empty *element*).

The function *createMenuPage* (not shown here) searches the Web page *home* for the *TagBlock MENU*. The list of elements contained in the *TagBlock MENU* is filtered, and only tags of type anchor (*A*-tags) are considered. Anchors are refined by adding the target frame (*target="R"*), to form the page *menu*. A fixed page *index*, loading *menu* into the left frame, and *home* into the right frame, is added to complete the transformation.

Migration to Dynamic Sites

Web sites of the first generation consist typically of a set of static HTML pages. Content and presentation are mixed and a same page structure is replicated every time a similar organization of the information is needed (for example, this happens for Web pages that are product-cards or personal pages). Such a practice poses several problems to the evolution of these sites: it is not easy to update the content, which is intermixed with formatting, and a change in the structure has to be propagated to all pages replicated in the Web site.

Figure 6 shows a (semi) automatic restructuring process aimed at transforming a portion of a static Web site into a dynamic one.

The process depicted in Figure 6 replaces a set of static pages having the same structure with a unique server script (*T.php*) that generates dynamic pages. The dynamic pages generated at run time have a fixed part (the template, *T.html*) and a variable part that is built using the information stored in a database.

Clustering is used to recognize Web pages with a common structure (Ricca & Tonella, 2003). Moreover, the output of clustering is used in the template extraction phase that provides the candidate template, *T.html*. In fact, the template is the Longest Common Subsequence (LCS) of HTML *elements* that can be found in the Web pages grouped inside a same cluster. A comparison between original pages and template provides the records to be inserted into the database (database generation phase). Variable parts in the original pages that are preceded by fixed parts shared with the template represent the candidate records. In the end, a script generates the migrated pages dynamically from the template and the database. Manual interventions (not shown in Figure 6) are limited to the refinement (when necessary) of the database and of the template.

The subject of the remaining of this section is the database generation phase. This process assumes that the template *T.html* has already been computed (by means of the LCS algorithm). Specifically, variable parts are replaced by a *DB* tag during LCS computation, so that the actual template has the form of the skeleton of an HTML page, with variable parts marked by *DB* tags. The following is an example of such a template:

```
<HTML>
 <BODY>
    <TABLE>
       <TR>
          <TH> Name </TH>
          <TD> <DB field='name'> </TD>
       </TR>
       <TR>
          <TH> Surname </TH>
          <TD> <DB field='surname'> </TD>
       </TR>
    </TABLE>
 </BODY>
</HTML>
```

Figure 6. Transformation of static pages into a dynamic Web application

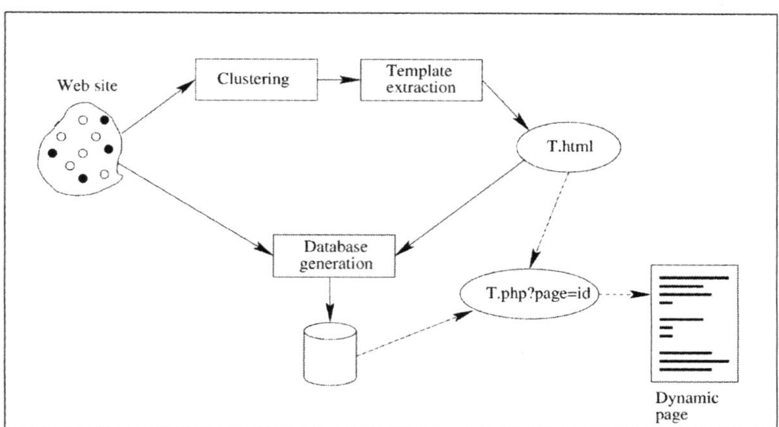

The TXL rule *createTableOfFields* (not shown), applied to the template, generates a table of fields. This rule just extracts the first *htmlText element*, which precedes each tag <*DB*>. Such an element becomes the name of a (potential) database field. In the example above, *Name* and *Surname* are the candidate fields of the database being constructed.

At this point, for each field in the table of fields and for each page in the Web site, the TXL function *buildFieldPlusValue* is called. This function, shown below, generates the couples field-value for each page. In the end, the sequence of values in these couples form the record to be inserted into the database.

```
function buildFieldPlusValue page [repeat element] field [htmlText]
    replace [couple]
     _
    deconstruct * page
      field restWithValue [repeat element]
    deconstruct * restWithValue
      value [htmlText] rest [repeat element]
    construct c [couple]
      field : value
    by
      c
end function
```

The two searching deconstructors applied in sequence inside *buildFieldPlusValue* respectively check the presence of an *element* (of type *htmlText*) equal to the parameter *field,* and recover the next following *element* of type *htmlText,* which is used as candidate value for the given field. The couple *c* produced by this function pairs *field* and *value* (using the colon as a separator).

Multilingual Sites

Multilingual Web sites are expected to provide the same information formatted in the same way and with the same interactive facilities in more than one language (e.g., Italian and English). For such sites, design, quality assurance, and evolution are more complicated than for monolingual sites. Multilingual contents have to be kept consistent with each other. The information provided should be the same for every language of the site: a change in a language has to be propagated to all other languages. Moreover, presentation and navigation should be language independent, still meaning that every change has to be properly propagated to all replications in different languages.

In Tonella, Ricca, Pianta and Girardi (2002), some techniques and algorithms have been proposed to support restructuring of multilingual Web sites so as to align the information provided in different languages and make it consistent across languages. The target of the restructuring process is an extension of XHTML (the new version of HTML supported by the W3C consortium) called MLHTML. Web pages written in MLHTML are ensured to provide multilingual information consistently. In fact, the page structure is shared, instead of being replicated for every supported language. Thus, any change in the structure (presentation, navigation, etc.) is automatically reflected in all languages. Moreover, the multilingual content is managed in a centralized way, so that alignment can be enforced easily.

MLHTML adds just one new tag to XHTML, the tag *<ML lang="L">*, where L is a language identifier. All language dependent page portions are embedded inside such a tag, while the remaining of the page is shared across languages. Thus, a set of Web pages written in different languages are migrated into a single MLHTML page, where language dependent parts are easily identified by the *ML* tag. The physical proximity of the multilingual information enclosed within *ML* tags helps keeping the content aligned over time. The HTML Web pages actually published by the Web site can be extracted from a single MLHTML page offline, once for all, or they can be generated dynamically by a server script on demand.

Existing Web sites can be migrated to MLHTML according to a process consisting of two steps:

- **Page Alignment**
- **Page Merging**

The first operation in this process, explained in detail in Tonella, Ricca, Pianta and Girardi (2002), aims at aligning the pages in the different languages. The outcome is a Web site where corresponding pages in different languages have exactly the same structure, with the same content translated into all supported languages. The second operation, the merging of multiple, aligned, HTML pages in different languages into a single MLHTML page, is the subject of this section.

The TXL transformation employed for page merging unifies a list of aligned pages into a single MLHTML page. The multilingual content is unified by embedding it into *<ML>* tags, while the XHTML code for the shared page structure is just kept. This transformation is obtained by means of the application, in sequence, of the following TXL functions/rules: *MLHTMLtransform, arrangeDoubleElements, arrangeMLblock* and *arrangeReferences* (not shown). For space reasons, the transformation will be described with reference to a bilingual site. However, its generalization to more than two languages is straightforward.

An example of transformation, involving the pages *Pit* (Italian) and *Peng* (English) is shown in Figure 7. The function *MLHTMLtransform* takes two pages (without *TagBlocks*) in input and produces a new page where each element is of type *TagBlock ML*. The *i*-th element of the resulting page is *Block(ML elP1_i elP2_i)ML* where *elP1_i* is the *i*-th element of the first input page and *elP2_i* is the *i*-th element of the second input page.

The rule *arrangeDoubleElements,* shown below, is applied to the result of *MLHTMLtransform* and transforms a *Block(ML elP1_i elP2_1)ML* into *elP1_i* only when *elP1_i* is equal to *elP2_i*. Since the page structure is shared across pages and only the content can change (when provided in different languages), the transformation applies only when *elP1_i* and *elP2_i* are either a same tag or a same text not translated in different languages (e.g., a proper name).

Figure 7. Two HTML pages (Pit and Peng) are merged into a single MLHTML page

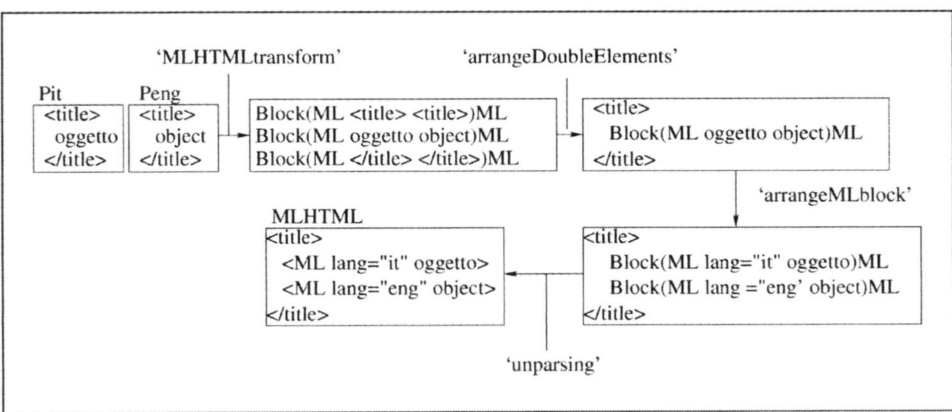

```
rule arrangeDoubleElements
    replace [element]
      Block( 'ML eTag [element] eTag)'ML
    by
      eTag
end rule
```

The rule *arrangeMLblock* splits each *TagBlock ML* into two *TagBlocks,* and adds the attribute *lang="L"*. The effect of this rule (with *e1* and *e2* two generic elements) is the following:

```
Block( 'ML e1 e2 )'ML  →  Block( 'ML lang="language1" e1)'ML
                          Block( 'ML lang="language2" e2)'ML
```

The rule *arrangeReferences* (not shown here) transforms the URL references to objects (such as HTML pages, images, etc.). URLs are replicated for all supported languages, and are embedded inside *ML* tags, with a suffix *'?lang=L'*, where *L* is each supported language. This last transformation is used only in case the HTML pages to publish are generated dynamically by a server script. In this case, the selected language becomes a parameter to be handled dynamically. It is propagated from page to page as an extra URL parameter.

An example of resulting URLs is the following:

```
<ML lang="it"> <A HREF="program.ml?lang="it"> Programma </A> </ML>
<ML lang="eng"> <A HREF="program.ml?lang="eng"> Program </A> </ML>
```

When the selected language is English ("*eng*"), only the second anchor is included in the dynamically generated page by the server script. Such a hyperlink has a parameter *lang="eng"*, which is used to filter the requested page (*program.ml*), so that only the *ML* embedded portions with *lang="eng"* are extracted. The other page portions, not embedded within *ML* tags, are transmitted to the Web browser unfiltered.

Related Works

Quality assurance is considered a central concern by the design methods that have been proposed to support the development of Web applications (Conallen, 2000; Isakowitz, Kamis & Koufar, 1997). However, only a few works have so far considered the problems related to the analysis and restructuring of Web applications.

One of the first systematic studies on Web site analysis is (Warren, Boldyreff & Munro, 1999), where the evolution of the entities in Web sites is characterized by means of a set of metrics traced over time. In (Ricca & Tonella, 2001), several structural analyses, derived from those used with software systems and based on a Web application model, are proposed and employed for restructuring. An experience of Web site reengineering is described in (Antoniol, Canfora, Casazza & De Lucia, 2000), where the target representation of the reverse engineering phase is based on RMM (Isakowitz, Kamis & Koufar, 1997). The recovering process and the following re-design activity were conducted almost completely manually.

A tool for interactively creating and updating HTML documents, preserving the DTD compliance, is described in (Bonhomme & Roisin, 1996). This tool, called *Tamaya*, is based on a transformation language tailored for HTML documents (presented in the paper), and can be used to restructure existing HTML pages which are non DTD-compliant.

In Graunke, Findler, Krishnamurthi and Felleisen (2001) an automated transformation tool converts traditional interactive programs into Web applications based on CGI programs. The authors extend a programming language with primitives that support saving and restoring the interaction state across successive interactions.

The document by Chisholm and Kasday (2001), taken from the W3C Web site (www.w3c.org), provides information about evaluation, repair and transformation tools that make the Web more accessible (see the *Web Content Accessibility Guidelines* at the W3C Web site). Tools in this document are classified into three different categories: *evaluation tools:* performing a static analysis of pages or sites, focused on their accessibility, and returning a report or a rating; *repair tools:* once the accessibility concerns of a Web page or site have been identified, these tools assist the author in making the pages more accessible; *filter and transformation tools:* these tools assist Web users rather than authors to either modify a page or handle a support technology.

Conclusion

Development and evolution of Web applications is one of the most challenging tasks in software engineering. The fast change-rate of requirements makes Web applications subject to continuous maintenance interventions. If this is not accompanied by periodic restructuring, the quality degrades and in the end the software becomes unmanageable. However, restructuring is not affordable if not supported by automated tools.

In this chapter, the possibility to automate restructuring of Web applications has been investigated. The general framework — that of program transformations — requires the ability to parse the source code of a Web application, and this is a non trivial task, given the multiplicity of standards and languages involved. An approach to solve this problem was described, with examples given in the TXL program transformation language. Based upon the parse tree produced by the syntactic analysis of a Web application, several restructuring transformations can be applied. The instances described in this chapter include an example of *design restructuring* (namely, the automatic reorganization into frames), an example of *dynamic page construction* (based on the usage of a template and on the migration of variable information to a database), and an example of *content management* (in case of multilingual content). Program transformations have the potential to (partially) automate the complex process of Web application restructuring.

References

Antoniol, G., Canfora, G., Casazza, G., & De Lucia, A. (2000). Web site reengineering using RMM. *In proceedings of the Int. Workshop on Web Site Evolution*, Zurich, Switzerland, March, 9-16.

Bonhomme, S. & Roisin, C. (1996). Interactively restructuring HTML documents. *In proceedings of the 5th International World Wide Web Conference (WWW5)*, Paris, May.

Chisholm, W. & Kasday, L. (2001). Evaluation, repair and transformation tools for Web content accessibility. *W3C Report* (*www.w3c.org*), 2001.

Conallen, J. (2000). *Building Web applications with UML*. Reading, MA, USA: Addison-Wesley Publishing Company.

Cordy, J. R., Dean, T. R., Malton, A. J., & Schneider, K. A. (2002). Source transformation in software engineering using the TXL transformation system. *Information and Software Technology, 44*(13), 827-837.

Graunke, P., Findler, R. B., Krishnamurthi, S., & Felleisen, M. (2001). Automatically restructuring programs for the Web. In *proceedings of the 16th International Conference on Automated Software Engineering*, Paris, November.

Isakowitz, T., Kamis, A., & Koufar, M. (1997). Extending RMM: Russian dolls and hypertext. *In proceedings of HICSS-30*.

Jeffries, R., Anderson, A., & Hendrickson, C. (2000). *Extreme programming installed*. Reading, MA, USA: Addison-Wesley Publishing Company.

Ricca, F., & Tonella, P. (2001). Understanding and restructuring Web sites with ReWeb. *IEEE MultiMedia, 8*(2), 40-51.

Ricca, F., & Tonella, P. (2003). Using clustering to support the migration from static to dynamic Web pages. In *proceedings of the International Workshop on Program Comprehension*, Portland, Oregon, USA, May, 207-216.

Ricca, F., Tonella, P., & Baxter, I. (2002). Web application transformations based on rewrite rules. *Information and Software Technology, 44*(13), 811-825.

Tonella, P., Ricca, F., Pianta, E., & Girardi, C. (2002). Restructuring multilingual Web sites. In *Proceedings of the International Conference on Software Maintenance*, Montreal, Canada, October, 290-299.

Warren, P., Boldyreff, C., & Munro, M. (1999). The evolution of Web sites. In *Proceedings of the International Workshop on Program Comprehension*, Pittsburgh, PA, USA, May 178-185.

Chapter XII

The Requirements of Methodologies for Developing Web Applications

Craig Standing
Edith Cowan University, Australia

Abstract

The Internet has had a significant impact on the process of developing information systems. However, there has been little research that has examined specifically the role of development methodologies in this new era. Although there are many new forces driving systems development many other issues are extensions of problems that have been there for some years. This study identifies the main requirements of methodologies for developing e-commerce applications. A number of e-commerce application development approaches are examined and a methodology is proposed which attempts to address a number of issues identified within the literature. The Internet Commerce Development Methodology (ICDM) considers evolutionary development of systems, provides a business and strategic focus and includes a management structure in addition to covering the engineering aspects of e-commerce application development. The methodology is evaluated by three focus groups. The results of the evaluations are used to highlight the factors that practitioners identify as important attributes of systems development methodologies for developing Web applications. These include emphasising a business focus, the consideration of organisational culture and management structures, and the importance of an external focus. Practitioners would ideally like methodologies to be relevant to their industry and provide detailed approaches for changing organisational culture. Many traditional systems development methodologies are perceived as being inadequate for dealing with the development of e-commerce systems. The research work proposes that there is a need for an overarching development framework where other more sub-system specific approaches can be integrated. However, any such framework should consider the strategic business drivers of the system, the evolutionary nature of systems, effective management structures, and the development of a conducive organisational culture.

Introduction

The popular assumption is that processes, methods, and techniques used for applications development have changed radically as the focus of applications has moved from the traditional information systems domain to the WWW (Howcroft & Carroll, 2000; Davies, 2000). In this research, we examine the requirements of development methodologies in the Web era. An Internet commerce development methodology is proposed which addresses many of these issues (ICDM). This is evaluated with three focus groups. From this we suggest a set of basic requirements that electronic commerce development approaches should address to be effective.

Methodologies for Web Applications Development

The Internet and the Web have had a profound impact on the business world. The changing business landscape has also impacted on the requirements of systems development approaches. As a developer it is important to be aware of these aspects so that the appropriate methods, design approaches and tools are employed in the development process. In this section of the chapter, the characteristics of electronic commerce applications are discussed with the implications for the development process and several e-commerce methodologies are analysed.

Characteristics of E-Commerce Applications

Web-based applications are frequently multi-functional systems. The multi-functionality of many systems forces organisations to transcend traditional functional boundaries. To meet the customers' needs, systems must be developed with a customer focus. This typically requires people from across the organisation to work in a collaborative manner, thereby breaking down functional boundaries (Rockwell, 1998).

Traditionally, development teams have consisted of IS professionals with a small number of user department representatives. Even teams made up of different business representatives may not be adequate for developing Web applications, especially if they are led by an information systems specialist (Kalin, 1998). The problems associated with representative teams are that members do not speak the same language and have different goals and expectations (Amor, 2000). The teams that are required for Internet applications development need to have a business focus and be led by a "producer" type figure who has expertise in the technical, marketing and business aspects of the organisation. The analogy of a film production team is apposite as such teams have one goal in mind but manage the diverse skills and tasks in the process (Schadler, 1998).

There are frequently diverse groups of stakeholders in relation to Web applications (McKeown and Watson, 1997). Stakeholders can include people internal or external to the organisation. Internal stakeholders could be specialised categories of employees and external stakeholders could be current customers or key suppliers. These stakeholder groups can live locally, or reside inter-state or overseas. Overseas users may have a different cultural and linguistic background and this may have to be considered in Web application development (Rockwell, 1998). As a result of the diversity of stakeholders, responsibility for the Web site applications within the organisation can be ambiguous with the potential for the overall management of the Web strategy to be given little consideration (Treese & Stewart, 1998; Davies, 2000).

The content and functionality of Web sites may change radically over time. Because of this, the notion of project completion is inappropriate. Even the standard six monthly update reviews used with traditional IS applications may be unsuitable for managing the rapid amount of change required. Web sites can be viewed as organic systems that are continually adapting to their environment (May, 2000).

Developments and amendments made to a Web site do not necessarily rely on IS experts (Davies, 2000). Web development can be done through HTML code or more likely web authoring tools like Macromedia Dreamweaver and Microsoft Frontpage that attempt to simplify the process of developing Web pages and applications. When the environment is one where the user departments or individual users have the skills, tools, and authority to make additions and amendments to the system, careful consideration needs to be given to the overall management process of the application to avoid chaos.

IS has been seen as a function supporting the running of the organisation (Gordon & Gordon, 1996). The combination of developments in technology and innovations in organisational structure have led to the development of organisations where the IS does not just play a supporting role but actually becomes the strategic driver. This is especially true of e-commerce applications, many of which are strategic in nature.

Examples of Web Development Approaches

E-Commerce applications development lacks the type of specialised methodologies that exist for more traditional IS applications. There are tools to document Web sites and monitor their activity, but they do not form an integrated suite of tools for the development process. Likewise, evaluation of Web site efficiency and effectiveness cannot be done in the same manner as IS professionals use with typical core business applications. There are few methodologies that are appropriate for the development of Web applications since most IS development methodologies traditionally focus on the technical and internal issues rather than business and organisational needs (Sauer & Lau, 1997). Table 1 presents a review of several Web applications development approaches. They have been chosen because they each represent a type of development approach in that each one takes a different view of the "system."

Fournier (1998) describes the factors involved in developing client server and Web-based systems. The methodology focuses on the development of an appropriate information architecture for an organisation. The method uses Joint Facilitated Sessions to determine user requirements and concentrates on the technical architecture design of the system. Strategic, organizational, and business issues are not given any attention in the approach. In this respect, the development process approach has an internal focus and more of a project view, rather than an evolutionary perspective.

The Intranet Design Methodology (IDM) (Lee, 1998), as its name suggests, is focused on intranet applications development. It has 10 stages, starting with a feasibility study. Three stages are devoted to gathering the requirements related to navigation through the intranet and content. The next four stages are concerned with design issues, and the final two stages cover implementation and testing. Overall, the focus of the methodology is on the design of the intranet. The key techniques used in IDM are the meta-information structure and the information structure. The meta-information structure is a method to organize information in abstract nodes with their links. The information structure defines the local structure of each node of the meta-information structure using classes, subclasses, instances, attributes, attribute values, and links.

Howcroft and Carroll (2000) propose a methodology for Web site development. In this respect, their understanding of the system is the Web site. The first phase of the methodology is the analysis phase which presents ideas for defining a Web site strategy and more specific objectives. The objectives analysis is sub-divided into six tasks:

- Technology analysis
- Information analysis
- Skills analysis
- User analysis
- Cost analysis
- Risk analysis

The second phase covers design issues, the third covers the steps in constructing the Web site, and phase four has three tasks related to implementing the Web site. Although the importance of an evolutionary perspective to development is mentioned in their chapter there are no specific details on how this is addressed. From the information provided the approach takes a project view, in other words, there is a relatively well defined end to the project. Users are mentioned but these seem to refer to internal people rather than customers. Also the strategy development component is narrow and related to the Web site only.

Web Application Extension (WAE) (Conallen, 2000) is concerned with the development of software for Web applications. It takes an object-oriented approach in the development process and involves system modeling with UML. One of the advantages of an object oriented approach is the emphasis on re-usability of software components, and this adds an evolutionary perspective on a software development level. Although focusing on software techniques may lead to reliable and effective software systems, it is unlikely to address the business issues which are the drivers of e-commerce applications.

Some researchers believe that new methodologies for information systems development need to be developed which recognise that "systems development is a first and foremost a social activity" (Myers, 1995, p. 68). Myers argues that formal engineering methods have an important role to play in IS development but they should be part of a much broader methodology which has a main aim of social and organisational change. The Internet Commerce Development Methodology discussed in this chapter is a methodology which attempts to address these issues within an e-commerce context.

It would appear that many of the issues being discussed in Electronic Commerce (EC) development are not particularly new. Taking a business perspective, the role of

Table 1. A comparison of Web development methodologies

	IDM (Lee, 200)	**Howcroft & Carroll, 2000**	**Fournier, R, 1998**	**Web Application Extension (Conallen, 2000)**
Scope	Feasibility to implementation	Strategy to implementation	Analysis to implementation	Analysis to implementation
Key Techniques and Tools	Meta-information structure Information structure Web page design	▪ Objectives analysis ▪ Web site design	▪ Technical architecture design ▪ Joint Facilitated Sessions	▪ Object oriented analysis and design
Focus of methodology	Intranet Application	Web Application	Information Architecture	Software Application
Systems Development View	Project/ evolutionary	Project view	Project view	Project/ evolutionary view
External/Internal Emphasis	Internal	Internal	Internal	Internal

methodologies, evolutionary development approaches, speed of development, and effective project management have all been topics of concern for many years (Boehm, 1988; Gilb, 1998; Avison & Fitzgerald, 1999). That is not to say that companies effectively developed systems with a business focus and with an evolutionary perspective. So rather than viewing Web commerce as a radically new development paradigm it can be viewed as an evolutionary stage in the discipline of information systems where many of same issues that were being discussed in the early nineties are just more critical and more significant now. However, the external focus of many e-commerce applications, alternatives to cost benefit analyses, effective management structures, and creating an appropriate organisational culture are issues which may be critical in e-commerce projects but which are not covered by more traditional IS methodologies. These issues are a consequence of the changing business environment and highlight the importance of developing methodologies that can transform the organisational environment as well as evolve an effective technical system.

Key Features of ICDM

In this section, the main features of the Internet Commerce Development Methodology (ICDM) are outlined (Standing, 1999; Standing, 2000). ICDM is aimed at business-to-consumer application development and provides a guiding framework for developers. It attempts to address the issues related to emphasising a business focus, external focus, and speed of change that business-to-consumer applications development requires. The description of the methodology is guided by the framework for analysing methodologies provided by Avison and Fitzgerald (1995).

Philosophy

ICDM views e-business developments as organisational initiatives and as such takes into account the need to address strategic, business, managerial, and organisational culture issues as well as the technical details of design and implementation. In this respect, the methodology takes a holistic subjectivist perspective, arguing that e-commerce applications will not be effective unless the organisational management and culture is conducive to change.

Defining an organisation's e-business strategy involves dealing with a range of information sources and opinions. A question such as "how can the organisation effectively employ e-commerce?" is inherently subjective in nature and any definition of *effective* will be socially constructed to a large extent. ICDM relies on competitive analysis to help shape the e-business direction (SWOT Analysis).

ICDM emphasises the organisational environment in that it considers the merging of functional boundaries and the political and cultural nuances of working in teams. The methods used for the development of business strategy and for the definition of requirements (brainstorming and groups requirements sessions) are intensely social in nature. This factor recognises strategy is a socially constituted process and is not static. Internet commerce should be a continually evolving feature of the organisation and as such any methodology to support it should be interwoven with a dynamic learning environment.

As a consequence of the changes in the business environment, organisations have had to change in form (Limerick, Cunnington, & Crowther, 1993). This has influenced organisational structure and management approaches. Flatter organisational structures have replaced many deep hierarchical organisational structures. Team based structures which frequently change according to the required skills-mix are an alternative to rigid departmental structures based upon functional lines. Teams are usually faster to adapt to a service and customer focus than large departments. The Internet Commerce Development Methodology (ICDM) can only be successful if its context is appropriate and effective. An organisational methodology, such as ICDM, is inextricably linked with the organisational structures, management strategies and approaches.

Scope

ICDM is a business analysis methodology as well as a systems development methodology. Many traditional information systems methodologies only cover the more technical aspects of systems development and do not start with any form of business analysis. Internet commerce is first and foremost a business direction and hence requires a thorough analysis of its place in the overall business strategy.

The Internet Commerce Development Methodology (ICDM) takes into account the wider trends in the business world and society in its strategy development phase with the SWOT analysis. The changing profile of the consumer is important and user or customer involvement is factored in at various points in the methodology. It is no longer sufficient for a methodology to be inwardly focused, it also must provide a mechanism for scanning the wider business environment. With the trend towards globalisation of economic markets, an organisation must be continually looking for opportunities and learning on a global level (Clarke & Clegg, 1998).

ICDM recommends a management structure for the evolution of Internet commerce in an organisation. Taking a project of electronic commerce is dangerous as the systems are continually changing. An evolutionary perspective is more apposite. The first tier of the three-tier management and development structure has the responsibility of overseeing the evolving form of e-business.

Techniques and Tools

ICDM has a number of component phases to guide the development of strategy and the Web site. Issues related to Web page design, database connections, security issues, and implementation tools and methods are addressed (Standing, 2000).

Framework

ICDM provides a framework for developing Internet commerce. It is not a prescriptive methodology with a large number of steps to be completed. It is a loose fitting framework for developing strategies and for the evolutionary development of Web based systems. As a result, it is applicable to a wide range of situations where organisations are looking to gain from investing in Internet commerce. The approach acknowledges that organisational development via Internet commerce is sufficiently complex and varied to warrant the use of guidelines rather than detailed tasks that lack general applicability. This allows the company to adapt the methodology to the specialised conditions of the organisation. A danger of using such an approach is that it could be adopted in a piecemeal fashion and damage the integrity of the methodology. The senior management and project teams would have to guard against this happening.

Overview of ICDM

This chapter proposes the Internet Commerce Development Methodology (ICDM) as a framework for the development of Internet Commerce in an organisational context (Figures 1, 2) (Standing, 2000). ICDM provides both a management strategy and a development strategy which are driven by the needs of the business. Studies have shown that methodologies have been chosen, frequently by the IS Department, which do not reflect the needs of the business (Sauer & Lau, 1997). Hence, ICDM gives particular attention to providing a business focus.

ICDM has the following components and features which are described in the remainder of this section (Figure 2).

- **Web Management Structure**
- **Strategy and Business Analysis Development Phase**
    - SWOT Analysis
    - Level of Change - Business Process Re-engineering or Value Chain Analysis
- **User Involvement**
- **Meta-Development Strategy**
- **Analysis Phase**
    - Requirements techniques
    - Functional requirements framework
- **Physical Architecture Framework**
- **Design Phase**
- **Component Implementation and Evolution**

Figure 1. Phases of ICDM

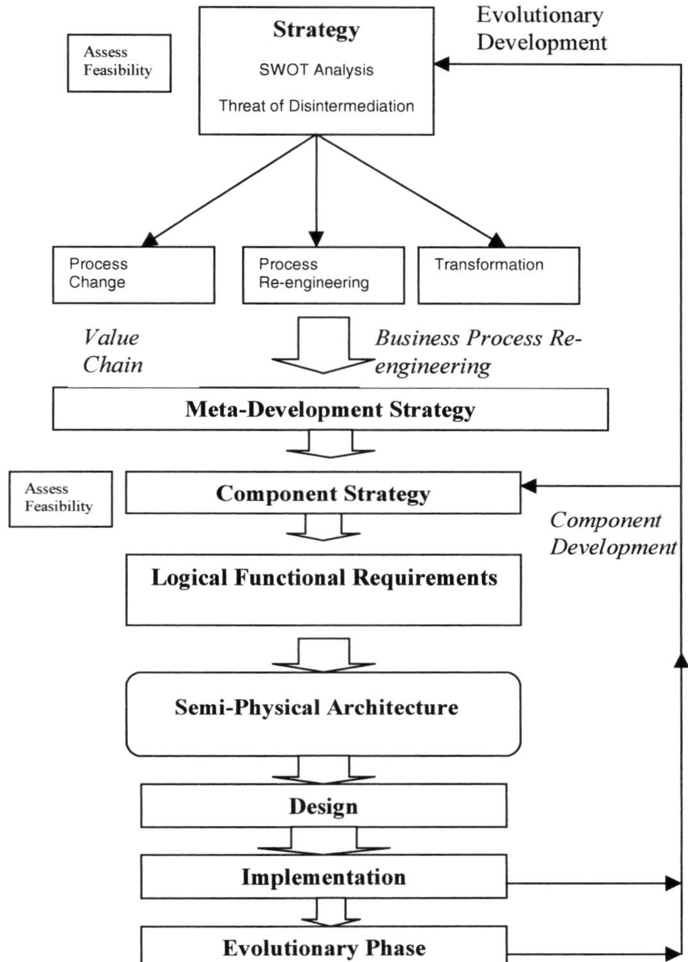

Web Management Strategy

ICDM recommends the management and development of e-business systems on three levels (Figure 3). The overall management and development of the entire Web strategy can be seen as an ongoing task as well as the development of the functional components of a Web application. The first tier is a meta-development and management perspective that provides a framework for development. The second tier concerns the development of the components of the Web site. At both levels the work must be seen as being evolutionary in nature, to cope with the inevitable changes that will have to be made. The

Figure 2. Key requirements and techniques of ICDM

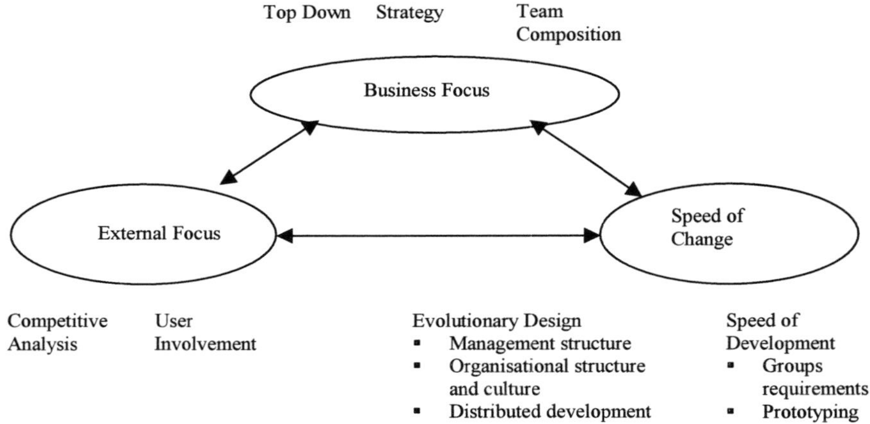

Figure 3. Web management and development structure

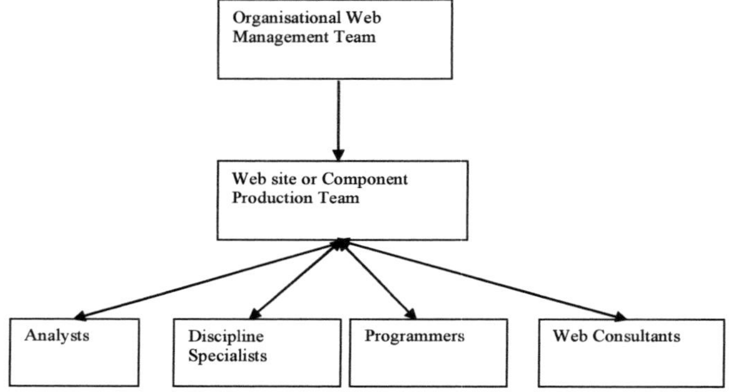

third tier in the management and development structure is concerned with developing and implementing the system and so includes technical development teams, analysts, content specialists, and Web development consultants.

Strategy Development Phase of ICDM

The use of the Internet for business purposes can take many forms. The Internet can be used strategically as a transformation agent to radically change the nature of the business. It can also be employed to improve processes or parts of processes over time and incrementally add value to the business. ICDM provides a strategic planning approach that considers which option is most appropriate for a given situation (Figure 4). ICDM draws upon Business Process Re-engineering (BPR) (Hammer & Champy, 1993) and Value Chain Analysis (Porter, 1985) for its core strategic planning tools.

To decide upon a strategy for a business, business unit, or functional area, managers need to assess an organisation's competitive situation. This involves assessing the organisation and its environment. The process is known as competitive analysis. SWOT analysis is one method of competitive analysis (Thompson & Strickland, 1995). The competitive situation for the company is assessed by examining its strengths (S), weaknesses (W), environmental opportunities (O) and threats (T). The competitive analysis will yield different results for each business examined (Figure 4).

The strengths examined in the SWOT analysis are the strengths of the business. The internal strengths are features of the organisation, such as streamlined administrative systems, or technologically adept staff. The internal weaknesses of the organisation can be detailed in much the same way. The wider environment can be scanned for economic, technological, and social trends that can be exploited. For example, new government legislation may create an opportunity for some organisations.

Besides performing a competitive analysis, organisations should assess the threat of disintermediation. Due to the ease with which suppliers of products and services can market and sell directly to consumers those companies that act as intermediaries in the distribution chain risk being by-passed. This would clearly have disastrous consequences for the intermediaries and is termed disintermediation. The businesses that are most at risk of disintermediation are those that do not significantly add value to the products and services they are distributing.

Figure 4. ICDM strategic planning phase

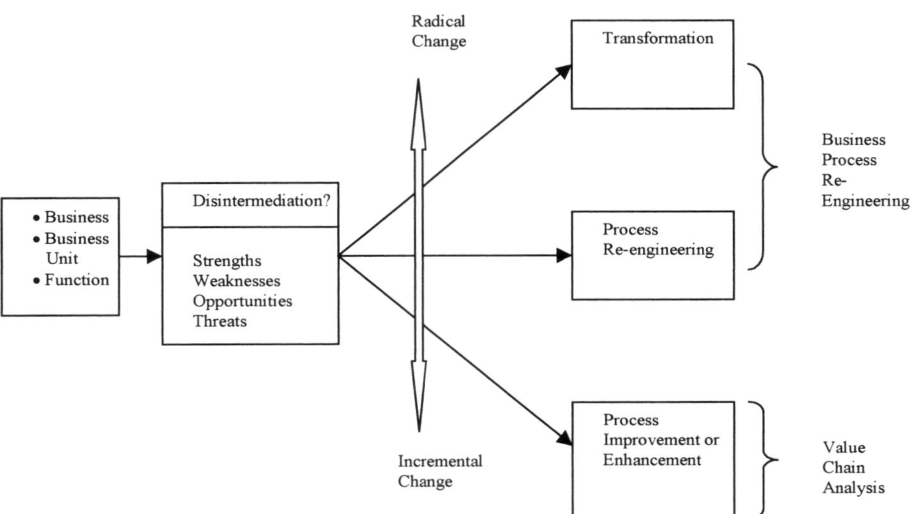

The scale and scope of the changes should fall into one of three categories: process change, process-re-engineering, or transformation. Process change is related to the enhancement or modification of an organisational process with the aid of the Internet. Value chain analysis can be used to identify where value can be added for the customer. Process re-engineering is the complete redesign of a process with the aid of the Internet. Transformation is the radical change of a business leveraging Internet technology.

Meta-Development Strategy

There are a number of strategies that can be employed by a company when managing the development of a Web site. The options depend upon the amount of regulation or control that is desired, both for content and design.

1. Plan the entire site and regulate its distributed development in consultation with business units.
2. Plan the core of the Web site and allow business units the autonomy to develop their own neighbourhoods.

ICDM proposes that the decision on which option to adopt should be made by the Web management team.

User Involvement

Customers or suppliers (users) of the systems should be involved at various stages of the e-business operations and be included in periodic reviews. Customer input is essential at the strategy development and business analysis stages and may involve the use of market research teams to obtain information on what customers require and barriers to using the Web. More detailed requirements can be obtained in Group Requirements Sessions (GRS), telephone interviews, or questionnaires. Customers can be involved in evaluating design issues through the use of prototype Web systems, and they should be included in testing and evaluation of the Web site. Feedback can be obtained from users once the Web site is "live." As the e-business strategy is likely to evolve through time, focus groups can be used to provide input through reviewing the current system and making recommendations.

Site and Component Development

Functional or divisional components of the Internet system can be approached as discrete projects. The implications of the integration with other components of the Web application still need to be considered. A functional component could be a component that provides customers with the option to interrogate a database of products, or to obtain details about customers for marketing purposes. Even so, a multi-disciplinary team is still required because any component of a Web site is still concerned with implementing business strategy not just technology.

Requirements Analysis Techniques

There are a number of information gathering techniques that are especially relevant to the process of defining the requirements of Web applications. These methods are useful for projects where some degree of innovation can substantially improve the success of the system by providing a competitive edge for the organisation.

Using group communication techniques can speed up the definition of the logical requirements for a Web application. The two group communication techniques used in the Internet Commerce Development Methodology (ICDM) are brainstorming and the Group Requirements Sessions (GRS). The first is used to define alternative ways of using Internet commerce in the business and the second is about obtaining the detailed requirements within a relatively fast time frame with involvement from customers, suppliers, and internal staff.

Prototypes can be developed to help in defining the requirements. In particular, the detailed information requirements of transaction and marketing systems can be trialled with customers. The prototypes, however, will be used to a greater extent in the design phase of development.

Functional Requirements Framework

Web applications fall into a number of categories. These functional applications need the detailed definition of their requirements. It is beyond the scope of this chapter to explain the detailed requirements of these systems but the analysts need to use the analysis techniques described earlier to make sure that the business objectives are being met (Standing, 2000).

Physical Architecture Framework

The techniques used for defining the requirements for an Internet project depend on the type of system and its functionality. There are three fundamental types of Web systems: document publishing systems, basic interactive systems, and complex transaction systems. It is not always the case that Web projects intending to transform the organisation require complex transaction systems. Useful information, clearly and effectively presented, with some simple database interactivity has the potential to make a major impact on a business.

Design Phase

The design phase, although not discussed in detail in this chapter, involves designing the network infrastructure, developing the Web site and developing security controls. The Web site design should consider:

- **Desired Image**
- **Usability**
- **Promotion**
- **Evaluation with Customers**

Implementation and Evolution Phases

The implementation of the Web site relates to the meta-development strategies discussed earlier. It is unlikely, unless the Web site is small, that the entire site will be designed and implemented in one project cycle. Web applications evolve and so rarely have a well-defined project completion. However, there are cases where components of the Web site, such as transaction modules can be implemented and remain reasonably stable. The continual evolution of the site also should be managed by the organisation's Web management team. This team should be made up of senior people from each functional unit of the organisation. It is their task to oversee the implementation of the Web strategy and changes in strategic direction. They should also set policy on who can add to the Web site and content and design guidelines.

Evaluation of ICDM

A development methodology can be evaluated in a variety of ways. The methodology could be trialled on a project and then assessed by the development team. A methodology could be evaluated in relation to its core concepts and functional components. Earlier sections of the chapter explained the core principles of ICDM and their rationale. A practical method of evaluation is to use focus groups to analyse and critically evaluate the methodology. In this section, the latter approach is used.

Three separate focus groups were used to evaluate ICDM. Each group was presented with extensive material documenting ICDM. A seminar lasting three hours was also conducted, at the end of which the participants discussed the methodology. The participants were then asked to list the strengths and weaknesses of the methodology for developing Internet commerce systems. The following describes the composition of each group and a summary of their findings.

Table 2. Singaporean-based focus group

Strengths	Weaknesses
Strategic Planning	***Strategic Planning***
Top down approach where the enterprise view and high-level objectives are being addressed	Not enough emphasis on the role of IT in the strategic formulation process (SWOT Analysis).
BPR provides a strategy to connect the strategy to the implementation.	A number of problems have been documented in relation to the use of BPR and this may influence perceptions of users.
The SWOT analysis involves a competitive analysis.	The time involved in developing a thorough business strategy and analysis.
The SWOT analysis considers external factors and therefore ICDM becomes externally focused.	Does not pay sufficient attention to company specific requirements or industry specific requirements.
Facilitates the development of a clear vision and strategy prior to Web development.	Internet commerce is one aspect of electronic commerce – EDI needs to be considered.
Organisational Environment	***Organisational Environment***
Emphasis on multi-disciplinary teams recognises the merging of functional boundaries.	Needs to incorporate more detail on fostering organisational learning.
Considers the politics and culture of organisations.	
Project Management	***Project Management***
Takes a process perspective.	Assumes a clean slate approach.
ICDM provides a series of phases and stages to follow and so serves as a project management tool.	
The loose framework provides a degree of flexibility.	
A balance between the simplicity of the methodology and the level of detail required to be of use.	
ICDM requires top management participation.	
Feasibility	***Feasibility & Evaluation***
Emphasises the importance of a feasibility study.	Needs to have more information on performance measures, assessing risks and potential benefits Needs to have more information on performance measures, assessing risks and potential benefits.
Evolutionary Approach	
The management structures facilitate an evolutionary approach.	

Table 3. Australian travel agency focus group

Strengths	Weaknesses
Clarifies the importance of strategic analysis.	So many stages it can be overwhelming.
Provides a map to help navigate from initial idea to implementation.	Maybe it is more relevant to large organisations than small businesses.
Explains that e-commerce is more than just a Web site.	Appears to be a costly process.
Puts everything in context, especially in relation to competition.	Detailed design issues are beyond most small business owners.
Stresses importance of keeping systems up to date.	

Focus Group A

The first group was composed of six IT/IS professional based in Singapore. Each member worked for a different company. The group had an average of eight years experience in the IT industry. The majority worked in project leader positions. Their comments are included in Table 2.

Focus Group B

A group of twelve travel consultants were provided with an overview of the methodology with specific examples from the travel industry. The comments made were generally less detailed than focus group A or C. The strengths and weaknesses of the methodology are listed in Table 3.

Focus Group C

This group consisted of five IT professionals in based in Perth, Western Australia. All had been substantially involved in e-commerce projects as part of their occupations. Their comments are outlined in Table 4.

Table 4. Australian-based focus group

Strengths	**Weaknesses**
SWOT analysis provides an internal and external competitive analysis.	More details on how to educate the rest of the organisation.
Takes into account evolutionary requirements of Web applications.	Transforming organisational culture needs further explanation.
Covers the full life-cycle including strategy.	More on business to business e-commerce.
Is more focused on the distinctive features of e-commerce than internal IS applications.	
Detailed design issues are important.	
Gets users and customers involved.	
Recognises politics and culture of organisations.	
Emphasises organisational issues.	
Includes evaluation of the Web applications.	
Management structures integrated.	
Provides a valuable project management framework.	

Discussion

Previous sections of the chapter have examined development issues in the electronic commerce environment with an analysis of several development approaches with an emphasis on ICDM. There are a number of general issues in relation to the use of methodologies and frameworks for e-commerce development which will now be discussed.

Different Views of the System

The scope of systems development approaches and methodologies varies greatly, and this is especially true of the e-commerce environment. With each methodology examined there is an implicit assumption about what the system constitutes. For example, the *system* may be understood to be the software applications, Web site, information architecture, intranet application, or business system.

- **Software application:** Takes the view of the system as the programs that form the e-commerce applications. These would typically include Web pages in HTML, client and server-side scripts, and programs ranging in complexity.
- **Web site:** Typically related to the design, creation, and management of Web pages and associated scripts.
- **Information architecture:** Includes the hardware, network, database, and software.
- **Specialist application:** Is related to the design, creation, and management of Web pages for a specialist application such as an intranet or extranet.
- **Business system:** This view sees the strategic business issues as drivers of the system.

The scope of the methodology or its implied understanding of the system highlights the level of specialisation in the IT environment. It is difficult for any one approach to give detailed guidance on all system views. However, the use of multiple methodologies would appear to be the only solution to this issue. A methodology or approach can serve as a guiding framework (this is the role of ICDM) and specialist methodologies can be integrated (such as object oriented development for software application development).

Methodology/Organisational Interface

Electronic commerce can be used to transform organizational processes in organization. Systems development methodologies rarely addressed the cultural transformation that was often required to support the changes in the processes. Business analysis methodologies such as Business Process Re-Engineering (Hammer, 1990; Hammer & Champy, 1993) explain the importance of transforming organizational culture to best take advantage of the introduction of new technology. What is required is a framework that includes business analysis approaches with systems development.

While the consideration of developing an effective organisational culture was listed as a strength of the ICDM by the focus groups, it was mentioned that more details need to be included on how to facilitate this. Creating an innovative organisational culture is not a simple task, and of course every company is at a different starting point. This highlights the recognition given by practitioners to the issue and the difficulties they face when introducing technology into organizations when the organizational culture is not conducive to maximizing the potential of a new system.

Perception of Methodologies

There is a perception that both in the academic and practitioner worlds we are in a post-methodology era. This has resulted from the disillusionment with traditional information systems development methodologies (Avison & Fitzgerald, 1999). This disillusionment results from the nature of many methodologies from previous eras in that they were seen as too inflexible for today's fast changing business environment. Criticisms included: the prescriptive form of many methodologies, the lack of industry/application specific features, and the emphasis on time consuming documentation. Whilst acknowledging this general disillusionment with methodologies, Avison and Fitzgerald do not disregard the need for and role of methodologies in systems development.

Conclusion

Developing electronic commerce systems in organization is a complex task. These systems have a number of sub-systems which include Web pages, software programs, IT and network systems and which are driven by the business system. There are methodologies for each of the systems but few that provide an overarching framework for development. ICDM aims to provide such a framework. However, feedback from focus groups and initial trials in industry suggest that further fine-tuning is required.

This chapter on electronic commerce development methodologies highlights a number of issues for developers. A recurring issue in relation to systems development methodologies is providing sufficiently flexible guidelines and providing support for industry specific factors. In addition, the methodology and organisational environment boundary is blurring. Practitioners require detailed guidelines on how to create a conducive organisational culture that will stimulate innovative thinking and wide-spread adoption of e-commerce initiatives. Both of these issues are difficult for methodology designers to adequately take on board but will nonetheless be essential if methodologies are to retain their sense of relevancy.

References

Amor, D. (2000). *The e-business revolution.* Upper Saddle River, NJ: Prentice Hall.

Avison, D. E. & Fitzgerald, G. (1999). Information Systems Development. In R., Galliers & W., Currie. (Eds.), *Rethinking management information systems.* Oxford University Press.

Avison, D. E. & Wood-Harper, A. T. (1990). *Multiview: An exploration in information systems development.* Oxford: Blackwell Scientific Publications.

Boehm, B. (1988). The spiral model of software development and enhancement. *Computer, 21*(5), 61-72.

Clarke, T. & Clegg, S. (1998). *Changing paradigms: The transformation of management knowledge for the 21st Century.* Harper Collins.

Davies, P. (2000). Survival of the fittest. *The Computer Bulletin,* Series 5, *2*(5), 28-29.

Fournier, R. (1998). *A methodology for client server and Web application development.* Yourdon Press.

Gilb, T. (1988). *Principles of software engineering management.* Addison-Wesley.

Gordon, S. R. & Gordon, J. R. (1996). *Information systems: A management approach.* Dryden.

Hammer, M. (1990). Re-engineering work - Don't automate obliterate. *Harvard Business Review,* July-August, 104-112.

Hammer, M. & Champy, J. (1993). *Reengineering the corporation - A manifesto for business revolution.* London: Nicholas Brierley publishing.

Howcroft, D. & Carroll, J. (2000). A proposed methodology for Web development. *Proceedings of the European Conference on Information Systems*, Vienna, 290-297.

Kalin, S. (1998). Conflict resolution. *CIO WebBusiness Magazine*, February 1, 1998. Online: *http://www.cio.com/archive/webBusiness/020198_Sales_content.html*

Lee, S. C. (1998). IDM: A methodology for intranet design. *Proceedings of the 1998 International Conference on Information Systems.* Helsinki, Finland, 51-67.

Limerick, D., Cunnington, B., & Crowther, F. (1993). *Managing the new organisation.* B & BP.

May, P. (2000). *The business of e-commerce.* Cambridge Press.

Myers, M. D. (1995). Dialectical hermeneutics: a theoretical framework for the interpretation for the implementation of information systems. *Information Systems Journal, 5,* 51-70.

Porter, M. (1985). *Competitive strategy.* New York: Free Press.

Rockwell, B. (1998). *Using the Internet to compete in a global marketplace.* Wiley & Sons.

Sauer, C. & Lau, C. (1997). Trying to adopt systems development methodologies - A case-based exploration of business users' interests. *Information Systems Journal, 7*(4), 255-275.

Schadler, T. (1998). Lights, Cameras, Apps! *CIO Magazine*, June 15, 1998. Online: *http://www.cio.com/archive*

Standing, C. (1995). Managing and developing Internet commerce systems with ICDM. *Proceedings of the 10th Australasian Conference on Information Systems*, Wellington, New Zealand, 850-862.

Standing, C. (2000). *Internet commerce development*. Boston: Artech House Publishers.

Standing, C., Vasudavan, T., & Borbely, S. (1999). A study of Web technology diffusion in travel agencies. *Proceedings of the Hawaii International Conference on System Sciences*.

Talwar, R. (1996). Re-engineering - A wonder drug for the 90s. In C. Coulson-Thomas (Ed.), *Business process re-engineering*. London: Kogan Page.

Thompson, A.A. & Strickland, A. J. III. (1995). *Strategic management: Concepts and cases* (8th ed.). Homewood: Richard D Irwin, Inc.

Treese, G. W. & Stewart, L. C. (1998). *Designing systems for Internet commerce*. Addison-Wesley.

Chapter XIII

A Customer Analysis-Based Methodology for Improving Web Business Systems

Choongseok Lee
Samsung, SDS Co., Korea

Woojong Suh
Inha University, Korea

Heeseok Lee
Korea Advanced Institute of Science and Technology, Korea

Abstract

The Web has enabled many companies to create new business from individual customers in a variety of forms, as well as to expand their traditional contact points with them into virtual workplaces dramatically. For the success of customer-oriented businesses on the Web, it is necessary to make a continuous effort to adapt Web business systems to ever-changing customers' needs. For this challenge, this chapter proposes a customer analysis-based improvement methodology (CAIM) to help evolve customer-oriented Web business systems; this methodology employs scenario-based and object-oriented approaches. The methodology consists of five phases: customer analysis, value analysis, Web design, implementation design, and construction. Scenarios are used to analyze customers' needs in a natural fashion. A real-life community Web site is illustrated to demonstrate the usefulness of the methodology.

Introduction

Web technologies have enabled many companies to take various beneficial opportunities for their business; the Web business makes possible commercial exchanges that cross physical, temporal, cultural, and legal boundaries on a scale that was technically complicated (Jarvenpaa & Tiller, 1999; Bajaj & Siau, 2000). It is even pointed out that successful players use Web technologies in every aspect of their business operations (Aissi, Malu, & Srinivasan, 2002; Barua, Whinston, & Yin, 2000). Accordingly, many companies have conceived Web business systems as a critical instrument for their business success and have made a lot of efforts to develop and maintain them. Especially through constructing the Web business systems, many companies have expanded their traditional contact points with individual customers into virtual workplaces dramatically and even created a variety of new business to them.

Under this Web business environment, individual customers are getting much smarter, and their needs are changing much faster than ever before. The customers can compare products and services with a variety of rich information, so that they can easily move to new products or services (Afuah & Tucci, 2000). As a result, companies tend to be more customer-oriented (Bishop, 2000; Cravens, Greenley, Piercy, & Slater, 1997); from this aspect, it is also addressed that companies should first analyze customers' experiences, and then respond to their needs online environment (Novak, Hoffman, & Yung, 2000). Even though a Web business system is developed (successfully from the customer aspects) in the well-suited forms to customers' needs, the companies should evolve for the business success their Web business systems agilely to meet the ever-changing customers' needs. On the other hand, the maintenance process generally requires a longer period and much more organizational resources than development process. Already, most companies with their Web business systems have spent a lot of time and money improving their Web business systems.

Nevertheless, the companies have not been supported by a systematic methodology for the improvement activities; most previous methodologies concerning Web business systems have focused on development rather than maintenance or improvement (Artz, 1996; Abels, White, & Hahn, 1997, 1999; Chen & Heath, 2001; Isakowitz, Stohr, & Balasubramanian, 1995; Isakowitz, Kamis, & Koufaris, 1997; Takahashi & Liang, 1997; Schwabe & Rossi, 1995; Faternali & Paolini, 2000; Bichler & Nusser, 1996a, 1996b; Troyer & Leune, 1998). Unlike the methodologies, Atzeni, Mecca, and Merialdo (1998) and Standing (2002) considered the maintenance as well as development, but their methodologies did not incorporate tightly the analysis of customers' needs into their major design phases. On the other hand, among the methodologies focusing on development, only Artz (1996), Troyer and Leune (1998), Abels et al. (1997, 1999), and Chen and Heath (2001) emphasized the importance of the analysis of customers' needs. However, these methodologies did not specify systematic steps for capturing the customers' needs. As customers' needs change dramatically, reflecting them is critical for sustaining competitive advantages. Accordingly, a customer-oriented methodology is required to support design activities ranging from the analysis of customers' needs to systems implementation and maintenance.

From this motivation, this chapter proposes a methodology, Customer Analysis-based Improvement Methodology (CAIM), that supports the development and maintenance of customer-oriented Web business systems. This methodology can help a series of activities required for iterative improvement as well as the first development, focusing on aligning customers' needs with implementation details. The outline of the chapter is as follows. The next section discusses the challenges in the development of Web business systems and explores the previous methodologies by comparing them. The following section provides an overview of the methodology, and the section after that describes the methodology in further detail using a real-life case.

Related Works

Web business systems employ hypermedia as a major technical principle; they can be conceived as one of the most popular applications of hypermedia (Lee & Suh, 2001). Accordingly, the methodologies for developing and designing hypermedia can be also directly applicable to Web business systems. The range of hypermedia applications is so broad that no single formal development methodology is relevant to the development of them all (Nanard & Nanard, 1995). In this context, a variety of Web business systems development methodologies have been proposed; they have their own advantages, but each among them has also some limitations in covering all the requirements for Web business systems satisfactorily.

The implementation of Web business systems typically requires several steps, such as information modeling for customers, navigation design to help customers find information, user interface design for Web page layout, and construction. Some implementation features such as navigation, contents, and user interfaces are not common in conventional software development (Gruhn & Schope, 2002). Building Web business systems is challenging because of the lack of developers' experiences, poorly defined processes, and unrealistic schedules (Barry & Lang, 2001; Powell, 2002).

To solve these problems, the Web engineering approach has been proposed. It attempts to solve important aspects of Web system development such as conceptual design, performance evaluation, and continual maintenance. Web engineering employs the methods from several areas such as software engineering (SE), human-computer interaction (HCI), project management, usability engineering, testing, and simulation (Gellersen, Wicke, & Gaedke, 1997; Ginige & Murugesan, 2001). The Web business system development methodology now needs to be handled in the area of Web engineering.

In order to help understand the previous methodologies for developing Web business systems, we will compare the features of the methodologies including our proposed methodology, CAIM. For the comparison, several criteria are of interest: customer analysis, system requirement analysis, source of navigation design, development supporting system, focus, and methodology phases. The comparison is summarized in Table 1.

Table 1. Methodology comparison

Classification	Informal Methodology				Formal Methodology							
					E-R Model Based				O-O Model Based			
Methodology / Criteria	Artz (1996)	Abels et al. (1997; 1999)	Chen and Heath (2001)	Standing (2002) ICDM	Isakowitz et al. (1995; 1997) RMM	Takahashi and Liang (1997)	Atzeni et al. (1998)	Fraternali and Paolini (2000) HDM-Lite	Schwabe and Rossi (1995); Schwabe, Pontes, & Moura (1999) OOHDM	Bichler and Nusser (1996a; 1996b) W3DT	Troyer and Leune (1998); Casteleyn and Troyer (2001) WSDM	This Methodology CAIM
Customer Analysis	Target Audience	Users' Task-related Information and Use Behavior	User Involvement	User Involvement	N/A	N/A	N/A	N/A	N/A	N/A	Audience Class Hierarchy	Correspon-dence Analysis
System Requirement Analysis	Objectives of Web Applications	User Criteria	Use Case	GRSs	N/A	Scenario	N/A	N/A	N/A	N/A	Audience Class Hierarchy	Scenario
Source of Navigation Design	N/A	Structure, Linkage, and Search	N/A	N/A	E-R Relationship	E-R Relationship	E-R Relationship	E-R Relationship	OO Relationship	OO Relationship	Navigation Track	Scenario and OO Relationship
Focus	Development	Development	Development	Development and Maintenance	Development	Development	Development and Maintenance	Development	Development	Development	Development	Development and Maintenance
Development Supporting System	N/A	N/A	N/A	N/A	RMCase	WebArchitect	PENELOPE	AutoWeb	OOHDM-Web	WebDesigner	N/A	eBizBench
Methodology Phases	1. Problem Statement 2. Constraining Requirements 3. Conceptual Model 4. Derived Requirements 5. Detailed Analysis 6. Detailed Design 7. Development	1. Information Gathering 2. Development 3. Evaluation 4. Implementation	1. Basic System Analysis and Design 2. Architecture Decision 3. Build Basic Functionality 4. Deployments	1. Strategy 2. Meta-Development Strategy 3. Component Strategy 4. Component Strategy 5. Logical Functional Requirements 6. Semi-Physical Architecture 7. Design 8. Implementation 9. Evolution	1. ER Design 2. Slice Design 3. Navigation Design 4. Conversion Protocol Design 5. UI Screen Design 6. Run-time Behavior Design 7. Construction and Testing	1. ER Analysis 2. Scenario Analysis 3. Architecture Design 4. Attribute Definition 5. Construction 6. Maintenance	1. Database Conceptual Design 2. Database Logical Design 3. Hypertext Conceptual Design 4. Hypertext Logical Design 5. Presentation Design 6. Hypertext to DB Mapping	1. Conceptualize 2. Generate Database 3. Implement and Deploy	1. Conceptual Design 2. Navigational Design 3. Abstract UI Design 4. Implementation	1. Requirement Analysis 2. Information Structuring 3. Navigational Design 4. Organizational Design 5. Interface Design 6. Implementation 7. Introduction and Maintenance	1. Mission Statement Specification 2. User Classification 3. User Class Description 4. Object Modeling 5. Navigational Design 6. Implementation Design 7. Implementation	1. Customer Analysis 2. Value Analysis 3. Web design 4. Implementa-tion Design 5. Construction

The methodologies can be categorized into formal and informal (Cunliffe, 2000), as shown in the classification part of Table 1. The informal methodologies do not specify detailed activities for each phase. These informal methodologies are flexible for formulating business strategies (Standing, 2002). Formal methodologies describe not only development activities but also linkages of inputs and outputs. Most formal methodologies adopt one of the two data modeling techniques such as Entity-Relationship (E-R) model and Object-Oriented (O-O) model. The O-O model provides semantic richness, reusability, and flexibility (Taylor, 1995; Wirfs-Brock, Wilkerson, & Wiener, 1990) HDM-Lite, RMM, and OOHDM were originally proposed for hypertext or hypermedia applications.

Customer analysis is a starting point for a customer-oriented Web business system development (Smart & Whiting, 2001). Artz (1996) places an emphasis on the analysis of customer groups using the system. Abels et al. (1997, 1999) propose that a Web site should be designed for the user, and user input be solicited throughout the process. Chen and Heath (2001) explore user involvement in the evolutionary design process. Troyer and Leune (1998) propose a user-modeling phase that consists of user classification and user description. However, this method is not sufficiently applicable to a dynamic Web business system because it focuses on the static information. CAIM includes systematic methods for customer analysis like the correspondence analysis. It helps developers capture customers' needs at an early stage and improve the system according to their needs.

To implement a usable system, system requirement analysis is important (Marquis, 2002). Artz (1996) suggests the exploration of objectives of a Web application to analyze system requirements and the objectives can be classified into seven categories in terms of business, information, functional, user interface, development, operational, and quality. Abels et al. (1997, 1999) propose user criteria that consist of use, content, structure, linkage, search, and appearance. These criteria can be used to provide specific suggestions for the Web business system design. Standing (2002) uses Group Requirements Sessions (GRSs) to obtain the detailed requirements with users' involvement. GRSs can lead to a compromised solution by striking balances between heterogeneous stakeholders. Takahashi & Liang (1997) use a scenario for the dynamic analysis. Their scenario does not describe interactions between the system and its customers. However, the scenarios employed in CAIM describe interactions between a Web business system and its customers, focusing on enhancing the service capabilities for current customers. Troyer and Leune (1998) focus on customer group's informational requirements.

The success of a Web business system is significantly associated with navigation capability (Schwabe, Esmereldo, Rossi, & Lyardet, 2001; Taylor, McWilliam, Forsyth, & Wade, 2002; Zang & Dran, 2002; Palmer, 2002). Most of the proposed methodologies use the relationships in data model as a major source of navigation design. Abels et al. (1997, 1999) use information derived from user criteria. Our methodology uses scenarios and relationships in object-oriented models to capture navigational requirements. The use of scenarios is likely to better reflect customers' navigational requirements.

For Web business systems, another important challenge is to reflect ever-changing customers' needs on them continuously and systematically. Standing (2002) also emphasizes the continual evolution of Web business systems from a managerial perspective, but specific procedures are not presented. Atzeni et al. (1998) propose a modeling method for a Web site structure and a supporting system for securing link consistency to help the maintenance. Similarly, our methodology, CAIM can improve Web business systems by monitoring customers' needs continuously.

A critical success factor for wider use of design methodologies is the availability of software tools (Barry & Lang, 2001; Killander, 2001). RMCase, WebArchitecture, PENELOPE, AutoWeb, OOHDM-Web, and WebDesigner have been developed to support the corresponding methodologies. For our methodology, *eBizBench* is developed (Lee et al., 2004).

Methodology Architecture

The architecture of our methodology, Customer Analysis-based Improvement Methodology (CAIM), is depicted in Figure 1. It consists of five phases: customer analysis, value analysis, Web design, implementation design, and construction. Customer analysis, value analysis, and Web design are independent of any specific technical platforms and details, while implementation design and construction depend on them. For the sake of better presentation, the feedback among phases is not depicted. However, feedback is of importance in our methodology because iterative design is essential for Web business system development (Preece, Sharp, Benyon, Holland, & Carey, 1994; Chen & Heath, 2001; Ginige & Murugesan, 2001).

The customer analysis phase analyzes customers' needs. Customers are categorized according to their shared needs. Each customer group has different needs. Customer groups and the corresponding needs are summarized in the customer need analysis table, and then their correspondence is analyzed by the use of a correspondence analysis technique.

The objective of the value analysis phase is to model value activities. This phase consists of value derivation and value activity modeling. In the value derivation, customers' needs are analyzed into customer value activities, and then prioritized. In the value activity modeling, customers' requests are identified in the form of events.

In the Web design phase, Web business to be implemented is logically designed. This phase consists of five subphases: scenario design, object modeling, view design, navigation design, and page design. In the scenario design, scenarios are designed in the form of natural language to describe customers' interactions with a Web business system from the customers' perspective. These scenarios lead to object modeling. In the view design, information units that customers want to find are designed. The navigation design subphase designs navigational paths for customers to access information conveniently. Finally, in the page design, users' information windows and the flow from one page to another are defined according to the views and their navigational paths.

During the implementation design, page specifications are determined and the object model is transformed into the physical database schema. Finally, the construction phase implements a physically running Web business system.

Figure 1. The architecture of CAIM

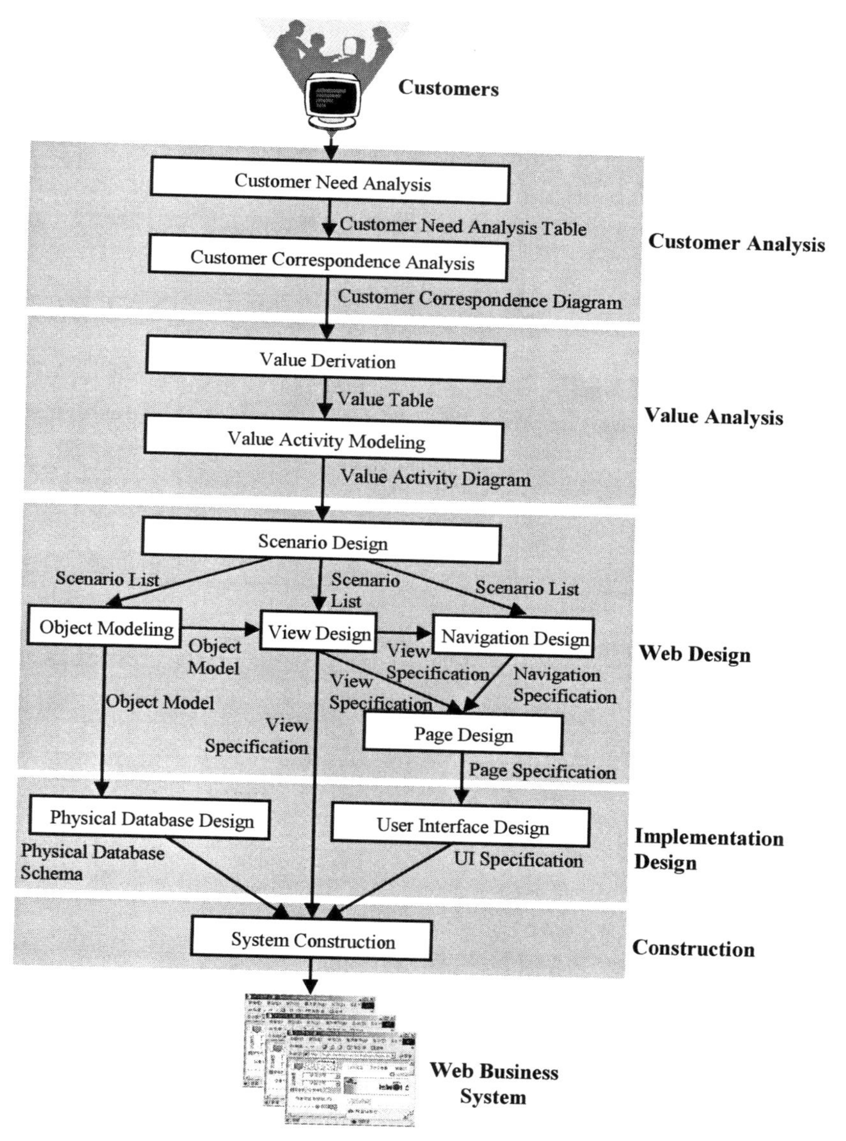

Methodology Details

Here, each phase of the CAIM is described in further detail by the use of a real-life case. This Web business site will be referred to as "*I site.*" I site (www.iloveschool.co.kr), a Web alumni association site, has provided a school-based community service since

October 1999. Its members can find any school friend who is also a member by locating the name of his or her school. They can leave messages via bulletin board and exchange e-mails. It has shown a dramatic network effect because its service becomes more valuable as more people use it. Drawn in by a rapid expansion of the Internet population, I site has turned into one of the top Korean community Web sites. In market surveys conducted by major private research institutes such as Samsung Economic Research Institute (www.koreaeconomy.org) and Yahoo! Korea (kr.yahoo.com), the site was picked as one of the best hit products in 2000. About 10 million customers are using the site and about 11,000 (almost 100 percent) Korean universities and schools are registered. I site has 400 million page views per month and its Alexa (www.alexa.com) ranking is the 47th in the world and the seventh in Korea as of April 2001. Its main service areas include schoolmate search, school BBS (Bulletin Board System), school club service, and club service.

The I site Web site laid out plans to become a serious player in the Internet community market. Customer loyalty has become more important than customer acquisition. Accordingly, our methodology, CAIM was employed to help developers improve I site. We will illustrate this application in details as follows.

Customer Analysis

Customer analysis includes customer need analysis and correspondence analysis. This phase can find creative ways to fulfill supplementary needs that may not involve the current company's offerings by building a detailed understanding of common customer needs.

Customer Need Analysis

The customer need analysis subphase analyzes customers on the basis of customers' data. First, data may be collected by observation, survey, or experimentation. Customers may be categorized according to their geographic, demographic, psychographic, or behavioral variables. Because behavioral variables are based on actual customer behavior toward products or service, they are more likely to be closely related to Internet business than other variables (Kotler & Armstrong, 1996).

In the case of I site, customers are categorized into five groups according to their roles: school club manager, club manager, school club member, club member, and member. In this site, communities can be categorized into two types such as school club and club. An example of school club is "soccer club in K school." Only the alumni of "K school" can join this school club. However, a club is not related to a particular school. To join a school club or club is not member's obligation. Accordingly, there may be members who join neither of these two clubs. A school club member is a customer who joins the school club, and a school club manager manages this school club. A club manager manages the club, and a club member joins the club.

To analyze customers' needs, we looked at 19,259 suggestions, which were made in the BBS by 11,240 volunteer customers between December 2000 and April 2001. I site ran the

BBS to listen to its customers. Because 18,956 suggestions are related to the existing services, the remaining 303 suggestions (from 291 volunteer customers) are analyzed. Customers' needs are grouped into nine categories according to their service characteristics, as shown in Table 2. For example, the schoolmate segmentation is most frequently suggested. This segmentation can divide schoolmates into various groups by their majors and graduation dates.

Customer Correspondence Analysis

The purpose of the customer correspondence analysis is to find the correspondence between customer groups and their needs. Different customer groups may have different needs. It is important to analyze the correspondence between customer groups and their needs. However, the previous customer need analysis provides the frequencies only. Typically, a correspondence analysis technique (Greenacre, 1984) is adopted for finding this correspondence. Third quantification method, reciprocal averaging, appropriate scoring, homogeneity analysis, dual scaling, and scalogram are all synonyms of correspondence analysis. The correspondence analysis provides a mathematical method for representing data in a Euclidian space so that the results can be visually examined. The correspondence analysis investigates simple two-way or multi-way tables containing some measure of correspondence between the rows and columns. It is similar to factor analysis techniques in statistics; it can explore the structure of categorical variables included in the table. For more information, refer to Greenacre (1984) and Greenacre and Hastie (1987).

The analysis results in the chi-square value, 93.2 (degree of freedom=32). This value confirms the correspondence. Figure 2 shows the customer correspondence diagram. In

Table 2. Customer need analysis table

Customer Group / Customer Need	School Club Manager	Club Manager	School Club Member	Club Member	Member	Total
Teacher Community	14	2	16	4	12	48
Schoolmate Segmentation	28	3	36	4	42	113
Post-graduate Community	12	2	19	3	18	54
Album Service	20	0	5	0	5	30
Schoolmate e-mail	10	1	3	0	4	18
Wireless Internet	11	5	0	0	0	16
Army Community	1	1	4	3	4	13
Off-line Support	3	1	0	0	3	7
Cooperative Purchase	0	0	1	0	3	4
Total	99	15	84	14	91	303

Figure 2. Customer correspondence diagram

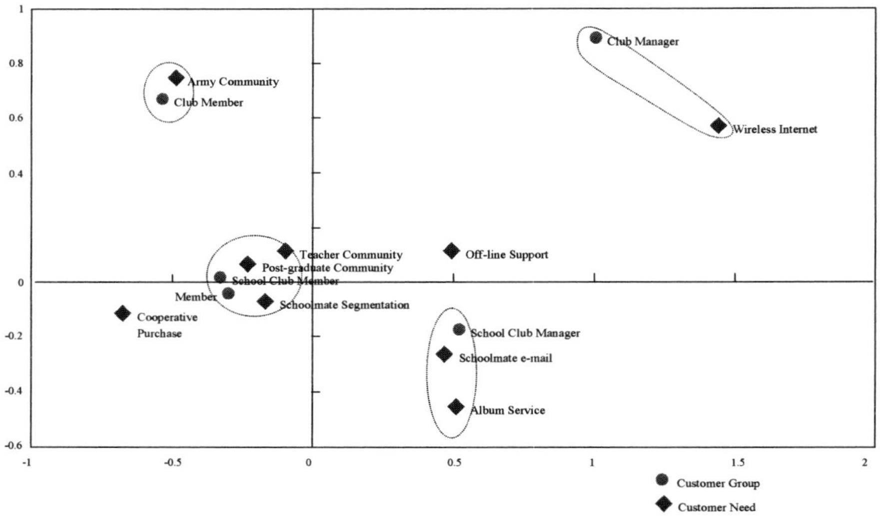

this diagram, the horizontal axis and vertical axis describe row and column coordinates, respectively. For example, the needs for school club members and members include teacher community, schoolmate segmentation, and post-graduate community.

Value Analysis

Web business systems are typically inventing new value propositions. The objective of the value analysis is to identify the values for customers and then describe the interactions between a Web business system and its customers.

Value Derivation

Customer values are explored on the basis of customers' activities with the system. The value derivation subphase employs a value analysis table to analyze customers' values, value activities, and implementation priorities. Customer value is defined as a bundle of benefits customers expect from a given product or service (Kotler, 1997). Customer value can be measured from financial, perceptual, and behavioral perspectives (Wheeler, 2002). Value activity is a customers' distinct event or integrated set of events to create customer value. Because customers may not be able to understand all of the new opportunities by new technologies or environments, implementation priorities are decided on the basis of technical feasibilities, business capabilities, and strategic importance.

Table 3 shows the result of value derivation. For example, school club members and members highly value "friendliness among teachers and students" in the teacher

Table 3. Value table

Customer Group	Customer Need	Customer Value	Value Activity	Implementation Priority
▪ Member ▪ School Club Member	▪ Teacher Community	▪ Friendliness among teachers and students	▪ Search for teachers ▪ Join teacher communities	○○○
	▪ Schoolmate Segmentation	▪ Friendliness among schoolmates	▪ Search for schoolmate segments ▪ Join schoolmate segments	○○
	▪ Post-graduate Community	▪ Friendliness among post-graduate schoolmates	▪ Search through post-graduate communities ▪ Join post-graduate communities	○
▪ School Club Manager	▪ Album Service	▪ Share of photos	▪ Manage on-line albums	○○○
	▪ Schoolmate e-mail	▪ Communication with all schoolmates	▪ Mail for all schoolmates	○
▪ Club Manager	▪ Wireless Internet	▪ Ease of management	▪ Manage community using wireless Internet	○○
▪ Club Member	▪ Army Community	▪ Friendliness among army colleagues	▪ Search through army communities ▪ Join army communities	○

community according to customers' perceptual perspective. "Search for teachers" and "join teacher communities" are activities for achieving this value. The implementation priorities of the teacher community and the album service are fairly high according to I site's current capabilities and strategic importance.

Value Activity Modeling

For the sustained customer loyalty, it is important to investigate the customers' activities to a system to be implemented. At the same time, the scope of the system is determined. A value activity diagram can capture these value activities. The diagram is based on events, customer groups, and subsystems. Events are identified for each customer group. An event is a trigger that starts a system (Booch, 1994).

In the value activity diagram, the needs for each customer group are depicted for the corresponding subsystem. Each customer group triggers events for this subsystem via value activities. The value activity diagram is similar to a use case diagram in standard UML notations (Fowler & Scott, 1999). Use cases describe the actions the system takes to deliver to the actor (Jacobson, Ericsson, & Jacobson, 1995). The emphasis of our value activity diagram is on finding detailed event activities between customer groups and the business Web system. The value activity diagram is thus simpler to depict a variety of activities between customer groups and the system.

Figure 3 shows the value activity diagram in our case. For the sake of simple presentation, it highlights two items for customer needs with top implementation priority ("teacher community" and "album service"). These two items are depicted as subsystems. Although the "search for teachers" activity is directly transformed into the "search for teachers" event, this activity can be subdivided into several activities, such as "search for teachers by teacher name" and "search for teachers by school name" to provide

Figure 3. Value activity diagram

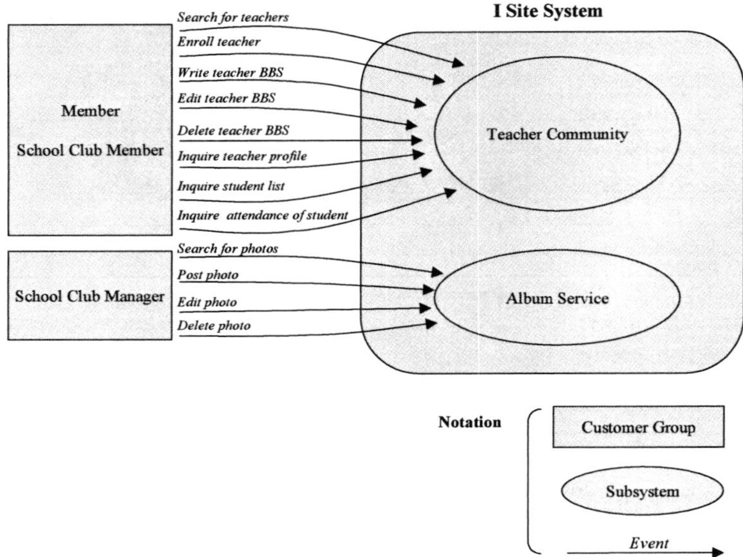

alternative search facilities for the members and the school club members. "Join teacher communities" activity is transformed into seven events: "search for teachers," "enroll teacher," "write teacher BBS," "edit teacher BBS," "delete teacher BBS," "inquire teacher profile," "inquire student list," and "inquire attendance of students."

Web Design

The Web design phase consists of five subphases: scenario design, object modeling, view design, navigation design, and page design.

Scenario Design

Our methodology, CAIM, employs scenarios to identify business system requirements from the earliest opportunity. Task analysis has often been adopted for capturing user activities in the human computer interaction studies (Preece et al., 1994; Dix, Finlay, Abowd, & Beale, 1998). A scenario is less formal than task analysis (Preece et al., 1994). Scenarios can be categorized into three types: descriptive, exploratory, and explanatory (Rolland & Anchour, 1998). Descriptive scenarios are typically employed to capture requirements. Exploratory scenarios are used to find possible solutions for satisfying given system requirements through the exploration and evaluation of alternatives. Explanatory scenarios are intended to support the explanation and argumentation of drawbacks, inefficiencies, or system performance problems. Our scenarios are descriptive to capture customers' requirements. A scenario is a description of customers' interactions with a subsystem from the perspective of customers. Although it is difficult to infer object classes or behaviors, our scenarios can better describe customers' interactions. Scenarios correspond to key business processes and thus can capture customers' requirements in a natural fashion.

In the scenario design subphase, the events drawn from the value activity diagram are described in the form of natural language. The natural language can enhance ease of use and understandability (Rolland & Anchour, 1998; Novak et al., 2000). In the I site case, 12 scenarios are generated from the 12 events. For example, Figures 4 through 6 show three scenarios from three events such as "search for teachers," "search for photos," and "post photo."

Figure 4. "Search for teachers" scenario

Event No: 1	Event Name: Search for teachers
1. A member or a school club member requests to search for teachers 2. The teacher community subsystem provides total number of present and former teachers for each school. And it requests to select either present or former teacher for a particular school. 3. A member or a school club member selects either present or former teacher for a particular school. 4. The teacher community subsystem provides the list of present or former teachers for a particular school. 5. The teacher community subsystem asks to select one of teacher's profile, memo, and e-mail. 6. A member or a school club member can select one of teacher's profile, memo, and e-mail. 7. When teacher's profile is selected, the teacher community subsystem provides teacher's profile such as ID, name, major, incumbency information, the first working date for the school, the last working date for the school, phone number, and address. 8. A member or a school club member reads teacher's profile	

Figure 5. "Search for photos" scenario

Event No: 9	Event Name: Search for photos
1. A school club manager requests to search for photos. 2. The album service subsystem requests to select photo search type such as search by photo title, search by photo description, and search by edited date. 3. A school club manager selects one of search by photo title, search by description, and search by edited date. 4-1. When search by title is selected, the album service subsystem requests input of photo title. 4-2. When search by description is selected, the album service subsystem requests input of photo description. 4-3. When search by edited date is selected, the album service subsystem requests input of photo edited date. 5-1. A school club manager inputs photo title. 5-2. A school club manager inputs photo description. 5-3. A school club manager inputs photo edited date. 6. The album service subsystem provides search result for the requested search condition. 7. A school club manager confirms the result.	

Figure 6. "Post photo" scenario

Event No: 10	Event Name: Post photo
1. A school club manager requests to post photo. 2. The album service subsystem requests input of photo file, title, and description. 3. A school club manager inputs photo file, title, and description. 4. The album service subsystem confirms photo. If photo file is missing, it requests input of photo file. If photo file is attached, the photo is posted and school club information is updated as current date. 5. The album service subsystem provides the information about the posted photo. 6. A school club manager confirms the information about the photo.	

Object Modeling

Next, we need to model a variety of information the Web provides for customers. An object-oriented modeling technique has several advantages (comprehensiveness, understandability, changeability, adaptability, and reusability) (Hutt, 1994; Booch, 1994). CAIM adopts the object-oriented modeling technique to inherit its advantages. Objects are derived from scenarios.

Notations for our object modeling technique are depicted in Figure 7. An object includes its name, attributes, and responsibilities. Attributes contain properties of the object. Responsibilities are behavioral properties of the object (Wirfs-Brock et al., 1990; Booch, 1994). Among objects, four types of object relationships are described: superclass/subclass, association, collaboration, and component. Any subclass can inherit or use the attributes and responsibilities of its superclass. The association relationship describes a linkage among objects with relationship properties: one-to-one (1:1), one-to-many (1:N), or many-to-many (N:N) (Batini, Ceri, & Navathe, 1992). The collaboration relationship describes a dynamic reference among objects through responsibilities (Maughan & Durnota, 1993). The object that can be used as an attribute in other objects is described by the use of the component relationship.

CAIM produces objects from scenarios as follows:

- **First, customer groups are primary candidates for objects.** Customer groups include important information for a customer-oriented Internet business system. All objects have basic attributes such as "ID" and "name" and responsibilities such as "create," "retrieve," "update," and "delete." For example, in the case of the "search for teachers" scenario, objects such as "member," "school club member," and "school club manager" are generated. "Member" object has "M_ID" and "M_Name" as its attributes and "Create_Member," "Retrieve_Member," "Update_Member," and "Delete_Member" as its responsibilities.

Figure 7. Notations for object model

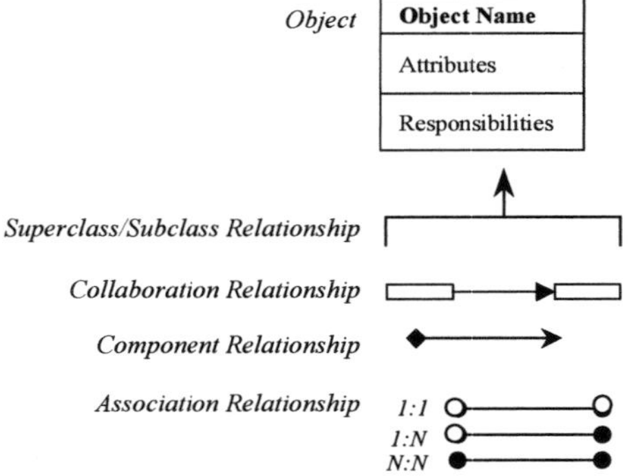

- **Second, information used in a subsystem can be a candidate.** For example, in case of the "search for teachers" scenario, "school" and "teacher" used in the "teacher community" subsystem can become the objects called "school" and "teacher." The "teacher history by school" object is generated for the teacher's history.
- **Third, additional attributes and responsibilities of objects and relationships among objects can be obtained.** For examples, in the "search for teachers" scenario, the association relationship between "member" object and "school" object is identified. Two attributes, "T_Phone" and "T_Address," are identified for the "teacher" object. From the "post photo" scenario, the "Update_School_Club" responsibility of the "school club album" object is found to have a collaboration relationship with the "Update_School_Club_Album_Edited_Date" responsibility in the "school club" object.

From three scenarios such as "search for teachers," "search for photos," and "post photo," eight objects ("member," "school club manager," "school club member," "teacher," "school," "school club," "school club album," and "teacher history by school") are generated. "School club manager" and "school club member" are the subclasses of "member" and thus can inherit attributes and responsibilities from "member." The resulting object model is depicted as shown in Figure 8.

Figure 8. Object model

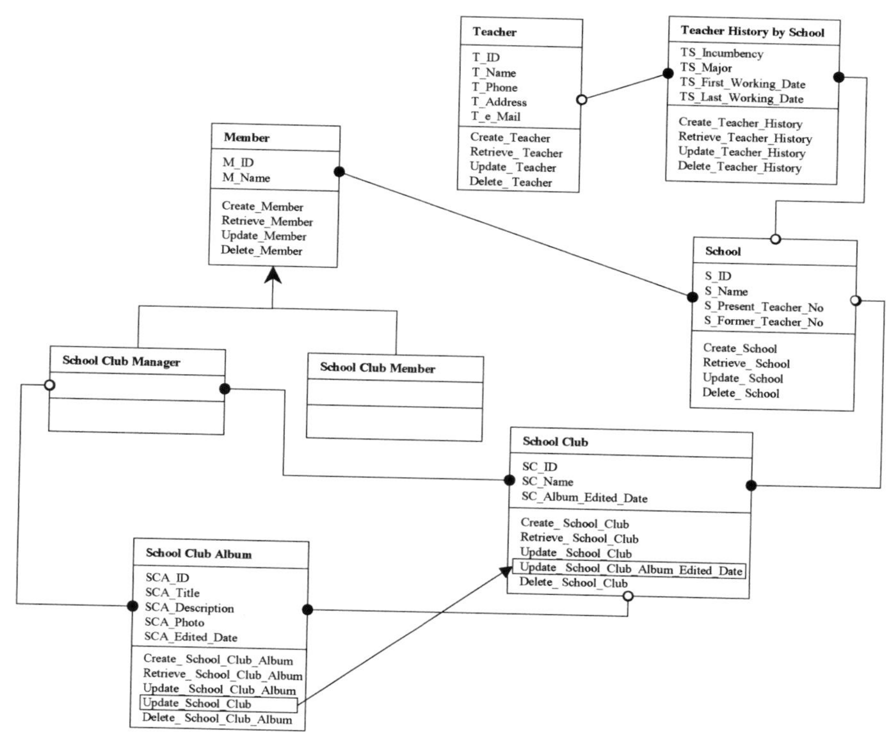

View Design

The view design subphase reorganizes information contents in the form of navigational units. A view is the information unit that customers want to find. These views may be referred to as O-O (object-oriented) views. These O-O views (Kim, 1995) are designed on the basis of responsibilities, attributes, and relationships in the object model. From our object model (eight objects), five views are generated, as shown in Figure 9.

Figure 9. View specification

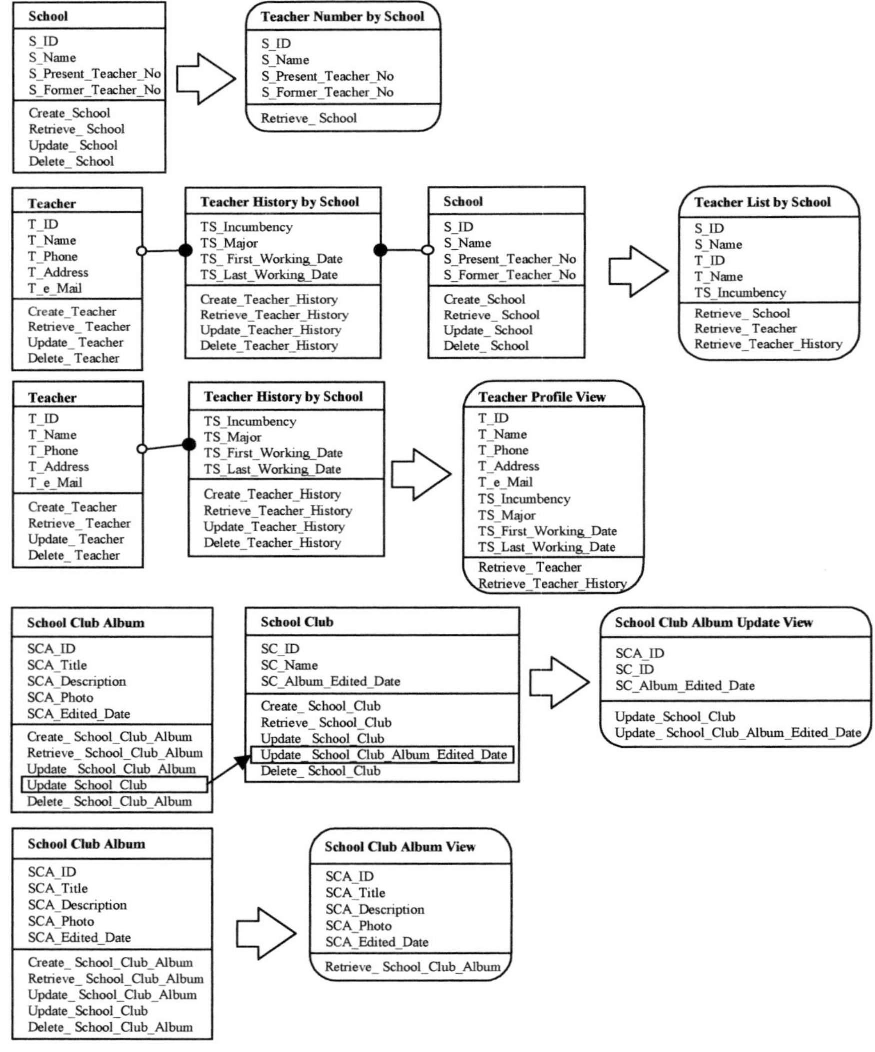

Views are categorized into three types: base view, association view, and collaboration view. First, a base view is generated from a single object. It is a subset of responsibilities and attributes in an object. It is a subset of responsibilities and attributes in an object. For example, in Figure 9, "teacher number by school" is a base view. It is generated from the attributes and responsibilities of the "school" object.

Second, an association view is extracted from the objects that have association relationship(s). It is a subset of responsibilities and attributes in these objects. "teacher list by school" and "teacher profile" are association views. The view, "teacher list by school," uses attributes and responsibilities in "teacher," "teacher history by school," and "school" objects.

Third, a collaboration view is generated from the objects having collaboration relationships. It is used not to provide information, but to change information. The origin of responsibilities for association views differs from that for collaboration views. In the case of collaboration view, the responsibilities required for collaboration are of importance. "School club album update" is a collaboration view extracted from the collaboration relationship between "school club album" and "school club." These three types of O-O views can be used in any type of Web business system. However, collaboration views are rarely generated in contents-oriented Internet business systems, like newspaper, since information is less dynamically updated according to customers' interaction.

From the object model in Figure 8, five views are generated as shown in Figure 9. "Teacher number by school," "teacher list by school," and "teacher profile" are generated from the "search for teachers" scenario sequentially. "School club album" and "school club album update" are generated from two scenarios, "search for photos" and "enroll photo," respectively.

Navigation Design

The navigation design subphase builds navigational links between nodes. The O-O view and Access Structure Node (ASN) are adopted for navigational units. The ASN differs from the O-O view in that ASN contains access paths to O-O views. The O-O view contains actual information that users want to obtain. These O-O views and ASNs correspond to nodes. A link denotes the relationship between the source node and destination node. These source and destination nodes may be O-O views or ASNs. Web pages are implemented on the basis of these O-O views and ASNs in the subsequent page design subphase.

From the scenarios, ASNs are found and then navigational links are determined. First, an event that begins with a scenario can become an event ASN. An event ASN starts navigation. For example, "search for teachers," "search for photos," and "enroll photo" events become "search for teachers ASN," "search for photos ASN," and "enroll photo ASN," respectively. Second, a selection ASN can be generated when a customer should select the next activities. For example, from the "search for photos" scenario, "condition for search for photos ASN" is built. Third, an input ASN can be generated when a customer needs to input contents. From the "enroll photo" scenario, "input photo ASN" is built.

Navigation specifications for I site are depicted in Figure 10. Linking ASNs and views together on the basis of scenario flows results in the navigation path. For example, according to the "search for teachers" scenario, "search for teachers ASN," "teacher number by school view," "teacher list by school view," "profile, memo, e-mail asn," and "teacher profile view" are linked sequentially.

Page Design

The page design subphase specifies Web pages. A page is a window having information and navigational guide. Web pages should be designed for customers to obtain necessary information in a convenient fashion. A page specification may be composed of many views and ASNs.

A page is designed according to the following steps: First, a view can be a page. Second, an input ASN and a selection ASN can be an individual page. Third, when an ASN follows a view, a page can include both this ASN and the following view. Fourth, an event ASN can be used with an anchor in other pages.

Pages are specified by organized anchors, O-O views, and additional description details (e.g., embedded components, text, images, sounds, etc.). Figure 11 illustrates page specifications. For example, the page "teacher list 001" entitled "teacher list by school" is derived from "teacher list by school view." It has three anchors that lead to "teacher profile 001," "memo 001," and "e-mail 001."

Implementation Design

The implementation design phase generates: (i) physical database schema and (ii) user interface (UI) specification for construction. A Web business system can be developed

Figure 10. Navigation specifications

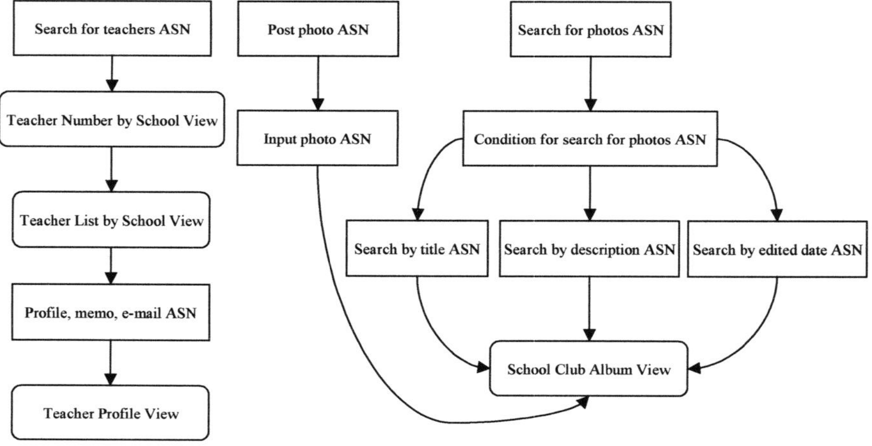

Figure 11. Page specification

Page ID: My Teacher 001	**Title:** My Teacher
Views Teacher Number by School View	
Description This page provides the number of present teachers and former teachers by each school.	
Anchors	
Other Components	

Page ID: Teacher List 001	**Title:** Teacher List by School
Views Teacher List by School View	
Description This page provides list of teachers for the selected school.	
Anchors Teacher Profile / Teacher Profile 001 Memo / Memo 001 e-mail / e-mail 001	
Other Components	

Page ID: Teacher Profile 001	**Title:** Teacher Profile
Views Teacher Profile View	
Description This page provides a profile of the selected teacher.	
Anchor	
Other Component	

under a variety of system environments. Implementation decisions are made according to the choice of technology. These technologies include DBMSs such as RDBMS or OODBMS, and development tools such as CGI, HTML, JAVA, Shockwave, Flash, DHTML, XML, and SGML. However, our implementation design phase is independent of these various system requirements.

Physical Database Design

Our methodology adopts the object model for data modeling. If OODBMS is used, this object model can be transformed directly. However, in many real-life cases, RDBMSs (Relational DBMSs) are most popular. Therefore, the transformation of the object model into relational schema is required. Here, designers need guidelines for this transformation. These transformation guidelines can be found in Blaha, Premerlani, and Rumbaugh (1988); Fong, (1995); and Lee, Lee, and Yoo (1999).

In addition to these guidelines, more views, SQL (Structured Query Language) stored procedures, or SQL triggers are required especially for the transformation of the collaboration relationship. An SQL stored procedure is a user-defined program module that is stored at the database server and can be invoked by client applications. An SQL trigger is usually in the form of SQL stored procedure and is automatically invoked by the data-related event. It is typically used to perform tasks related to changes in a table (Orfali, Harkey, & Edwards, 1996). For example, the collaboration relationship between "school club album" and "school club" can be transformed into a trigger as depicted in Figure 12. The collaboration view, "school club album view" (Figure 9), will be implemented by the use of the "Update_School_Club_Edited_ Date" trigger.

Transforming the object model (Figure 8) results in 10 tables, as shown in Figure 13. For example, the "school cub member" and "school club manager" tables inherit their fields from the "member" table.

User Interface Design

For construction, the page specification should be extended to incorporate data location, interface component choice, and component properties. The user interface design phase maps the page specification to user interface components like choice box, list box, button, check box, and scroll bar, which are supported in various implementation tools. Figure 14 shows the notation of user interface components and transitions.

A caption is a description of components. An action is an interactive procedure. Items are sets of data included in the user interface component. Two notations are proposed

Figure 12. Collaboration relationship transformation

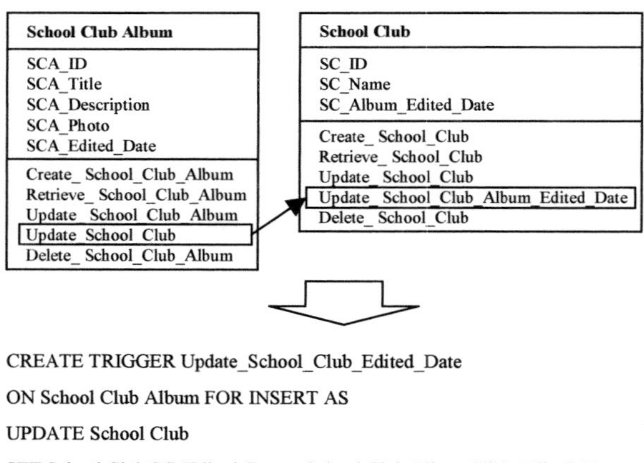

Figure 13. Physical database schema

Table Name	Field Name
Member	M_ID, M_Name
Teacher	T_ID, T_Name, T_Phone, T_Address, T_e_Mail
Teacher History by School	T_ID, S_ID, TS_ Incumbency, TS_Major, TS_First_Working_Date, TS_Last_Working_Date
School	S_ID, S_Name, S_Present_Teacher_No, S_Former_Teacher_No
School Club	SC_ID, SC_Name, SC_Ablum_Edited_Date
School Club Member	SCMe_ID, SCMe_Name
School Club Manager	SCM_ID, SCM_Name
School Club Album	SCA_ID, SCA_Title, SCA_Description, SCA_Photo, SCA_Edited_Date, SCM_ID, SC_ID
Member by School	M_ID, S_ID
Manager by School Club	SC_ID, SCM_ID

Figure 14. User interface component

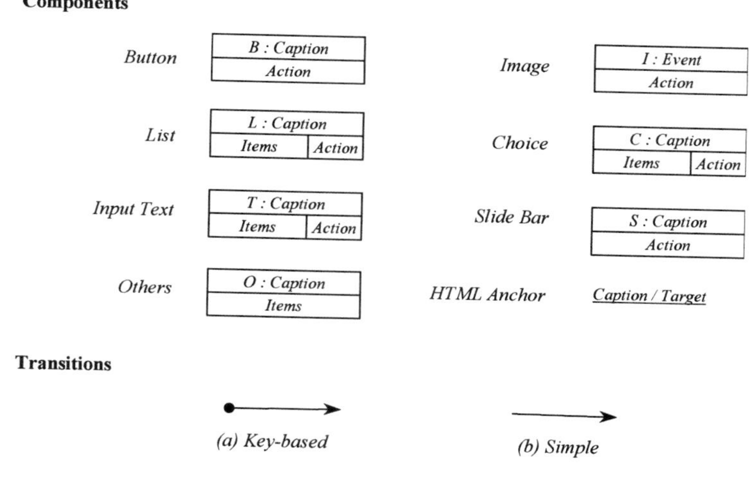

for transitions. The key-based transition refers to the current state of the component while the simple transition does not. These user interface components may be determined according to the access structure in the navigational design. All anchors may be transformed into a set of HTML anchors.

The page specification ("My Teacher" in Figure 11) can lead to the UI specification (Figure 15) by the use of UI components. This UI specification consists of: (i) the "My club & School Club" HTML anchor that provides customers with a link to access "My club & School Club" screen, (ii) the "MyTeacher.gif" image for the description of this screen, (iii) the "Teacher Number by School" list composed of four items such as "S_ID,"

Figure 15. User interface specification

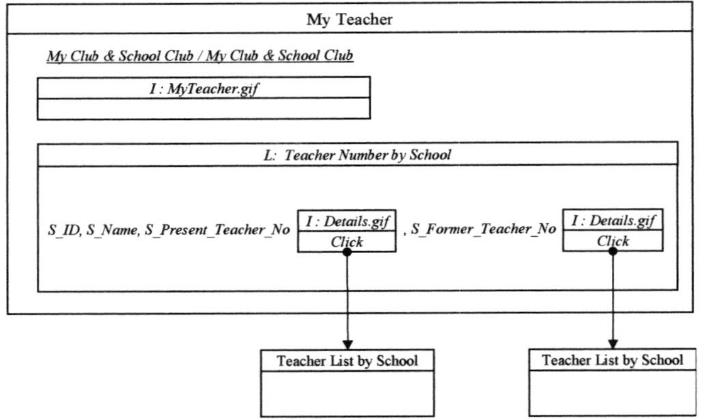

Figure 16. Main page screen of I Site

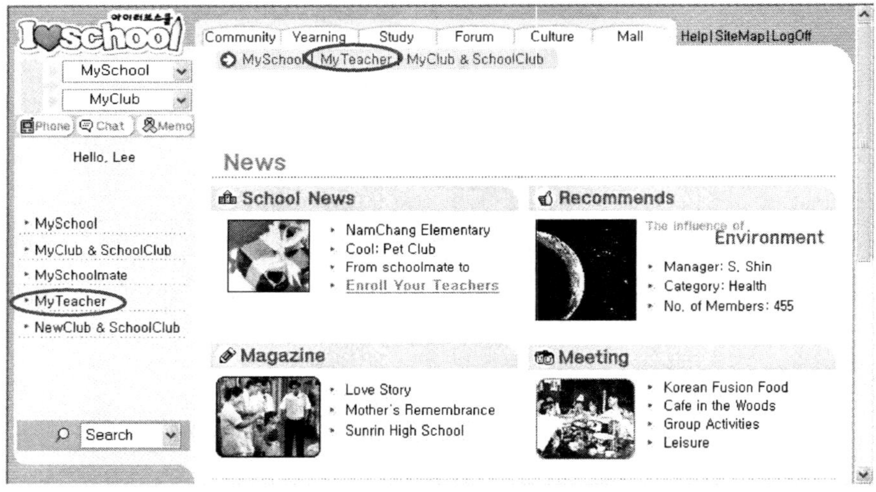

"S_Name," "S_Present_Teacher_No," and "S_Former_Teacher_ No," and (iv) two "Details.gif" images for the key-based transition to the "Teacher List by School" screen.

Construction

The construction phase implements a physically running Web business system. All of the outputs during the implementation design phase should be mapped to physical components. For example, Figure 16 shows the main page of I site. To implement

Figure 17. "My Teacher" screen

customers' "Teacher Community" needs, a new menu entitled "My Teacher" is added on the left hand side as well as the upper side. Customers can access "Teacher Community" by using the "My Teacher" menu. Figure 17 shows the "My Teacher" screen that is constructed by using the UI specification as shown in Figure 15. In this screen, customers can execute the "search for teachers" scenario as shown in Figure 4. Our design results in 7 newly implemented pages for improving I site.

Conclusion

This chapter reviewed the previous methodologies for developing Web business systems and proposed a new methodology, CAIM (Customer Analysis-based Improvement Methodology), illustrating how the methodology was employed to improve a real-life case. Although the CAIM focuses on improving customer-oriented Web business systems, it can also be employed successfully in the first development of the system if the effort to capture the types of potential customers and their requirements is made.

The CAIM provides seamless and systematic processes to help align customers' needs with implementation details for developing a Web business system. Scenarios are employed to analyze customers' requirements in a natural fashion. Scenarios are better able to monitor customers' requirements, and thus enhance the feasibility of our methodology. By using our methodology, companies are more likely to capture the context in which customers interact with their Web business systems. This is especially true if shifts in customer needs mandate some sort of reintegration of the system.

Our methodology has its limitations. The following future research avenues will be able to alleviate these possible weaknesses. First, it is noted that our scenarios are descriptive. They can be extended to cover exploratory or explanatory designs. Furthermore, the direct incorporation of customers' experiences into the Web site may be able to make our methodology more powerful (Seybold, 2001). Second, adaptive Web design is of interest. Analyzing customer profiles will be able to enhance the adaptability of presentation or navigation. Web server logs on the basis of customers' profiles may help find more convenient navigation (Perkowitz & Etzioni, 2000). Finally, our current mechanism for determining the implementation priority is not systematic. Quality Function Deployment (QFD) may be applied to evaluating this priority. QFD can transform what the customer wants into how the company plans to provide it (Brady, 2001; Govers, 2001). QFD can help analyze the value via cross-functional teams in a collaborative fashion.

References

Abels, E.G., White, M.D., & Hahn, K. (1997). Identifying user-based criteria for Web pages. *Internet Research: Electronic Networking Applications and Policy, 7*(4), 252-262.

Abels, E.G., White, M.D., & Hahn, K. (1999). A user-based design process for Web sites. *OCLS Systems & Services, 15*(1), 35-44.

Afuah, A. & Tucci, C.L. (2000). *Internet business models and strategies: Text and cases.* McGraw-Hill.

Aissi, S., Malu, P., & Srinivasan, K. (2002). E-business process modeling: The next big step. *IEEE Computer, 35*(5), 55-62.

Artz, J.M. (1996). A top-down methodology for building corporate Web applications. *Internet Research: Electronic Networking Applications and Policy, 6*(2/3), 64-74.

Atzeni, P., Mecca, G., & Merialdo, P. (1998). Design and maintenance of data-intensive Web sites. *EDBT'98 Lecture Notes in Computer Science*, 436-450.

Bajaj, A. & Siau, K. (2000). An introduction to the area of e-commerce systems: Architecture, infrastructure, model, and development methodology. *Proceedings of the America's Conference on Information Systems (AMCIS)*, Los Angeles.

Barry, C. & Lang, M. (2001). A survey of multimedia and Web development techniques and methodology usage. *IEEE Multimedia*, 8(2), 52-60.

Barua, A., Whinston, A.B., & Yin, F. (2000). Value and productivity in the Internet economy. *IEEE Computer, 33*(5), 102-105.

Batini, C., Ceri, S., & Navathe, S. (1992). *Conceptual database design: An entity-relationship approach.* The Benjamin/Cummings.

Bichler, M. & Nusser, S. (1996a). SHDT: The structured way of developing WWW-Sites. *Proceedings of the 4th European Conference on Information Systems*, Lisbon, 1093-1101.

Bichler, M. & Nusser, S. (1996b). Modular design of complex Web-applications with W3DT. *Proceedings of 5th International Workshops on Enabling Technologies: Infrastructure for Collaborative Enterprises (WET ICE'96)*, 328-333.

Bishop, B. (2000). *The strategic enterprise*. Stoddart Publishing.

Blaha, M.R., Premerlani, W.J., & Rumbaugh, J.E. (1998). Relational database design using an object-oriented methodology. *Communication of the ACM, 31*(4), 414-427.

Booch, G. (1994). *Object-oriented analysis and design with application*. The Benjamin/Cummings.

Brady, J. (2001). Systems engineering and cost as an independent variable. *Systems Engineering, 4*(4), 233-241.

Casteleyn, S. & Troyer, O.D. (2001). Structuring Web sites using audience class hierarchies. *Proceedings of 20th International Conference on Conceptual Modeling (ER 2001)*.

Chen, J.Q. & Heath, R.D. (2001). Building Web applications: challenges, architectures, and methods. *Information Systems Management, 18*(1), 68-79.

Cravens D.W., Greenley, G., Piercy, N.F., & Slater, S. (1997). Integrating contemporary strategy management perspective. *Long Range Planning, 3*(4), 493-506.

Cunliffe, D. (2000). Developing usable Web sites: A review and model. *Internet Research: Electronic Networking Applications and Policy, 10*(4), 295-307.

Dix, A.J., Finlay, J.E., Abowd, G.D., & Beale, R. (1998). *Human-Computer Interaction*. Prentice Hall.

Fong, J. (1995). Mapping extended entity relationship model to object modeling technique. *SIGMOD Record, 24*(3), 18-22.

Fowler, M., & Scott, K. (1999). *UML distilled: A brief guide to the standard object modeling language* (2nd ed.). Addison-Wesley.

Fraternali, P. & Paolini, P. (2000). Model-driven development of Web applications: The Autoweb system. *ACM Transaction on Information Systems, 28*(4), 323-382.

Gellersen, H., Wicke, R., & Gaedke, M. (1997). WebComposition: An object-oriented support system for the Web engineering lifecycle. *Computer Networks and ISDN Systems, 29*, 1429-1437.

Ginige, A. & Murugesan, S. (2001). Web engineering: An introduction. *IEEE Multimedia, 8*(1), 14-18.

Govers, C.P.M. (2001). QFD not just a tool but a way of quality management. *International Journal of Production Economics, 69*, 151-159.

Greenacre, M.J. (1984). *Theory and applications of correspondence analysis*, Academic Press.

Greenacre, M.J. & Hastie, T.J. (1987). The geometric interpretation of correspondence analysis. *Journal of the American Statistical Association, 82*, 437-447.

Gruhn, V. & Schope, L. (2002). Software processes for the development of electronic commerce systems, *Information and Software Technology, 44*, 891-901.

Hutt, A.T.F. (1994). *Object analysis and design: Description of methods*. John Wiley & Sons.

Isakowitz, T., Kamis, A., & Koufaris, M. (1997). Extending RMM: Russian dolls and hypertext. *Proceedings of the 30th Hawaii International Conference on System Sciences,* 177-186.

Isakowitz, T., Stohr, E.A., & Balasubramanian, P. (1995). RMM: A methodology for structured hypermedia design. *Communications of the ACM, 38*(8), 34-44.

Jacobson, I., Ericsson, M., & Jacobson, A. (1995). *The object advantage: Business process reengineering with object technology*. Addison Wesley.

Jarvenpaa, S.L & Tiller, E.H. (1999). Integrating market, technology, and policy opportunities in e-business strategy. *Journal of Strategic Information Systems, 8*(3), 235-249.

Killander, A.J. (2001). Why design methodologies are difficult to implement. *International Journal Technology Management, 21*(3/4), 271-276.

Kim, W. (1995). *Modern Database Systems: The object model, interoperability, and beyond.* Addison Wesley.

Kotler, P. (1997). *Marketing management analysis, planning, and control.* Prentice Hall.

Kotler, P. & Armstrong, G. (1996). *Principles of marketing*. Prentice-Hall.

Lee, C., Choi, B., & Lee, H. (2004). Development environment for customer-oriented Internet business: eBizBench. *Journal of Systems and Software, 72*(2), 163-178.

Lee, H., Lee, C., & Yoo, C. (1999). A scenario-based object-oriented hypermedia design methodology. *Information and Management, 36*(3), 121-138.

Lee, H. & Suh, W. (2001). A workflow-based methodology for developing hypermedia information systems. *Journal of Organizational Computing and Electronic Commerce, 11*(2), 77-196.

Maughan, G. & Durnota, B. (1993). MON: An object relationship model incorporating roles, classification, publicity and assertions. *Proceedings of OOIS'94, International Conference on Object Oriented Information Systems.*

Nanard, J. & Nanard, M. (1995). Hypertext design environments and the hypertext design process. *Communications of ACM, 38*(8), 49-56.

Novak, T.P., Hoffman, D.L., & Yung, Y-F. (2000). Measuring the customer experience in online environments: A structural modeling approach. *Marketing Science, 19*(1), 43-62.

Orfali, R., Harkey, D., & Edwards, J. (1996). *The essential client/server survival guide.* John Wiley & Sons.

Palmer, J.W. (2002). Web site usability, design, and performance metrics. *Information Systems Research, 13*(2), 151-167.

Perkowitz, M. & Etzioni, O. (2000). Towards adaptive Web sites: Conceptual framework and case study. *Artificial Intelligence, 118*(1-2), 245-275.

Powell, T.A. (2002). *Web design: The complete reference.* Osborne/McGraw-Hill.

Preece, J., Sharp, H., Benyon, D., Holland, S., & Carey, T. (1994). *Human-computer interaction.* Addison-Wesley.

Rolland, C.R. & Anchour, C.B. (1998). Guiding the construction of textual use case specifications. *Data & Knowledge Engineering, 25*(1), 125-160.

Schwabe, D., Esmeraldo, L., Rossi, G., & Lyardet, F. (2001). Engineering Web applications for reuse. *IEEE Multimedia, 8*(1), 20-31.

Schwabe, D., Pontes, R.A., & Moura, I. (1999). OOHDM-Web: An environment for implementation of hypermedia applications in the WWW. *SigWEB Newsletter.*

Schwabe, D. & Rossi, G. (1995). The object oriented hypermedia design model. *Communications of the ACM, 38*(8), 45-46.

Seybold, P.B. (2001). Get inside the lives of your customers. *Harvard Business Review*, May, 81-88.

Smart, K.L. & Whiting, M.E. (2001). Designing systems that support learning and use: a customer-centered approach. *Information and Management, 39*(3), 177-190.

Standing, C. (2002). Methodologies for developing Web applications. *Information and Software Technology, 44*, 151-159.

Suh, W. & Lee, H. (2001). Hypermedia document management: A metadata and meta-information system. *Journal of Database Management, 12*(2), 25-35.

Takahashi, K. & Liang, E. (1997). Analysis and design of Web-based information systems. *Proceedings of 6th World Wide Web Conference.*

Taylor, D.A. (1995). *Business engineering with object technology*. John Wiley & Sons.

Taylor, M.J., McWilliam, J., Forsyth, H., & Wade, S. (2002). Methodologies and Web site development: A survey of practice. *Information and Software Technology, 44*(6), 381-391.

Troyer, M.F.D. & Leune, C.J. (1998). WSDM: A user centered design method for Web sites. *Proceedings of the Seventh International WWW Conference*, Brisbane, Australia.

Wheeler, B.C. (2002). NEBIC: A dynamic capabilities theory for assessing net-enablement. *Information Systems Research, 13*(2), 125-146.

Wirfs-Brock, R., Wilkerson, B., & Wiener, L. (1990). *Designing object-oriented software.* Prentice Hall.

Zang, P. & Dran, G.M. (2002). User expectation and rankings of quality factors in different Web site domains. *International Journal of Electronic Commerce, 6*(2), 9-34.

Section VI

Web Intelligence:
Techniques and Applications

Chapter XIV

Analysis and Customization of Web-Based Electronic Catalogs

Benjamin P.-C. Yen
The University of Hong Kong, China

Abstract

Electronic catalogs are at the core of information system support for electronic commerce. Unlike traditional paper-based product catalogs which are limited by size, access method, high production cost, and obsolete information, electronic catalogs promise up-to-date information, more flexible methods of search and retrieval, interactive multimedia user interface, and automated linkage and support for various procurement functions. As the World Wide Web became more popular, a tremendous amount of information flooded the cyberspace resulting in the problem of information overload. To attract and retain users, a Web site should be adaptive on information content, information organization and information display. In this chapter, a Personalized Electronic Catalog (PEC) system is proposed to synthesize the Web-based electronic catalog customization on information content, organization, and display; as well as to demonstrate the analysis and improvement of information access for electronic catalogs in an industrial application.

Introduction

Electronic catalogs are a central component of the procurement process in e-commerce. Traditionally, product catalogs are the references for product selection and are also used in supporting other steps of procurement including source selection, price negotiation, ordering, and order fulfillment. Electronic catalogs are more powerful than paper-based catalogs because they carry up-to-date information. Furthermore, they can be searched in numerous ways other than by product name and identification number, and can be configured to satisfy the different information needs of various functions involved in each step of the procurement process such as marketing and sales, as well as different industry roles such as supplier and manufacturer. Electronic catalogs inherit the advantages of the Internet technology for easy update, economical development, and full-scale information. If defined according to standards, they can also potentially participate in a multi-catalog framework allowing buyers to search across multiple catalogs.

The Internet has emerged as the media for a market with the greatest potential. Many organizations have established their Web sites as a business frontier in order to gain the strategic advantages of competition in the electronic business. Most commercial sites provide information about the company, products and services, well-organized electronic catalogs, or transaction functions. Many Web sites are loaded with large amounts of information, such as electronic catalogs in shopping malls (Yahoo! Shopping, shopping.yahoo.com) and auction sites (eBay, www.ebay.com). It is not surprising that users often feel lost and frustrated due to the disorganized, obsolete, and irrelevant information when they surf the information sphere. The situation is getting worse as the number of Web sites and the volume of data associated soar. Even though various search engines are provided in many of these sites, they cannot guarantee that the user can really find what he is looking for, because he may not be able to specify some attributes or keywords in the query (NUA Internet Surveys). The ultimate goal of an EC Web site is to attract and retain the visitors by providing better services rather than just providing more information, an attractive layout, or flashy advertisements. One solution is to provide a customized Web site for individual visitor where customization is based on the user preferences for information content, product display, and supporting functions.

Research in electronic catalogs has been fragmented. Issues that have been investigated include search and information retrieval mechanisms, architectures of multi-catalog systems supporting supplier/buyer networks, information presentation, and user interfaces. An integration of extant research into a comprehensive definition and structural design of electronic catalogs facilitates to specify the components, content, features, functions, and inter-component relationships. Since different stakeholders of the procurement process would have different needs for these components, it would be beneficial for designers to be aware of these needs. A prototype based on the structural design allows different stakeholders to evaluate the components hands-on. Systematic analysis of their evaluations can derive design guidelines for electronic catalogs.

Background

Many researchers have been seeking ways to resolve the problem of information overload. In this section, a literature review of research on electronic catalogs and information access on the Web is provided.

Electronic catalogs are at the core of information system support for electronic commerce. It is the component that provides product information for customers to order goods, make payments, access customer support, and provide feedback. It is also used in the marketing function for advertising, marketing, sales, distribution, and support channels. Unlike traditional paper-based product catalogs which are limited by size, access method, high production cost, and obsolete information, electronic catalogs promise up-to-date information, more flexible methods of search and retrieval, accessibility at any time and anywhere, interactive multimedia user interface, joint search with other catalogs, and automated linkage and support for various procurement functions. These promises, however, have yet to be realized. Customization is a way to improve the performance of electronic catalogs. As the WWW became popular, more information flooded cyberspace, resulting in the problem of information overload, especially for some information intensive Web sites like electronic catalogs.

Lots of research were carried out in the electronic catalog area related to EC. Ginsburg, Gebauer, & Segev (1999) introduced three electronic catalog models. In the Do-It-Yourself Model, the buyer company initializes the development of electronic catalogs; while in the Third-Party E-catalog Integrator Model, the firm seeks help from a third-party to develop the master electronic catalog and then rent the access service. In the Real-Time Knowledge Discovery model, the buyer firm uses the advanced software technique, such as agents, to carry out the real-time information discovery on the Internet. Garcia Gosalvez (1997) pointed out the need for integrating the electronic product catalog into the technological, organizational, and strategic aspects of a company in order to gain the real advantages of electronic catalogs, which is capable of helping the day-to-day organization management. Koch and Turk (1997) illustrated the development process of the electronic product catalog and presented the architecture of the EPK-fix system, which constructs electronic production catalogs systematically. Handschuh, Schmid, and Stanoevska-Slabeva (1997) described the concept of Mediating Electronic Product Catalog (MEPC) based on the Q-Technology. MEPC is an intermediary between buyers and sellers, which adds value to both suppliers and customers through the formation of a federated system of autonomous electronic product catalogs. Palmer (1997) conducted a survey to compare the similarity and difference among four different B2C electronic catalog sites (beverage, music, computer and clothing) with ordering capabilities either through online or telephone purchasing. The research (Segev, Wan, & Beam, 1995; Keller & Genesereth, 1997; Stanoevska-Slabeva & Schmid, 2000) has given the definition of electronic catalogs in information and functional prospective, as well as the role of electronic catalogs in electronic commerce.

Sung, Yang, Yiu, Ho, Cheung, and Lam (2002) tackled the problem of automating the re-organization of Web sites from scratch. They modeled online catalog organization as a decision tree structure and proposed a metric, based on the popularity of products and the relative importance of product attribute values, to evaluate the quality of a catalog organization. The problem is then formulated as a decision tree construction problem. An efficient greedy algorithm (GENCAT) is developed and the experimental results show that it produces better catalog organizations. Joh and Lee (2002) focused on the integration with multiple sellers' e-catalogs and maintaining consistency with the dynamically changing sellers' e-catalogs to solve the mismatched level of details, directory depths unbalance, and changed category names. They adopted the logic programming approach to represent the structures of both buyers' and sellers' directories and devised a top-down control algorithm that improves the depth and balance of the directory significantly and results in automatically generating more effective buyer's directory. Lee, Wang, & Lee (2001) discussed the interface of online product catalogs, focusing on its ability to help shoppers navigate and analyze product information. They presented a new interactive interface for online product catalogs that is effective in navigating through the product information space and analytically selecting suitable products, where the interface is a multi-dimensional visualization mechanism based on parallel coordinates and augmented by a number of visual facilities for filtering, color-coding, and dynamic querying. Oh, Park, Kim, Lee, and Wu (2001) discussed the catalog interoperability and catalog sharing. They proposed an extended catalog model of e-catalogs and presented a view-integrated architecture for an electronic catalog library, named CatalogStop. The Live Catalog in CatalogStop is a virtual catalog that can be bound directly to the contents in the catalog repository or to a query that will retrieve the contents from possibly distributed and heterogeneous catalog sources using a standard protocol.

The research for information access on the Web is mainly divided into four groups based on their application and scope — Web site customization based on the user access information, agents based intelligence search for information retrieval and discovery, intelligence browser and agent to support user navigation on the Internet based on user preferences, and collection of user information on the Web.

Perkowitz and Etzioni (2000a; 2000b) proposed an artificial intelligence (AI) approach to create the adaptive Web site, which can improve site organization based on the users' access log with the assumption of each originating computer corresponding to a particular user. PageGather, based on the clustering algorithm, processes the access log and measures the co-occurrence frequencies between pages to generate a similar matrix and the corresponding graph. Clusters are then extracted from the graph and ranked to eliminate the overlap. The Webmaster selects clusters that each is associated with an index page of links within it. Yan, Jacobsen, Garcia-Molina, and Dayal (1996) proposed the use of user access patterns to generate hyperlinks, which are captured in the access log and analyzed offline in an interval basis, to improve the information access. Each user session is formulated as an n-dimensional vector where each element refers to a page of interest. A clustering algorithm is used to discover the cluster of users with similar interest from the vectors. When a user browses through the Web site, the matched cluster is used for the corresponding hyperlinks. Sarukkai (2000) used a Markov Chain model based on the user access information for link prediction and path analysis. The URL or HTTP request is formulated as the Markov states and the transition matrix is estimated for path prediction. In addition to link prediction, the Markov Chain model also provides Web server HTTP request prediction, adaptive Web navigation, Web tour generation, and personalized hub/authority. Wang, Siew, and Yi (2000) proposed a personalized product information filtering model to filter and rank the product information with linear functions on the user preference. Only matched items are presented to user for selection. The user preference is updated with inductive learning method in the selection process.

The research in the second group focuses on intelligence agents to help the user seek for information on the Internet. Cheung, Dao, and Lee (1998) proposed a model of four-level classification tool where the level-4 tool has property of learning the behavior of both information user and information source. The Web tool is composed of three agents to help user retrieve the desired information on WWW: the learning agent, the monitor agent, and the suggestion agent. Chen and Kuo (2000) proposed a personalized information retrieval system based on the user profile modelled as the semantic relevance (SR) and co-occurrence (CO) of keywords to capture the real meaning of user query. The process is composed of issuing query, enhancing query, selecting document, and updating profile. Chang, Hun, and Hou (1998) identified that the manually constructed hyperlinks have the property of decreasing relevance as the number of hyperlinks between two pages increase and some relevant information far from the root page is difficult to discover. They presented a site traveling algorithm (STA) to discover the relevant information, in which the relevance of the retrieved document is evaluated with the content popularity and richness (CPR). Yang, Yen, and Chen (2000) presented the development of intelligent personal Internet agent based on automatic textual analysis of Internet document and hybrid simulated annealing algorithm. With the capability of comparison of similarity for Internet documents, the hybrid simulated annealing algorithm is used to search for the relevant Internet document for the user. Tu and Hsiang (2000) proposed an interactive information retrieval (IIR) agent architecture made up of a group agent that handles group knowledge and preference, and a personal agent that keeps track of the individual user profile. Each agent operates and achieves its goal through the collaboration of its subagents to generate category knowledge of group and individual preferences through the document vector model and clustering algorithm.

The third group of research concerns navigation assistant for user during the browsing process. Joachims, Freitag, & Mitchell (1997) introduced the Web-Watcher, based on a learning approach with the user feedback to improve the quality of advice for navigation interactively. Similarly, Liaberman (1995) introduced the intelligent agent, Letiza, which works with conventional Web browser to keep track of the user browsing behavior and interests. Furthermore, Berghel, Berleant, Foy, and McGuire (1999) presented a Web browser called the "Cyberbrowser" to customize the information access for the content within the Web page, which include keyword and sentences extraction according to user selection.

In addition to the three groups of research mentioned above, some papers are mainly about gathering user information on the Internet. Lin, Huang, and Chen (1999) described an approach for capturing user access patterns on the WWW to address the problem that the Web server will only recognize the proxy server instead of the individual user. The method used is called "page conversion" and each page on the site is encoded into a cipher on the server side. When a user requests a page, a client-side program (deciphering module) is downloaded from the server and reports the event of page access to the Access Pattern Collection Server (APCS) before deciphering the encoded page and presenting it to the user. Richardson (2000) did a comparison on the existing tools to access information on the Internet, such as visitor counters and guest books.

From the review above, although many researches have been done on information retrieval and site organization, there is a conspicuous lack of integration of these two aspects. The research mainly considers general Web information retrieval rather than the electronic catalogs in electronic commerce. In addition, little research has been carried out on the customization for electronic catalogs on the WWW, which is one of the major sources for information overload. Furthermore, the customization of electronic catalogs should include the personalization of information presentation that is critical for product selection and evaluation. In this chapter, a Personalized Electronic Catalog (PEC) System is proposed to synthesize the customization on information content, organization, and display for electronic catalogs.

Main Thrust of the Chapter

Electronic catalogs should be designed to produce maximum business value. The value of each catalog component, for example the usefulness or relevance of its functions and features as perceived by different stakeholders, should be the basis for determining whether to develop a component and how it should be designed. The definitions, functions, and structures of electronic catalogs are reviewed as follows.

Issues, Controversies, Problems

Traditionally, product catalogs contain pictures, drawings, and photographs of the products and descriptive words next to them (1993). According to Muldoon (1995), there are two types of catalogs: consumer and business-to-business. Consumer catalogs may be further classified into unaffiliated, retail, manufacturer-supported, incentive, non-profit, co-op, syndicated and international. To date, many definitions of electronic catalogs exist. For example, Segev et al. (1995) defined electronic catalogs as "any WWW page that contains information about the products and services a commercial entity offer. A typical electronic catalog contains detailed pricing information, which potential customers can use to help make purchasing decisions. Moreover, it may also support online shopping, ordering, and payment capabilities…" Baron, Shaw, and Bailey (2000) defined them broadly as "electronic representations of information about the products and/or services of an organization." A narrower definition is provided by Timm and Rosewitz (1998): "... allow customers to browse through multimedia product representations and to get relevant information concerning the product…" Keller (1997) defined them "as the reference for product selection and which can assist with source selection and description of terms and conditions." Some definitions contain descriptions of the purpose, system functions, and contents of electronic catalogs, while others describe their users, business functions, and value.

In their investigation of the impact on consumers, Jones and Vijayasarathy (1998) compared individual's perceptions of Internet catalog shopping and print catalog shopping. They found that their perceptions differed based on personality differences (level of need for cognition) and influence of other important people. They also compared individuals' attitudes and intentions to shop using print and Internet catalogs (Jones & Vijayasarathy, 2000a), and examined intentions to shop using Internet catalogs by product types, shopping orientations, and attitudes toward computers (Jones & Vijayasarathy, 2000b). Some researchers have focused on studying the information layout/page design (Koch & Turk, 1997; Luedi, 1997; Spiller & Lohse, 1998; Marcus, 1997; Nielsen, 1996; Richtel, 1998; Gehrke & Turban, 1999; Zhang, Small, von Dran, & Barcellos, 1999; Fink & Laupase, 2000; Lohse & Wu, 2001; Liu, Arnett, & Litecky, 2000; Miles, Howes, & Davies, 2000). They studied the effectiveness of using different media in the product presentation, such as text, image, photo-realistic virtual reality object, 3D virtual object, animation, and video. For example, Chau, Au, and Tam (2000) reported that pictures are not definitely better than text. Westland and Au (1998) found that a significant difference produced by a virtual reality storefront interface is the time spent shopping. The amount of money spent and number of items purchased did not vary. On the other hand, the Sharper Image reported increased sales after the introduction of 3D virtual object (1999). Johnson (1998) found that users browsed through and enjoyed both conventional Web pages (which contain text and 2D images) and 3D virtual objects.

From a management perspective, Gebauer, Beam, and Segev's research (1998) showed that the impact of the Internet and related technologies had been to change the role of purchasing department from a transaction-oriented one to a more managerial one that focuses on establishing and maintaining relationships with related parties. The above impact studies provided piecemeal evidence on the effectiveness of electronic catalog features and hence piecemeal advice on catalog design. To provide comprehensive guidelines for designers of electronic catalogs, it is necessary to have different stakeholders of the procurement process evaluate first hand the different components of an electronic catalog built according to a comprehensive structural design. Their evaluation of the value of each catalog component, such as the usefulness and relevance of its functions and features, should be the basis for developing comprehensive design guidelines for electronic catalogs.

Structural designs of information systems may be viewed as physical definitions of systems. A structural design specifies the components, their content, features, functions, and inter-component relationships. Current research in the structural design of electronic catalog design has focused on both the front-end and the back-end (Garcia Gosalvez, 1997; Koch & Turk, 1997; Palmer, 1997; Stanoevska-Slabeva and Schmid, 2000; Baron et al., 2000; Luedi, 1997; Spiller & Lohse, 1998). Front-end design typically focuses on information organization and media presentation (Hoffman, Novak, & Chatterjee, 1996), while back-end design focuses on the system functionality. In front-end design, for example, Stanoevaka-Slabeva and Schmid (2000) introduced an Internet-based Electronic Product Catalog (IEPC) that reduced online customers' difficulties in navigating the catalog while searching for products. Personalization strategies were incorporated into product searching mechanisms in the Participatory Electronic Product Catalog (PEP) and the Intelligent Catalog Search System (ICSS) (Schubert, 2000; Glezer and Yadav, 2001). Research on back-end design focuses on support for user functions and features such as search engines (Handschuh et al., 1997; Keller, 1997), shopping carts (Lim and Lee, 2000), personalization of information and interface layout (Keller, 1997; Luedi, 1997; Schubert, 2000), as well as system administrator functions such as product information retrieval and storage, communication, and collaboration with organizational parties and customers (Baron et al., 2000; Schubert, 2000), and mediation with other databases and electronic catalogs (Ginsburg et al., 1999; Keller, 1997; Lincke & Schmid, 1998). Although much work has been done in designing individual front-end and back-end components, a comprehensive structural design for an electronic catalog is still lacking.

From the discussions above, the definitions, functions, and structures of electronic catalogs are summarized as follows.

Electronic Catalogs: Definitions

Catalogs originated from the library as descriptive lists of the library collection about two thousand years ago (The Concise Columbia Electronic Encyclopedia). As time goes by, the use of catalogs becomes more popular and is no longer restricted to books in the library. The styles and facilities of the catalogs are changing along with the media carrying the catalogs. Paper catalogs provide product information, colorful photos, and an index for searching. With the adoption of computer technology, catalogs evolved to electronic media (such as CD-ROM) for its cost effective and large storage capacity nature. In electronic media, catalog style is no longer restricted to pictures and text; audio, video, and hypertext are also used for information presentation. In addition to simple indexes, sophisticated functions (such as keyword/image search engines) are also added for users to search information in catalogs. As the Internet technology emerges, catalogs are also migrating onto the Web for online access, quick updates, and easy distribution. In general, the definition of electronic catalog can be viewed in two aspects — function and structure.

Electronic Catalogs: Functions

In a broad view, the function of electronic catalogs can be seen as virtual gateways for the buyer to obtain information about the product, purchase the product, make payments, access support services, and cooperate with the sellers (Segev et al., 1995). In a narrow view, electronic catalogs help the buyer to browse through the collection of product information in multimedia and retrieve the relevant subset of product information (Keller & Genesereth, 1997). It enables the buyer to retrieve the reference for the selection of product from the entire collection to assist the sourcing process (Handschuh et al., 1997). A functional definition of electronic catalogs provided by Stanoevska-Slabeva and Schmid (2000) is as "… interactive and multimedia interface between buyers and sellers on the Internet, which support product representation, search and classification and have interface to market services as negotiation, ordering and payment …"

In addition, the functional definition of electronic catalogs can be viewed from the perspective of both the seller and the buyer. For the seller, it is an integrated back-end system for data update, customization of catalog layout, and collection of customer information; while for the buyer, the searching and browsing functions help the product selection and ordering process (Garcia Gosalvez, 1997). In this chapter, we define the *electronic catalog* as an interactive and multimedia information space on the Internet with information creation, update, browsing, searching, presentation, classification, and customization facilities to assist catalog users to construct, maintain, and retrieve the product information. On top of the primitive information processing functions mentioned above, electronic catalogs also provide negotiation functions for communication and transaction functions for purchasing to facilitate the procurement business processes. In general, sellers are more concerned about creating and updating information in the electronic catalog. On the other hand, buyers are more interested in browsing, searching, presenting, and customizing the electronic catalog. The classification, negotiation, and transaction function are important for both parties.

Electronic Catalogs: Structures

From a structural point of view, an electronic catalog is defined as a collection of classified information in forms of a catalog tree as shown in Figure 1. In a catalog, each *record*, representing a product or a collection of products, consists of a set of attributes and the corresponding values, $\{(A, v)\}$, to denote the product information, such as price, manufacturer, functions, and images. The records are classified according to attribute and value pair (A, v). The records may share some common set of attributes for classification. The attributes of a record can be denoted as a set $\{\{A_a\},\{A_c\},\{A_o\}\}$, where $\{A_a\}$ is the set of common attributes for all records and must not be an empty set, $\{A_c\}$ is a set of common attributes for some records, and $\{A_o\}$ is a set of attributes only for a particular record. For example, there are three records α, β, γ in the catalog, and $A_{\{s\}}$ is denoted as the common attribute for the set of records(s). The records can be classified by the values of the common attributes in the catalog as follows (refer to Figure 2):

$$\alpha = \{(A_{L11}, v_{111}), (A_{L12}, v_{121}), (A_1, v_\alpha)\}$$
$$\beta = \{(A_{L11}, v_{112}), (A_{L12}, v_{121}), (A_{L2}, v_{21}), (A_2, v_\beta)\}$$
$$\gamma = \{(A_{L11}, v_{112}), (A_{L12}, v_{122}), (A_{L2}, v_{22}), (A_3, v_\gamma)\}$$
$$\{A_{\alpha\beta\gamma}\} = \{A_{L11}, A_{L12}\}$$
$$\{A_{\beta\gamma}\} = \{A_{L2}\}$$
$$\{A_\alpha\} = \{A_1\}$$
$$\{A_\beta\} = \{A_2\}$$
$$\{A_\gamma\} = \{A_3\}$$

The catalog tree can be constructed by taking the common attribute in the set of record, for example, A_{L11} and A_{L12} for α, β and γ. Based on the value of attribute A_{L11} of each record, two groups with value v_{111} and v_{112} are formed. Similarly further classification can be done on the record set (β, γ). The classification process is shown in Figure 3. Therefore, searching down the catalog can uniquely identify a record. The classification process can be based on the similar criteria for query optimization in database. According to the structural definition, the scope of electronic catalog not only includes the ordinary electronic catalog of product, service or information, but also the Internet directory

Figure 1. Example of a catalog tree

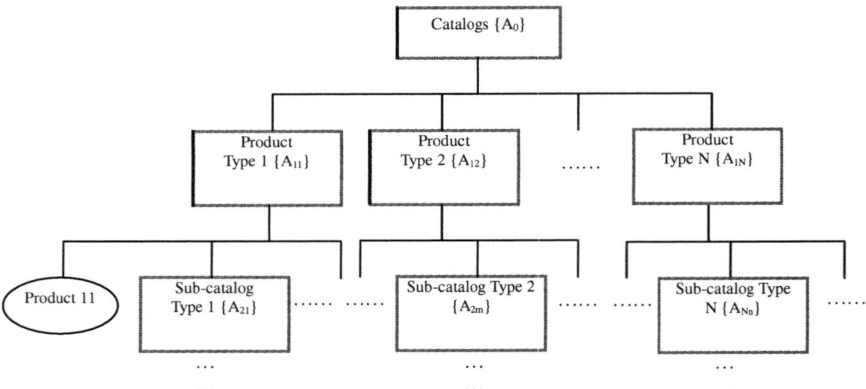

Figure 2. Example of attribute set for three record α, β, γ

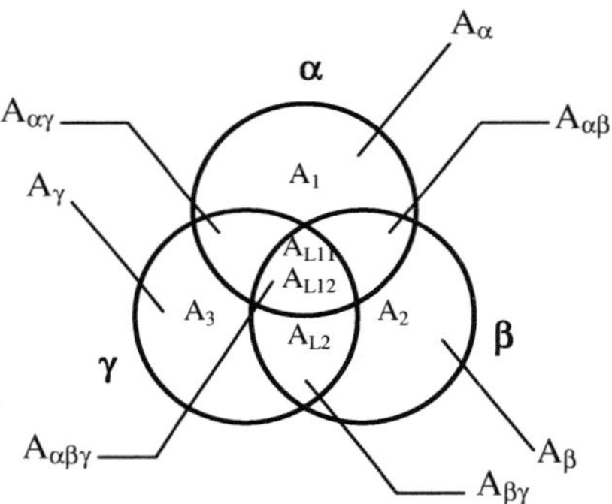

Figure 3. Record classification process

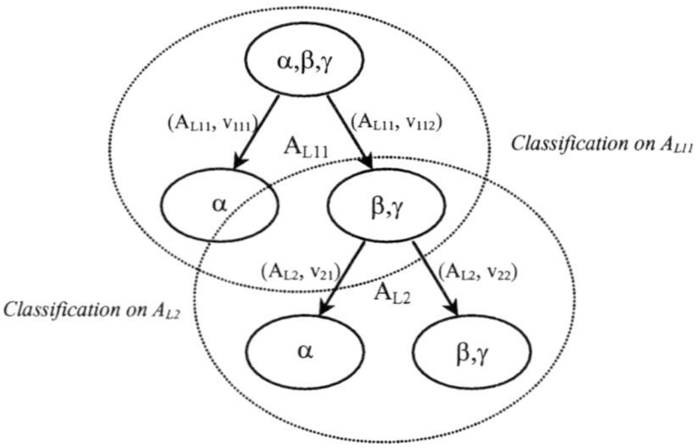

service, such as Yahoo, a catalog of URL's. Therefore, although a standard product catalog is used to demonstrate the personalization of an electronic catalog, the similar techniques can also be applied to other kinds of electronic catalogs.

Solutions and Recommendations: Personalization of Electronic Catalogs

The approach of Web site customization on information content, access, and presentation is proposed to tackle the information overload on the Internet. The customization process starts with the information compilation online during the catalog navigation. The compilation results then are analyzed for constructing profiles, which are used in various personalization approaches. There are three main steps for catalog customization, namely information collection, information analysis, and personalization. The whole process repeats as a cycle shown in Figure 4.

Electronic Catalog Personalization Cycle

There are two main issues for information compilation: *what* and *how*. The information collected can be date, time, file accessed, and the IP address of the remote machine, which normally are available in the Web server log. Many commercial software packages, such as WebTrends Log Analyzer (WebTrends), are available for analyzing and extracting valuable information from the server log and generating reports of the access patterns and statistics. However, due to the common use of the proxy server for reasons of security and resource utilization, analyzing the Web server log has one major drawback in that normally it is not able to track the access pattern of individual users. The proxy server functions as a middleman between the user and the Web server. The server log will only record the access from the proxy server, not from the user directly, so the log only represents the aggregated access patterns of all users. Though solution like Page Conversion (Lin et al., 1999) can partially solve this problem, additional downloading of

Figure 4. Electronic catalog personalization cycle

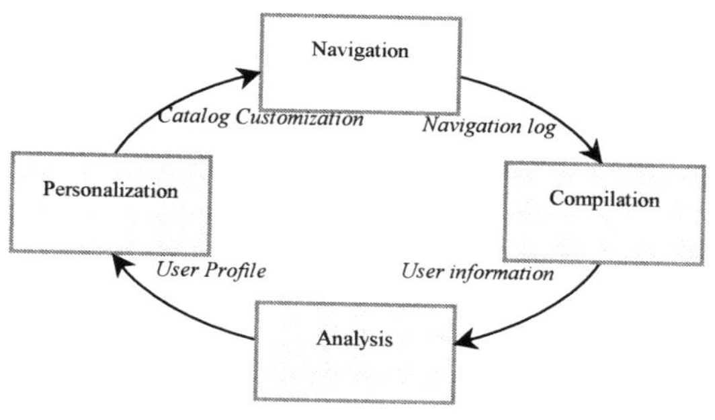

decryption programs and processing time of page conversions are required. In addition, the information collected is normally restricted to file level. On the other hand, Common Gateway Interface (CGI) can be used to keep track of user access patterns and record the information in databases. This approach can guarantee that all levels of information can be gathered from the user if login functions and dynamic construction of Web pages are provided, which is suitable for the application of electronic catalogs that is normally constructed in nature. The additional information collected can be the access sequence, time spent on each page, searching query and criteria, and the preference of Web page layout.

The personalization of electronic catalogs can be viewed in three different aspects: information retrieval, site organization, and information presentation. In information retrieval, the focus is on the information content selected from the electronic catalog. In order to customize the search result based on user preferences, the information can be filtered or ranked. The main objective of site organization is to provide a well-organized site structure for users to access the pages containing the information desired. Since physically there are only few pages in CGI and the pages are inter-connected, improving the physical structure of the Web site is not as critical as page prediction. The query result can be described as a set of pages or specified by various searching criteria. By applying statistic analysis on the user profile, a set of searching criteria can be created to describe the query goals to generate personalized hyperlinks that lead the user to the desired page. Information presentation mainly concerns how the retrieved information is presented in the pages of electronic catalogs. There are two ways that the user can customize the information presentation in form of templates: system-guided modularization of elements inside the page and user-defined templates in HTML and standard marking.

System Design and Specification

The PEC (Personalized Electronic Catalog) system consists of the system database, the user profile manager, the information retrieval (IR) engine, the user goal prediction (UGP) engine, and the page generation (PG) engine. In general, a user is required to login before he can access the electronic catalog through various supporting functions. Upon the system's receipt of the request, the user profile manager first updates the user profile in the system database and then forwards the profile to the IR engine and UGP engine. The IR engine returns the ranked and highlighted information based on the user profile and the catalog information in the system database. At the same time, the UGP engine performs data analysis on the user profile and generates a set of predicted goals. The result from the IR engine and the UGP engine together with the user presentation profile from the user profile manager is sent to the PG engine to generate catalog Web pages for the client browser. The PEC system architecture and the process flow for electronic catalog personalization are shown in Figure 5.

The user profile denotes the interests toward the information in the electronic catalog, and is classified into two parts, namely the catalog information profile and the presentation profile. The information structure of catalog is in form of the attribute and value pair (A, v). Although the user may not be concerned with all the attributes of a particular record of interest, a set of (A, v) that user is really interested in can be formed in a long

Figure 5. Architecture and process flow of PEC system

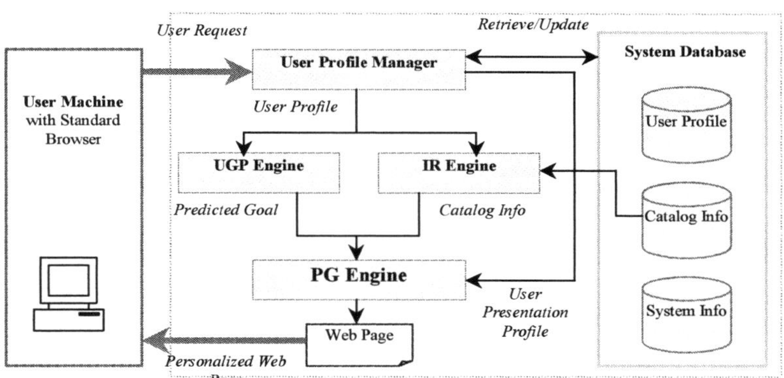

run. The catalog information profile {(A, v, f)} is a collection of tuples of an attribute (A), a value (v), and a preference degree (f) to represent the degree of interest on user preferences. The presentation profile is defined as how the information is presented in the catalog Web pages. The information of the presentation profile is based on user input and a collection of templates for the generation of catalog Web pages.

- **System database:** The system database, as the central information repository, mainly consists of three parts, namely catalog information, user profile, and system supporting information. The catalog is subject to modification or new addition. The user profile is composed of the catalog information profile, the set of attributes, value, and preference degree, and user presentation profile, a collection of templates. The system supporting information includes the basic user information, authentication information, a list of available modules and parameters for the generation of templates, and other system information.
- **User profile manager:** The main function of the user profile manager is to retrieve and update the user profile. In the process of updating the user profile, upon a user request for catalog information, a set of searching criteria in the form of attribute and value pairs is forwarded to the user profile manager which checks each pair in the searching criteria in the user profile. If the pair is found in the user profile, the corresponding preference degree will be updated; otherwise, the pair is added to the user profile. The pair whose preference degree is less than a given *low-level* threshold will be removed from the user profile for management and performance. The user can interact with the user profile manager by choosing the modules for display on the Web page, where the customization is based on the Bus Modularity (Pine, 1993) approach. The Web page itself functions as a bus and various modules are plugged into the bus. The user may configure the parameters with a default value in each module being selected. The user may accept the resulting template or generate the template through HTML and standard marking which will be

validated and interpreted by the user profile manager for final document generation.

- **IR engine:** The function of the IR engine is to retrieve information based on the search criteria and rank/highlight the result based on the catalog information profile. The records whose preference degree is greater than certain high-level threshold are highlighted or ranked at the top of the list.
- **UGP engine:** The UGP engine is used to generate a set of hyperlinks to the target pages as the predicted goal of the user. As the target pages are dynamically generated, the hyperlinks actually are represented by the searching criteria. By performing the statistical analysis, such as clustering algorithms (Yan et al., 1996; Hartigan, 1975), on the preference degree in the user profile, a set of attribute and value pairs can be found to predict the user target page. In order to have better performance and resource utilization, non-significant information is filtered prior to the generation process. It is also suggested to perform a pre-checking of the number of return records in order to avoid too many or too few return records.
- **PG engine:** The function of the PG engine is to generate the Web pages from the templates in the user presentation profile, and forward the resulting pages to the client browser. The user templates define the presentation of the Web page, including the element, style, and location. Therefore, the PG engine integrates the information from the IR engine and UGP engine with the templates.

System Development

The modular approach is adopted for the implementation of the PEC System. IIS (Internet Information Server) or PWS (Personal Web Server) of Microsoft is used as the Web server. The System Database is implemented with Microsoft Access or an SQL Server. ASP (Active Server Page) is used to dynamically create the Web pages as well as the remaining modules. Furthermore, ADO (ActiveX Data Object) with ODBC (Open Database Connectivity) is used to link between the ASP and the System Database. The schematic diagram of the system is shown in Figure 6. The Web pages can be divided into four groups, namely the public, the catalog, the catalog maintenance, and the user profile maintenance pages. Among the four groups of pages, only the catalog pages need to be customized. The user first needs to login or register. The main catalog page is displayed and the user can access the catalog through the searching functions, create/update their catalog in the catalog maintenance page, and create/update the presentation profile in the user profile maintenance page.

The system database is divided into three parts: the catalog database, the user profile database, and the system-supporting database. In the catalog database, the basic catalog information (B-Info) stores all the common catalog information for all records and additional catalog information (A-Info) for new attributes of records. Therefore, for each item in the electronic catalog, there is only one record in the B-Info, which is mapping to multiple records in A-Info. The user profile database is also divided into two parts: the user catalog information profile and the user presentation profile. The catalog information profile is similar to the A-Info in the catalog database, including the user identity, the attribute, the value, and the preference degree. The user presentation profile is a collection of templates and parameters including the user identity, the template, and the content. The system-supporting database consists of the user information, module information, and other system-supporting information. The user information table includes the user name, user identity, and password; whereas the module information is made up of basic module tables, the parameter tables and the parameter list tables. These two tables are used in the template generation process by the special tag embedded in the module information.

The user profile manager is composed of the catalog information profile and the presentation profile. The main function of this part is to set or update the preference degree to capture the previous user behavior, while being sensitive enough to detect the shift of user interest. To update the preference degree, the notations are defined as follows: where f is the pervious preference degree; R, constant; f, current preference degree after updating; f_o, the initial preference degree for a new attribute and value pair being added, and m, a constant. If $f < m$, the corresponding record pair is removed from the catalog information profile. The new preference degree f is the sum of the pervious preference degree and the adjusted value R. The sensitivity toward change in the preference is depending on the value R. The initial preference degree f_o, m and R determine how long an un-accessed record can stay in the user profile. The updating process of the preference degree is implemented as an independent component for any plug-in update methods of preference degree. The three constants are like system environmental variables in order to provide an easy way for configuration in the update process.

The user profile manager also functions as an interface to guide the user in the module selection and configuration process of template generation. There are three types of catalog pages, namely the main catalog page, the sub catalog page, and the detail page. The page content can be classified into the toolbar, keyword search engine interface, catalog search engine interface, search result listing area, and detail information area. The user interface as the guidance for the template generation process in the user profile manager is presented as a series of Web pages. The user first selects the catalog page to be customized and chooses the modules in the page. Each module is required to configure parameters and then a preview of resulting template is provided.

The major functions of the IR engine are to retrieve information based on searching criteria and rank/highlight the result based on catalog information profile. Together with the information retrieved in the first step, the corresponding aggregated preference degree of each result record is calculated as well. A comparison between the aggregated preference degree and a given configurable threshold value is performed to determine rank. The result is then sent to the PG engine. The UGP engine is used to generate a set of hyperlinks as user goal, based on the catalog information profile. A simple clustering algorithm, the leader algorithm (Hartigan, 1975), is employed in the profile analysis to generate the predicted user goals. Although the leader algorithm is dependent on the result of the vector order and the unbounded distance between the cluster vector and cluster medium, the algorithm is fast and memory efficient in only one pass, which can guarantee quick response and low memory usage for each user session. The modular approach of implementation enables plug-in functions for new algorithms. The PG engine

Figure 6. Schematic diagram of PEC system

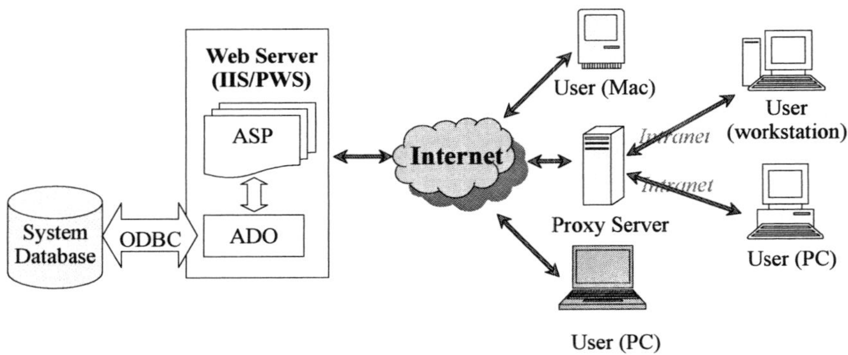

generates the Web pages by integrating the catalog information from the IR engine, hyperlinks from the UGP engine, and the template from user presentation profile information. The PG engine template reader parses the template line by line for special tags and interpreter in the remaining line. The line is sent to a Web page buffer first and the interpreter determines plug-in information and retrieves the information from the IR engine and the UGP engine.

Performance Evaluation

The HKTAIGA.COM site (www.hktaiga.com) originates from the Electronic Commerce Front End for Hong Kong Apparel Industry Community (EC) Project funded by the HKSAR Government. The objective of the project is to build up the information technology and electronic commerce infrastructure for the apparel industry in Hong Kong. At HKTAIGA.COM, the user is able to search for accessory information (such as buttons, zippers, and shoulder pads) and fabric information (such as woven). In addition, he can also create/update his own company Web page and product catalog. There are approximately 1,000 members and 7,000 products in about 20 categories in the catalog. Following is a scenario used to illustrate the comparison between a PEC system, a personalized electronic catalog, and HKTAIGA.COM, an ordinary electronic catalog. The minimum number of page accessed (Min NPA) from the catalog root is used as the comparison variable.

In the scenario, the user is a merchandiser for a garment manufacturer who searches for various types of buttons and buckles, especially those made of plastic. As the merchandiser always searches for plastic buttons and buckle, the PEC system will recognize user preference for product type to be buttons and buckles made of a plastic material. Consequently, when the merchandiser searches for the plastic button again in the PEC system, he only needs to click on the button category in the main catalog with all the plastic buttons being displayed on the first page, and the system recognizes the preference to rank the plastic buttons at the top of the list. On the other hand, if the merchandiser chooses to use HKTAIGA.COM, he needs to specify searching criteria for plastic material after clicking on the button category. The Min NPA for the PEC system

Figure 7. Search example: New plastic button and buckle

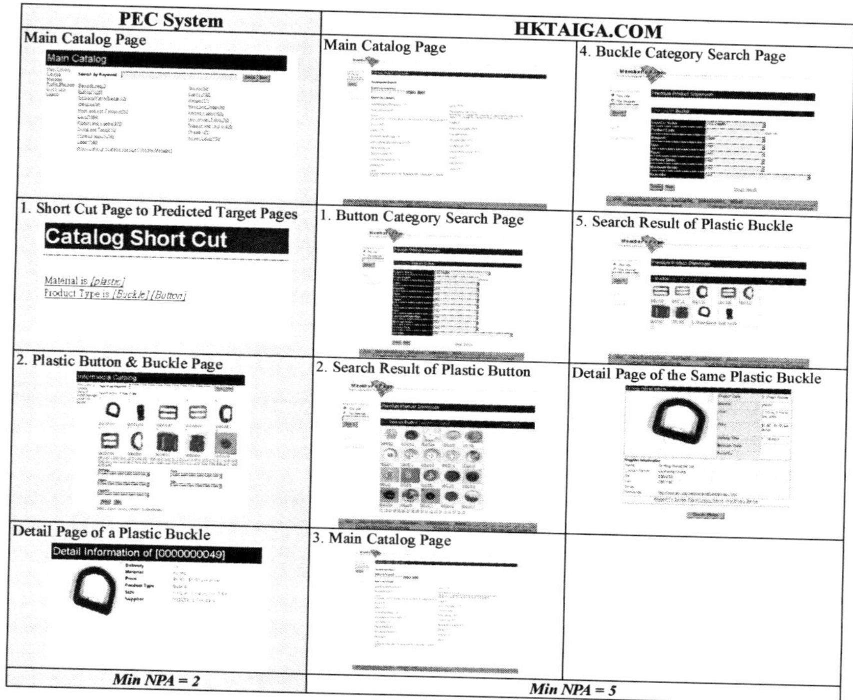

and HKTAIGA.COM is one and two respectively. When the merchandiser searches for all the plastic buttons and buckles, the PEC user only needs to access the shortcut page anytime during navigation, which is based on the input information forming a cluster and the corresponding Min NPA is only two. In contrast, the HKTAIGA.COM user needs to click either button or buckle category first, specify the searching criteria, go back to the root page, access the other category, and specify the searching criteria again. In this case, the Min NPA is equal to five (as shown in Figure 7). In the case of a keyword search, the PEC system ranks the resulting information according to user preference, while the HKTAIGA.COM user needs to go through all the return information as usual. The above examples illustrate two more important aspects of PEC system: continuously updated user profiles that ensure that personalization can evolve according to the shift of user interest, and customizable catalog interfaces that provide a personal and user-friendly working interface.

Future Trends

Electronic catalogs are often directly transplanted from printed catalogs with little added functionality other than keyword searches on product descriptions and multimedia product illustrations. Each company designs its own electronic catalog, with little regard to common standards that could support joint searching of catalogs by buyers. Research in the design of electronic catalogs is fragmented, with streams in the development of innovative search and retrieval methods, mostly exploratory works in business needs and value, and conceptual architectures of catalog systems. The future directions can be addressed in the following seven aspects:

1. **Empirically derived design guidelines.** Different stakeholders of the procurement process will find different value from each component of an electronic catalog. Their evaluation of the value of each catalog component, such as the usefulness and relevance of its functions and features, should be the basis for determining whether to develop the component and how it should be designed.
2. **Flexible logon mechanism.** The logon process can be more flexible in order to accommodate a large domain of applications where the user can access catalog information without a logon. For example, the server can generate a unique identity for each user and store it as cookies on the user's computer.
3. **User profile in marketing.** The user profile can be used for target marketing and focus on only those users interested in the corresponding promotion. The user profile can also be utilized to "push" the preferred, updated, real-time information to the individual user for online response.
4. **Impact study of customization on catalogs management.** The customization of electronic catalogs impacts both the catalog usage and administration. The tradeoff between service quality and management workload is critical for the catalog adoption in electronic commerce.
5. **Catalog evolution cycle analysis.** The popularity of products in a catalog may change over time due to marketing promotion, seasonal demand, and other issues. The strategy to maintain balance between popularity and accessibility of product information is imperative for electronic catalog management.
6. **Information quality evaluation.** The evaluation of electronic catalogs is similar to that for general Web applications and information product. The information quality framework (Wang et al., 1998) can be applied to assess the accessibility, intrinsic, contextual, and representational information quality of electronic catalogs.
7. **Efficient catalog record classification.** The performance for the classification of catalog records depends on the selection sequence of common attribute. The information classification and query optimization are two exemplary areas for solution exploration.

Conclusion

Electronic catalogs are at the core of information system support for electronic commerce. It is the component that provides product information for customers to order goods, make payments, access customer support, and provide feedback. It is also used in the marketing function for advertising, marketing, sales, distribution, and support channels. Unlike traditional paper-based product catalogs which are limited by size, access method, high production cost, and obsolete information, electronic catalogs promise up-to-date information, more flexible methods of search and retrieval, accessibility at any time and anywhere, interactive multimedia user interface, joint searching with other catalogs, and automated linkage and support for various procurement functions. These promises, however, have yet to be realized.

Information overload and access performance on the Internet are critical in most EC applications. To attract and retain people to the Web site is one of the major challenges in electronic commerce. Doing more advertisement, providing more useful information, or designing more flashy pages cannot prevent the Internet surfers from getting lost in the huge amount of information, especially in the case of electronic catalogs. One solution is to customize the Web site for each individual user through the analysis of preferences and interests in the user profile. The site should be able to customize itself on information content, information organization and information display. Information collection, analysis, and customization form a process to improve and customize the Web site for each user, without Webmaster interference in normal operation.

In this chapter, we focused on the issues related to the customization for electronic catalogs from the aspects of information organization, retrieval, and presentation. A system, called Personalized E-Catalog (PEC), was proposed to customize and personalize information access of electronic catalogs on the Web. The system design and implementation is presented with an industrial example. The minimum number of page accessed (Min NPA) is used as the comparison variable to demonstrate that the PEC system can improve performance in two examples. An industrial application is used to demonstrate the improvement of information access for electronic catalogs.

References

Baron, P., Shaw, M.J. & Bailey, A.D. (2000). Web-based e-catalog systems in B2B procurement. *Communications of ACM, 43*(5), 93-100.

Berghel, H., Berleant, D., Foy, T., & McGuire, M. (1999). Cyberbrowsing: information customization on the Web. *Journal of the American Society for Information Science, 50*(6), 505-513

Bond, W.J. (1993). *Home-based catalog marketing*, McGraw-Hill, Inc.

Chang, C.H., Hun, C.C. & Hou, C.L. (1998). Exploiting hyperlinks for automatic information discovery on the WWW. *Proceedings Tenth IEEE International Conference on Tools with Artificial Intelligence*, 156-63.

Chau, P.Y.K., Au, G. & Tam, K.Y. (2000). Impact of information presentation modes on online shopping: An empirical evaluation of a broadband interactive shopping service. *Journal of Organizational Computing and Electronic Commerce, 10*(1), 1-22.

Chen, P.M & Kuo, F.C. (2000). An information retrieval system based on user profile. *The Journal of System and Software, 54*(1), 3-8.

Cheung, D.W., Kao, B. & Lee, J. (1998). Discovering user access patterns on the World Wide Web. *Knowledge-Based Systems, 10*(7), 463-70.

The Concise Columbia Electronic Encyclopedia, 3rd ed. (*http://www.encyclopedia.com/articles/02414.html*).

Fink, D. & Laupase, R. (2000). Perceptions of Web site design characteristics: A Malaysian/Australian comparison. *Internet Research, 10*(1), 44-55.

Garcia Gosalvez, M. (1997). Electronic product catalog: What is missing? *Electronic Market, 7*(3), 3-5.

Gebauer, J., Beam, C. & Segev, A. (1998). Impact of the Internet on procurement. *Acquisition Review Quarterly, 5*(2), 167-184.

Gehrke, D. & Turban, E. (1999). Determinants of successful Web site design: Relative importance and recommendations for effectiveness. *Proceedings of the 32nd HICSS*, Hawaii.

Ginsburg, M., Gebauer, J., & Segev, A. (1999). Multi-vendor electronic catalogs to support procurement: Current practice and future directions. *Proceedings of Global Networked Organization 25th International Bled Electronic Commerce Conference.*

Glezer, C. & Yadav, S. (2001). A conceptual model of an intelligent catalog search system. *Journal of Organizational Computing and Electronic Commerce, 11*(1), 31-46.

Goff, L. (1999). The Sharper Image. *Catalog Age*, S15-S16.

Handschuh, S., Schmid, B.F., & Stanoevska-Slabeva, K. (1997). The concept of mediating electronic product catalog. *Electronic Market, 7*(3), 32-35.

Hartigan, A.J. (1975). *Clustering algorithms*. New York: Wiley.

Hoffman, D.L., Novak, T.P. & Chatterjee, P. (1996). Commercial scenarios for the Web: Opportunities and challenges. *Journal of Computer-Mediated Communication, 1*(3).

Joachims, T., Freitag, D. & Mitchell, T. (1997). WebWatcher: A tour guide for the World Wide Web. *Proceedings of IJCAI-97*, Nagoya, Janpan, 770-775.

Joh, Y.H. & Lee, J.K. (2002). Buyer's customized directory management over sellers' e-catalogs: Logic programming approach. *Decision Support Systems, 34,* 197-212.

Johnson, C. (1998). On the problems of validating DesktopVR. In H. Johnson, L. Nigay & C. Roast (Eds.), *People and Computers XIII: Proceedings of HCI'98*, Springer-Verlag London Ltd., 327-338.

Jones, J.M. & Vijayasarathy, L.R. (1998). Internet consumer catalog shopping: Findings from an exploratory study and directions for future research. *Internet Research, 8*(4), 322-330.

Keller, A.M. (1997). Smart catalogues and virtual catalogues. In R. Kalakota & A.B. Whinston (Eds.), *Reading in electronic commerce*, Addison-Wesley, 259-271.

Keller, A.N. & Genesereth, M.R. (1997). Using Infomaster to create housewares virtual catalogs. *The International Journal of Electronic Commerce and Business Media*, *7*(4), 41-44.

Koch, N. & Turk, A. (1997). Towards a methodical development of electronic catalogs. *Electronic Market*, *7*(3), 28-31.

Lee, J.Y., Wang, P. & Lee, H.S. (2001). A Visual One-Page Catalog Interface for Analytical Product Selection, *Lecture Notes of Computer Science*, LNCS2115, pp. 240-249, Springer-Verlag.

Liaberman, H. (1995). Letizia: An agent that assists Web browsing. *Proceedings of the 14th International Joint Conference on Artificial Intelligence (IJCAI-95)*, 1, 924-929.

Lim, G.G. & Lee, J.K. (2000). Buyer-carts for B2B EC: The b-Cart approach. *Proceedings of the International Conference on Electronic Commerce*, Seoul, Korea, 54-63.

Lin, I.Y., Huang, X.M. & Chen, M.S. (1999). Capturing user access patterns in the Web for data mining. *Proceedings 11th International Conference on Tools with Artificial Intelligence*, 345-348.

Lincke, D.M. & Schmid, B. (1998). Mediating electronic product catalogues, *Communications of ACM*, *41*(7), 86-88.

Liu, C., Arnett, K.P. & Litecky, C. (2000). Design quality of Web sites for electronic commerce: Fortune 1000 webmasters' evaluations. *Electronic Markets, 10*(2), 120-129.

Lohse, G.L. & Wu, D.J. (2001). Eye movement patterns on Chinese yellow pages advertising. *Electronic Markets, 11*(2), 87-96.

Luedi, A.F. (1997). Personalize or perish. *Electronic Markets, 7*(3), 22-25.

Marcus, A. (1997). History lesson: The Web discovers user interface design. *Proceedings of the 7th International Conference on Human-Computer Interaction*, San Francisco.

Miles, G.E., Howes, A. & Davies A. (2000). A framework for understanding human factors in Web-based electronic commerce. *International Journal of Human-Computer Studies, 52*, 131-163.

Muldoon, K. (1995). *How to profit through catalog marketing.* NTC Business Books.

Nielsen, J. (1996). Top ten mistakes in Web design. *Alertbox*, *http://www.useit.com/alertbox/9605.html*

NUA Internet Surveys, Catalog Shopping Beats Online Shopping. (*http://www.nua.ie/surveys/?f=VS&art_id=905355366&rel=true*)

Oh, J., Park, G., Kim, K., Lee, S.G. & Wu, C. (2001). Catalog sharing through catalog interoperability. *Lecture Notes of Computer Science*, LNCS2105, 61-77, Springer-Verlag.

Palmer, J.W. (1997). Retailing on the WWW: The use of electronic product catalog. *Electronic Market, 7*(3), 6-9.

Perkowitz, M. & Etzioni, O. (2000a). Towards adaptive Web sites: Conceptual framework and case study. *Artificial Intelligence, 118*(1-2), 245-75.

Perkowitz, M. & Etzioni, O. (2000b). Examining the potential use of automated adaptation to improve Web sites for visitors. *Communication of ACM, 43*(8), 152-158.

Pine, B.J. (1993). *Mass customization: A new frontier in business competition.* Boston: Harvard Business School Press.

Richardson, O. (2000). Gathering accurate client information from World Wide Web sites. *Interacting with Computers, 12*(6), 615-22.

Richtel, M. (1998). Making Web sites more 'usable' is former Sun engineer's goal. *The New York Times, http://www.nytimes.com/library/tech/98/07/cyber/articles/13usability.html*

Sarukkai, R.R. (2000). Link prediction and path analysis using Markov Chains. *Computer Network, 33*(1-6), 377-386.

Schubert, P. (2000). The participatory electronic product catalog: Supporting customer collaboration in e-commerce applications. *Electronic Markets, 10*(4), 229-236.

Segev, A., Wan, D., & Beam, C. (1995). Designing electronic catalogs for business value: Results the CommerceNet pilot, CITM Working Paper CITM-WP-1005. (*http://haas.berkeley.edu/citm/publications/papers/wp-1005.pdf*)

Spiller, P. & Lohse, G.L. (1998). A classification of Internet retail stores. *International Journal of Electronic Commerce, 2*(2), 29-56.

Stanoevska-Slabeva, K. & Schmid, B. (2000). Internet electronic product catalogs: An approach beyond simple keywords and mulitmedia. *Computer Networks, 32*, 701-715.

Sung, W.K., Yang, D., Yiu, S.M., Ho, W.S., Cheung, D. & Lam, T.W. (2002). Automating construction of online catalog topologies. *IEEE Transactions on Systems, Man, and Cybernetics*, Part C, *32*(4), 382-391.

Timm, U., & Rosewitz, M. (1998). Electronic sales assistance for product configuration. *Proceedings of the 11th International Bled Electronic Commerce Conference.*

Tu, H.C. & Hsiang, J. (2000). An architecture and category knowledge for intelligent information retrieval agents. *The Journal of Decision Support Systems, 28*(3), 255-268.

Vijayasarathy, L.R. & Jones, J.M. (2000a). Print and Internet catalog shopping: Assessing attitudes and intentions. *Internet Research, 10*(3), 191-202.

Vijayasarathy, L.R. & Jones, J.M. (2000b). Intentions to shop using Internet catalogues: Exploring the effects of product types, shopping orientations, and attitudes towards computer. *Electronic Markets, 10*(1), 29-38.

Wang, R., Lee, Y. & Strong, D. (1998). Manage your information as a product. *Sloan Management Review*, Summer, 95-105.

Wang, Z., Siew, C.K., & Yi, X. (2000). A new personalized filtering model in Internet Commerce. *Proceedings of SSGRR (Scuola Superiore G. Reiss Romoli)*, Rome, Italy.

WebTrends Log Analyzer. *http://www.webtrends.com/*

Westland, J.C. & Au, G. (1998). A comparison of shopping experience across three competing digital retailing interfaces. *International Journal of Electronic Commerce, 2*(2), 57-69.

Yan, T.W., Jacobsen, M., Garcia-Molina, H., & Dayal, U. (1996). From user access patterns to dynamic hypertext linking. *Computer Networks & ISDN Systems, 28*(7-11), 1007-14.

Yang, C.C., Yen, J. & Chen, H. (2000). Intelligent Internet searching agent based on hybrid simulated annealing. *Decision Support Systems, 28*(3), 269-277.

Zhang, P., Small, R.V., von Dran, G.M., & Barcellos, S. (1999). Web sites that satisfy users: A theoretical framework for Web user interface design and evaluation, *Proceedings of the 32nd HICSS*, Hawaii.

Chapter XV

Data Mining Using Qualitative Information on the Web

Taeho Hong
Pusan National University, Korea

Woojong Suh
Inha University, Korea

Abstract

Data mining has drawn much attention in generating the useful information from Web data. Data mining techniques have typically considered quantitative information rather than qualitative, though the qualitative information can often be used to improve the quality of a result. This chapter provides a hybrid data mining application, KBNMiner (Knowledge-Based News Miner), to predict interest rates on the basis of qualitative information on the Web as well as quantitative information stored in a database. The KBNMiner is developed through the integration of cognitive maps and neural networks. To validate the effectiveness of the KBNMiner, an experiment with Web news information is conducted and its results are discussed.

Introduction

Recently, the number of large-scale repositories linked to the Web has been increased enormously. The expectations and dependencies on Web resources have also increased rapidly. Nevertheless, it is getting more difficult to collect and generate the useful information from the resources. Concerning this difficulty, the importance of data mining is being addressed more now than ever before, and many applications employing statistical and machine learning techniques are being developed (Changchien & Lu, 2001; Chiang, Chow, & Wang, 2000; Fayyad, Piatesky-Shapro, &Smith, 1996a; Park, Piramuthu, & Shaw, 2001).

Although both techniques have their own strengths and weaknesses, machine learning has typically been employed in data mining applications (Bose & Mahapatra, 2001). Machine learning includes various techniques such as neural networks, rule induction, case-based reasoning, and genetic algorithms. These techniques are typically applied to analyze quantitative information rather than qualitative because the quantitative information is usually represented in the form of words or images. Qualitative information on the Web can be included primarily in a variety of text-based documents. As the most popular example, news on the Web can be considered; news typically consists of text and images. Unlike the quantitative information, in most cases, the qualitative information is not ready for use in data mining.

Among the techniques mentioned above, the neural networks have shown more considerable success in modeling financial data series (Refenes, Burgess, & Bentz, 1997; Walczak, 1999; Zhang et al., 1998). Neural networks have a flexible nonlinear function-mapping capability that can be used to approximate any continuous function with any desired accuracy (Cybenko, 1989; Hornik, Stinchcombe, & White, 1989). Neural networks are also nonparametric data-driven models that impose few prior assumptions on the underlying processes from which data are generated. This is an important advantage in financial data series forecasting. Neural networks have the ability to scan the data for patterns and can be used to construct nonlinear models. However, in financial data series forecasting, most neural network models are constructed on the basis of only quantitative information stored in database as the form of numeric, though qualitative information is able to improve the performance of the forecasting. For example, the qualitative information on the political situations, social conditions, international events, government policies, and traders' psychology has influenced the movement of the financial data series (Kohara, Ishikawa, Fukuhara, & Nakamura, 1997; Kuo, Chen, & Hwang, 2001).

Considering this background, the following research questions may be addressed:

- How can the qualitative information be used in modeling financial data series?
- What is the effective tool in knowledge processing for utilizing the qualitative information in modeling financial data series?
- What is the effect of the qualitative information on the neural network performance when compared to the neural network model with only quantitative information?
- Is it more effective to train neural networks by separating the learning data into two groups on the basis of event information, which can be acquired from news information, than to apply traditional learning methods?

As a solution to get answers to the questions, this chapter proposes a data mining application to predict interest rates on the basis of qualitative information on the Web. The application named KBNMiner (Knowledge-Based News Miner) is designed to adopt a prior knowledge base, representing expert knowledge, as a foundation on which to probe and collect news, then to apply this news information to a neural network model of interest rate prediction. A cognitive map (CM) is used to build the prior knowledge base. CM is a representation perceived to exist by a human being in a visible or conceptual target world. CM manages the causality and relation of the qualitative information mentioned above. The KBNMiner retrieves the event information from news information on the Web utilizing CM and prior knowledge. Event information is divided into two types in the KBNMiner. One is positive event information, which affects the increase of interest rates, and the other is negative event information, which affects the decrease of interest rates. A neural network forecaster is developed and an empirical analysis is performed on the use of event information.

The organization of this chapter is as follows: the next section briefly reviews the studies of data mining including the neural networks in financial data series and the CM method employed in the KBNMiner. The following section introduces the conceptual framework of the KBNMiner and presents a detailed description of KBNMiner. The section after that does an experiment on KBNMiner by the use of Web news information and discusses its results.

Related Works

Data Mining

Data mining, also known as "knowledge discovery in database" (Fayyad et al., 1996a), has become a research area with increasing importance with the amount of data greatly increasing (Fayyad, Piatetsky-Shapiro, & Smyth, 1996b; Chiang et al., 2000; Changchien & Lu, 2001; Park et al., 2001). Furthermore, data mining has come to play an important role since research has come to improve many methods used in data mining applications including statistical pattern recognition, association rules, recognizing sequential or temporal patterns, clustering or segmentation, data visualization, and classification. Berry and Linoff (1997) defines data mining as the exploration and analysis, by automatic or semiautomatic means, of large quantities of data in order to discover meaningful patterns and rules. Frawley and his fellows (1991) refer to the entire process involving data mining as ***knowledge discovery in database (KDD)***. Fayyad and Stolorz (1997) draw a distinction between the KDD and data mining. They view the term data mining as referring to a single step in the process that involves finding patterns in the data. However, Allen (1996) notes data mining is the entire process of knowledge discovery. Knowledge discovery in database is a non-trivial process of identifying valid, novel, potentially useful and ultimately understandable pattern in data (Fayyad et al., 1996a).

Fayyad & his fellows (1996b) outline a practical view of the data mining process emphasizing its interactive and iterative nature in Figure 1. The core of the knowledge

Figure 1. Overview of the steps constructing the KDD process

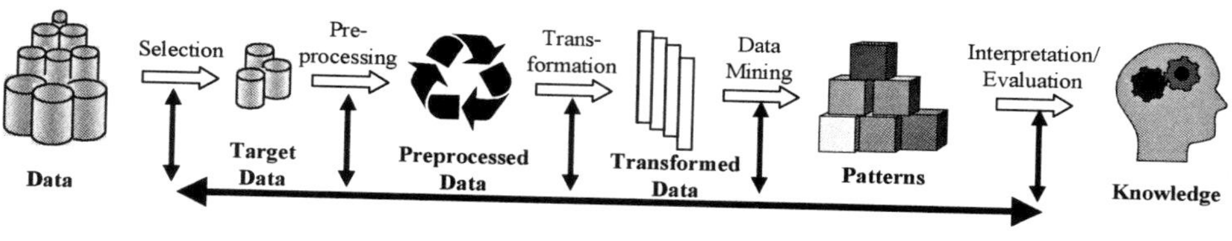

discovery process is the set of data mining tasks used to extract and verify patterns in data. However, this core typically composes only a small part (estimated at 15 - 25 percent) of the effort of the overall process (Brachman, Khabaza, Kloesgen, Piatesky-Shapiro, & Simoudis, 1996).

Data mining applications utilizing statistical and machine learning techniques are being developed (Changchien & Lu, 2001; Chiang et al., 2000; Fayyad et al., 1996a; Park et al., 2001). A number of algorithms have been developed in domains, such as machine learning, statistics, and visualization, to identify patterns in data. The data set must confirm to rigid distribution criteria to employ statistical modeling methods. Pattern discovery algorithms based on machine learning techniques, on the other hand impose fewer restrictions and produce patterns that are easy to understand. Machine learning is the study of computational methods to automate the processes of knowledge acquisition from examples (Langley & Simon, 1995). Major categories of machine learning techniques are Neural Networks (NN), Inductive Learning (IL), Case-Based Reasoning (CBR) and Generic Algorithms (GA). Data mining applications and prototypes have been developed for a variety of domains, including finance, telecom, marketing, and Web analysis. (Bose & Mahapatra, 2001). A majority of the applications use a predictive modeling approach, although a few notable applications utilize other methods (Brachman et al., 1996). Table 1 shows data mining research in financial area and identifies the techniques used and the type of data mining problem addressed.

Neural Networks for Financial Data Series

Neural networks were first inspired by an attempt to mimic the neural functions of human brain (Rumelhart, Hinton, & Williams, 1986). They are powerful prediction and classification tools, and provide new opportunities for solving difficult problems that have been traditionally modeled using statistical approaches. Among the numerous neural networks that have been proposed, backpropagation networks are probably the most popular and widely used. The usage of the term "backpropagation" appears to have evolved after 1985. The basic idea of backpropagation was first described by Werbos in his Ph.D. thesis (1974). The idea has been invented by many researches such as Bryson and Ho (1969), Parker (1985), and Rumelhart et al. (1986).

Overall, neural networks are comparable to their statistical counterparts. For real world problems with high nonlinearity and short memory dynamics, neural networks usually

Table 1. List of data mining applications in financial area (adapted from Bose & Mahapatra, 2001)

Problem type	Application	Method(s) used
Prediction	Forecasting bankruptcies	NN (Tam & Kiang, 1992; Altman et al., 1994; Wilson & Sharda, 1994) IL (Sung et al., 1999)
	Forecasting defaulting loans	IL (Messier & Hansen, 1998)
	Forecasting stock price	NN (Barr & Mani, 1997; Walczak, 1999; Shi et al., 1999) NN and GA (Kim & Han, 2000; Leigh et al., 2002)
	Credit assessment	IL (Carter & Catlett, 1987)
	Forecasting foreign exchange rates	NN (Zhang & Hu, 1998; Shin & Han, 2000)
	Portfolio management	IL (John et al., 1996)
	Forecasting interest rates	NN (Hong & Han, 1996) NN and CBR (Kim & Noh, 1997) NN and Pettitt test (Oh & Han, 2000)
	Forecasting price of index futures	IL and NN (Tsaih et al., 1998; Tay & Cao, 2001)
	Forecasting mutual fund	NN (Indro, 1999)
	Loan approval	IL and visualization (Becker, 1997)
	Corporate bond rating	CBR and IL (Buta, 1994; Shin & Han, 2001)
Classification	Risk classification	IL (Shaw, 1990) NN (Piramuthu, 1998)
	Financial customer classification	IL (Rauch & Berka, 1997)
Detection	Detecting delinquent bank loans	NN and visualization (John & Zhao, 1997)
	Identifying suspicious transactions	NN (Brachman et al., 1996) IL (Kokkinaki, 1997; Senator et al., 1995)
	Risk management	Visulaization (Gershon & Eick, 1997)

IL: Inductive Learning, NN: Neural Networks, CBR: Case-Based Reasoning, GA: Genetic Algorithms

perform better at prediction and classification accuracy. Furthermore, neural network models are more robust, more easily adaptive to a changing environment, and less sensitive to the changes in sample size, number of variables, and data distribution. They work well when the form of the mapping function is unknown (Sun et al., 1997). Due to its faulty tolerance and adaptability to noisy data, neural networks are being used in a growing number of industrial and research applications including pattern recognition in engineering, control, manufacturing, and financial investment (Tam & Kiang, 1992; Chu & Widjaja, 1994; Desai, Crook, & Overstereet, 1996; Zhu & Padman, 1997).

Utilizing neural networks with financial data in their database, many studies have focused on improved accuracy of forecasting financial data series over the past few decades. The previous studies were performed through various approaches for improving the performance of neural networks. We classified them into three types. First, the integration of neural networks and other machine learning and statistical techniques have been tried in order to obtain synergistic results. These studies proposed the integrated approaches using neural networks and case-based reasoning (Kim & Noh, 1997), genetic algorithms (Leigh, Purvis, &Ragusa, 2001; Shin & Han, 2000), and the Ptetitt test (Oh & Han, 2000). The second is how to select learning samples from historical database of a data series. Several methods have been used. Included among them are the similar data selective learning method (Peng, Hubele, & Karady, 1992), and the correlation coefficient based similar data selection method (Shimodaira, 1996). Moreover, Cheng, Low, Chan, and

Motwani (2001) demonstrated the method which separated data in a set into good and bad data sets through fuzzy linear regression. Deco, Neuneier, and Schurmann (1997) present a non-parametric data selection approach for detecting nonlinear statistical dependencies in a non-stationary time series. They insisted that the predictive performance by neural networks depends on learning samples. The last is related to preprocessing data for reducing noises (Kim & Han, 2000; Shin & Han, 2000).

However, not all of the financial data series, such as interest rates, stock prices, and foreign exchange rates, are explained only by quantitative information such as financial data or the autoregressive model even though they are more effective. Meanwhile another approach was attempted in the prediction of the stock price index where Kohara & his fellows (1997) took into account non-numeric factors such as political and international events from news information. They insist that, with event information acquired from newspapers, this method improves prediction ability of neural networks. Also, Kuo et al. (2001) proposed genetic-algorithm based fuzzy neural network to capture the stock experts' knowledge. They divided the factors, which affect the stock price, into two categories, quantitative, and qualitative factors. The qualitative factors, which may influence the stock market, were identified from the related economic journals, government technical reports, and newspapers. Although their proposed methods outperform the traditional neural network models considering only the quantitative factors, it is, however, not easy for people to search and retrieve the vast amount of information simply through knowledge and capacity. To overcome this weakness, Hong and Han (2002) proposed a system using information retrieval techniques. We thus believe that the qualitative information will improve the performance of the neural network forecaster in financial data prediction.

Qualitative Information and Cognitive Maps

Knowledge is an interesting concept that has attracted the attention of philosophers for thousands of years. In more recent times, researchers have investigated knowledge in a more applied way with the chief aim of bringing knowledge to life in machines. Artificial intelligence has contributed to the perceived challenge by developing new tools to produce knowledge from data. However, knowledge is a complex concept and is itself, invisible. These two factors lead to difficulties in the attempt to manage knowledge. One of the more serious problems is that knowledge is built differently in each human being corresponding to common experiences. People have knowledge consisting of their own views of things and events. It may be difficult to communicate the full meaning of such views to others. The other problem is that knowledge is invisible. Knowledge is represented differently in the process of visualization even though it comes from the same concept. Despite the difficulties faced in artificial intelligence, it is the most effective means for discovering knowledge in data or human beings.

When knowledge is represented in the system through data mining, a problem arises in contexts where the precise numerical information is not available to represent the qualitative description of a domain. When precise numeric information is available, quantitative analysis is still considered the most appropriate and efficient method. However, most of the time, precise quantitative information is not available in the real world contrary to the physical world. The possible reasons for not having accurate numeric information arise from incomplete and imprecise knowledge (Harmcher, Kiang, & Lang, 1995). Qualitative information such as news information on the Web, which affects the movement of financial data directly or indirectly, is not highlighted in previous data mining methods.

CM, introduced by Axelrod (1976) for representing social scientific knowledge, has originally been used for representing knowledge in many studies, representing the cause-effect relationships which are perceived to exist among the elements of a given environment. Although the term "cognitive map" is used in many different ways, all CMs can be categorized by their target worlds. One category is physical and visible, while another is conceptual and invisible (Zhang, Chen, Wang, & King, 1992). Thus, a CM is a representation perceived by a human being to exist in a visible or conceptual target world. From the perspective of knowledge representation, the cognitive map is the proper tool by which the perception of human beings can be captured (Park & Kim, 1995; Taber, 1991; Zhang et al., 1992).

Knowledge-based expert systems usually employ domain experts. The knowledge engineer is responsible for converting experts' knowledge into the knowledge base. Therefore, the knowledge engineer extracts CMs and has two or more maps of the domain. He generally tries to combine CMs into one. But domain experts sometimes cannot agree with one other. Taber (1991) notes that experts have varied credentials and experience. There is little justification for assuming that experts are equally qualified. Although combined CMs would always be stronger than an individual CM because the information is derived from a multiplicity of sources and make point errors less likely, it is not easy to give each of equal weight. Even when experts address the same topic, a map will differ in content and edge weight. For example, three experts estimate the weights at (+0.8, +0.8, 0.2), making the average 0.6. This is the error resulting from weights. On the other hand, the direction of the arc among nodes can be derived more easily through their agreement since the arc has polarity. In this case, the direction is (1, 1, 1) and the result is 1. More sophisticated knowledge representation is not always better than a simple.

Conceptual Framework of KBNMiner

Integration of knowledge and machine learning has been extensively investigated, because such integration holds great promise in solving complicated real-world problems. One method is to insert prior knowledge into a machine learning mechanism and to refine it with learning through examples (Frasconi, Gori, Maggini, & Soda, 1991; Giles & Omlin, 1993; Towell, Shavlik, & Noordewiser, 1990). Kohara and his fellows (1997) suggested another method by which the prediction ability can improve with prior knowledge and event information. They take into account qualitative information such as political and international events with newspaper information. In stock price prediction, they categorize event information influencing the stock price into two types: negative event information, which tends to reduce the stock price, and positive event information, which tends to raise the stock price. Based on their research, our approach, the KBNMiner, is constructed by adopting the positive and negative event information.

Figure 2. System architecture of KBNMiner

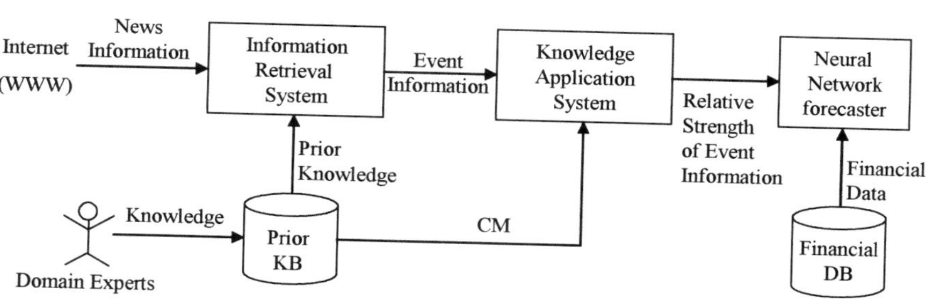

The KBNMiner is designed to utilize CMs as a representation of expertise on interest rate movements, to search and retrieve news information on the Internet according to prior knowledge and expertise and to further apply this news information to a neural network model in order to achieve more accurate interest rate predictions. The KBNMiner consists of several modules including a prior-knowledge base, an information retrieval system, a knowledge application system, and a neural network forecaster as illustrated in Figure 2. The KBNMiner is developed by Microsoft Visual Basic 6.0 and Microsoft Access 97. In addition, the neural network module is integrated into the KBNMiner with NeuroShell 2 provided by Ward Systems Group, Inc.

The procedure of the KBNMiner is shown in Figure 3. Prior knowledge is built by using CMs of specific domains as its primary source of solving problems in those domains. The KBNMiner receives the knowledge built by using CMs and deposits it in the prior knowledge base. The information retrieval system is used to retrieve news information on the Internet by drawing on prior knowledge. The results of the retrieved information are applied to CMs. Knowledge application systems apply the retrieved event information to CMs and perform the causal propagation with a causal connection matrix. The final result of the causal propagation is input into a neural network model as positive or negative information along with other financial variables. The details of the KBNMiner is described in the next section.

Prior Knowledge Base

Representing an application domain involves much effort, in which experts of the application domain provide knowledge for knowledge engineers, who then have to represent it in an appropriate form suitable for the application. Although domain experts' needs are kept in mind, they seldom take part in the construction of the knowledge base. The knowledge base cannot ceaselessly be updated, so the updating process becomes a discrete process where the time interval between updates can be lengthy. Thus, the knowledge acquisition process should be systematic or semi-systematic al least by applying automatic tools. To overcome this problem, we proposed the KBNMiner as a system for knowledge acquisition and processing.

Figure 3. Procedure of KBNMiner

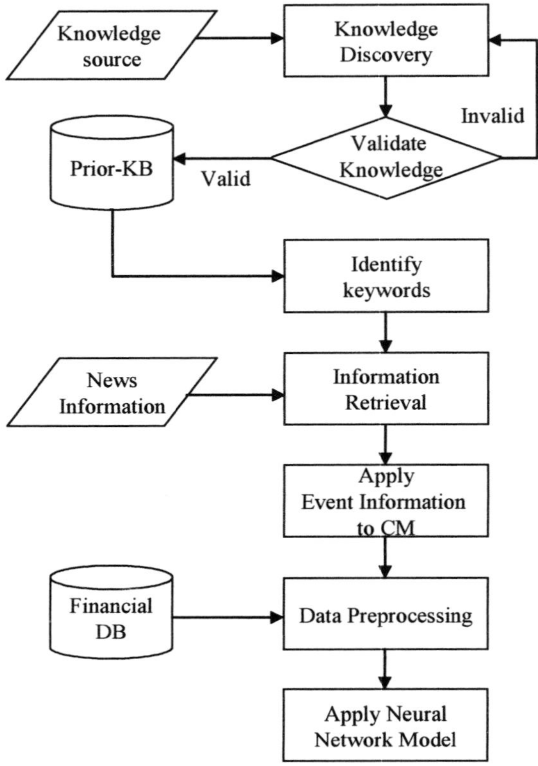

We defined the knowledge into two types. One can be acquired from domain experts and the other can be discovered from data. The knowledge generated by domain experts is stored in a prior knowledge base. And new knowledge is discovered on the basis of the prior knowledge by the data driven method. In our approach, the prior knowledge base is constructed by CMs and the final knowledge is presented through neural networks. First, we will explain the way how to construct a prior knowledge base in this section. The data driven method, neural networks, will be presented in the next section. The CMs in the KBNMiner take on the role of discovering from experts' learning and experiences. The knowledge is converted into symbolic types in a prior knowledge base after it is discovered. Then the acquired prior knowledge is converted into information to be further applied in information retrieval systems. Thus we utilized CMs for the purpose of knowledge engineering and storing prior knowledge base with knowledge previously acquired.

Human experts consider their experiences and learning about the specified domain and convert their knowledge to a prior knowledge base. The human expert knowledge is deposited into the prior knowledge base and used for retrieving news information in the information retrieval system. We built the prior knowledge base using the CM for the

Figure 4. Cognitive map for the movement of the interest rates

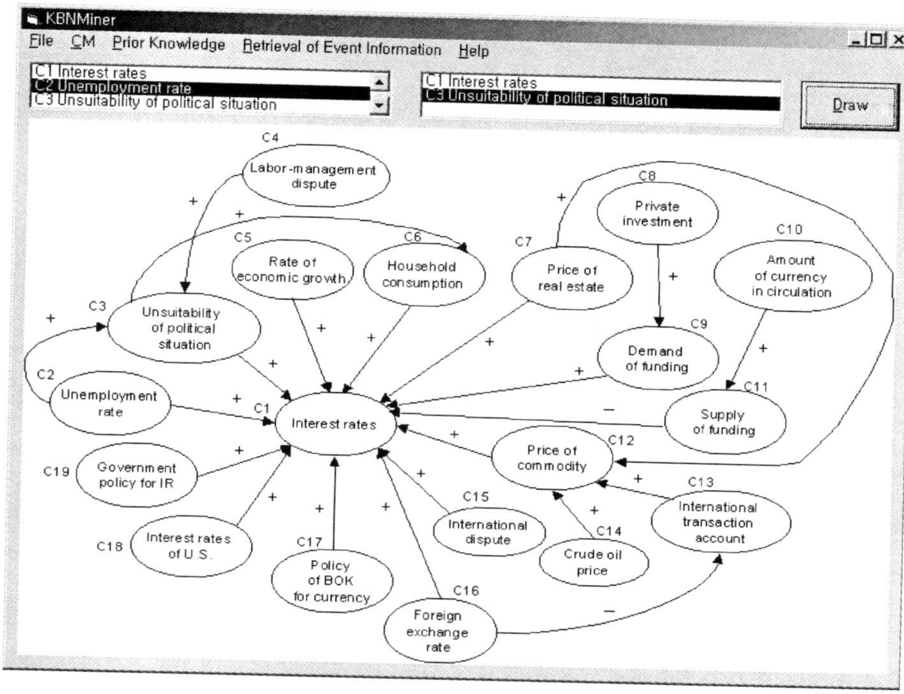

prediction of interest rates. The CM is constructed in two phases. In the first phase, we define candidate concept nodes affecting the movement of interest rates without any direction among concept nodes. These candidate nodes affect each trader's behavior directly or indirectly when news events including information related to the concept node arise in a newspaper. The second phase is to determine the final nodes and the direction among them for the CM. The five domain experts, who are senior fund managers in trust and investment companies, determined the concept nodes of the CM through discussion. They selected the final nodes for the candidate nodes through brainstorming. After the concept nodes are finally determined, they are discussed by the experts and the directions are modified for each node until the conclusions are passed unanimously. To acquire a credible CM, no weight was used here. As mentioned previously, we use only polarity among nodes in our CM to avoid the biased weights which result from the diversity in the experience of experts. The CM is shown in Figure 4.

Information Retrieval System

There is much research on information retrieval (IR) and improved IR techniques such as neural networks and genetic algorithms. And we however deployed and adopted the classical IR model which is called n-gram matching and modified it to apply Korean characters because our study is focused on the application of the results of IR with prior knowledge, not on IR models. The next examples of n-gram are explained in the following. We represent the following sentence in the form of the following set of 3-grams:

> The new printer does not work.
>
> {the, new, pri, rin, int, nte, ter, doe, oes, not, wor, ork}

To retrieve information from Korean news, we defined a keyword set representing concept nodes in CMs (Figure 5) and built thesauri according to the keyword set. The thesauri are compared to the words in texts in order to find information according to the meaning of concept nodes, and we regard those texts which completely match the thesauri as having the same meaning as those concept nodes. In the above case, we represent the set of the thesauri as {the, new, printer, does not, work} according to the keyword set representing concept, "The new printer does not work." This approach is applied in the Korean language. Let's look at Figure 4. The C_2 node means the unemployment rate. The positive information of C_2 increased the C_1 (interest rates) and C_3 (unsuitability of the political situation). And the negative information of C_2 decreases

Figure 5. KBNMiner: Setting screen for prior knowledge keywords

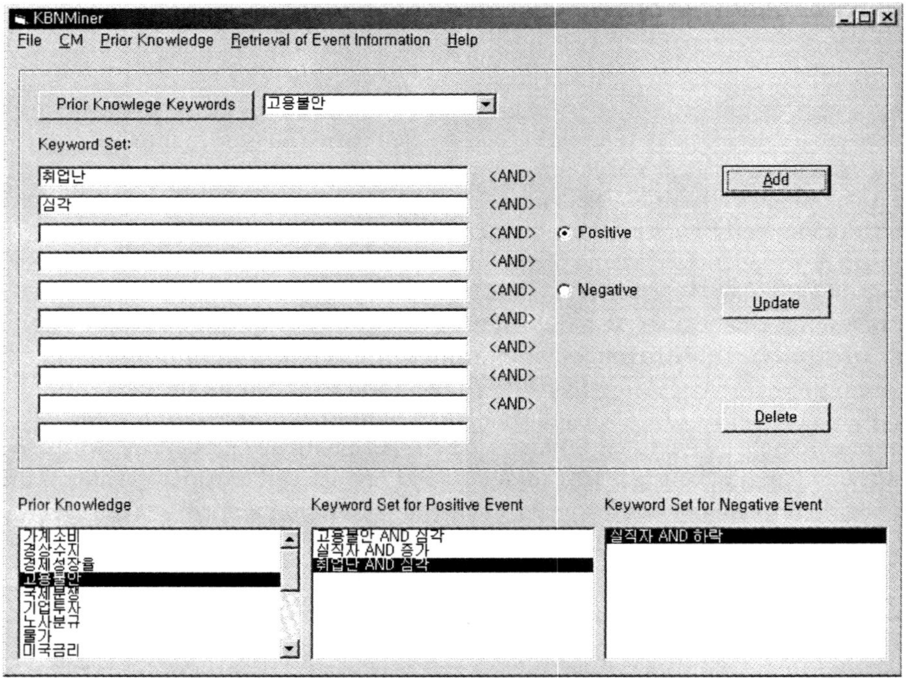

the C_1 and C_3. Thus Figure 5 gives an example where the keyword set for positive events is defined as {unemployment & increase, unemployed person & increase, the state of unemployment & decrease}. The keyword set for negative events is {unemployed person & decrease} according to the C_2 node, defined here as prior knowledge. This example is merely a translation from Korean into English to assist in the understanding of our information retrieval method.

Our study uses major newspapers in Korea as the information source to validate our proposed system (the KBNMiner). These are the newspapers stored in a database in the form of documents.

Knowledge Application System

We consider the 19-by-19 causal connection matrix E that represents the CM in Figure 4 (Figure 6). We can apply this causal connection matrix to causal propagation (Kosko, 1986; Zhang et al., 1989). Event information, which is gathered by the information retrieval system, is applied to the causal propagation by a causal connection matrix. Let us consider the input vector D. For example, the information retrieval results of the news on 6 January 1998 is represented by the vector, D=(1 0 0 1 1 1 1 1 1 0 0 1 0 1 0 -1 0 0 0), then

Figure 6. Causal connection matrix from cognitive map

$$
E = \begin{array}{c} \\ C_1 \\ C_2 \\ C_3 \\ C_4 \\ C_5 \\ C_6 \\ C_7 \\ C_8 \\ C_9 \\ C_{10} \\ C_{11} \\ C_{12} \\ C_{13} \\ C_{14} \\ C_{15} \\ C_{16} \\ C_{17} \\ C_{18} \\ C_{19} \end{array}
\begin{array}{c}
\begin{array}{ccccccccccccccccccc} C_1 & C_2 & C_3 & C_4 & C_5 & C_6 & C_7 & C_8 & C_9 & C_{10} & C_{11} & C_{12} & C_{13} & C_{14} & C_{15} & C_{16} & C_{17} & C_{18} & C_{19} \end{array} \\
\begin{pmatrix}
0 & 0 & 0 & 0 & 0 & 0 & 0 & 0 & 0 & 0 & 0 & 0 & 0 & 0 & 0 & 0 & 0 & 0 & 0 \\
1 & 0 & 1 & 0 & 0 & -1 & 0 & 0 & 0 & 0 & 0 & 0 & 0 & 0 & 0 & 0 & 0 & 0 & 0 \\
1 & 0 & 0 & 0 & 0 & 0 & 0 & 0 & 0 & 0 & 0 & 0 & 0 & 0 & 0 & 0 & 0 & 0 & 0 \\
0 & 0 & 1 & 0 & 0 & 0 & 0 & 0 & 0 & 0 & 0 & 0 & 0 & 0 & 0 & 0 & 0 & 0 & 0 \\
1 & 0 & 0 & 0 & 0 & 0 & 0 & 0 & 0 & 0 & 0 & 0 & 0 & 0 & 0 & 0 & 0 & 0 & 0 \\
1 & 0 & 0 & 0 & 0 & 0 & 0 & 0 & 0 & 0 & 0 & 0 & 0 & 0 & 0 & 0 & 0 & 0 & 0 \\
1 & 0 & 0 & 0 & 0 & 0 & 0 & 0 & 0 & 0 & 0 & 1 & 0 & 0 & 0 & 0 & 0 & 0 & 0 \\
0 & 0 & 0 & 0 & 0 & 0 & 0 & 0 & 1 & 0 & 0 & 0 & 0 & 0 & 0 & 0 & 0 & 0 & 0 \\
1 & 0 & 0 & 0 & 0 & 0 & 0 & 0 & 0 & 0 & 0 & 0 & 0 & 0 & 0 & 0 & 0 & 0 & 0 \\
0 & 0 & 0 & 0 & 0 & 0 & 0 & 0 & 0 & 0 & 1 & 0 & 0 & 0 & 0 & 0 & 0 & 0 & 0 \\
-1 & 0 & 0 & 0 & 0 & 0 & 0 & 0 & 0 & 0 & 0 & 0 & 0 & 0 & 0 & 0 & 0 & 0 & 0 \\
1 & 0 & 0 & 0 & 0 & 0 & 0 & 0 & 0 & 0 & 0 & 0 & 0 & 0 & 0 & 0 & 0 & 0 & 0 \\
0 & 0 & 0 & 0 & 0 & 0 & 0 & 0 & 0 & 0 & 0 & 1 & 0 & 0 & 0 & 0 & 0 & 0 & 0 \\
0 & 0 & 0 & 0 & 0 & 0 & 0 & 0 & 0 & 0 & 0 & 1 & 0 & 0 & 0 & 0 & 0 & 0 & 0 \\
1 & 0 & 0 & 0 & 0 & 0 & 0 & 0 & 0 & 0 & 0 & 0 & 1 & 0 & 0 & 0 & 0 & 0 & 0 \\
1 & 0 & 0 & 0 & 0 & 0 & 0 & 0 & 0 & 0 & 0 & 0 & 0 & 0 & 0 & 0 & 0 & 0 & 0 \\
1 & 0 & 0 & 0 & 0 & 0 & 0 & 0 & 0 & 0 & 0 & 0 & 0 & 0 & 0 & 0 & 0 & 0 & 0 \\
1 & 0 & 0 & 0 & 0 & 0 & 0 & 0 & 0 & 0 & 0 & 0 & 0 & 0 & 0 & 0 & 0 & 0 & 0 \\
1 & 0 & 0 & 0 & 0 & 0 & 0 & 0 & 0 & 0 & 0 & 0 & 0 & 0 & 0 & 0 & 0 & 0 & 0
\end{pmatrix}
\end{array}
$$

the output vector is (1 0 1 0 0 0 0 0 1 0 0 1 -1 0 0 0 0 0 0) as the results of causal propagation. For more information on casual inference, see Kosko (1986) and Zhang et al. (1989).

Finally, we gathered the positive and negative information for each of the seven days. The results of the causal propagation of positive and negative event information are converted into the relative strength of effects on interest rates (see Table 1). We defined the variable CBY, KOSPI, FX as quantitative information and EK as qualitative information acquired from news information using our CM and casual propagation. If the relative strength $EK_t = PK_t/(PK_t + NK_t)$ is over 0.5, then it can be stated that the positive effect on interest rate is stronger than the negative effect. If the relative strength is under 0.5, then the negative effect on interest rates is weaker than the positive effect. The relative strength is input into neural networks as meaningful signals in application systems.

Experiments and Results

Case

The KBNMiner is applied to Korean newspapers in the way mentioned above. There are about 180,000 articles related to national politics, business and international affairs in the news database. The KBNMiner found 3,731 events in all the articles matching prior knowledge. We compared the daily Corporate Bond Yields (CBY) with event knowledge on each date and finally got 252 samples after preprocessing. Our research model was developed for predicting one month ahead.

Selecting Learning Samples

The predictive performance of multi-layer feedforward neural networks depends on how to select learning samples from the historical database of a time series (Shimodaira, 1996) and on the data condition of a training data set (Klein & Rosin, 1999). This means that a more homogeneous training set promise higher performance of neural networks. Cheng et al. (2001) propose a way to improve the accuracy of the neural network by separating training data using the fuzzy regression method for classification.

The KBNMiner retrieves the event information from news information on the Web utilizing CM and prior knowledge. Event information is divided into two types in the KBNMiner. One is positive event information, which affects the increase of interest rates, and the other is negative event information, which affects the decrease of interest rates. By using the event information, the KBNMiner separated the training data into two groups and utilized two neural network forecasters accordingly.

To acquire a more reliable approach, we used the k-fold cross-validation method with k = 10. For our sample, with 252 test cases, 10 repetitions are used. In each repetition 225 cases are used for the training set and 25 cases as a holdout set for testing. In order to cover the whole samples, merely the 10th fold consists of 27 cases for testing set. Holdout

Table 2. Variable description

Variable	Description
CBY_{t+n}	N days ahead of the Corporate Bond Yield
CBY_t	Average of Corporate Bond Yield in the previous 7 days
$KOSPI_t$	Average of Korea Stock Price Index in the previous 7 days
FX_t	Average of the foreign exchange rate for Korean Won/ US dollar in the previous 7 days
EK_t	Relative strength in the previous 7 days $EK_t = Pk_t/(Pk_t + Nk_t)$,where PK: Number of positive events NK: Number of negative events

sets are selected so that their union over all repetitions presents the entire training set. This resulting error estimate provides a reliable estimate of the true error rate and the proposed model is robust enough with respect to sampling variation (Hu, Zhang, Christine, & Patuwo, 1999).

Experimental Design

We utilized a neural network model to illustrate our approach with the above data and test the results of the KBNMiner statistically. Three-layer feedforward neural networks are used to forecast the Korean interest rates. Logistic activation functions are employed in the hidden layer and linear activation is utilized in the output layer. The number of output nodes is one, and this is targeted in the neural network forecaster.

The input variables of the neural networks are described in Table 2. The prediction model is designed to predict 30 days ahead of time. We set the input variables as CBY, KOSPI and FX while considering autoregressive characteristics and correlation to the target variable. These variables are averaged for the previous seven days.

We designed three models to compare the performance of event knowledge in the neural network forecaster: 1.) NN1 is the neural network model without event information; 2.) NN2 is the neural network model with event information; and 3.) NN3 is the neural network model using separated learning sample with event information. NN3_P is trained by the learning samples from positive event information and NN3_N is trained from negative event information.

Results and Analyses

Table 3 shows the results using MAE (Mean absolute error) as the performance measure. The results show the effect of event information comparing a 10-fold validation. The

Table 3. Performance of prediction results based on MAE

Sample Sets for cross-validation	NN1		NN2		NN3_P		NN3_N		NN3	
	Train	Test	Train	Test	Train	Test	Train	Test	Train	Test
Set 1	0.452	0.557	0.554	0.652	0.346	0.448	0.543	0.445	0.413	0.449
Set 2	0.531	0.627	0.464	0.520	0.501	0.404	0.333	0.283	0.444	0.363
Set 3	0.547	0.624	0.505	0.586	0.584	0.483	0.459	0.164	0.154	0.373
Set 4	0.551	0.503	0.537	0.479	0.326	0.565	0.331	0.587	0.328	0.573
Set 5	0.602	0.665	0.471	0.579	0.482	0.514	0.287	0.486	0.416	0.505
Set 6	0.517	0.652	0.447	0.483	0.565	0.642	0.356	0.432	0.494	0.570
Set 7	0.555	0.626	0.493	0.585	0.326	0.296	0.425	0.445	0.359	0.348
Set 8	0.540	0.528	0.435	0.465	0.383	0.530	0.302	0.277	0.355	0.443
Set 9	0.545	0.569	0.499	0.448	0.469	0.355	0.367	0.295	0.435	0.334
Set 10	0.573	0.500	0.454	0.469	0.593	0.833	0.436	0.575	0.540	0.744
Average	0.541	0.586	0.486	0.527	0.457	0.507	0.384	0.399	0.432	0.470

Table 4. Performance of prediction results based on MAPE (%)

Sample Sets for cross-validation	NN1		NN2		NN3_P		NN3_N		NN3	
	Train	Test	Train	Test	Train	Test	Train	Test	Train	Test
Set 1	3.59	4.03	4.31	4.36	2.48	3.34	4.07	4.70	3.23	3.81
Set 2	4.02	0.99	3.56	4.34	3.61	3.07	2.90	2.19	3.37	2.76
Set 3	4.32	0.85	4.00	4.60	4.60	3.31	4.14	0.98	4.44	2.50
Set 4	4.18	3.71	4.04	3.51	2.35	4.07	2.91	4.67	2.54	4.28
Set 5	4.84	5.44	3.70	4.63	3.48	3.92	2.53	4.69	3.16	4.18
Set 6	3.96	4.89	3.46	3.72	4.31	4.36	3.08	3.41	3.89	4.03
Set 7	4.40	5.01	3.91	4.65	2.42	2.26	3.80	3.96	2.89	2.85
Set 8	4.23	4.12	3.36	3.50	2.82	3.81	2.64	2.21	2.76	3.26
Set 9	4.25	4.63	3.87	3.59	3.44	2.38	3.19	2.56	3.36	2.44
Set 10	4.51	4.18	3.55	3.85	4.54	7.36	3.79	5.96	4.28	6.87
Average	4.23	4.59	3.78	4.08	3.40	3.79	3.37	3.53	3.39	3.70

Table 5. Paired t-test for the prediction results of NN1, NN2, and NN3

Comparison	Paired-t Statistics	Error Measure: MAE	Error Measure: MAPE
NN1 vs. NN2	Difference	3.272	3.722
	p-value	0.001***	0.000***
	Number of Cases	252	252
NN1 vs. NN3	Difference	4.061	3.761
	p-value	0.000***	0.000***
	Number of Cases	252	252
NN2 vs. NN3	Difference	2.046	1.703
	p-value	0.042**	0.090*
	Number of Cases	252	252

* Significant at the 10% level, ** Significant at the 5% level, *** Significant at the 1% level

columns represent the neural network model for comparing the effect of qualitative information. The NN2 model with qualitative information has 0.527 in average error, which is the minimum error in comparison to the NN1 model with only quantitative information. We found that the neural network forecaster is improved by the qualitative information acquired from news information and that the effect of qualitative information does exist. It illustrates that the information from news previously mentioned is useful in the prediction of interest rates. It is easy to understand that the same results also appear in table 4, measuring the errors by MAPE (Mean absolute percent error).

The NN3_P and NN3_N models are constructed by separating the learning samples according to the signal of event information. The learning samples are divided into positive and negative sets. The relative strength of the sets in Table 2 is over 0.5 for positive, under 0.5 for negative as results from casual propagation of our CM. The NN3 model is aggregated from the NN3_P and NN3_N models for all samples. The NN3_P and NN3_N models all show superior performance to the NN2 model, which is inserted with qualitative information additionally with respect to the NN1 model. Thus, the NN3 model is greatly superior to other neural network models. In addition, we found that the neural network forecast method learned by the separated learning samples using the signal of relative strength presented from qualitative information is very effective in here.

We attempted to test the results of our experiments statistically. Absolute percentage error (APE) is commonly used (Carbone & Armstrong, 1982) and highly robust (Armstrong & Collopy, 1992). As the forecasts are not statistically independent or always normally distributed, we compare the AEs (absolute errors) and APEs of the forecast using the paired *t*-test. Paired *t*-test results for NN1 and NN2 show a significant difference at the 1 percent level in table 5. Also, the results for NN1 and NN3 are significant at the 1 percent level statistically. This means that the qualitative information is very useful in a neural network forecaster. To analyze the results of NN2 and NN3, MAE and MAPE are at least significant at the 10 percent level for measuring error. We conclude that event information affects our forecaster model significantly. Also, another research question, proposed in the introduction, is proved that the positive and negative information is more effective for improving the learning capacity of neural networks when learning samples are separated into two groups according to the event information. This supports our suggested method, by which the qualitative information is integrated into neural networks with CMs. And our integrated method provides a decision maker with meaningful knowledge to aid in effective decision making related on the movement of interest rates.

Conclusion

We proposed a way to improve the performance of neural networks using qualitative information acquired from news information on the Web. The event information, acquired by the KBNMiner, is applied into a neural network model for the validation of our suggested method. The KBNMiner was developed as a means of applying current information gained on the World Wide Web for the prediction of interest rates. The KBNMiner provides traders or those who are concerned about the movement of interest rates with more relevant knowledge from data and aids in effective decision making. It is designed to apply not only experts' knowledge, but also knowledge of events and conditions influencing interest rate dynamics. The process involves the formation of a prior knowledge base, derived from the CMs of professional experience and learning, upon which the system draws in the search and retrieval of news information to further be applied in a neural network forecaster.

Our research questions are answered through this study. The CMs are the effective tool in knowledge processing for representing knowledge and reflecting the causality of knowledge. Based on our empirical results, the qualitative information has a significant effect on the neural network performance in the prediction of interest rates. We have also described how to apply the event information to the neural network forecaster for gaining a competitive edge through separated learning. The separated learning method, proposed herein, improves the performance of neural network model compared to the traditional learning method.

Our method needs to refine CMs and improve the algorithm of the information retrieval system for acquiring more precise results. In the point of information retrieval, the more progressive approach should be considered in the future although our methods are designed and developed from conservative points, which accompany minimal errors and risks. In addition, the other machine learning techniques could be employed to validate the effectiveness of the qualitative information in the prediction of financial data series. We expect that the valid results will be gained likewise, when our method is deployed with other data mining techniques such as case based reasoning and inductive learning.

References

Allen, L.E. (1996). Mining gold from database. *Mortgage Banking, 56*(8), 99-100.

Altman, E., Macro, G., & Varetto, R. (1994). Corporate distress diagnosis comparing using linear discriminant analysis and neural networks. *Journal of Banking and Finance, 18*(3), 505-529.

Armstrong, J.S., & Collopy, F. (1992). Error measures for generalizing about forecasting methods: empirical comparisons. *International Journal of Forecasting, 8*, 69-80.

Axelrod, R. (1976). *Structure of decision: The cognitive maps of political elites.* New Jersey: Princeton University Press.

Barr, D.S., & Mani, G. (1994). Using neural nets to manage investments. *AI Expert*, 16-21.

Becker, B.G. (1997). Using MineSet for knowledge discovery. *IEEE Computer Graphics and Application*, 75-78.

Berry, M.J.A., & Linoff, G. (1997). *Data mining techniques for marketing, sales and customer support*. New York: John Wiley.

Bose, I., & Mahapatra, R.K. (2001). Business data mining – a machine learning perspective. I*nformation & Management, 39*, 211-225.

Brachman, R.J., Khabaza, T., Kloesgen, W., Piatesky-Shapiro, G., & Simoudis, E. (1996). Mining business database. *Communications of the ACM, 39*(11), 42-48.

Bryson, A.E., & Ho, Y.C. (1969). *Applied optimal control*. New York: Blaisdel.

Buta, P. (1994). Mining for financial knowledge with CBR. *AI Expert*, 34-41.

Carbone, R., & Armstrong, J.S. (1982). Evaluation of extrapolative forecasting methods: results of academicians and practitioners. *Journal of Forecasting, 1*, 215-217.

Carter, C., & Catlett, J. (1987). Assessing credit card applications using machine learning. *IEEE Expert*, Fall, 71-79.

Changchien, S.W., & Lu, T. (2001). Mining association rules procedure to support on-line recommendation by customer and products fragmentation. *Expert Systems with Applications, 20*(4), 325-335.

Cheng, C., Low, B., Chan, P., & Motwani, J. (2001). Improving the performance of neural networks in classification using fuzzy linear regression. *Expert Systems with Applications, 20*(2), 201-206.

Chiang, D., Chow, L.R., & Wang, Y. (2000). Mining time series data by a fuzzy linguistic summary system. *Fuzzy Sets and Systems, 112*, 419-432.

Chu, C.H., & Widjaja, D. (1994). A neural network system for forecasting method selection. *Decision Support Systems, 12*, 13-24.

Cybenko, G. (1989). Approximation by superpositions of a sigmoid function. *Mathematical Control Signals Systems, 2*, 203-314.

Deco, G., Neuneier, R., & Schurmann, B. (1997). Non-parametric data selection for neural learning in non-stationary time series. *Neural Networks, 10*(3), 401-407.

Desai, V.S., Crook, J.N., & Overstreet, G.A. (1996). A comparison of neural networks and linear scoring models in the credit union environment. *European Journal of Operational Research, 95*, 24-37.

Fayyad, U., Piatetsky-Shapiro, G., & Smyth, P. (1996b), From data mining to knowledge discovery: An overview. In U., Fayyad, G., Piatesky-Shapiro, P., Smyth, & R., Uthurusamy. (Eds.), *Advances in knowledge discovery and data mining*. Menlo Park, CA : AAAI/MIT Press, 1-34.

Fayyad, U., & Stolorz, P. (1997). Data mining and KDD: Promise and challenges. *Future Generation Computer Systems, 13*, 99-115.

Fayyad, U.M., Piatesky-Shapiro, G., & Smith, P. (1996a). The KDD processes for extracting useful knowledge and learning from volumes of data. *Communications on the ACM, 39*(11), 27-34.

Frasconi, P., Gori, M., Maggini, M., & Soda, G. (1991). A unified approach for integrating explicit knowledge and learning by example in recurrent neural networks. *Proceedings of International Joint Conference on Neural Networks,* Seattle, I-811-I-816.

Frawley, W.J., Piatesky-Shapiro, G., & Matheus, C.J. (1991). Knowledge discovery in database: An overview. In Fayyad, G., Piatesky-Shapiro, P., Smyth, (Eds.), *Knowledge discovery in database,* Cambridge MA: AAAI/MIT Press, 1-27.

Gershon, N., & Eick, S.G. (1997). Information visualization applications in the real world. *IEEE Computer Graphics and Application*, 66-70.

Giles, C., & Omlin, C. (1993). Rule refinement with recurrent neural networks. *Proceedings of International Conference on Neural Networks*. San Francisco, 801-806.

Harmcher, W., Kiang, M.Y., & Lang, R. (1995). Qualitative reasoning in business, finance, and economics: Introduction. *Decision Support Systems*, *15*(2), 99-103.

Hong, T., & Han, I. (1996). The prediction of interest rates using artificial neural network. *Proceedings of The First Asian Pacific Decision Science Institute Conference*. Hong Kong, 975-984.

Hong, T., & Han, I. (2002). Knowledge-based data mining of news information on the Internet using cognitive maps and neural networks. *Expert Systems with Applications*. 23, 1-8.

Hornik, K., Stinchcombe, M., & White, H. (1989). Multilayer feedforward networks are universal approximators. *Neural Networks, 2*, 359-366.

Hu, M.Y., Zhang, G., Christine, X.J., & Patuwo, B.E. (1999). A cross-validation analysis of neural network out-of-sample performance in exchange rate forecasting. *Decision Sciences*, *30*(1), 197-216.

Indro, D.C., Jiang, C.X., Patuwo, B.E., & Zhang, G.P. (1993). Predicting mutual fund performance using artificial neural networks. *Omega*, *27*, 373-30.

John, G.H., Miller, P., & Kerber., R. (1996). Stock selection using rule induction. *IEEE Expert*, 52-58.

John, G.H., & Zhao, Y. (1997). Mortgage data mining. *Proceedings of the IEEE/IAFE Conference on Computational Intelligence for Financial Engineering,* 232-236.

Kim, K., & Han, I. (2000). Genetic algorithms approach to feature discretization in artificial neural networks for the prediction of stock price index. *Expert Systems with Applications*, *19*(2), 125-132.

Kim, S.H., & Noh, H.J. (1997). Predictability of interest rates using data mining tools: a comparative analysis of Korea and the US. *Expert Systems with Applications*, *13*(2), 85-95.

Klein, B.D., & Rosin, D.F. (1999). Data quality in neural network models: effect of error rate and magnitude of error on predictive accuracy. *Omega*, *27*, 569-582.

Kohara, K., Ishikawa, T., Fukuhara, Y., & Nakamura, Y. (1997). Stock price prediction using prior knowledge and neural networks. *Intelligent System in Accounting, Finance and Management*, 6, 11-22.

Kokkinaki, A.I. (1997). On atypical database transactions: identification of probable frauds using machine learning for user profiling. *Proceedings of the IEEE Knowledge and Data Engineering Exchange Workshop*, Newport Beach, CA, 107-113.

Kosko, B. (1986). Fuzzy cognitive maps. *International Journal of Man-Machine Studies*, *24*, 65-75.

Kuo, R.J., Chen, C.H., & Hwang, Y.C. (2001). An intelligent stock trading decision support system through integration of genetic algorithm based fuzzy neural network and artificial neural network. *Fuzzy Sets and Systems*, 118, 21-45.

Langley, P., & Simon, H.A. (1995). Application of machine learning and rule induction. *Communication of ACM*, *38*(1), 55-64.

Leigh, W., Purvis, R., & Ragusa, J.M. (2002). Forecasting the NYSE composite index with technical analysis, pattern recognizer, neural network, and genetic algorithm: a case study in romantic decision support. *Decision Support Systems*, *32*(4), 361-377.

Messier, Jr., W.F., & Hansen, J.V. (1988). Inducing rules for expert system development: an example using default and bankruptcy data. *Management Science*, *34*(2), 1403-1415.

Oh, K.J., & Han, I. (2000). Using change-point detection to support artificial neural networks for interest rates forecasting. *Expert Systems with Applications*, *19*(2), 105-115.

Park, K.S., & Kim, S.H. (1995). Fuzzy cognitive maps considering time relationships. *International Journal of Human-Computer Studies, 42*, 157-168.

Park, S.C., Piramuthu, S., & Shaw, M.J. (2001). Dynamic rule refinement in knowledge-based data mining systems. *Decision Support Systems*, *31*(2), 205-222.

Parker, D.B. (1985). Learning-logic: casting the cortex of the human brain in silicon. *Technical Report TR-47. Center for Computational Research in Economics and Management Science*. Cambridge, MA: MIT Press.

Peng, T.M., Hubele, N.F., & Karady, G.G. (1992). Advancement in the application of neural networks for short-term load forecasting. *IEEE Transactions on Power Systems*, *7*(1), 250-257.

Piramuthu, S., Ragavan, H., & Shaw, M.J., Using feature construction to improve the performance of neural networks. *Management Science*, *44*(3), 416-429.

Rauch, J., & Berka, P. (1997). Knowledge discovery in financial data – A case study. *Neural Network World*, *4*(5), 427-437.

Refenes, A.N., Burgess, A.N., & Bentz, Y. (1997). Neural networks in financial engineering: a study in methodology. *IEEE Transactions Neural Networks*. *8*(6), 1222-1266.

Rumelhart, D.E., Hinton, G.E., & Williams, R.J. (1986). Leaning internal representations by error propagation in parallel distributed processing. In D.E. Rumelhart, & J.L. McClelland. (Eds.), *Parallel distributed processing: exploration in the micro-structure of cognition. Vol. 1*, Chapter 8, Cambridge, MA: MIT Press.

Senator, T.E., Goldberg, H.G., Wooton, J., Cottini, M.A., Umar Khan, A.F., Klinger, C.D., Llamas, W.M., Marrone, M.P., & Wong, E.W.H. (1995). The financial crimes enforcement network AI systems (FAIS) identifying potential money laundering from reports of large cash transactions. *AI Magazine, 21*, 39.

Shaw, M.J., & Gentry, J.A. (1990). Inductive learning for risk classification. *IEEE Expert*, 47-53.

Shi, S.M., Xu, L.D., & Liu, B. (1999). Improving the accuracy of nonlinear combined forecasting using neural networks. *Expert Systems, 16*, 49-54.

Shimodaira, H. (1996). A method for selecting similar learning data in the prediction of time series using neural networks. *Expert Systems with Applications*, *10*(34), 429-434.

Shin, K, & Han, I. (2001). A case-based approach using inductive indexing for corporate bond rating. *Decision Support Systems, 32*, 41-52.

Shin, T., & Han, I. (2000). Optimal signal multi-resolution by genetic algorithms to support artificial neural networks for exchange-rate forecasting. *Expert Systems with Applications*, *18*(4), 257-269.

Sung, T.K., Chang, N., & Lee, G. (1999). Dynamics of modeling in data mining: interpretive approach to bankruptcy prediction. *Journal of Management Information Systems, 16*(1), 63-85.

Taber, R. (1991). Knowledge processing with fuzzy cognitive maps. *Expert Systems with Applications, 2*, 83-87.

Tam, K., & Kiang, M. (1992). Managerial applications of neural networks: The case of bank failure prediction. *Management Science*, *38*(7), 926-947.

Tay, F.E.H., & Cao L. (2001). Application of support vector machines in financial time series forecasting. *Omega, 29*, 309-317.

Towell, G., Shavlik, J., & Noordewiser, M. (1990). Refinement of approximate domain theories by knowledge-based neural networks. *Proceedings of National Conference on Artificial Intelligence,* Boston, 861-866.

Tsaih, R., Hsu, Y.,& ai, C.C. (1998). Forecasting S&P 500 stock index futures with a hybrid AI system, *Decision Support Systems, 23*, 161-174.

Walczak, S. (1999). Gaining competitive advantage for trading in emerging capital markets with neural networks. *Journal of Management Information Systems*, *16*(2), 177-192.

Werbos, P.J. (1974). Beyond regression: new tools for prediction and analysis in the behavioral science. Ph.D. Thesis. Harvard University.

Wilson, R.L., & Sharda, R. (1994). Bankruptcy prediction using neural networks. *Decision Support Systems, 11*, 545-557.

Zhang, G., & Hu, M.Y. (1998). Neural network forecasting of the British pound/US dollar exchange rate. *Omega, 26*(4), 495-506.

Zhang, G., Patuwo, B.E., & Hu, M.Y. (1998). Forecasting with artificial neural networks: the state of the art. *International Journal of Forecasting*, *14*(1), 35-62.

Zhang, W.R., Chen, S.S., & Bezdek, J.C. (1989). Pool2: A generic system for cognitive map development and decision analysis. *IEEE Transactions on Systems, Man, and Cybernetics*, *19*(1), 31-39.

Zhang, W.R., Chen, S.S., Wang, W., & King, R.S. (1992). A cognitive-map-based approach to the coordination of distributed cooperative agents. *IEEE Transactions on Systems, Man, and Cybernetics*, *22*(1), 103-114.

Zhu, D., & Padman, R. (1997). Connectionist approaches for solver selection in constrained project scheduling. *Annals of operations Research, 72*, 265-298.

About the Authors

Woojong Suh is an assistant professor of the MIS/e-business field in the College of Business Administration at Inha University, Korea. He received his PhD in MIS from the Graduate School of Management at the Korea Advanced Institute of Science and Technology (KAIST), Seoul, Korea. He earned his BA and MA in applied statistics from Yonsei University, Seoul. He has performed large-scale projects concerned with e-Biz and KM, as a senior consultant of e-KM team at PricewaterhouseCoopers (PwC) Consulting Korea and as a research fellow of e-Biz Research Center at POSCO Research Institute (POSRI). His research has been published in journals such as *Journal of Organizational Computing and Electronic Commerce, Journal of Systems and Software, Journal of Database Management, Journal of Expert Systems and Applications, Information and Software Technology,* and *Journal of Knowledge Management.* His research interests include Web engineering, hypermedia design, Web-based information system (WIS) development and improvement methodology, workflow modeling, knowledge management, and Web mining.

* * * *

Stuart J. Barnes is an associate professor at the School of Information Management, Victoria University of Wellington, New Zealand. He has been teaching and researching in the information systems field for more than a decade. His academic background includes a first class degree in economics from University College London and a PhD in business administration from Manchester Business School. He has published more than 60 articles including those in journals such as *Communications of the ACM*, the *International Journal of Electronic Commerce*, the *e-Service Journal*, *Electronic Markets*, and the *Journal of Electronic Commerce Research.* He has published three books: *E-Commerce and V-Business* (2001), a best-seller for Butterworth Heinemann, *Knowledge Management Systems* (2002), and *M-Business* (2003).

Javier Bazzocco holds a computer science analyst degree from the Universidad de La Plata, Argentina. His main areas of interest include: object oriented design and development; Web applications design; geographic information systems; object oriented databases; object-relational mapping; and software engineering issues—especially those related to Web environments. He also teaches object oriented paradigm and object oriented databases at the Faculty of Informatics of the National University of La Plata.

Michael Bieber is an associate professor in the information systems department of the college of computing sciences at the New Jersey Institute of Technology, USA. He teaches both on-campus and in the distance learning program, often combining the students in both modes. Bieber is conducting research in several related areas: hypermedia functionality, automatically generating hypermedia links and services for analytical applications and for digital libraries, Web engineering, incorporating hypermedia into WWW applications, relationship analysis (as part of the software engineering process), supporting knowledge and learning within virtual communities, asynchronous learning networks and distance education, and infrastructures for future educational software. He has published many articles in these and other areas. He also is active in several of these research communities, co-organizing conference minitracks and other activities, and co-editing special journal issues. Bieber co-directs NJIT's Collaborative Hypermedia Research Laboratory. He is affiliated with the New Jersey Center for Multimedia Research and the National Center for Transportation and Industrial Productivity. He holds a PhD in decision sciences from the University of Pennsylvania, USA.

Joseph Catanio earned his PhD in information systems from the College of Computing Sciences at the New Jersey Institute of Technology in May 2004. His primary area of research has been in systems analysis techniques and software engineering. He has worked as a professional software engineer for 15 years managing and performing application development and embedded systems. His research interests include software engineering, systems analysis, creativity and innovation, the learning process, educational software tools and environments, collaborative systems, and group support systems. He has received an assistant professor appointment from LaSalle University to begin in the Fall 2004. There he will continue his research endeavors.

Jim Q. Chen is an associate professor of business computer information systems at St. Cloud State University, USA. He received his PhD in management information systems in 1995 from University of Nebraska-Lincoln, USA. His current research interests include Web application development methodologies, E-commerce, and executive decision support systems. His recent publications appeared in *Communications of the ACM, Decision Support Systems, Journal of Internet Commerce, Information Systems Management, Journal of Computer Information Systems, Systems Development Management, Logistics Information Management, Review of Accounting Information Systems*, and *Total Quality Management*, among other journals.

Sotiris P. Christodoulou received a BSc in computer engineering and informatics from the University of Patras, Greece in 1994. He also received a PhD from the University of Patras in 2004. He is currently a senior researcher of Web engineering at HPCLab at the University of Patras. His research interests include Web engineering, hypermedia, Web information systems development, XML. He has participated in several Greek and European R&D projects in the fields of hypermedia technologies since 1994, including: unified cultural information system, numerous WWW infrastructures, intranets, multimedia CDROMs, ESPRIT projects, IST projects, etc. Most projects combined applied research and development, emphasizing on applying cutting-edge technologies to real-world problems. His research publications include two book chapters, and eight conference papers, two of which are strongly refereed.

Athula Ginige is a professor in the School of Computing and IT at the University of Western Sydney, Australia. He is also director of the AeIMS (Advanced enterprise Information management Systems) research center. He has done extensive research in the areas of development of large-scale Web-based information systems, multimedia systems, next generation information retrieval strategies for the Web, and electronic business systems for small to medium enterprises. Ginige has authored publications in the areas of Web engineering, multimedia and e-commerce. He is the main author of three chapters in the book *Hypermedia and the Web: An Engineering Approach*, John Wiley, 1999. He is a co-guest editor of the special issues of *IEEE Multimedia* on Web engineering, part 1 and 2 (January 2001 and April 2001) and chair of the International Workshop on Web Engineering held in conjunction with the Conference of Software Engineering and Knowledge Engineering, 2002 and 2003.

Silvia Gordillo earned a PhD in computer science from the University Claude Bernard Lyon, France, and a Master's in software engineering from the Universidad de La Plata, Argentina. She is a full professor at the Universidad Nacional de La Plata in the database area and one of the directors of LIFIA. Her research interests include: geographic information system and mobile applications. She has published papers in these areas.

Richard D. Heath, PhD, is a professor in the business computer information system department of the G.R. Herberger College of Business at the St. Cloud State University. He teaches in the area of application program development specializing in the area of Web applications. He has published and does research and graduate thesis advising in the area. He was president and CEO of Royal Oaks Information Systems.

Taeho Hong is an assistant professor of MIS field in the College of Business Administration at Pusan National University, Korea. He received his PhD in management engineering from the Graduate School of Management at the Korea Advanced Institute of Science and Technology (KAIST), Seoul, Korea. His research interests are Web mining, data mining for network intrusion detection, intelligent agent, and financial application using artificial intelligence. His research has been published in journals of expert systems with applications and expert systems.

Geun-Sik Jo is currently a professor in the department of computer science and information engineering, Inha University, Korea. He is a chief information officer at Inha Univeristy. Jo received his BS from the department of computer science, Inha University, in 1982; his MS in computer science from Queens College/CUNY in 1985; and his PhD in computer science from the City University of New York in 1991. His research interests include semantic web, intelligent electronic commerce systems, intelligent agents, intelligent scheduling, and constraint programming. He may be contacted at: gsjo@inha.ac.kr

Jason J. Jung is a PhD candidate at the School of Computer and Information Engineering, Inha University in Korea. He received his Bachelor degrees in computer engineering and mechanical engineering from Inha University in 1999, and his Master's degree in computer and information engineering from Inha University in 2002. His research interests are in the areas of semantic Web mining, distributed recommendation systems, and collaborative knowledge management systems. He is currently visiting Fraunhofer FIRST in Berlin, Germany.

Jinwoo Kim isprofessor of HCI in the School of Business at Yonsei University, Korea. He is also working as director of Human Computer Interaction Lab at Yonsei University. His research interests include three types of issues in three different domains. The three issues include navigation structures for interactive systems, cross-cultural value of IT and its impact on usability, and evaluation metrics and framework for digital contents. The three platforms include traditional e-business systems, mobile Internet and digital TV. He has published several papers in *Information Systems Research, Decision Support Systems, International Journal of Human Computer Studies, International Journal of Human Computer Interaction, ACM Transaction on Human Computer Interaction, Communications of ACM*, and other related journals and conferences.

Robert Laurini is currently the head of SIMA/CASSINI, French CNRS Research Group on Geographic Information Systems. He has served as deputy head of the LIRIS Research Center for Images and Information Systems since January 1, 2003 and is a member of the INSA board with the rank of vice president for the reduced board. He is a full distinguished professor at the computing department of the National Institute for the Applied Sciences (INSA), Lyon, France. Previously, he carried out research at the University of Cambridge, UK (1976-1977) and at the University of Maryland, USA (1986-1987). He was taught in the computing department of the University Institute of Technology, Claude Bernard University of Lyon for several years. For five years, he was head of the Laboratory for Information System Engineering (LISI), shared by the INSA and Claude Bernard University of Lyon, France. He has published dozens of papers in the area of geographic information systems.

Choongseok Lee is a senior consultant in the media and communications business consulting cell, business integration division at Samsung SDS Co. Ltd., Seoul Korea. He received a PhD in management information systems from the Graduate School of Management at Korea Advanced Institute of Science and Technology (KAIST), Seoul

Korea. He earned his BA and MA degrees from KAIST. His research centers on Web engineering, especially Web system design methodology. His work has appeared in *Information & Management, Information and Software Technology,* and *Journal of Systems and Software.*

Heeseok Lee is a professor of the Graduate School of Management, Korea Advanced Institute of Science and Technology, Korea. He received his PhD in management from the University of Arizona, USA. He was previously on the faculty at the University of Nebraska at Omaha, USA. His research interests include performance management, knowledge management, and IS strategy. His recent publications appeared in *Journal of Management Information Systems, Information and Management, Information Systems, Journal of Organizational Computing and Electronic Commerce* and *Journal of Database Management.*

Jae Kyu Lee is the professor of e-Commerce and management information systems in the Graduate School of Management at the Korea Advanced Institute of Science and Technology, Korea. He is a director of the International Center for Electronic Commerce, and editor-in-chief of Electronic Commerce Research and Applications (Elsevier). He may be contacted at: jklee@kgsm.kaist.ac.kr.

Emilia Mendes is a senior lecturer in computer science at the University of Auckland, New Zealand. She has active research interests in the areas of Web engineering, hypermedia, machine learning, software engineering, and computer science and software engineering education. In particular, she focuses on Web quality and metrics, measurement, effort prediction and productivity benchmarking for Web applications, object-oriented metrics and measurement, software and Web engineering education and case-based reasoning, in which areas she has published widely. She has taught postgraduate courses in software measurement and Web engineering for several years. She has consulting experience in the areas of Web cost estimation and productivity benchmarking, object-oriented development and usability, as well as running an industry workshop in Web cost estimation and productivity benchmarking. She has been on numerous conference program committees, including recent international Web conferences, and is on the editorial board of the International Journal of Web Engineering Technology.

Nile Mosley is experienced in the area of software development, Web measurement and metrics. He is currently company director of OKKI Software in Auckland, New Zealand, specializing in software development, software measurement and training. Mosley is also Technical Director of MetriQ Limited, New Zealand, a software company that specialises in the development of measurement tools. Mosley has taught courses in software development at several Universities and has more than 12 years of experience in software development. He has published his research in reputable conferences such as IEEE Software Metrics Symposium, ACM/IEEE International Symposium Empirical Software Engineering, and journals such as *IEEE Multimedia* and *Empirical Software Engineering.*

San Murugesan is professor of information technology in the School of Multimedia and Information Technology at Southern Cross University, Australia. He also worked at NASA Ames Research Centre, USA, as a NRC senior research fellow. His areas of interest include Web engineering, Web intelligence, information retrieval and personalization. He is a distinguished visitor and tutorial speaker of the IEEE Computer Society. He is a co-guest editor of the special issues of *IEEE Multimedia* on Web Engineering, part 1 and 2 (January 2001 and April 2001) and a co-editor of the book, *Web Engineering: Managing the Diversity and Complexity of Web Application Development* (Springer Verlag, 2001). He is general chair of International Conference on Web Engineering 2005, Sydney, Australia, and served as co-chair and organizer of many international workshops and conferences. He also serves as associate editor of the *Journal of Web Engineering*.

Theodore S. Papatheodorou received his BSc in mathematics from the University of Athens, Greece, in 1968. He also received his MSc in mathematics (1971), MSc in civil engineering (1975) and PhD in numerical analysis (1973), all from Purdue University, USA. He has held several academic and consulting positions in Greece and the United States. Since 1984, he has been professor of computer engineering and informatics in the University of Patras, Greece. He initiated the establishment of the Computer Technology Institute (CTI), where he served as the first director (1985-1990) and led the institute's research and organizational development. He is the founder and director of the High Performance Computing Laboratory (HPCLab) of the University of Patras, where he leads the research and development work on system and application software for parallel and distributed computing, scientific computing, web and multimedia applications, 3D virtual reconstruction of monuments and other applications for culture and education. He has published numerous scientific articles and a book on algorithms. He has been serving as member or chairman of international scientific committees and is the recipient of several academic awards for research and cultural multimedia applications.

Filippo Ricca received his degree in Computer Science from the University of Genova, Italy, in 1994, with a thesis in the field of analysis and design of concurrent systems. From 1995 to 1998 he worked at Comune di San Lorenzo al Mare, Imperia, Italy, as computer operator and accountant. In 1999, he joined the Software Engineering group (STAR) at ITC-irst. He received a PhD from the University of Genova in 2003, with the thesis "Analysis, Testing and Restructuring of Web Applications." His current research interests include Web application analysis and testing.

Gustavo Rossi holds a PhD from PUC-Rio, Brazil. He is the head of LIFIA (a computer science research lab in Argentina) and is a full professor at the Universidad Nacional de La Plata, Argentina. He has published papers on design patterns and frameworks and is one of the developers of the object-oriented hypermedia design method (OOHDM)—a mature method for Web engineering.

Mye M. Sohn is an assistant professor in the College of Systems Management Engineering at the Sungkyunkwan University, Korea. He may be contacted at: myesohn@skku.edu..

Craig Standing is professor of strategic information management at Edith Cowan University, Western Australia. He was born in the UK and achieved his PhD at the University of Western Australia. His research interests include development methods and the impact of e-marketplaces on organizations. He may be contacted at: c.standing@ecu.edu.au.

Paolo Tonella received his laurea degree cum laude in electronic engineering from the University of Padua, Italy in 1992, and his PhD in software engineering from the same university in 1999, with the thesis "Code Analysis in Support to Software Maintenance." Since 1994, he has been a full-time researcher of the Software Engineering group at ITC-irst, Trento, Italy. He participated in several industrial and European Community projects on software analysis and testing. His current research interests include reverse engineering, aspect-oriented programming, Web applications, and testing.

Richard Vidgen is a reader in information systems in the School of Management, University of Bath, UK. After working in industry in information systems development for many years he joined the University of Salford, UK, in 1992, where he completed a PhD in systems thinking and IS quality. His current research interests include Web site quality, e-commerce transformation in the automotive industry, IS development methodologies, and XML/Web Service based information systems. He is the author of *Developing Web Information Systems* (Butterworth Heinemann, 2002) and has published many research papers in leading international journals.

Benjamin P.-C. Yen is an associate professor in the School of Business at The University of Hong Kong. He received his PhD degrees from Columbia University, USA. His research interests include electronic catalogs, supply chain management, and Web information accessibility. He has papers published in major journals of information systems and operations research, including *IEEE Transactions on Systems, Man, and Cybernetics*, *Journal of Organizational Computing and Electronic Commerce*, *Information & Management*, *Electronic Commerce Research Journal*, *International Journal of Electronic Markets*, *Information Processing Letters*, *Annals of Operations Research*, and *European Journal of Operational Research*, etc.

Index

D

E

F

G

H

I

Q

R

S

T

U

V

W

X